POSUKA DEMIZU

I hope you enjoy volume 18. For this volume cover, I have the Japanese logo placed vertically for the first time. It was a challenge I'd never attempted before! I have various challenges for the next volume and the ones after that too.

Please look forward to the future *The Promised Neverland* volumes! By the way, people who are reading this, are you reading it in a physical book? Or in the digital version? Recently I bought the entire series of *One Piece* for my Kindle. I can read it anytime on my phone, and it's very convenient. Physical books are good, and so are the digital versions. I often can't choose which version to buy. And when you can't choose...you buy both! That's what being an adult is all about!

I'll see you again in volume 19!

Posuka Demizu debuted as a manga artist with the 2013 *CoroCoro* series *Oreca Monster Bouken Retsuden*. A collection of illustrations, *The Art of Posuka Demizu,* was released in 2016 by PIE International.

KAIU SHIRAI

Writer Shirai's interesting tidbits for *The Promised Neverland* fanatics, part 6!

The most important thing to me when naming a character is how the name sounds rather than its meaning.

So when I get comments like "I never thought I'd be able to remember Legravalima, but I keep wanting to say it out loud," I feel happy.

For demon names, I try to find unfamiliar sounds as much as possible. From my brain.

Please enjoy this volume!

Kaiu Shirai debuted in 2015 with *Ashley Gate no Yukue* on the *Shonen Jump+* website. Shirai first worked with Posuka Demizu on the two-shot *Poppy no Negai,* which was released in February 2016.

THE PROMISED NEVERLAND

VOLUME 18
SHONEN JUMP Manga Edition

STORY BY KAIU SHIRAI
ART BY POSUKA DEMIZU

Translation/Satsuki Yamashita
Touch-Up Art & Lettering/Mark McMurray
Design/Julian [JR] Robinson
Editor/Alexis Kirsch

YAKUSOKU NO NEVERLAND © 2016 by Kaiu Shirai, Posuka Demizu
All rights reserved.
First published in Japan in 2016 by SHUEISHA Inc., Tokyo.
English translation rights arranged by SHUEISHA Inc.

The stories, characters and incidents mentioned in this publication are
entirely fictional.

No portion of this book may be reproduced or transmitted in any form or
by any means without written permission from the copyright holders.

Printed in the U.S.A.

Published by VIZ Media, LLC
P.O. Box 77010
San Francisco, CA 94107

10 9 8 7 6 5 4 3 2 1
First printing, January 2021

viz.com

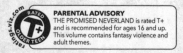

PARENTAL ADVISORY
THE PROMISED NEVERLAND is rated T+
and is recommended for ages 16 and up.
This volume contains fantasy violence and
adult themes.

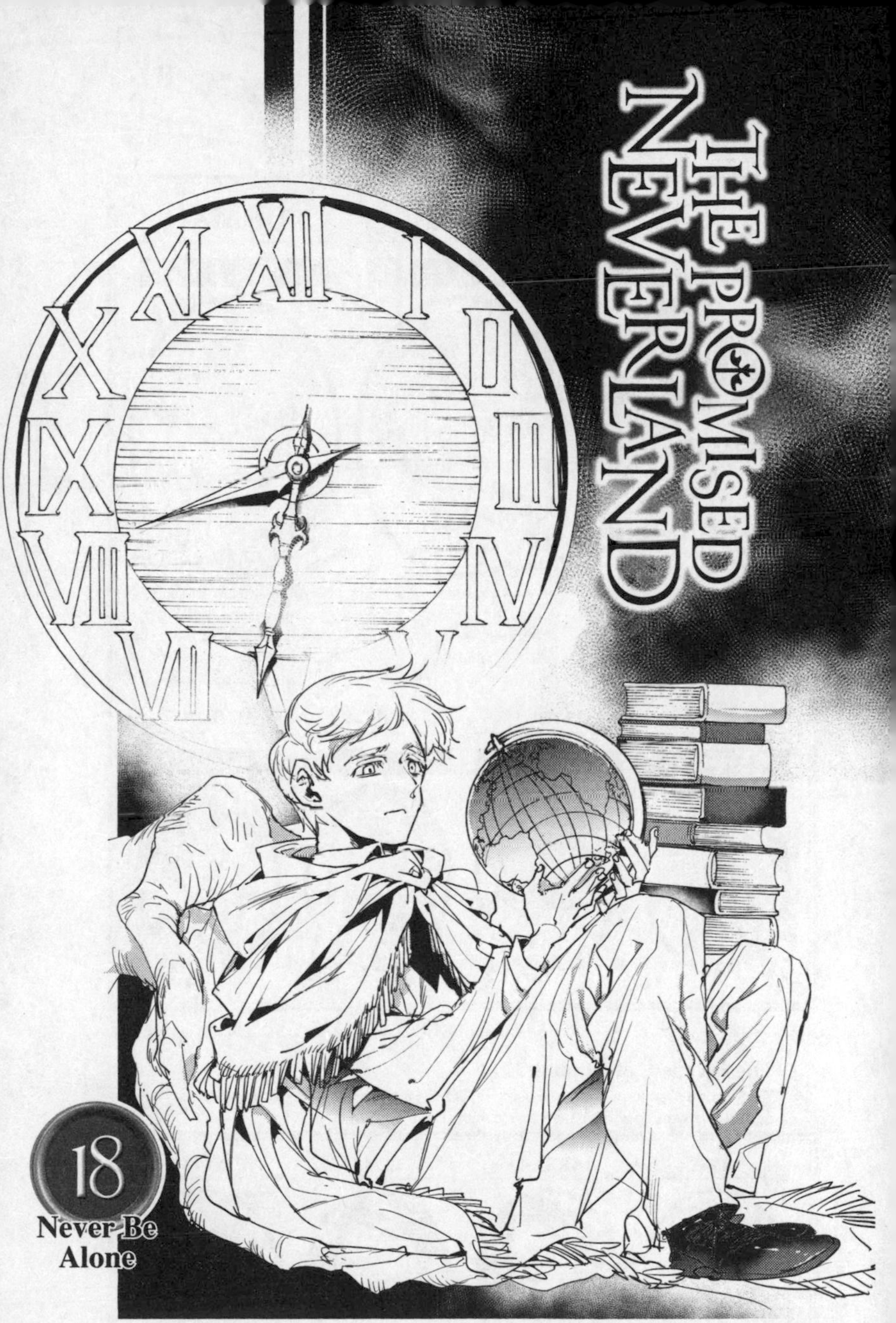
THE PROMISED NEVERLAND
18
Never Be Alone

STORY	KAIU SHIRAI
ART	POSUKA DEMIZU

CHARACTERS

The Children of Grace Field House

They aim to free all of the children who are trapped in Grace Field House within the next two months.

RAY

On the Run

The only one among the Grace Field House children who can match wits with Norman.

EMMA

On the Run

An enthusiastic and optimistic girl with superb athletic and learning abilities.

NORMAN

On the Run

A boy with excellent analytical and decision-making capabilities. He is the smartest of the children from Grace Field House.

CAROL

In Grace Field House

PHIL

In Grace Field House

GILDA

On the Run

DON

On the Run

The Escapees of Lambda 7214

They obtained superpowers from being repeatedly experimented on by the demons. They are devoted to Norman and have destroyed many farms with him.

ZAZIE

BARBARA

CISLO

VINCENT

Geelan Clan

Joined an alliance with Norman to get revenge on the royal family and aristocrats.

GEELAN

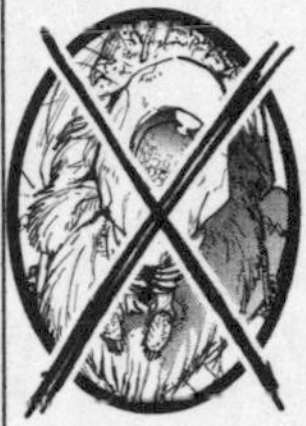

Evil-Blooded Girl Group

Thought to have been killed by the royal family for her ability to maintain human form, but she has secretly survived.

MUJIKA

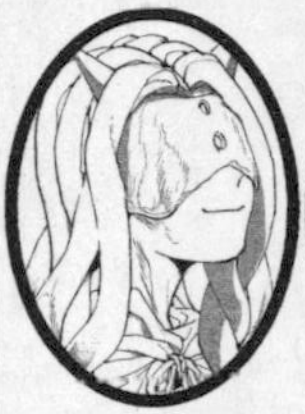

SONJU

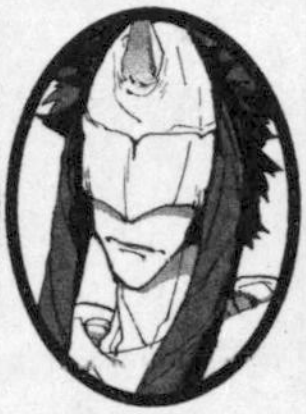

Disposed Child

Stolen from a farm and raised by a demon.

AYSHE

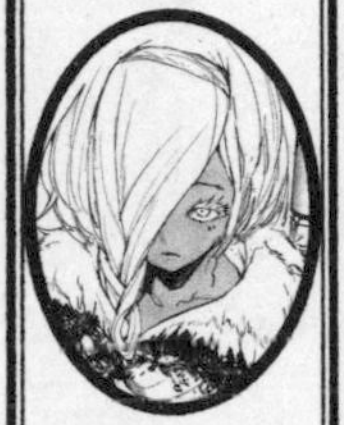

Royal Family

The queen who rules the many subjects of the demon world.

LEGRAVALIMA

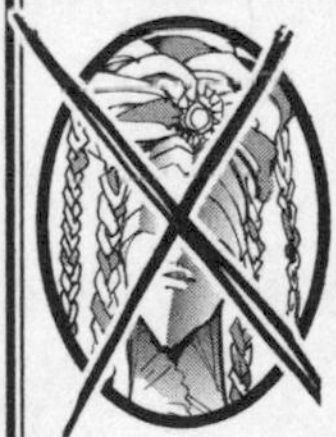

The Five Regent Houses

They govern the demon world with the royal family. They also operate the farms that raise humans.

LORD DOZZA

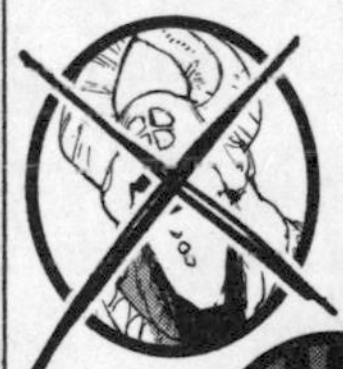

DUKE YVERK

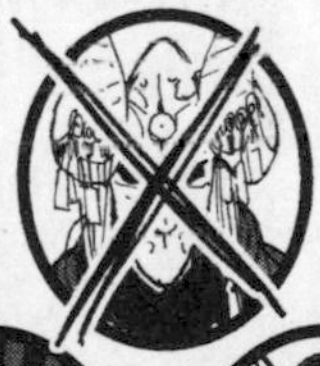

LADY NOUM

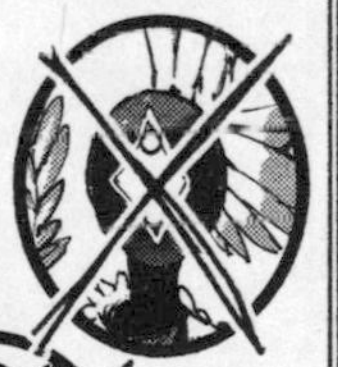

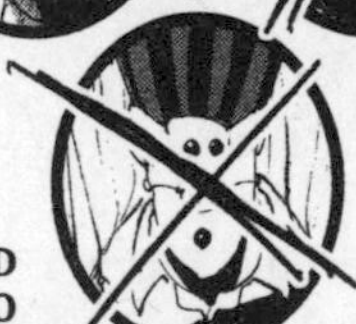

LORD PUPO

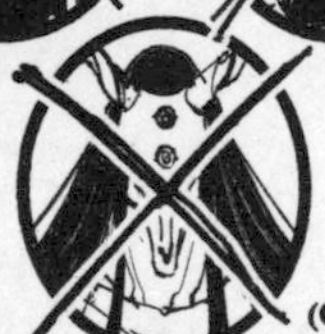

LORD BAYON (CURRENT)

The Story So Far

Emma is living happily at Grace Field House with her foster siblings. One day, she realizes that they are being bred as food for demons and escapes with a group of other children. After meeting new friends and gaining further information, she decides to free all of the children raised in the farms. Her group researches the Seven Walls, the key to making a new promise, and after a lot of hard work they find the way. Emma makes another move toward her goal and is reunited with Norman, who is alive after all. He reveals his plan to annihilate the demons, and Emma sets out to create a new promise that can allow for humans and demons to both exist. In the meantime, Norman continues with his plan and marches his men to the imperial capital, where they kill the demon queen. Emma meets up with Norman there, but...

THE PROMISED NEVERLAND 18

Never Be Alone

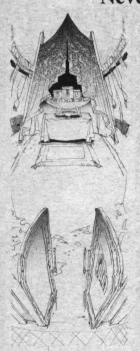

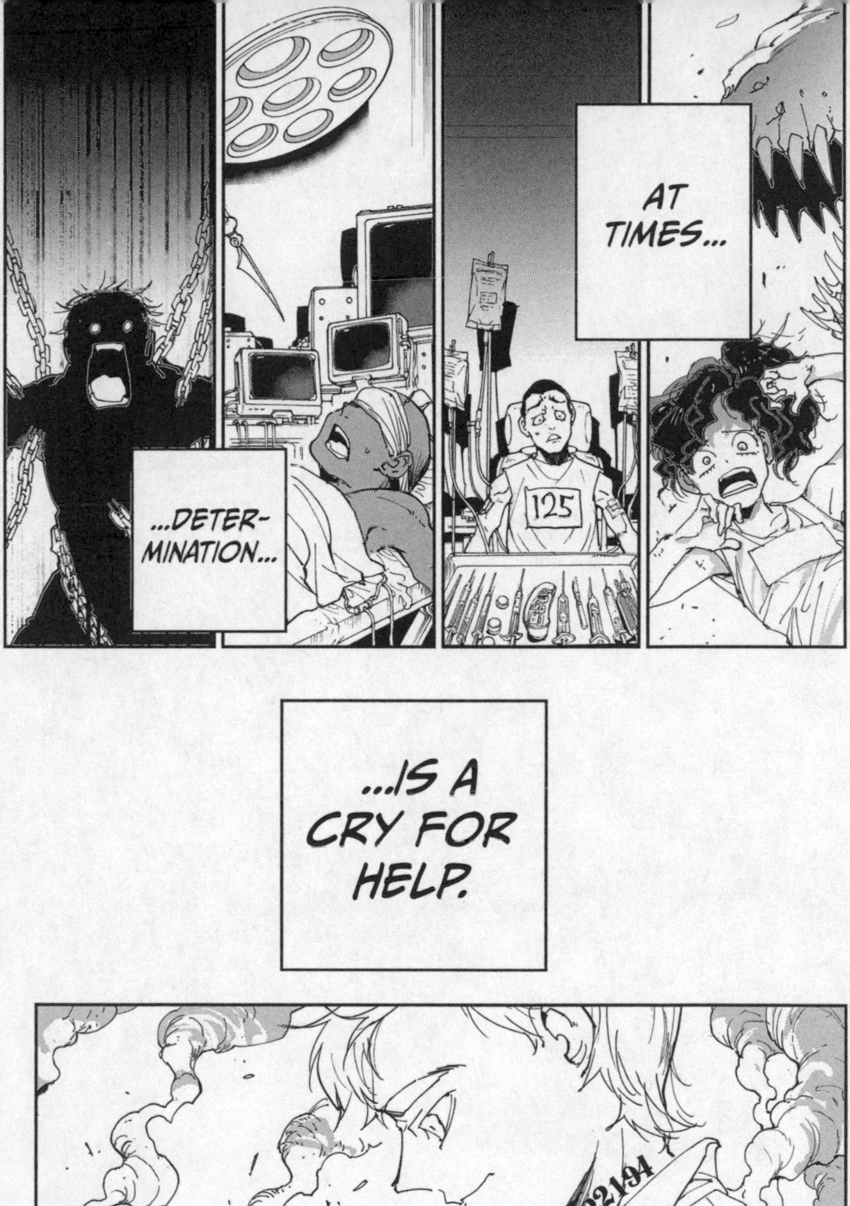
AT TIMES...
125
...DETER-
MINATION...
...IS A CRY FOR HELP.
22194

CHAPTER 153: COWARD

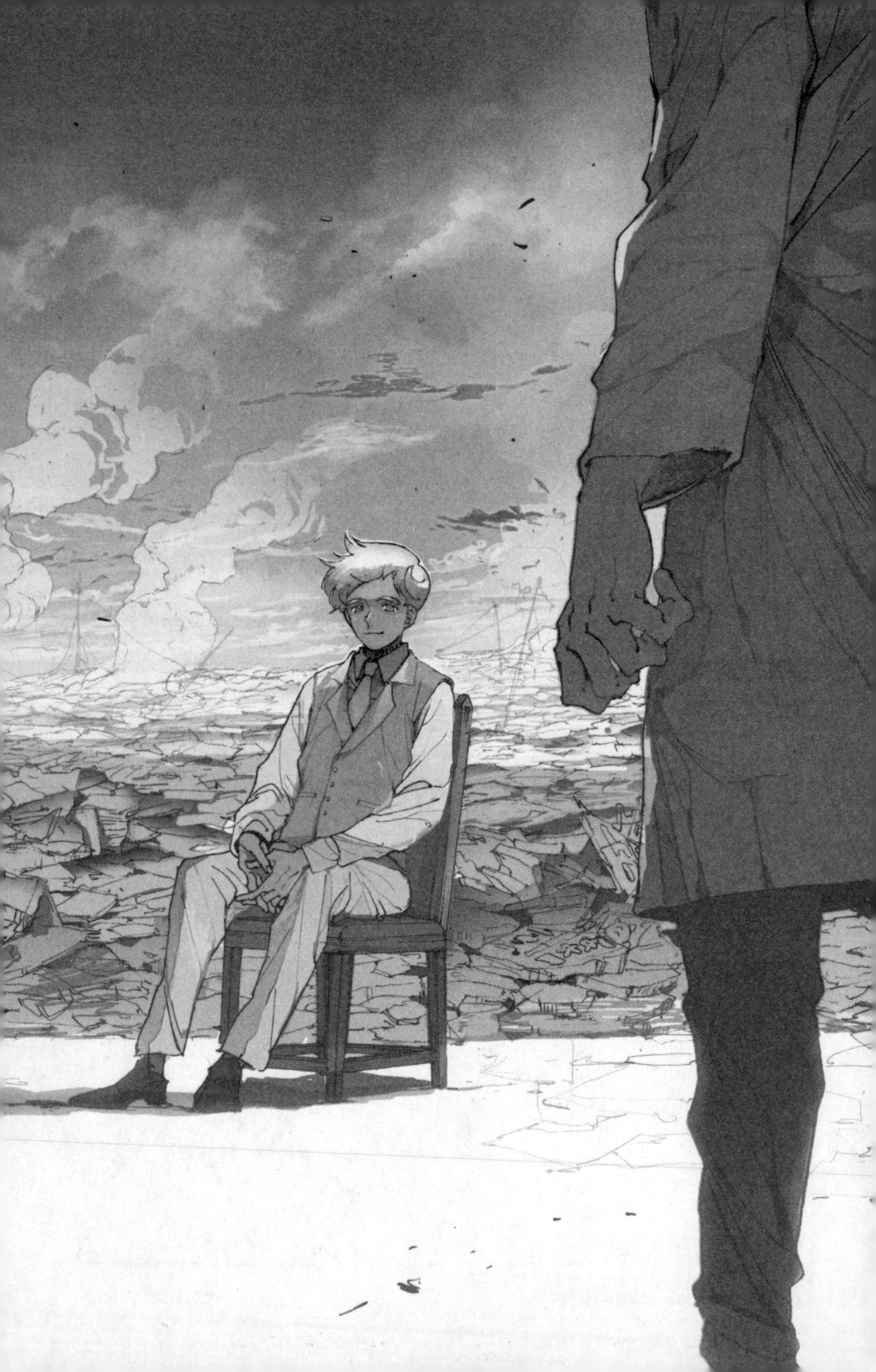

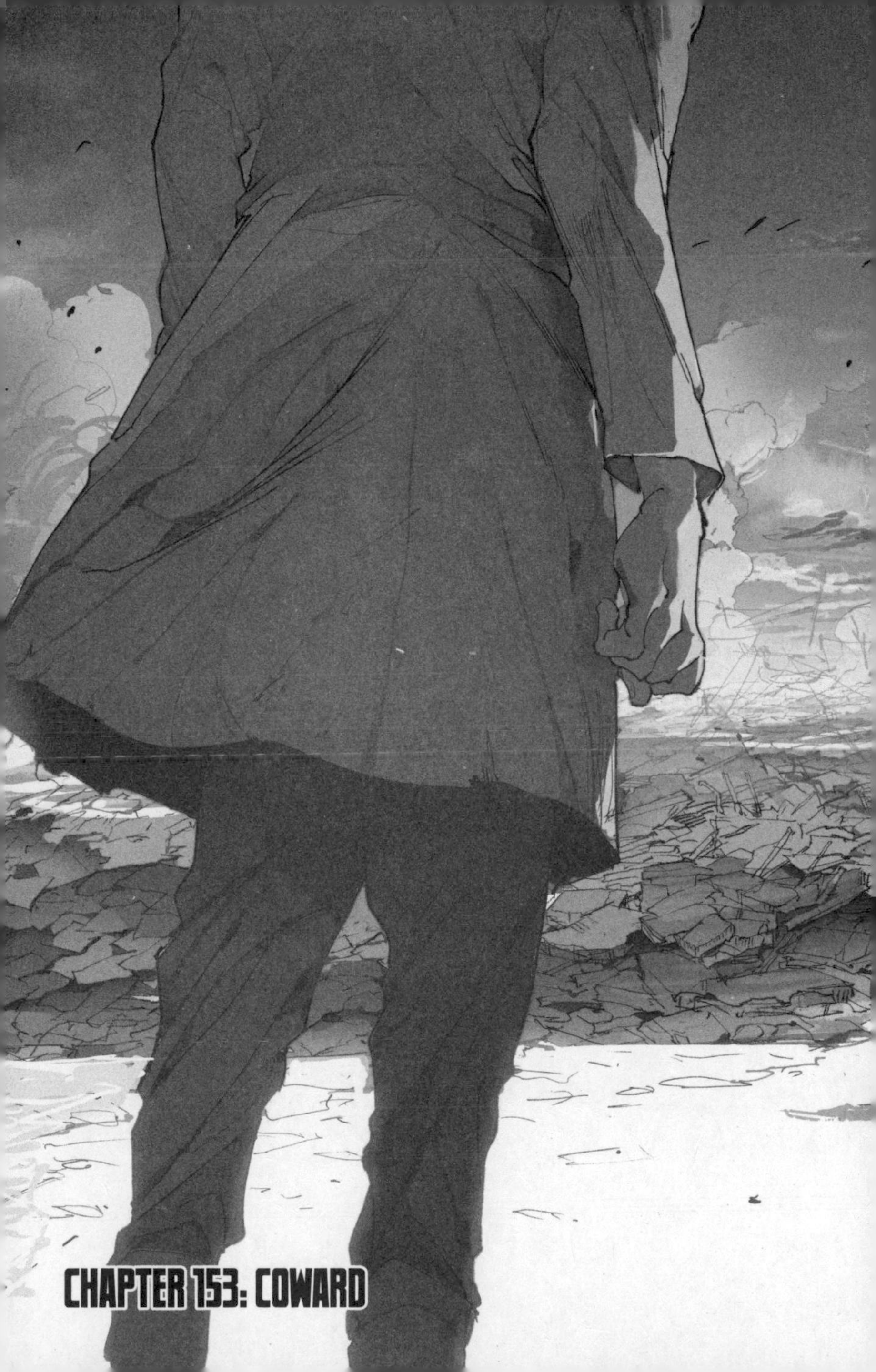
CHAPTER 153: COWARD

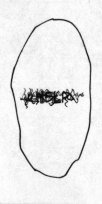

NORMAN!

EMMA. RAY.

YOU WERE A BIT TOO LATE.

BUT I'M SORRY.

GOOD. YOU BOTH WERE ABLE TO COME BACK SAFELY.

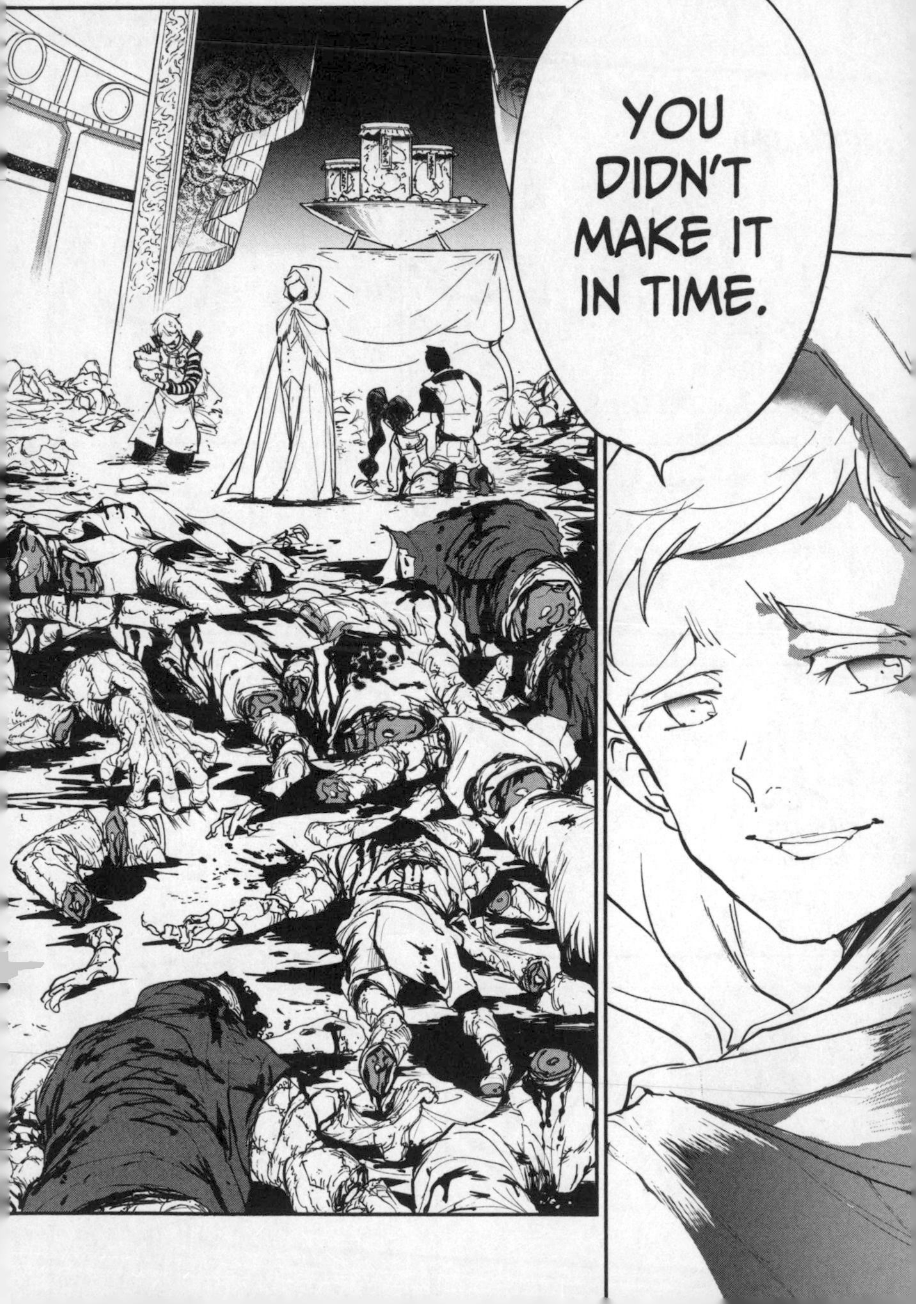
YOU DIDN'T MAKE IT IN TIME.

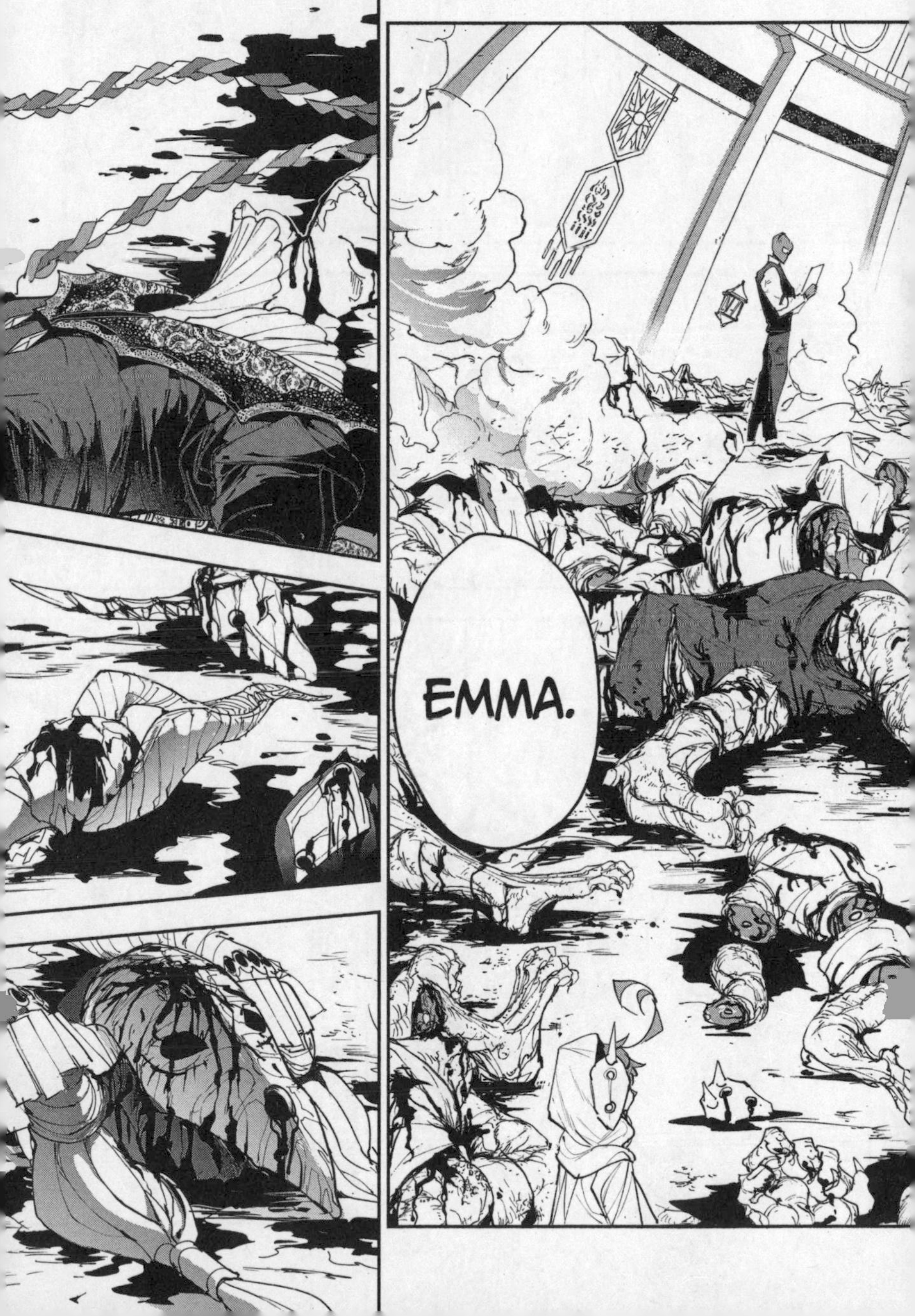
EMMA.

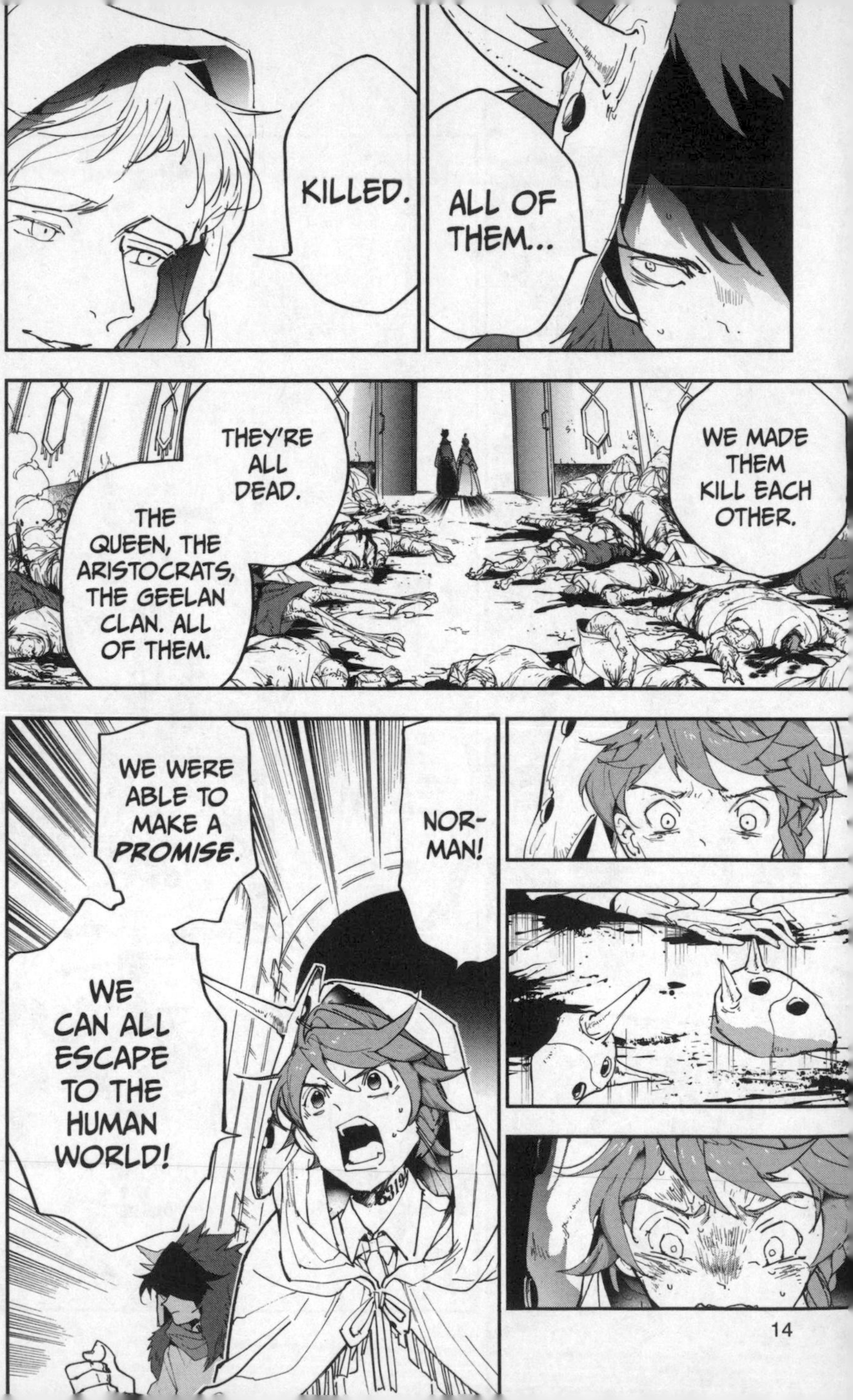
ALL OF THEM...
KILLED.
WE MADE THEM KILL EACH OTHER.
THEY'RE ALL DEAD.
THE QUEEN, THE ARISTOCRATS, THE GEELAN CLAN. ALL OF THEM.
NOR-MAN!
WE WERE ABLE TO MAKE A *PROMISE*.
WE CAN ALL ESCAPE TO THE HUMAN WORLD!

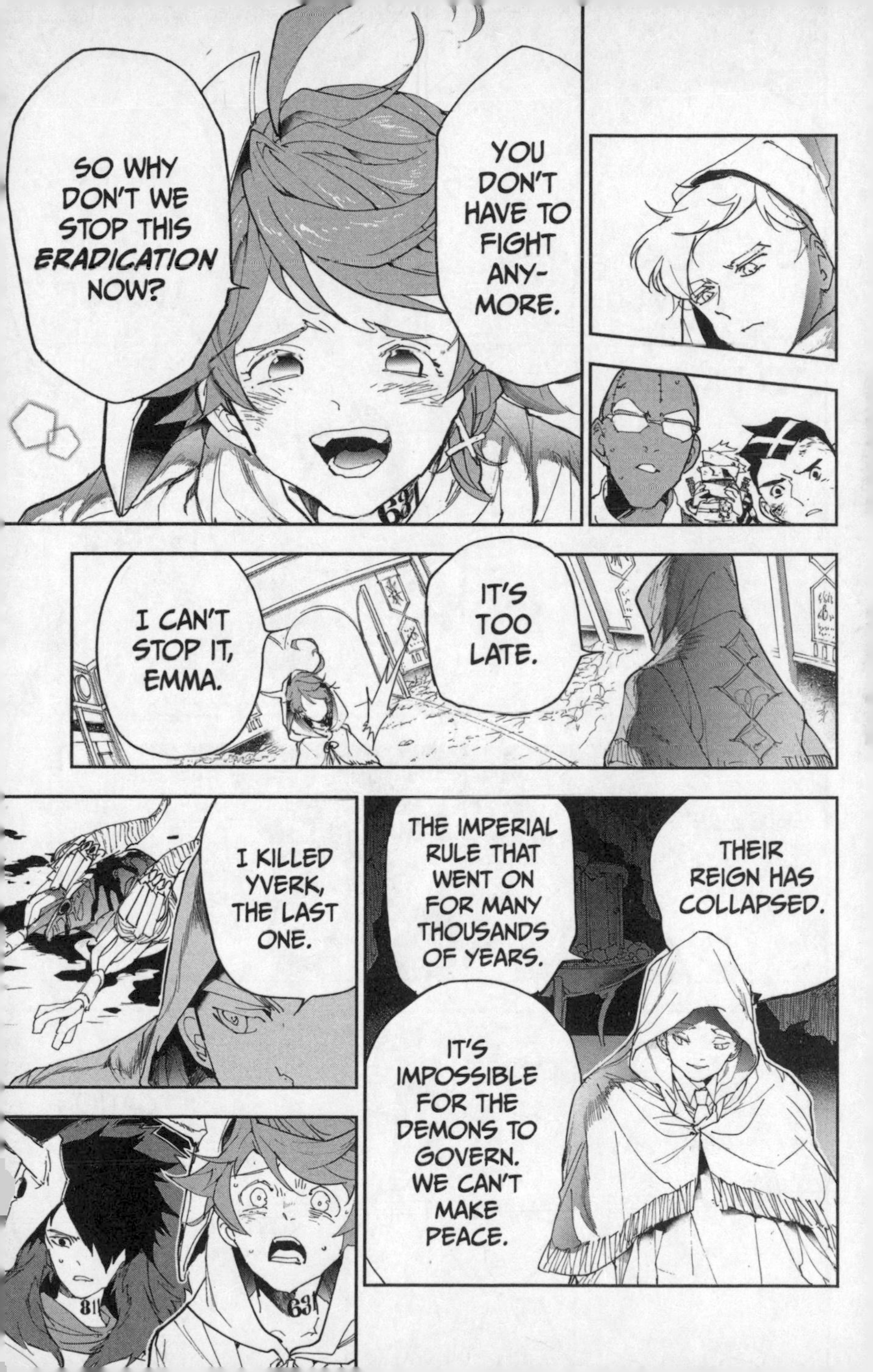
YOU DON'T HAVE TO FIGHT ANYMORE.
SO WHY DON'T WE STOP THIS *ERADICATION* NOW?
IT'S TOO LATE.
I CAN'T STOP IT, EMMA.
THEIR REIGN HAS COLLAPSED.
THE IMPERIAL RULE THAT WENT ON FOR MANY THOUSANDS OF YEARS.
IT'S IMPOSSIBLE FOR THE DEMONS TO GOVERN. WE CAN'T MAKE PEACE.
I KILLED YVERK, THE LAST ONE.
81
63

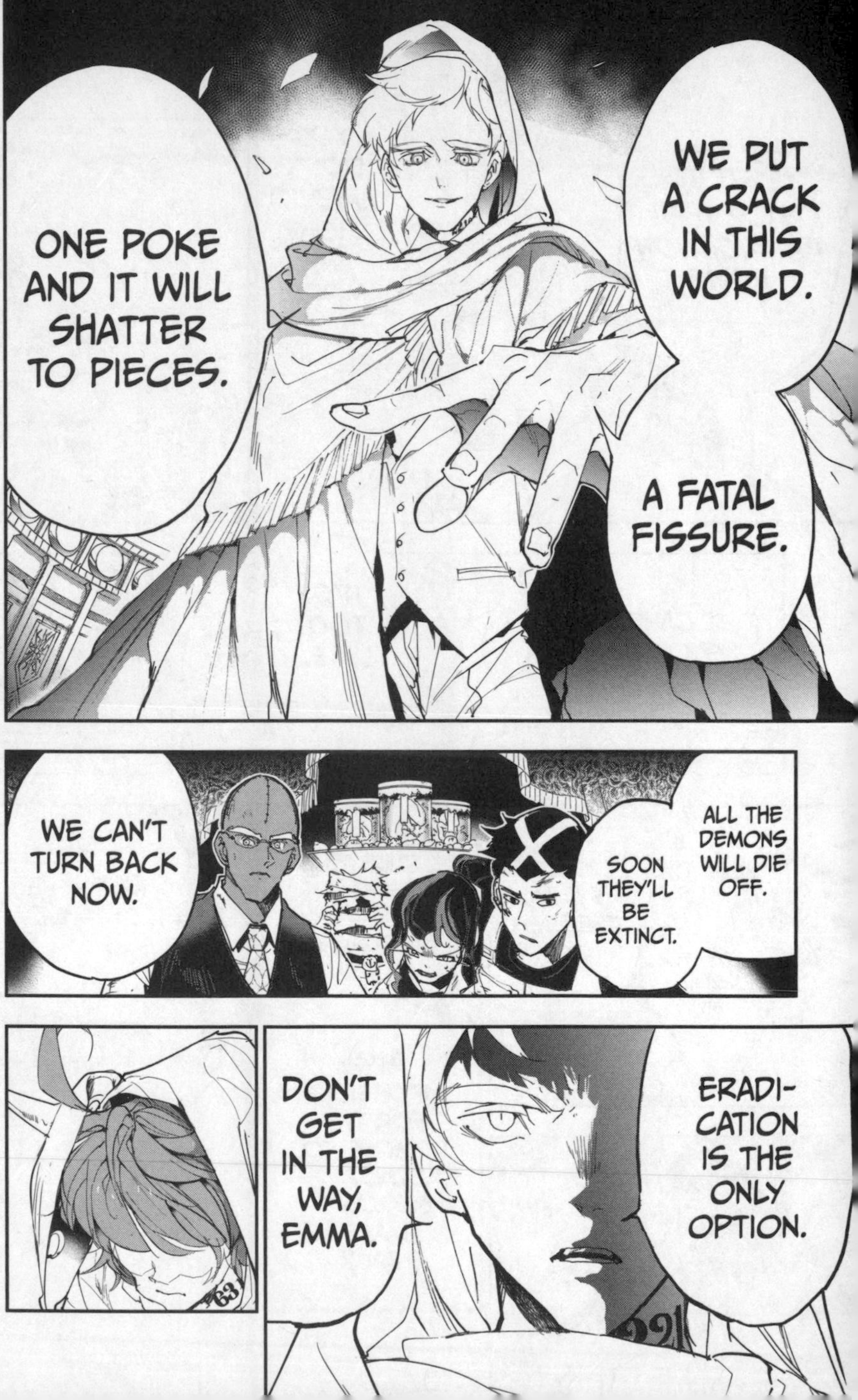
WE PUT A CRACK IN THIS WORLD.
A FATAL FISSURE.
ONE POKE AND IT WILL SHATTER TO PIECES.
ALL THE DEMONS WILL DIE OFF.
SOON THEY'LL BE EXTINCT.
WE CAN'T TURN BACK NOW.
ERADI-CATION IS THE ONLY OPTION.
DON'T GET IN THE WAY, EMMA.

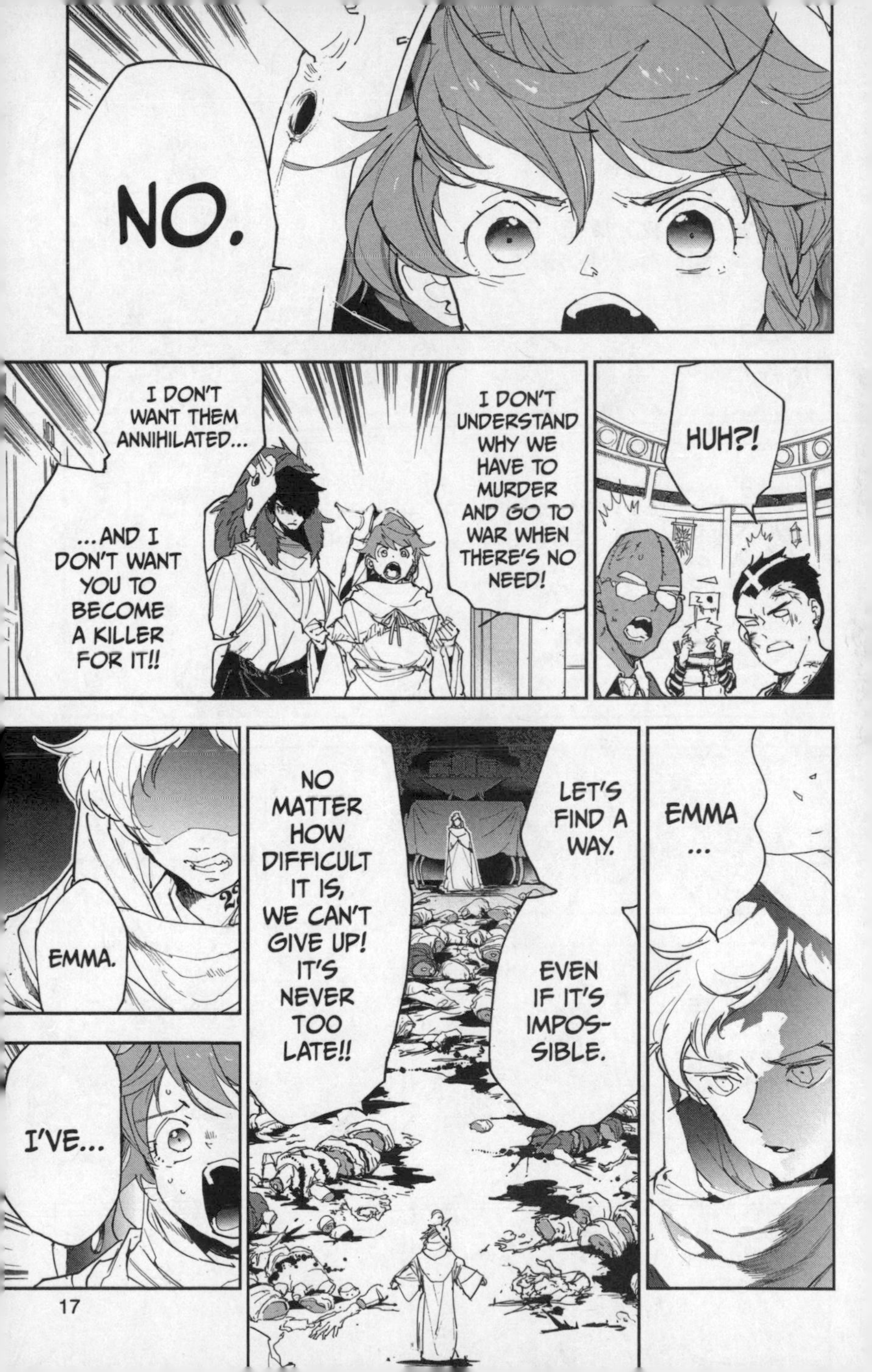
NO.
HUH?!
I DON'T UNDERSTAND WHY WE HAVE TO MURDER AND GO TO WAR WHEN THERE'S NO NEED!
I DON'T WANT THEM ANNIHILATED...
...AND I DON'T WANT YOU TO BECOME A KILLER FOR IT!!
EMMA...
LET'S FIND A WAY.
EVEN IF IT'S IMPOS-SIBLE.
NO MATTER HOW DIFFICULT IT IS, WE CAN'T GIVE UP! IT'S NEVER TOO LATE!!
EMMA.
I'VE...

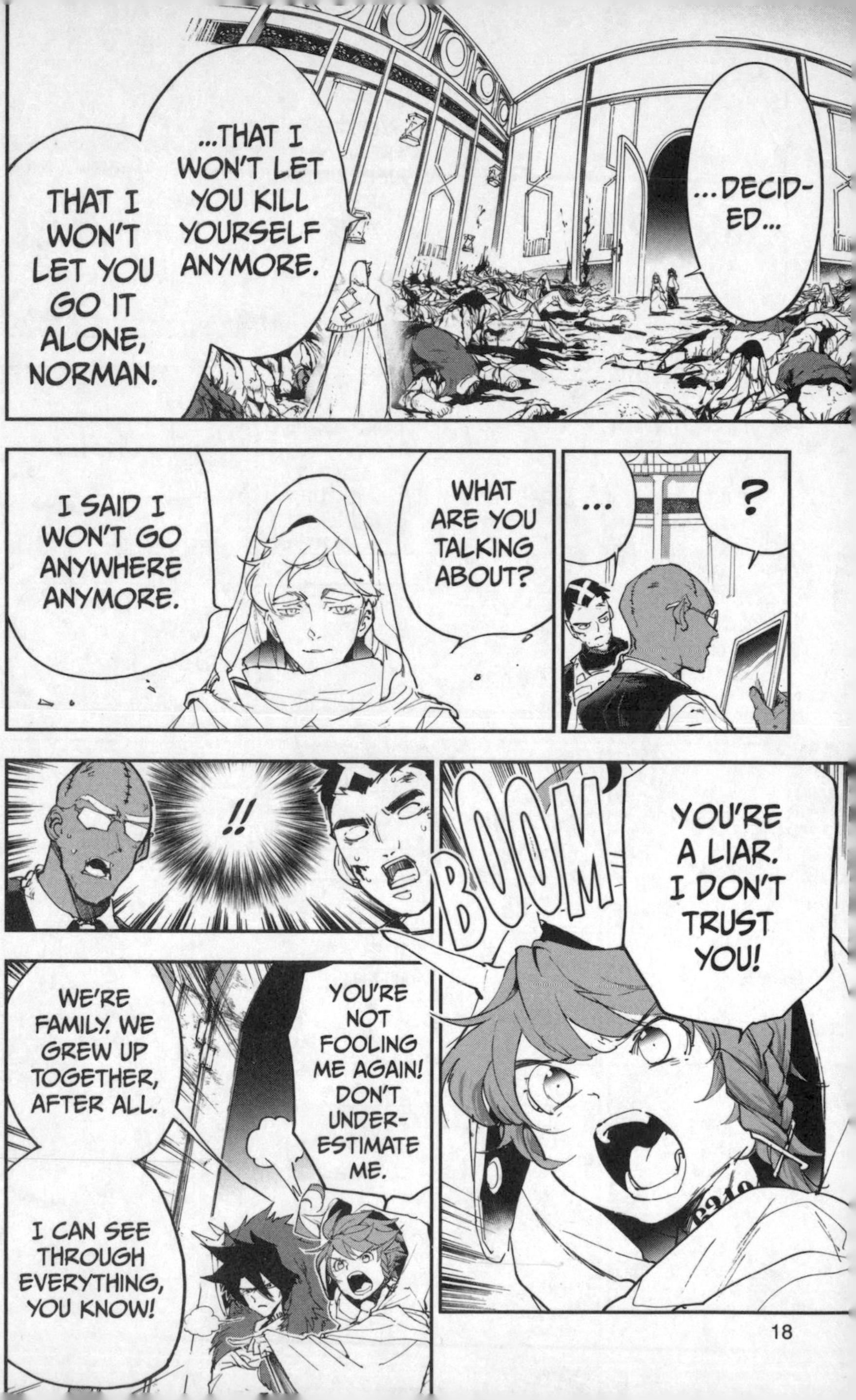
...DECIDED...
...THAT I WON'T LET YOU KILL YOURSELF ANYMORE.
THAT I WON'T LET YOU GO IT ALONE, NORMAN.
?
...
WHAT ARE YOU TALKING ABOUT?
I SAID I WON'T GO ANYWHERE ANYMORE.
BOOM
YOU'RE A LIAR. I DON'T TRUST YOU!
!!
YOU'RE NOT FOOLING ME AGAIN! DON'T UNDER-ESTIMATE ME.
WE'RE FAMILY. WE GREW UP TOGETHER, AFTER ALL.
I CAN SEE THROUGH EVERYTHING, YOU KNOW!

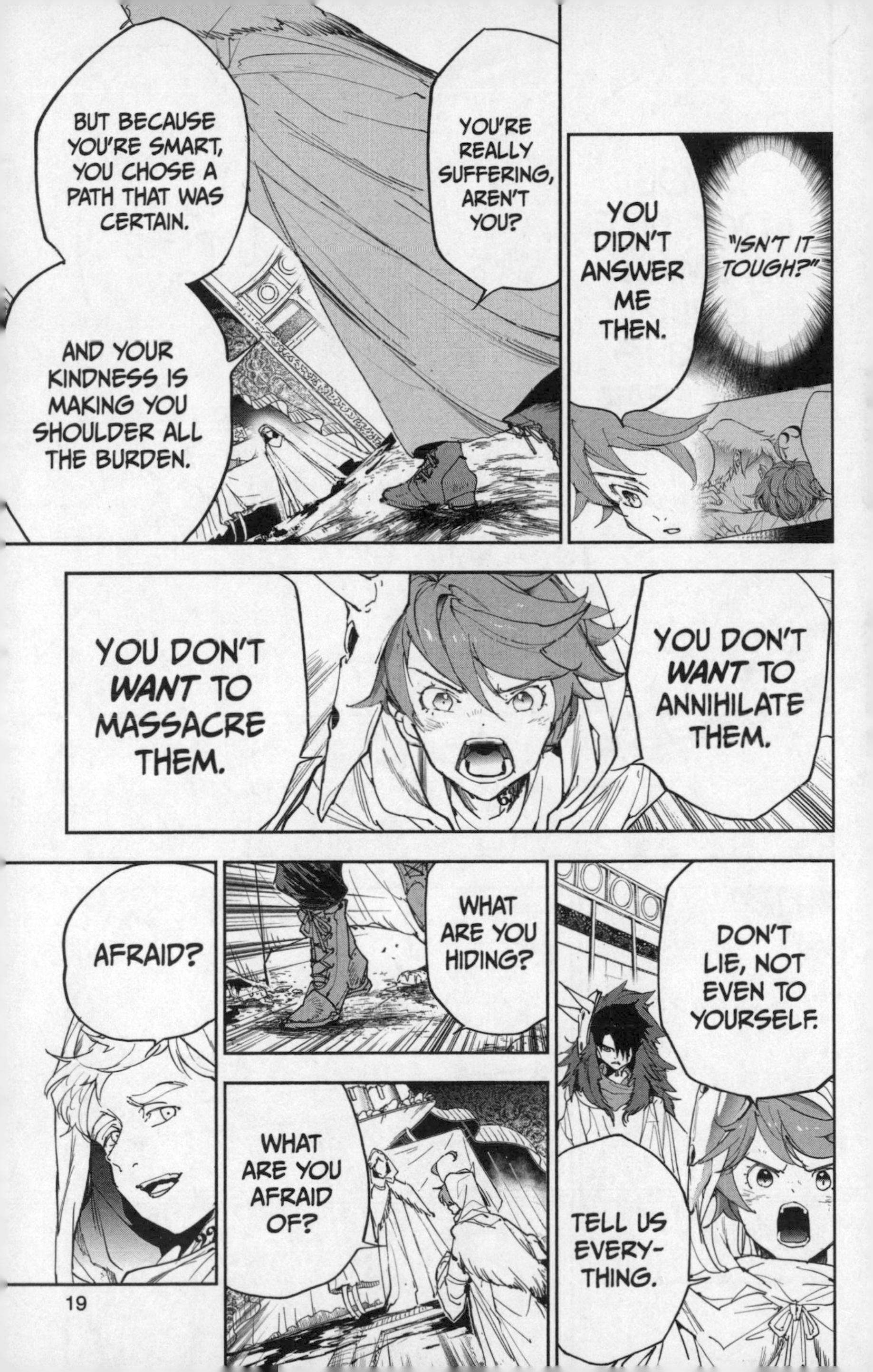
"ISN'T IT TOUGH?"
YOU DIDN'T ANSWER ME THEN.
YOU'RE REALLY SUFFERING, AREN'T YOU?
BUT BECAUSE YOU'RE SMART, YOU CHOSE A PATH THAT WAS CERTAIN.
AND YOUR KINDNESS IS MAKING YOU SHOULDER ALL THE BURDEN.
YOU DON'T *WANT* TO ANNIHILATE THEM.
YOU DON'T *WANT* TO MASSACRE THEM.
DON'T LIE, NOT EVEN TO YOURSELF.
TELL US EVERY-THING.
WHAT ARE YOU HIDING?
WHAT ARE YOU AFRAID OF?
AFRAID?

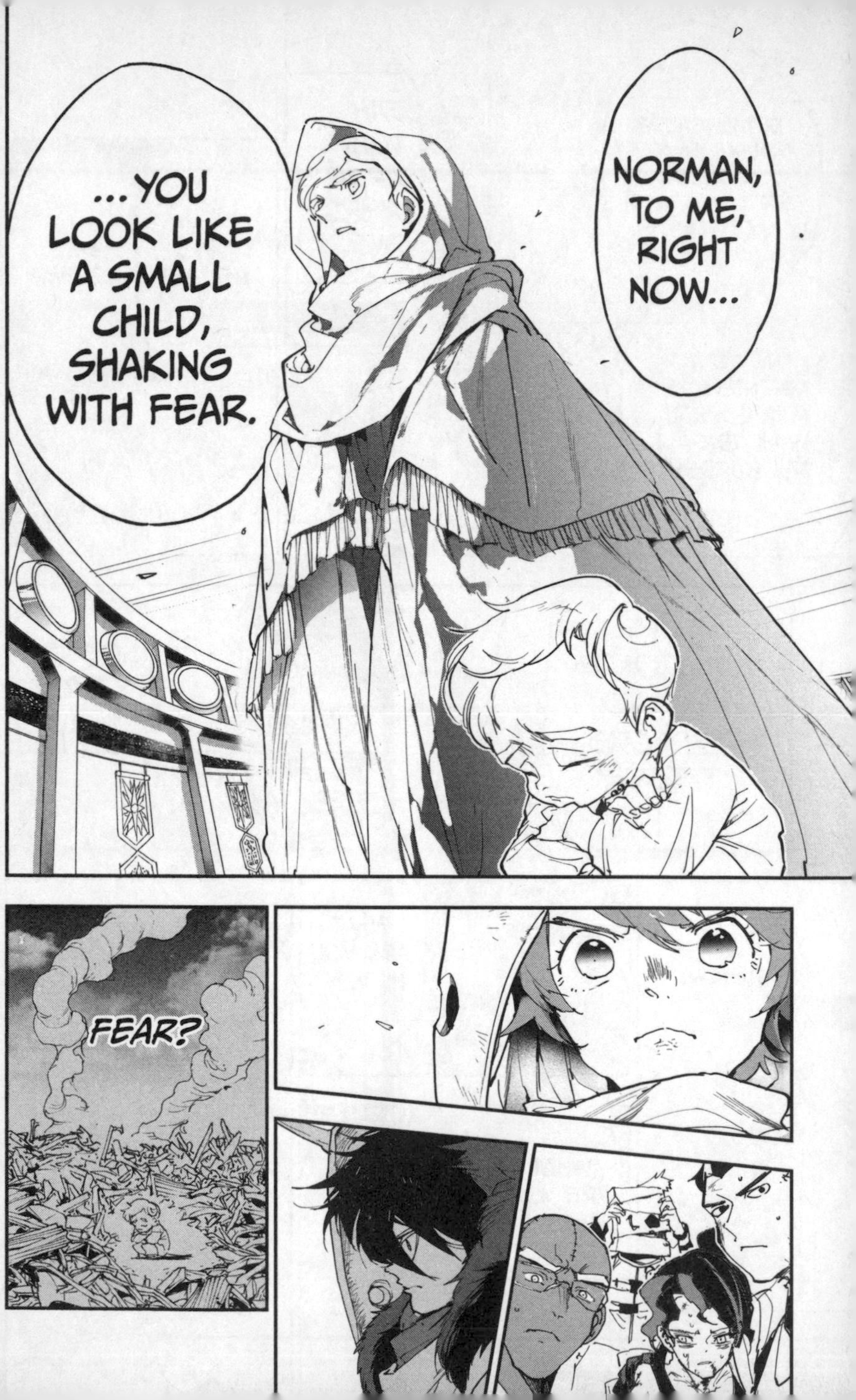
NORMAN, TO ME, RIGHT NOW...
...YOU LOOK LIKE A SMALL CHILD, SHAKING WITH FEAR.
FEAR?

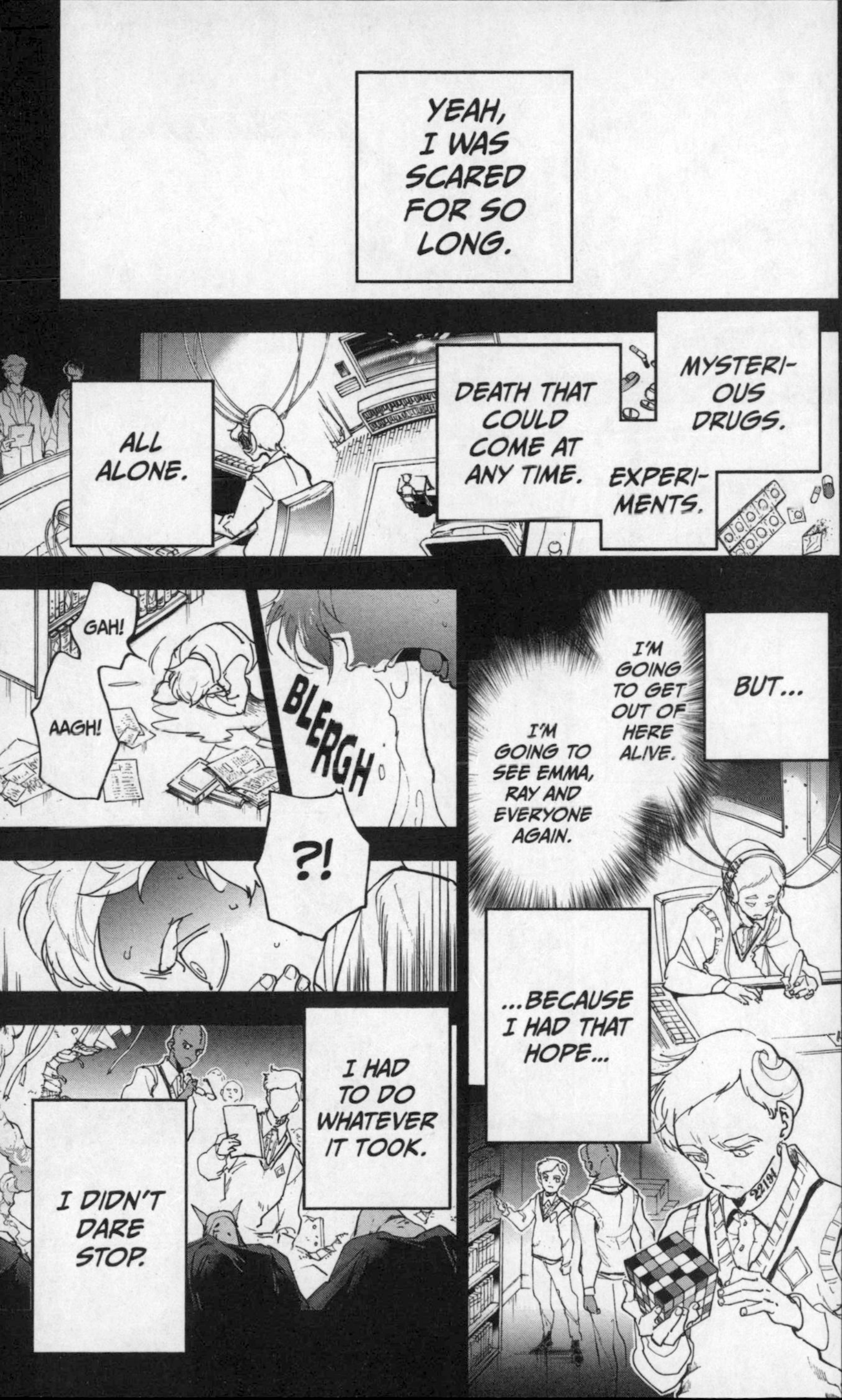
YEAH, I WAS SCARED FOR SO LONG.
MYSTERIOUS DRUGS.
DEATH THAT COULD COME AT ANY TIME.
EXPERIMENTS.
ALL ALONE.
BUT...
I'M GOING TO GET OUT OF HERE ALIVE.
I'M GOING TO SEE EMMA, RAY AND EVERYONE AGAIN.
...BECAUSE I HAD THAT HOPE...
BLERGH
GAH!
AAGH!
?!
I HAD TO DO WHATEVER IT TOOK.
I DIDN'T DARE STOP.

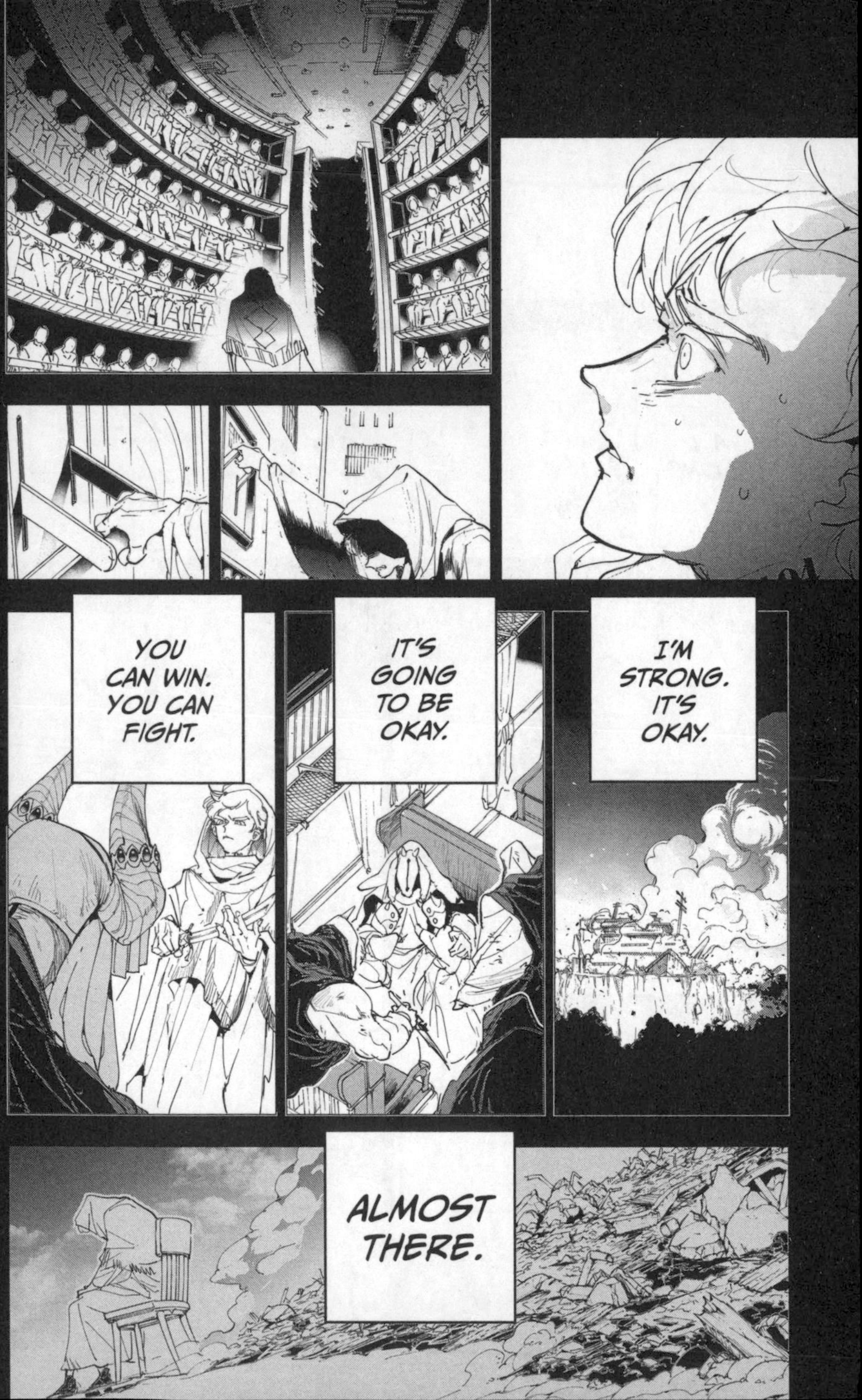
I'M STRONG. IT'S OKAY.
IT'S GOING TO BE OKAY.
YOU CAN WIN. YOU CAN FIGHT.
ALMOST THERE.

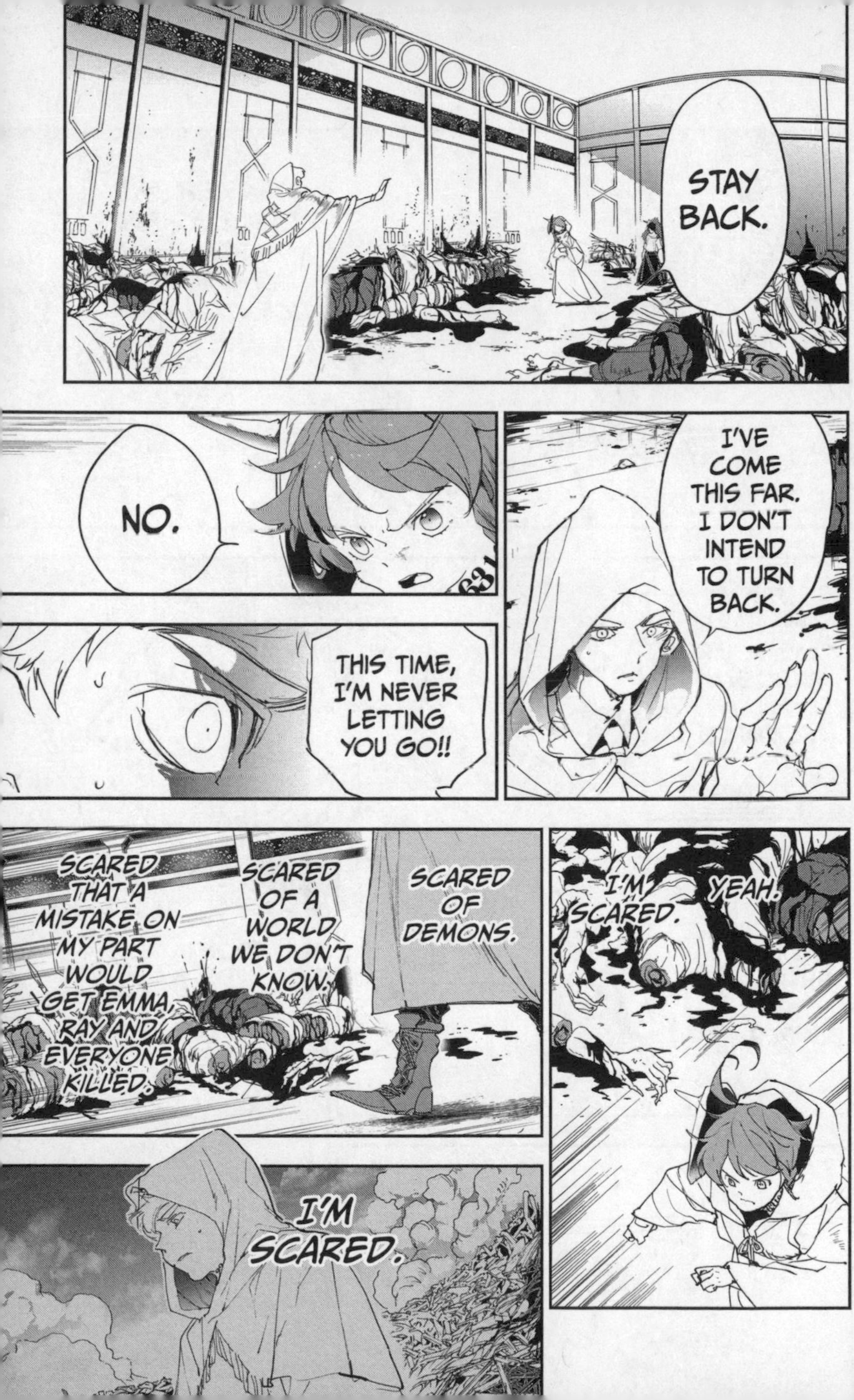
STAY BACK.
I'VE COME THIS FAR. I DON'T INTEND TO TURN BACK.
NO.
THIS TIME, I'M NEVER LETTING YOU GO!!
YEAH.
I'M SCARED.
SCARED OF DEMONS.
SCARED OF A WORLD WE DON'T KNOW.
SCARED THAT A MISTAKE ON MY PART WOULD GET EMMA, RAY AND EVERYONE KILLED.
I'M SCARED.

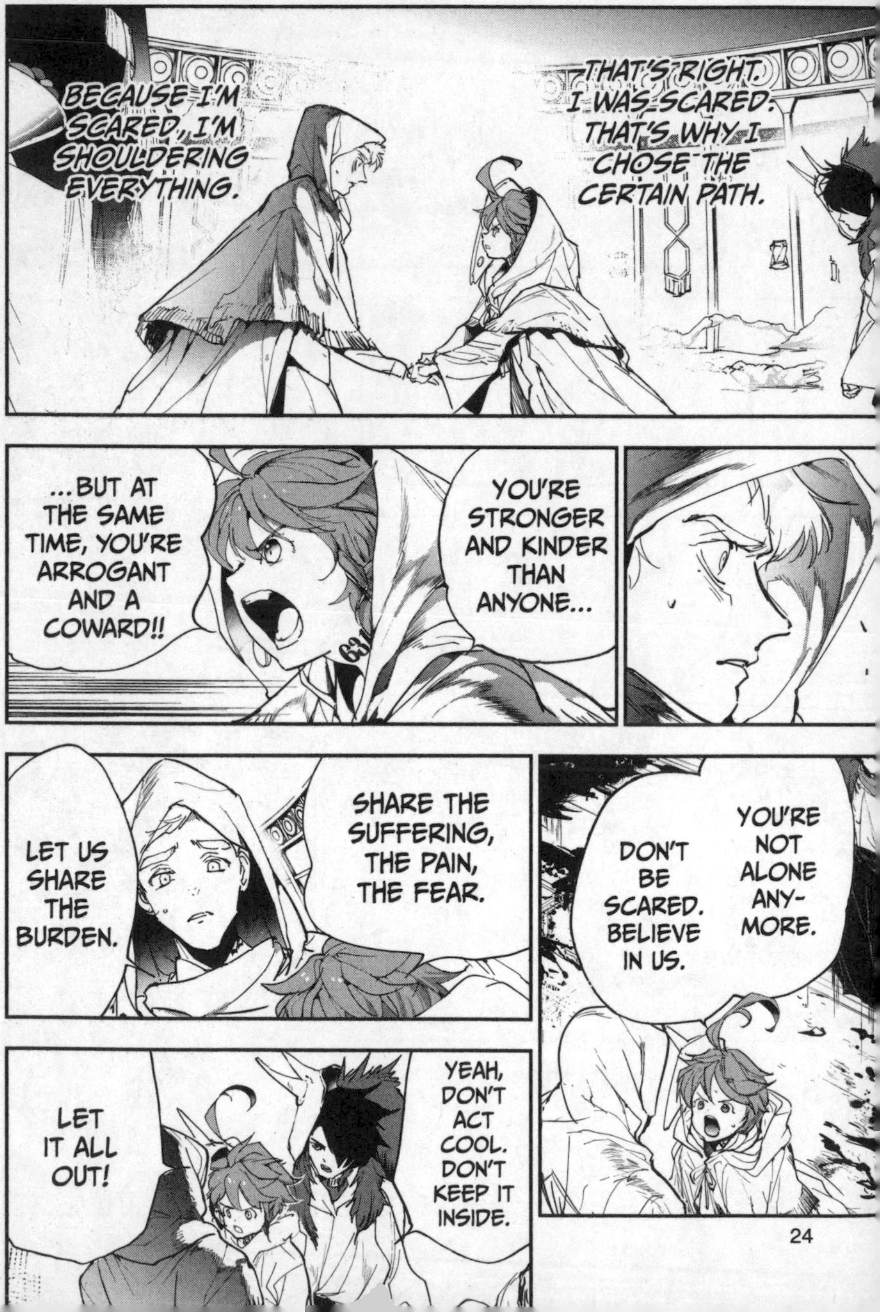
THAT'S RIGHT. I WAS SCARED. THAT'S WHY I CHOSE THE CERTAIN PATH.
BECAUSE I'M SCARED, I'M SHOULDERING EVERYTHING.
YOU'RE STRONGER AND KINDER THAN ANYONE...
...BUT AT THE SAME TIME, YOU'RE ARROGANT AND A COWARD!!
YOU'RE NOT ALONE ANYMORE.
DON'T BE SCARED. BELIEVE IN US.
SHARE THE SUFFERING, THE PAIN, THE FEAR.
LET US SHARE THE BURDEN.
YEAH, DON'T ACT COOL. DON'T KEEP IT INSIDE.
LET IT ALL OUT!

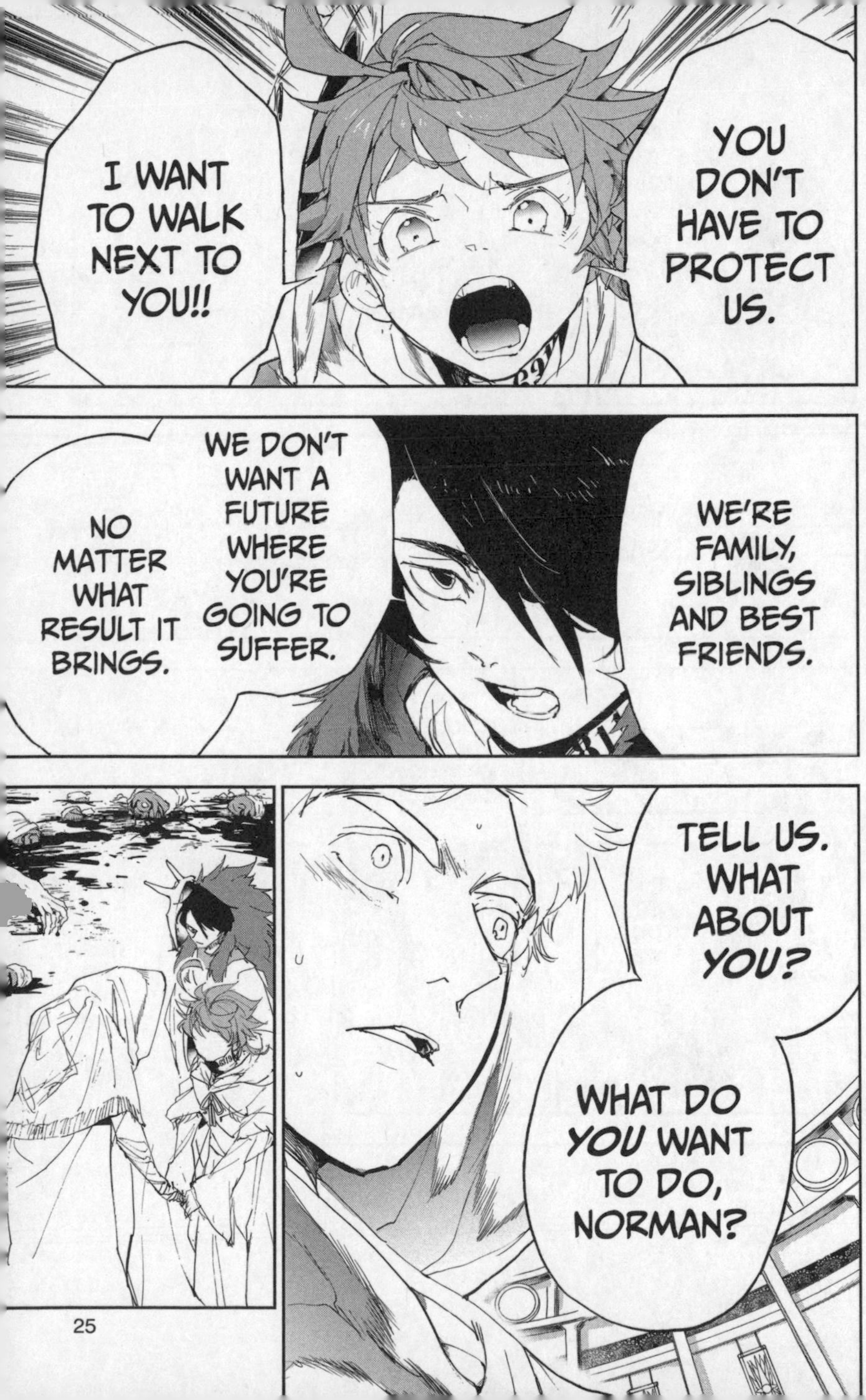
YOU DON'T HAVE TO PROTECT US.
I WANT TO WALK NEXT TO YOU!!
WE'RE FAMILY, SIBLINGS AND BEST FRIENDS.
WE DON'T WANT A FUTURE WHERE YOU'RE GOING TO SUFFER.
NO MATTER WHAT RESULT IT BRINGS.
TELL US. WHAT ABOUT *YOU?*
WHAT DO *YOU* WANT TO DO, NORMAN?

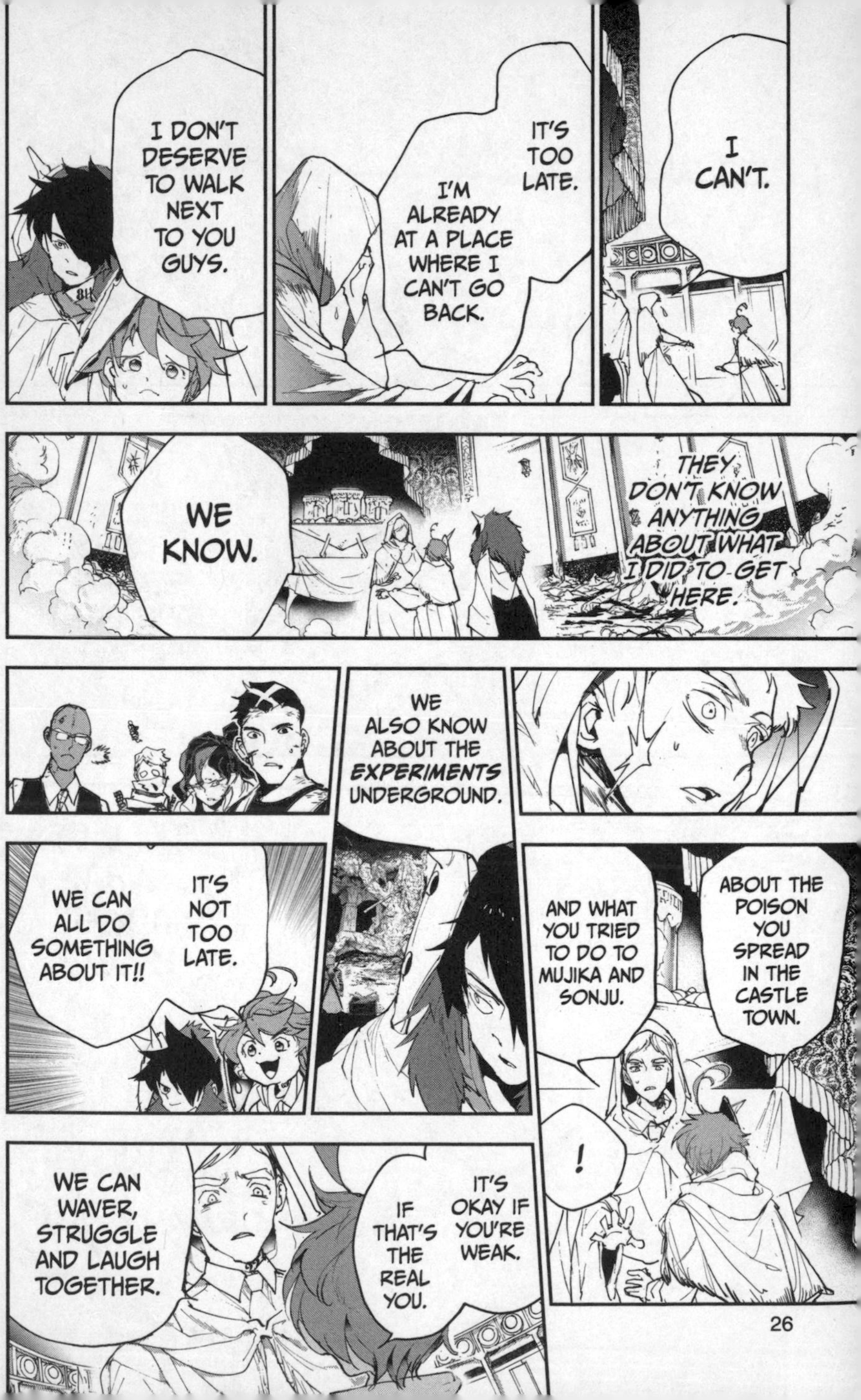
I CAN'T.
IT'S TOO LATE.
I'M ALREADY AT A PLACE WHERE I CAN'T GO BACK.
I DON'T DESERVE TO WALK NEXT TO YOU GUYS.
THEY DON'T KNOW ANYTHING ABOUT WHAT I DID TO GET HERE.
WE KNOW.
WE ALSO KNOW ABOUT THE *EXPERIMENTS* UNDERGROUND.
ABOUT THE POISON YOU SPREAD IN THE CASTLE TOWN.
AND WHAT YOU TRIED TO DO TO MUJIKA AND SONJU.
!
IT'S NOT TOO LATE.
WE CAN ALL DO SOMETHING ABOUT IT!!
IT'S OKAY IF YOU'RE WEAK.
IF THAT'S THE REAL YOU.
WE CAN WAVER, STRUGGLE AND LAUGH TOGETHER.

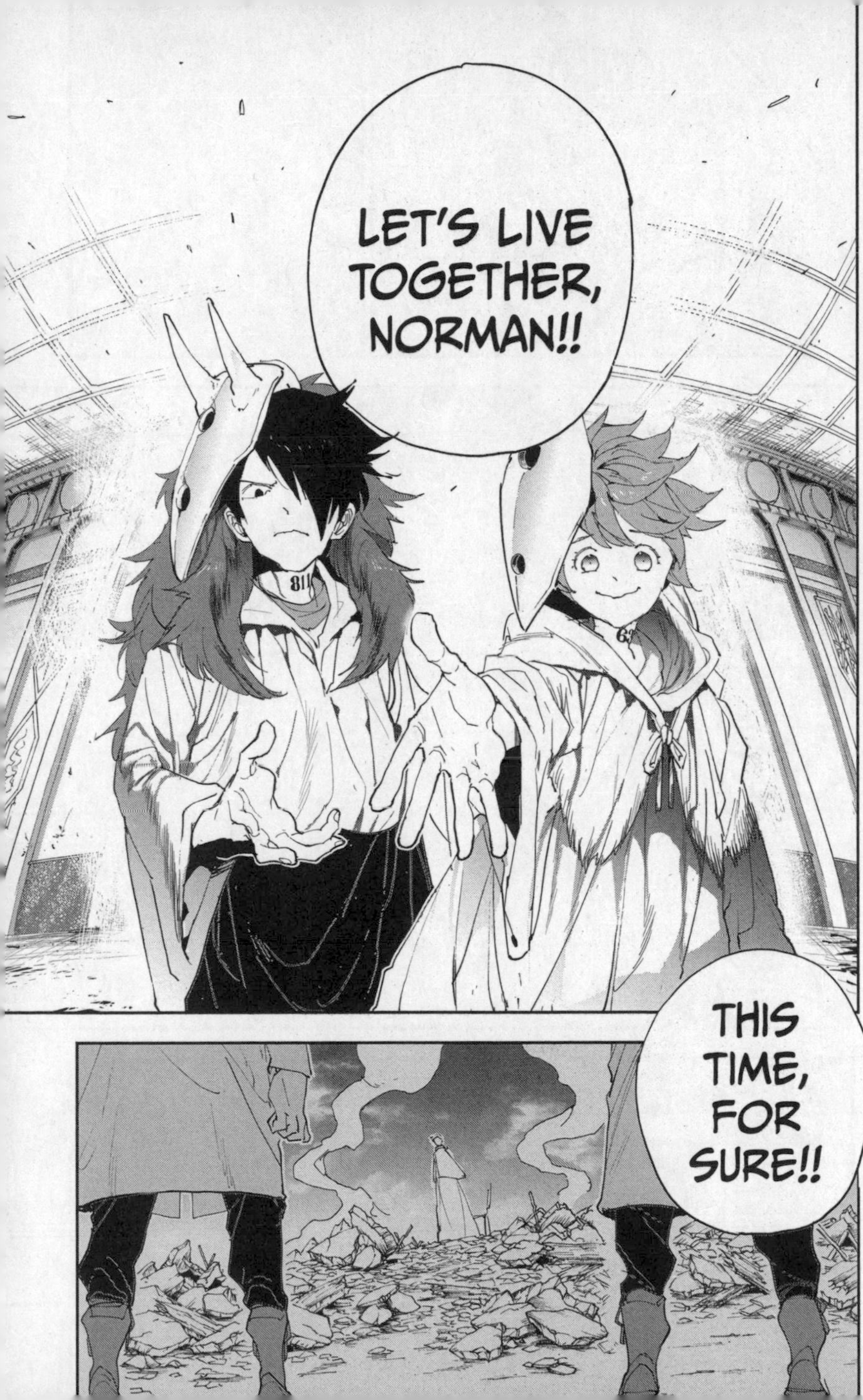
LET'S LIVE TOGETHER, NORMAN!!
THIS TIME, FOR SURE!!

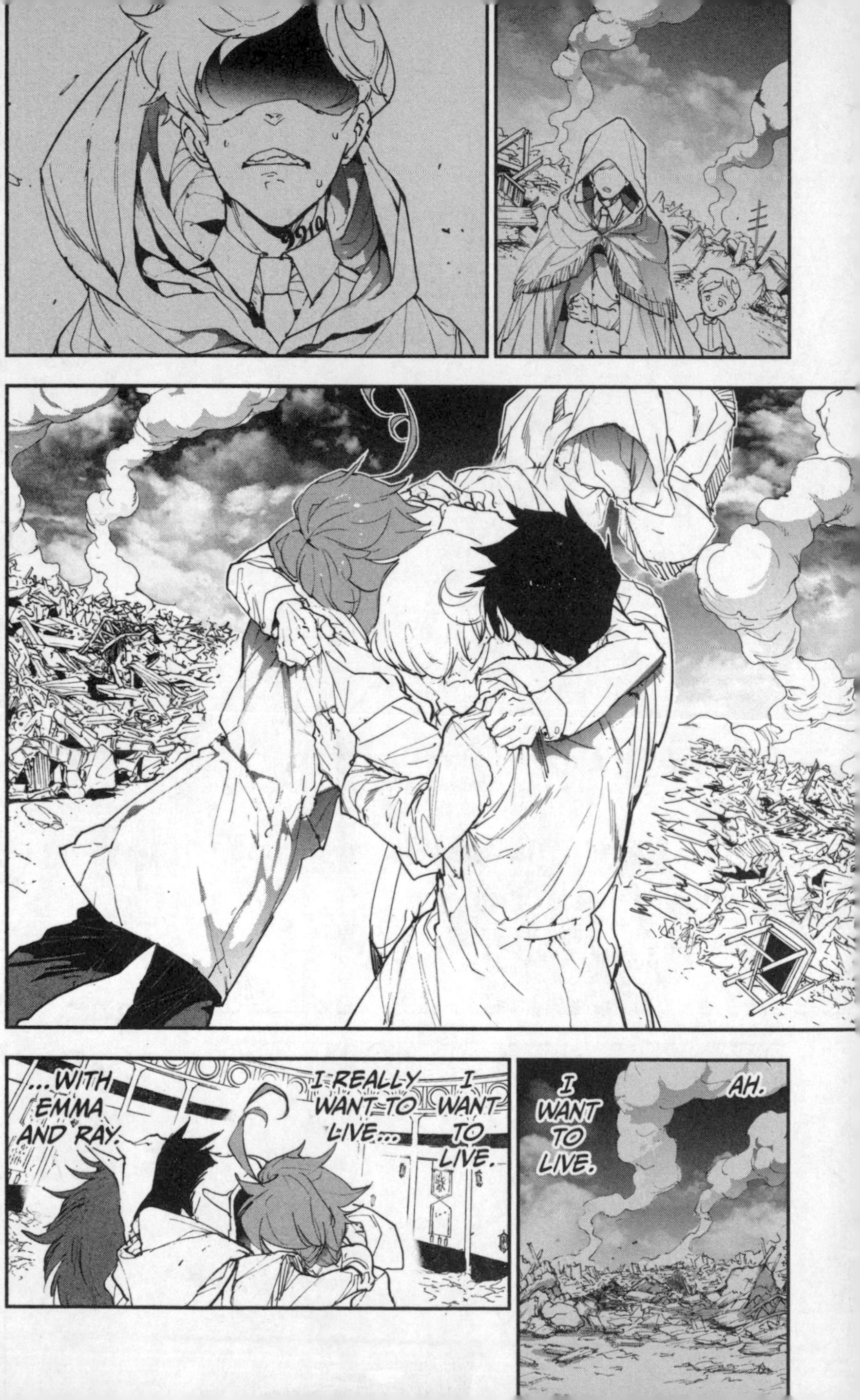
AH.
I WANT TO LIVE.
I WANT TO LIVE.
I REALLY WANT TO LIVE...
...WITH EMMA AND RAY.

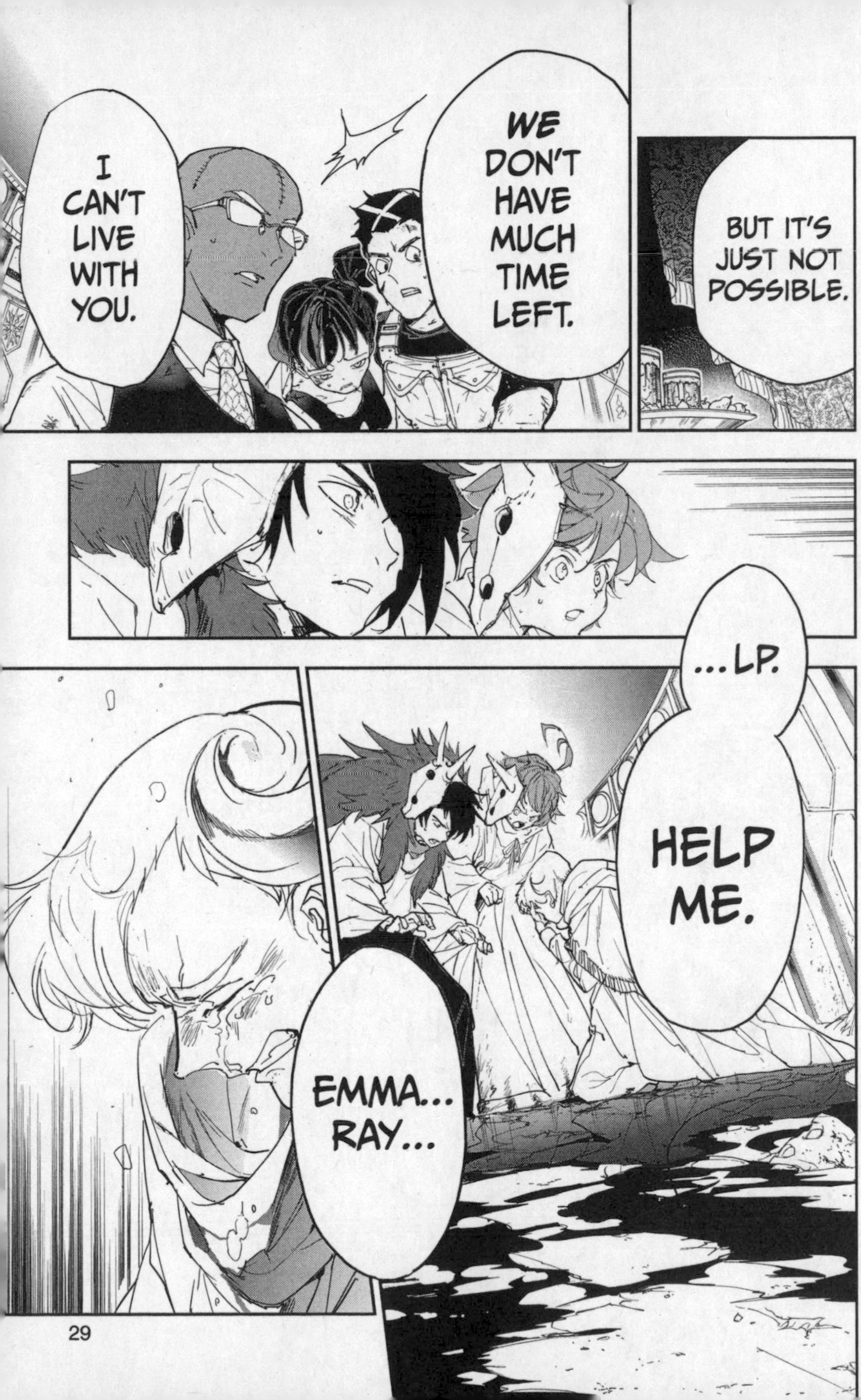
BUT IT'S JUST NOT POSSIBLE.
WE DON'T HAVE MUCH TIME LEFT.
I CAN'T LIVE WITH YOU.
...LP.
HELP ME.
EMMA... RAY...

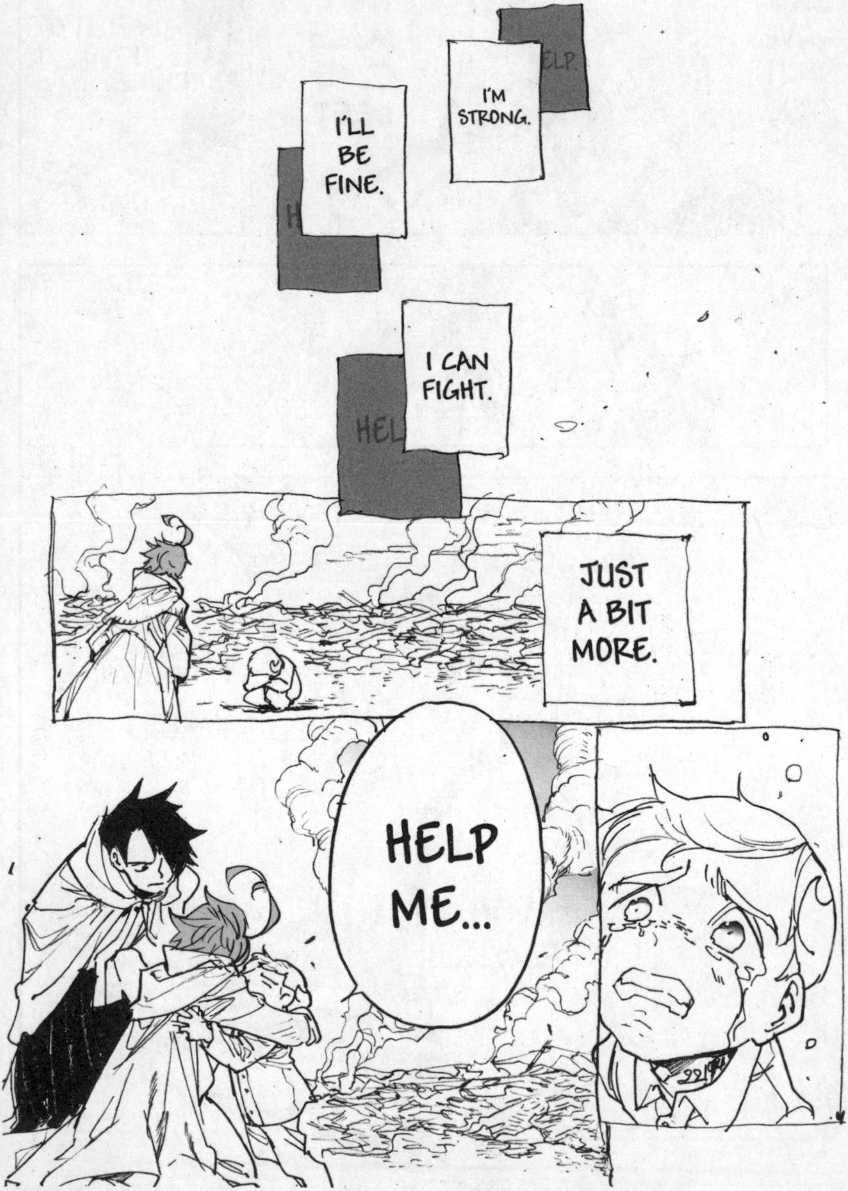

I'M STRONG.
ELP.
I'LL BE FINE.
H
I CAN FIGHT.
HEL
JUST A BIT MORE.
HELP ME...

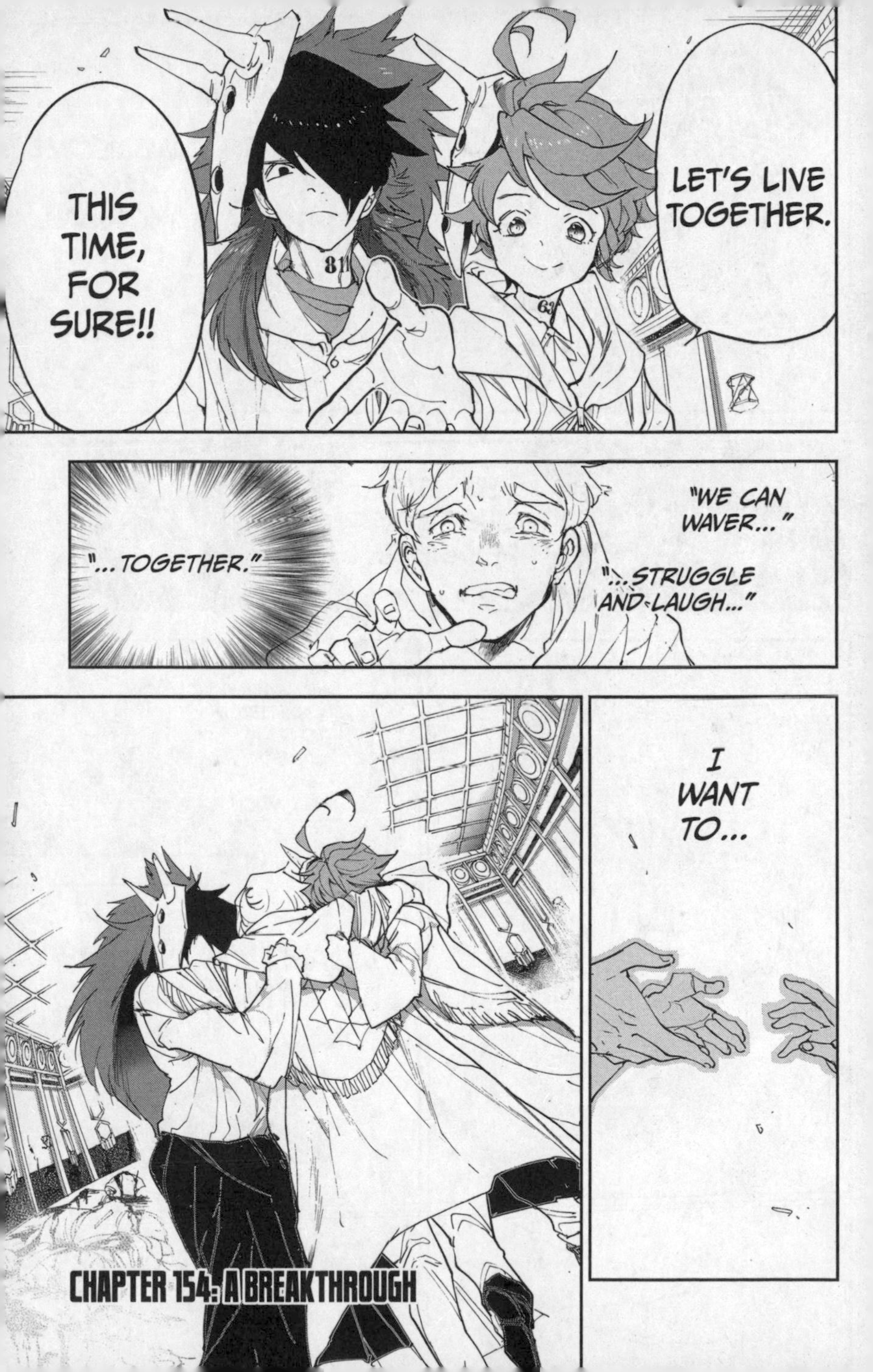
LET'S LIVE TOGETHER.
THIS TIME, FOR SURE!!
"WE CAN WAVER..."
"...STRUGGLE AND LAUGH..."
"...TOGETHER."
I WANT TO...
CHAPTER 154: A BREAKTHROUGH

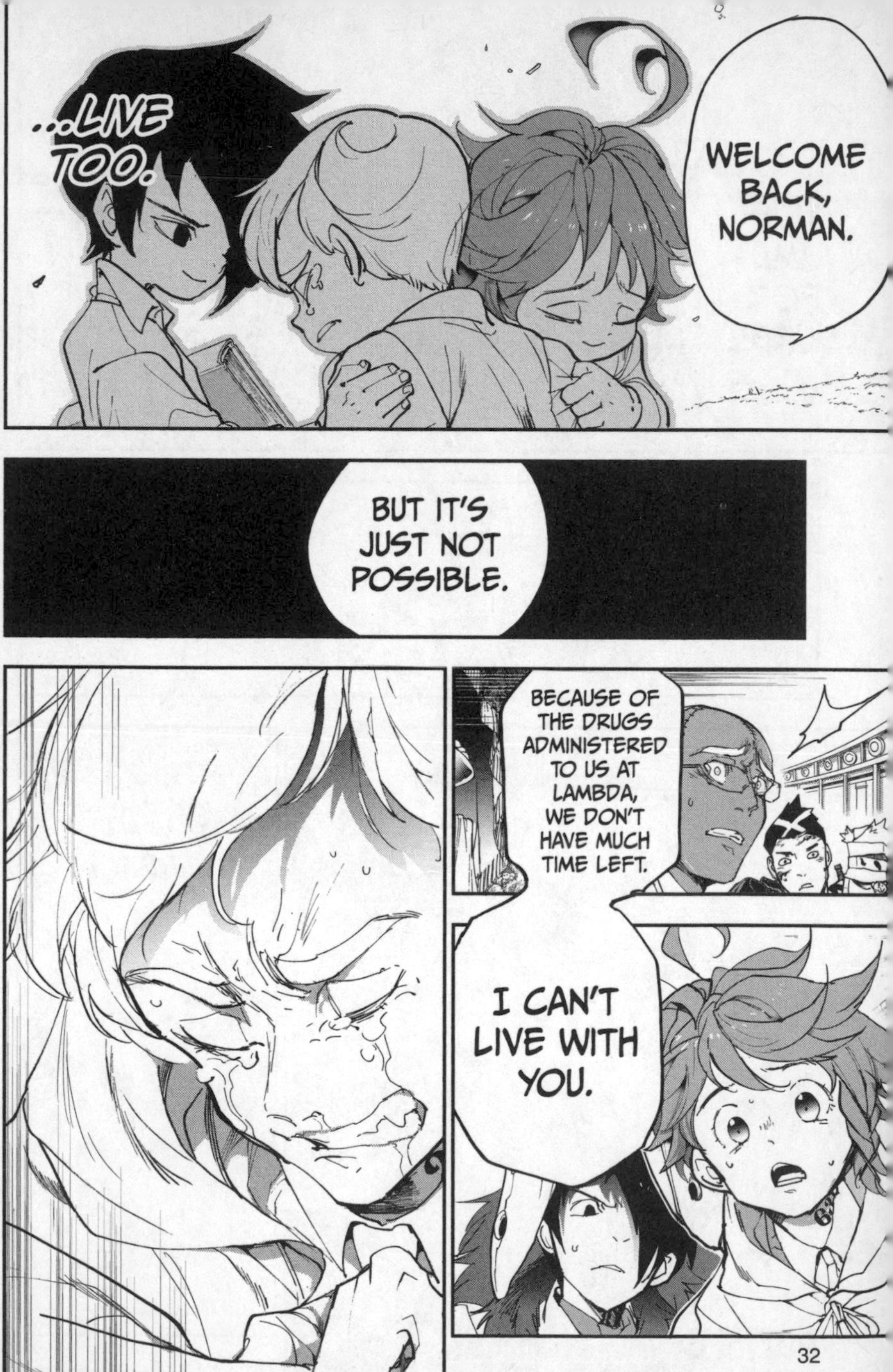
WELCOME BACK, NORMAN.
...LIVE TOO.
BUT IT'S JUST NOT POSSIBLE.
BECAUSE OF THE DRUGS ADMINISTERED TO US AT LAMBDA, WE DON'T HAVE MUCH TIME LEFT.
I CAN'T LIVE WITH YOU.

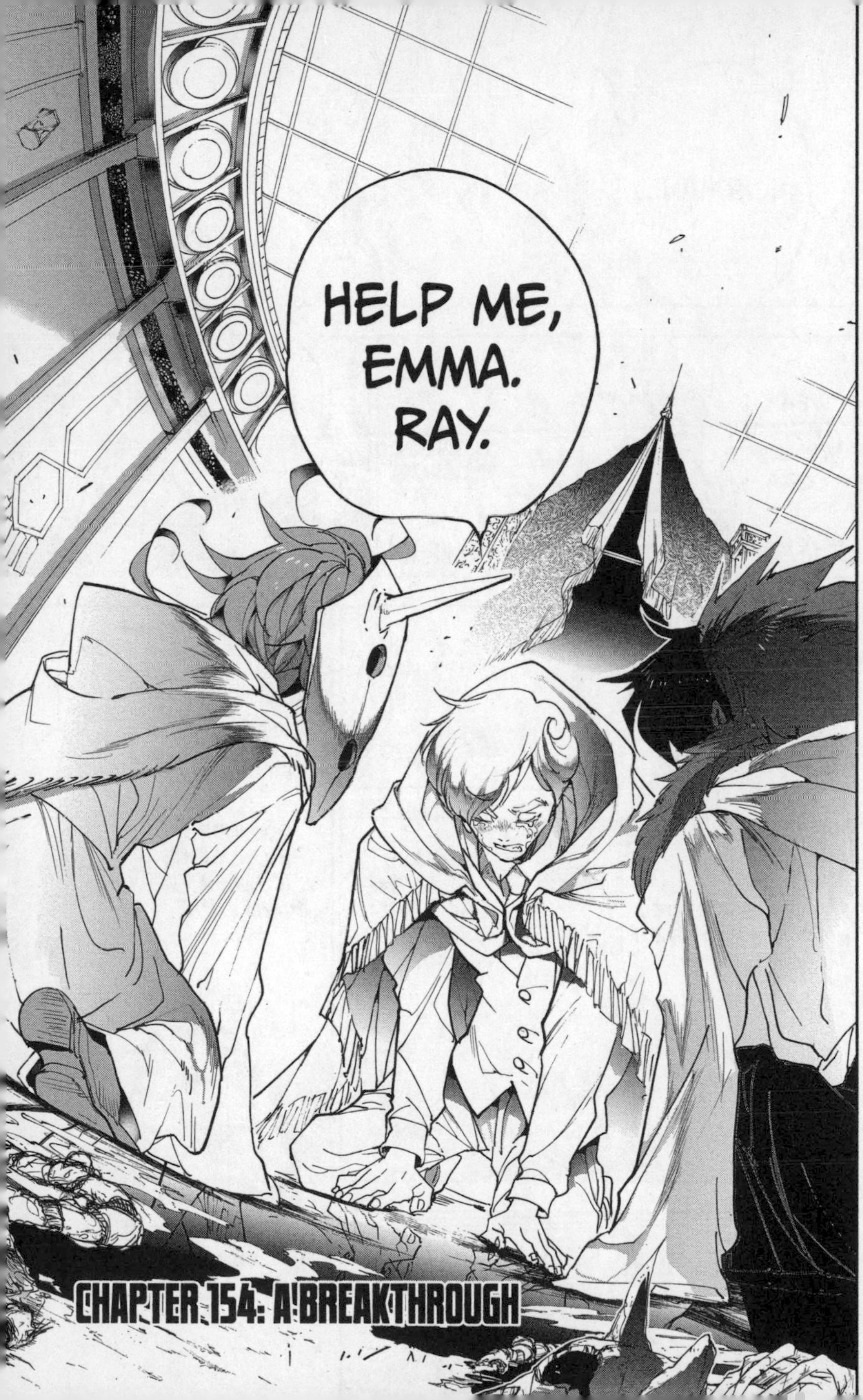
HELP ME, EMMA. RAY.
CHAPTER 154: A BREAKTHROUGH

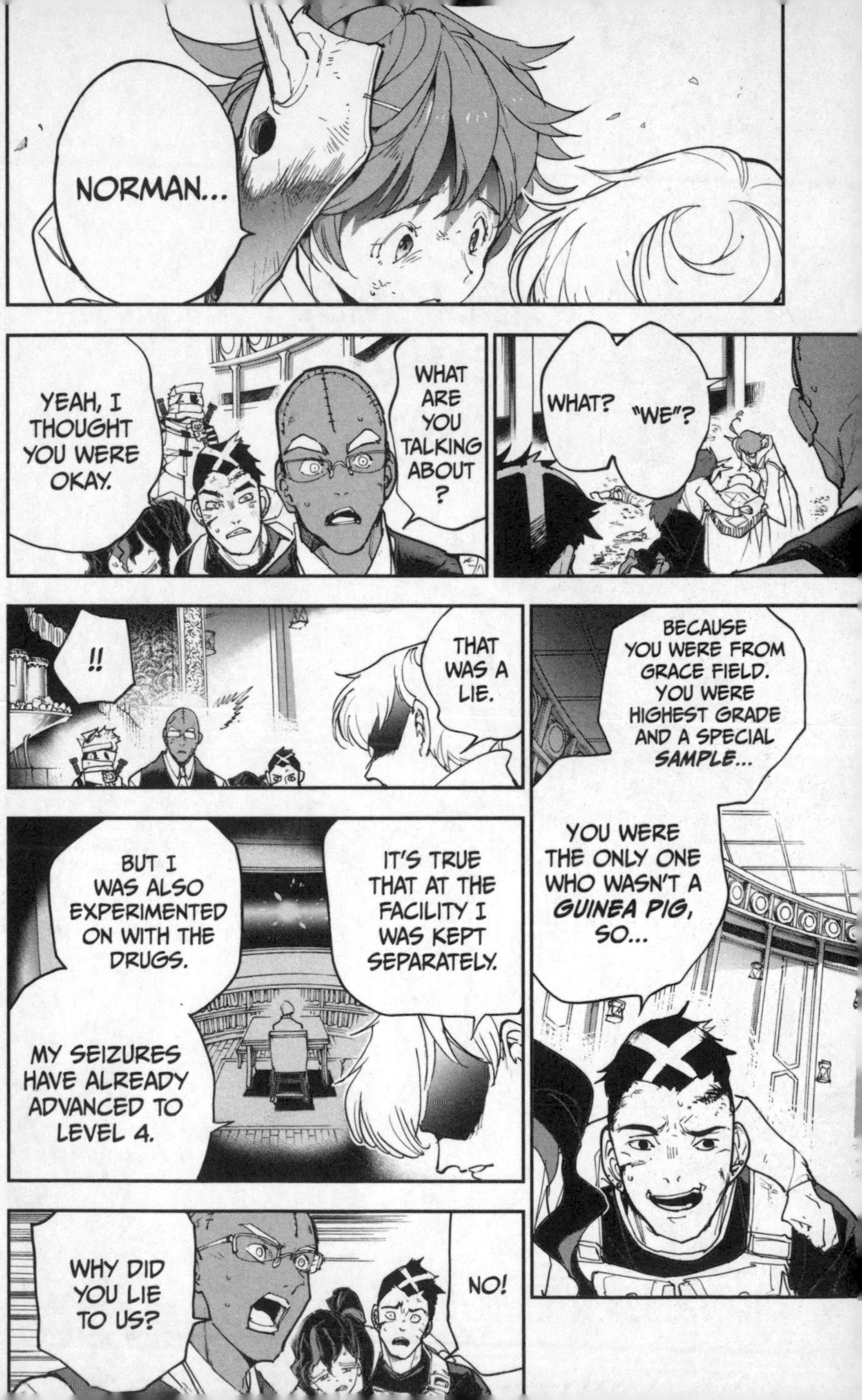
NORMAN...
WHAT? "WE"?
WHAT ARE YOU TALKING ABOUT?
YEAH, I THOUGHT YOU WERE OKAY.
BECAUSE YOU WERE FROM GRACE FIELD. YOU WERE HIGHEST GRADE AND A SPECIAL *SAMPLE*...
YOU WERE THE ONLY ONE WHO WASN'T A *GUINEA PIG*, SO...
THAT WAS A LIE.
!!
IT'S TRUE THAT AT THE FACILITY I WAS KEPT SEPARATELY.
BUT I WAS ALSO EXPERIMENTED ON WITH THE DRUGS.
MY SEIZURES HAVE ALREADY ADVANCED TO LEVEL 4.
NO!
WHY DID YOU LIE TO US?

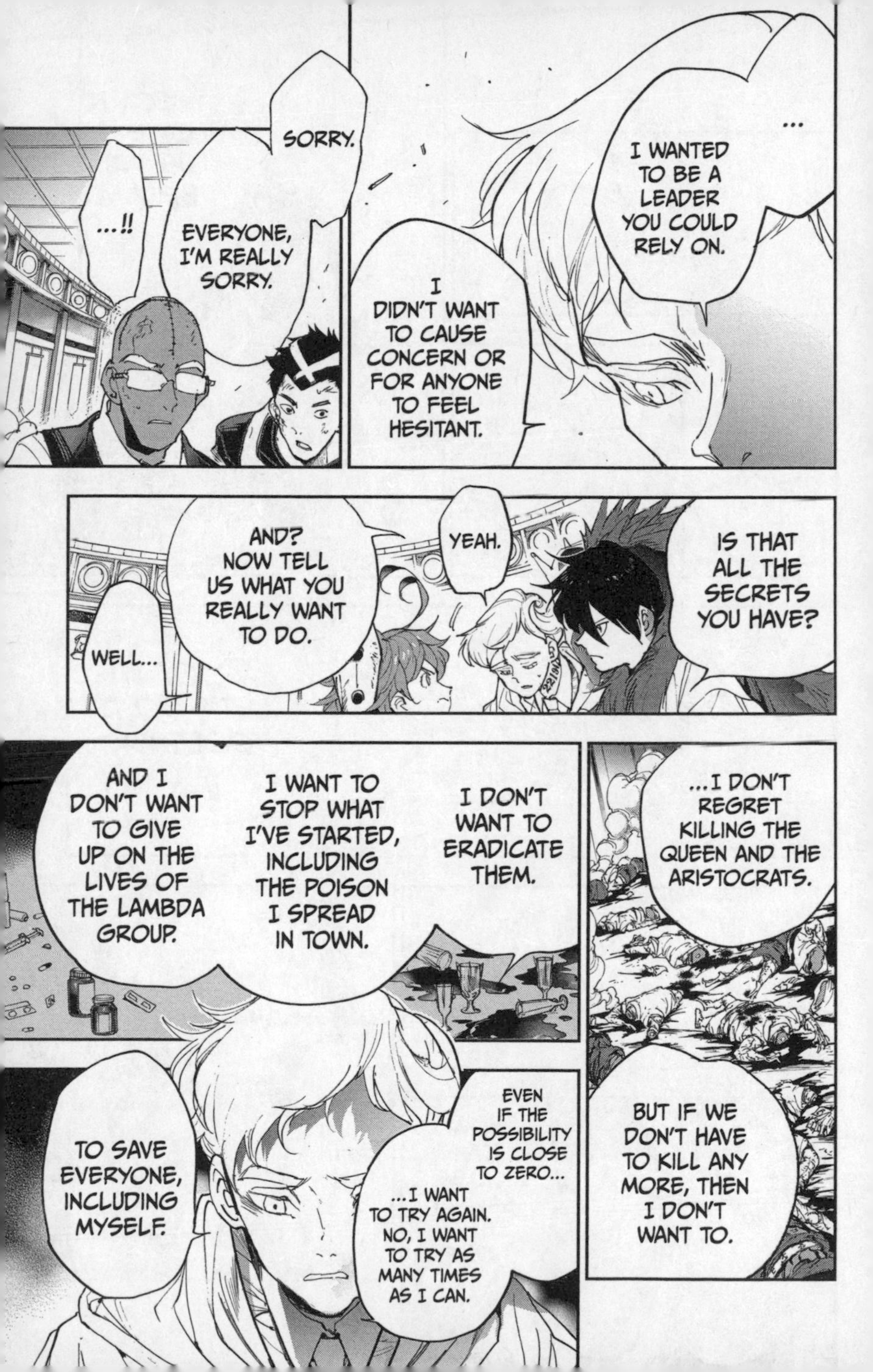
...
I WANTED TO BE A LEADER YOU COULD RELY ON.
I DIDN'T WANT TO CAUSE CONCERN OR FOR ANYONE TO FEEL HESITANT.
SORRY.
EVERYONE, I'M REALLY SORRY.
...!!
IS THAT ALL THE SECRETS YOU HAVE?
YEAH.
AND? NOW TELL US WHAT YOU REALLY WANT TO DO.
WELL...
...I DON'T REGRET KILLING THE QUEEN AND THE ARISTOCRATS.
BUT IF WE DON'T HAVE TO KILL ANY MORE, THEN I DON'T WANT TO.
I DON'T WANT TO ERADICATE THEM.
I WANT TO STOP WHAT I'VE STARTED, INCLUDING THE POISON I SPREAD IN TOWN.
AND I DON'T WANT TO GIVE UP ON THE LIVES OF THE LAMBDA GROUP.
EVEN IF THE POSSIBILITY IS CLOSE TO ZERO...
...I WANT TO TRY AGAIN. NO, I WANT TO TRY AS MANY TIMES AS I CAN.
TO SAVE EVERYONE, INCLUDING MYSELF.

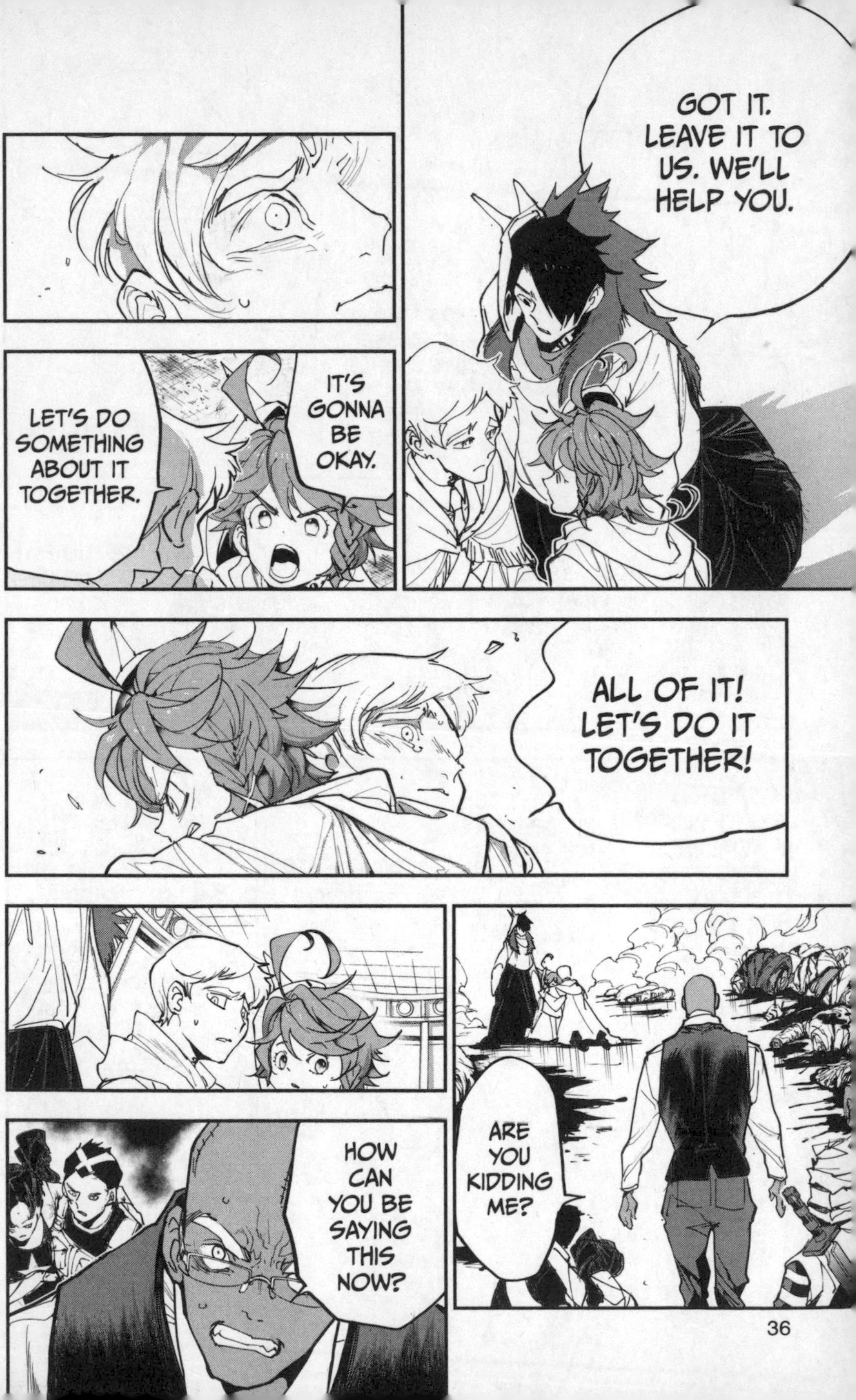
GOT IT. LEAVE IT TO US. WE'LL HELP YOU.
IT'S GONNA BE OKAY.
LET'S DO SOMETHING ABOUT IT TOGETHER.
ALL OF IT! LET'S DO IT TOGETHER!
ARE YOU KIDDING ME?
HOW CAN YOU BE SAYING THIS NOW?

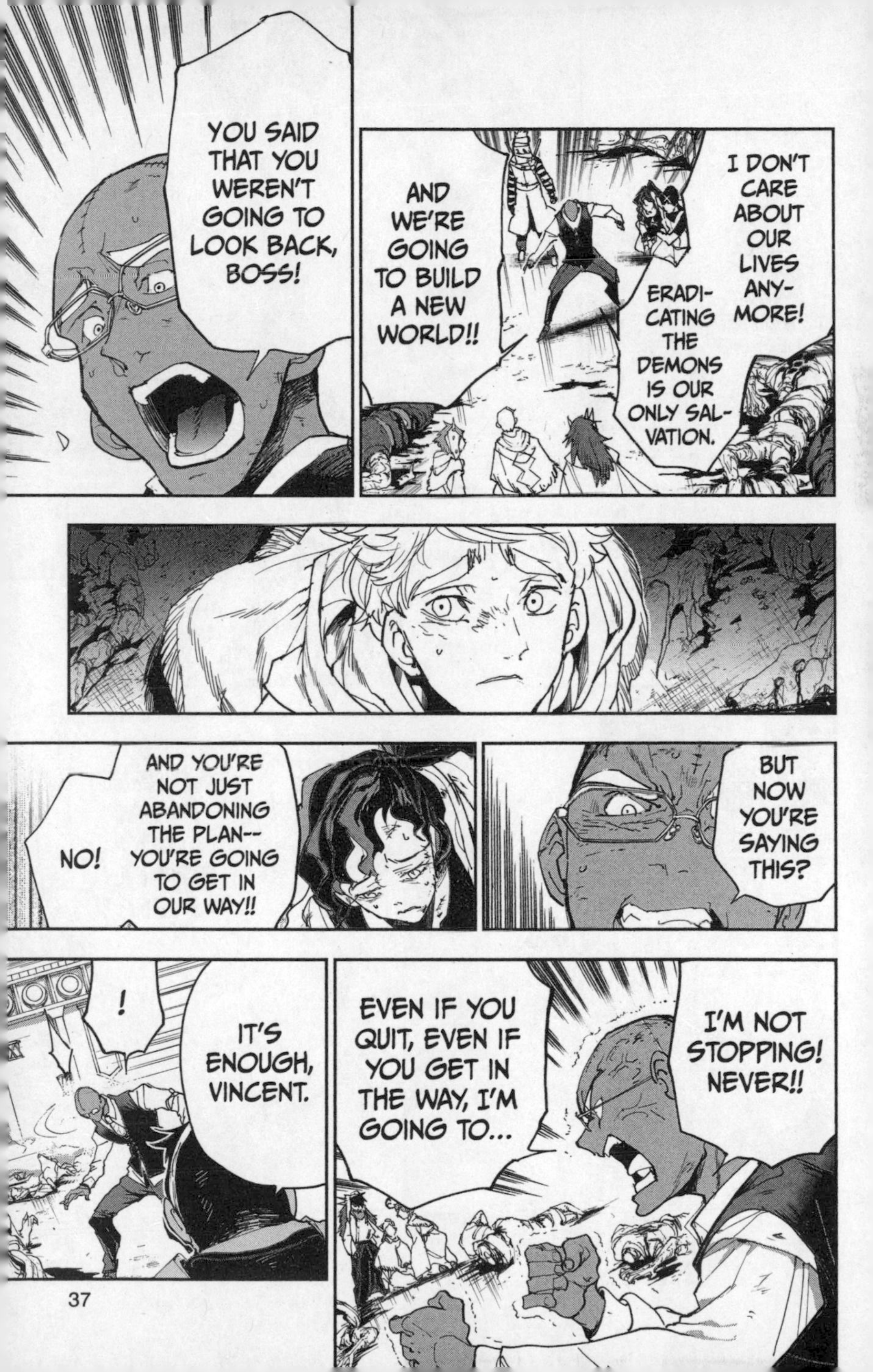
I DON'T CARE ABOUT OUR LIVES ANYMORE!
ERADICATING THE DEMONS IS OUR ONLY SALVATION.
AND WE'RE GOING TO BUILD A NEW WORLD!!
YOU SAID THAT YOU WEREN'T GOING TO LOOK BACK, BOSS!
BUT NOW YOU'RE SAYING THIS?
AND YOU'RE NOT JUST ABANDONING THE PLAN-- YOU'RE GOING TO GET IN OUR WAY!!
NO!
I'M NOT STOPPING! NEVER!!
EVEN IF YOU QUIT, EVEN IF YOU GET IN THE WAY, I'M GOING TO...
!
IT'S ENOUGH, VINCENT.

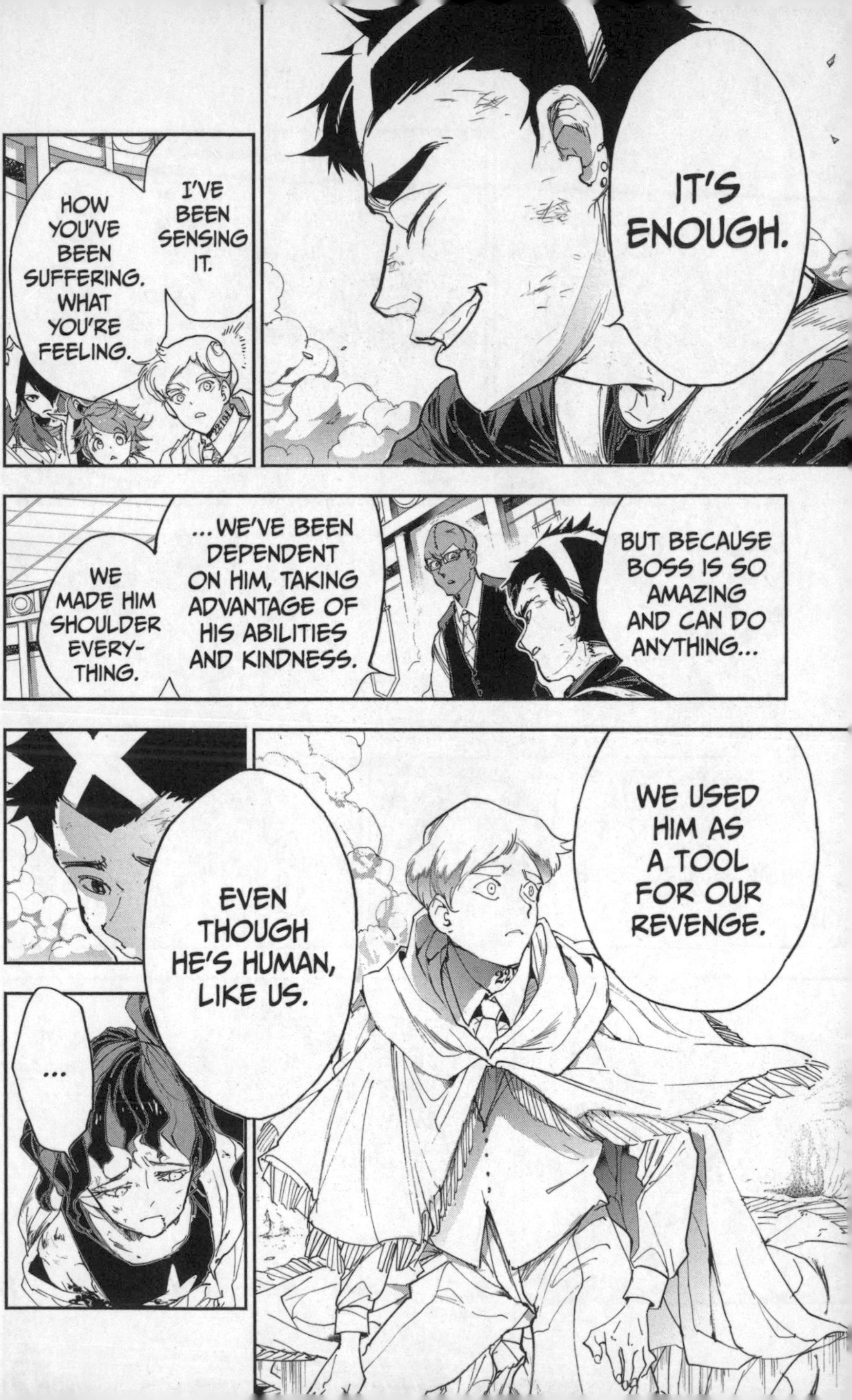
IT'S ENOUGH.
I'VE BEEN SENSING IT.
HOW YOU'VE BEEN SUFFERING. WHAT YOU'RE FEELING.
BUT BECAUSE BOSS IS SO AMAZING AND CAN DO ANYTHING...
...WE'VE BEEN DEPENDENT ON HIM, TAKING ADVANTAGE OF HIS ABILITIES AND KINDNESS.
WE MADE HIM SHOULDER EVERY-THING.
WE USED HIM AS A TOOL FOR OUR REVENGE.
EVEN THOUGH HE'S HUMAN, LIKE US.
...

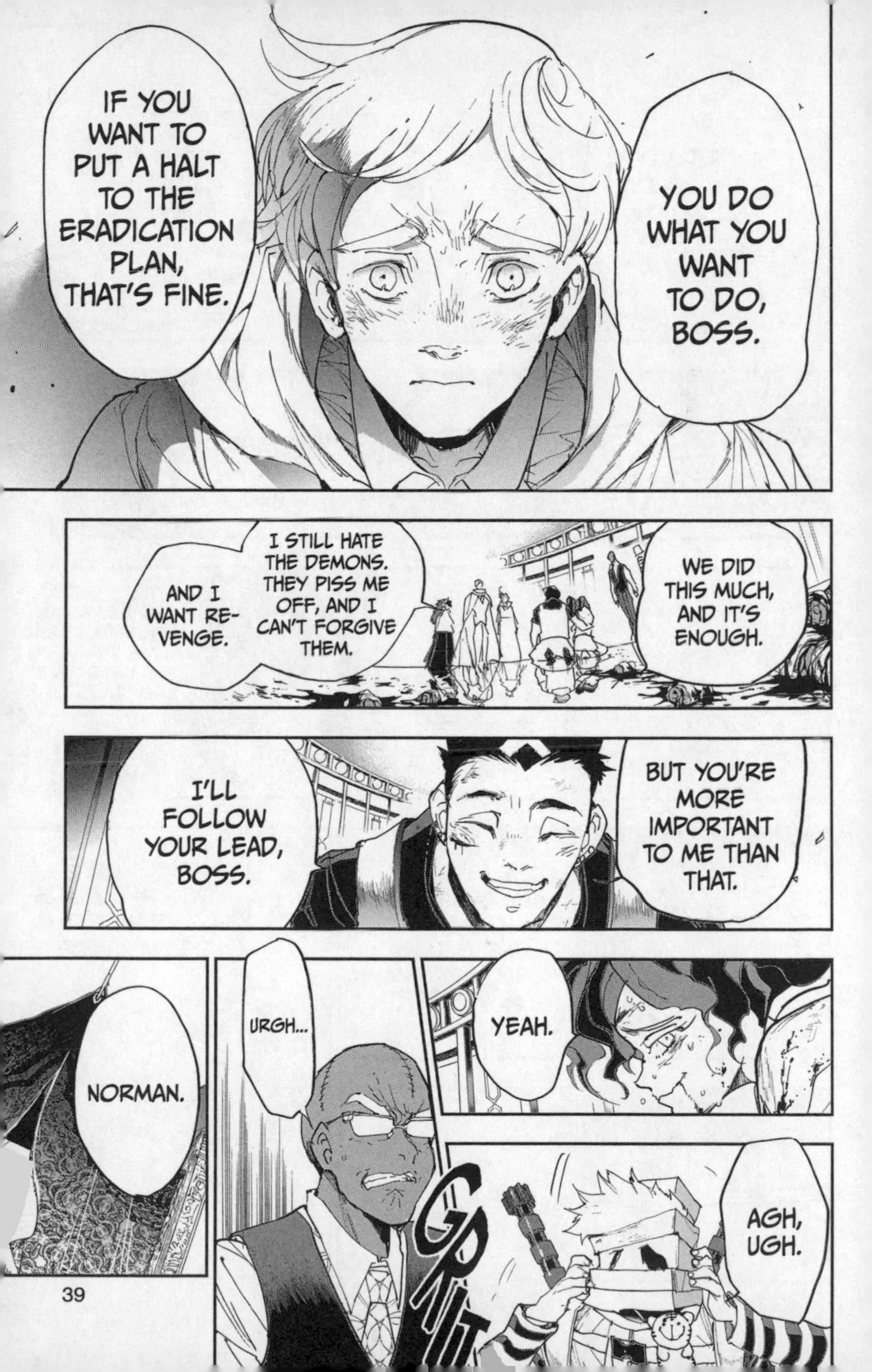
IF YOU WANT TO PUT A HALT TO THE ERADICATION PLAN, THAT'S FINE.
YOU DO WHAT YOU WANT TO DO, BOSS.
WE DID THIS MUCH, AND IT'S ENOUGH.
I STILL HATE THE DEMONS. THEY PISS ME OFF, AND I CAN'T FORGIVE THEM.
AND I WANT RE-VENGE.
BUT YOU'RE MORE IMPORTANT TO ME THAN THAT.
I'LL FOLLOW YOUR LEAD, BOSS.
YEAH.
AGH, UGH.
URGH...
GRIT
NORMAN.

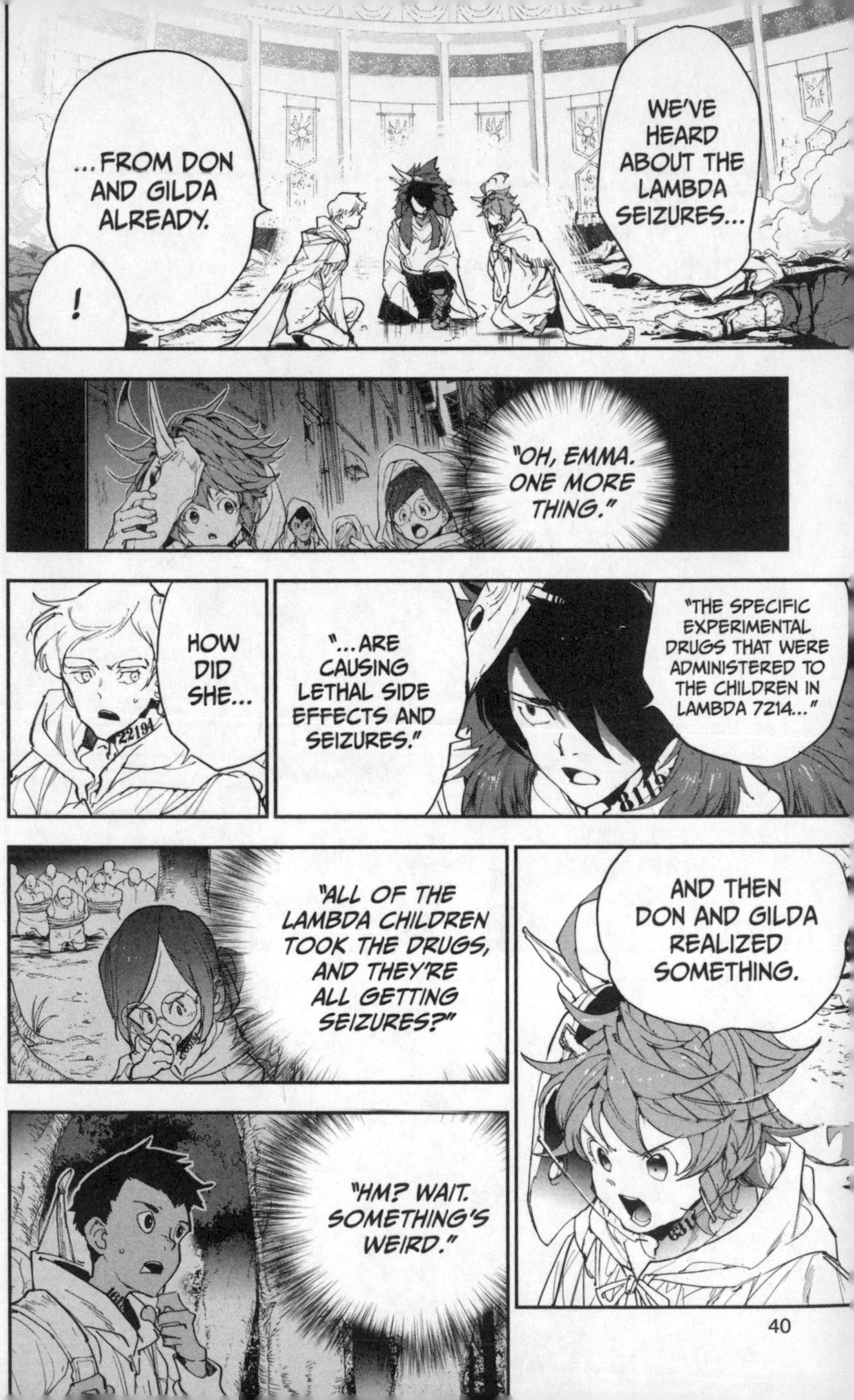
WE'VE HEARD ABOUT THE LAMBDA SEIZURES...
...FROM DON AND GILDA ALREADY.
!
"OH, EMMA. ONE MORE THING."
"THE SPECIFIC EXPERIMENTAL DRUGS THAT WERE ADMINISTERED TO THE CHILDREN IN LAMBDA 7214..."
"...ARE CAUSING LETHAL SIDE EFFECTS AND SEIZURES."
HOW DID SHE...
AND THEN DON AND GILDA REALIZED SOMETHING.
"ALL OF THE LAMBDA CHILDREN TOOK THE DRUGS, AND THEY'RE ALL GETTING SEIZURES?"
"HM? WAIT. SOMETHING'S WEIRD."

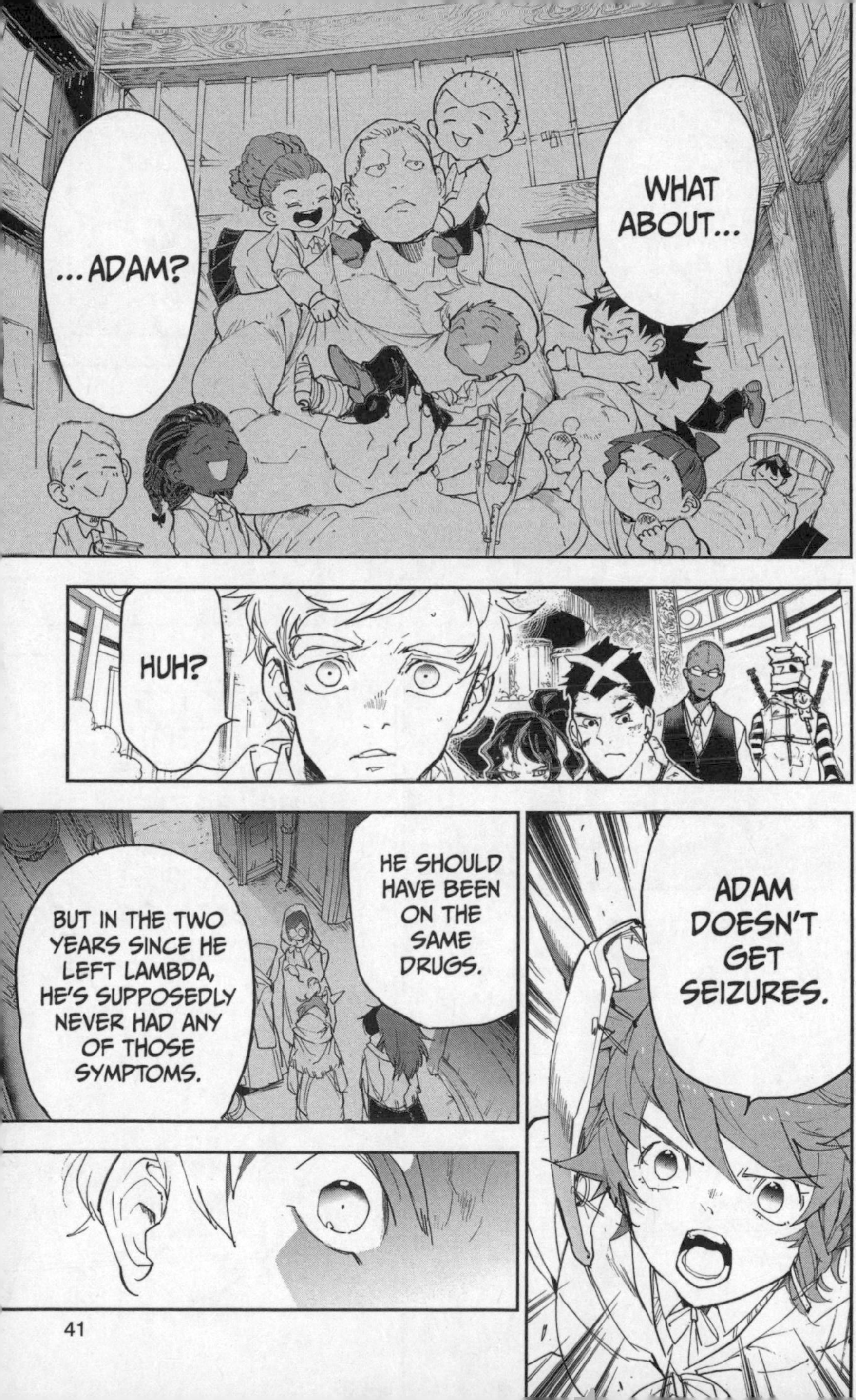
WHAT ABOUT...
...ADAM?
HUH?
ADAM DOESN'T GET SEIZURES.
HE SHOULD HAVE BEEN ON THE SAME DRUGS.
BUT IN THE TWO YEARS SINCE HE LEFT LAMBDA, HE'S SUPPOSEDLY NEVER HAD ANY OF THOSE SYMPTOMS.

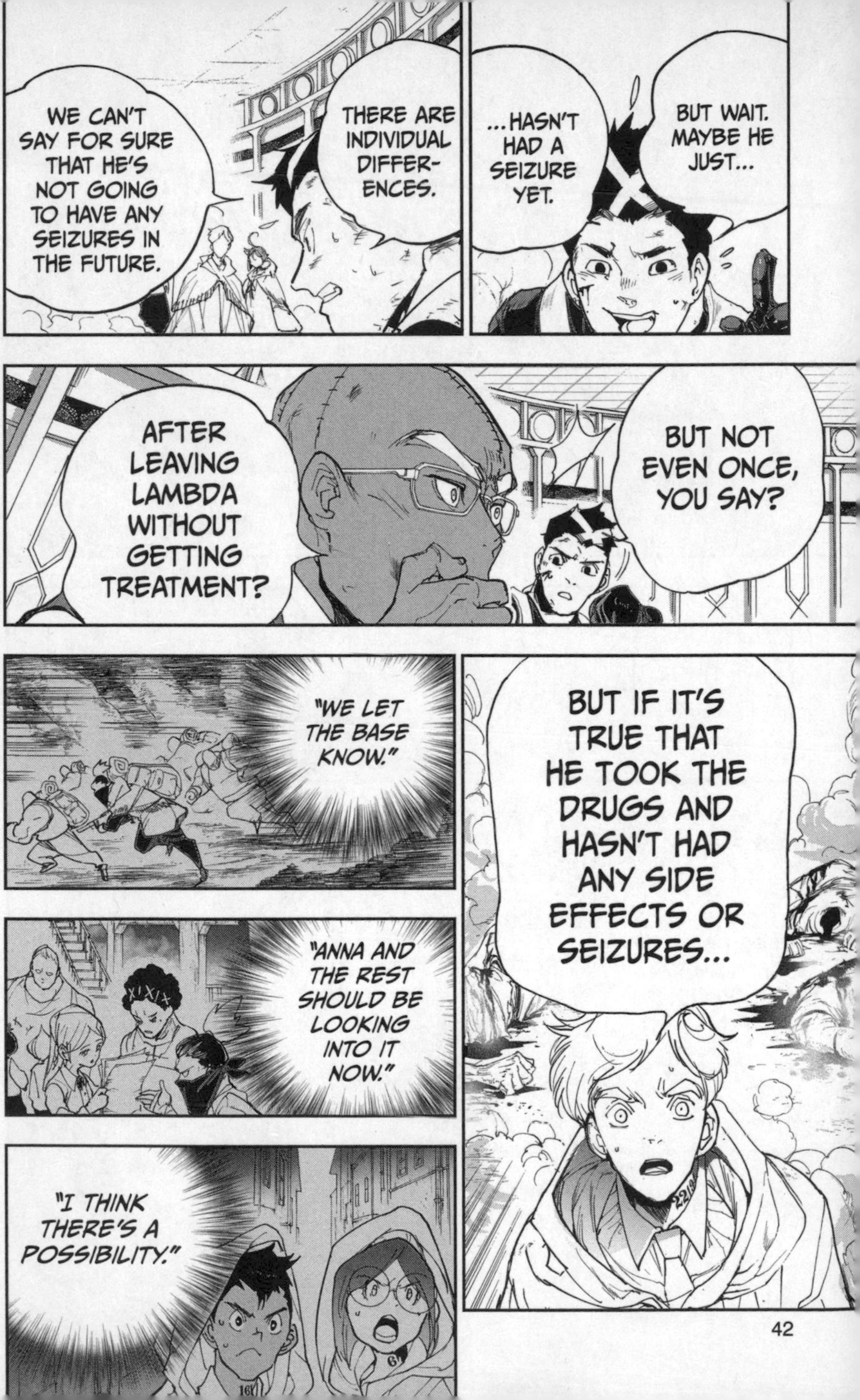
BUT WAIT. MAYBE HE JUST...
...HASN'T HAD A SEIZURE YET.
THERE ARE INDIVIDUAL DIFFER- ENCES.
WE CAN'T SAY FOR SURE THAT HE'S NOT GOING TO HAVE ANY SEIZURES IN THE FUTURE.
BUT NOT EVEN ONCE, YOU SAY?
AFTER LEAVING LAMBDA WITHOUT GETTING TREATMENT?
BUT IF IT'S TRUE THAT HE TOOK THE DRUGS AND HASN'T HAD ANY SIDE EFFECTS OR SEIZURES...
"WE LET THE BASE KNOW."
"ANNA AND THE REST SHOULD BE LOOKING INTO IT NOW."
"I THINK THERE'S A POSSIBILITY."

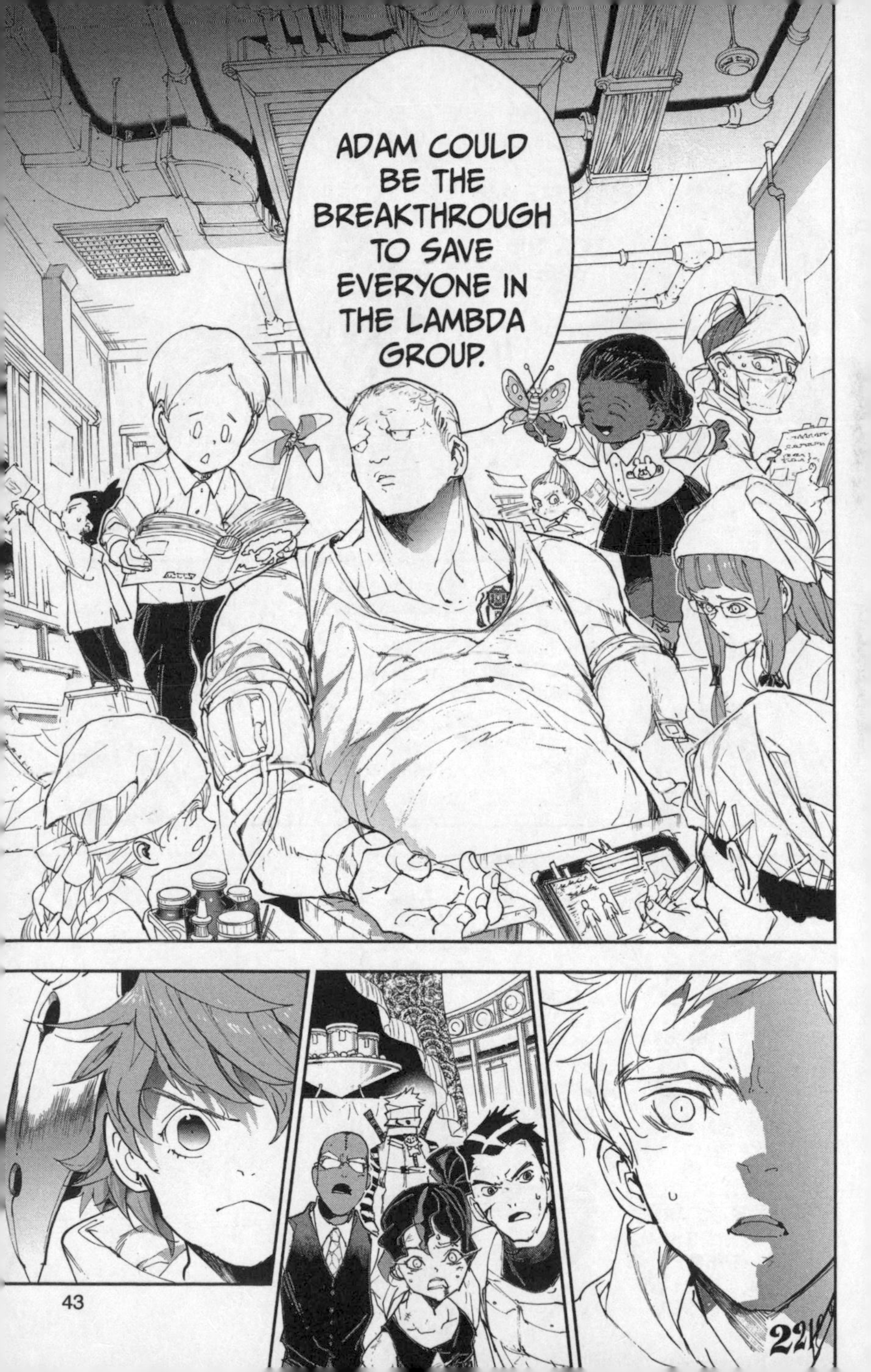
ADAM COULD BE THE BREAKTHROUGH TO SAVE EVERYONE IN THE LAMBDA GROUP.

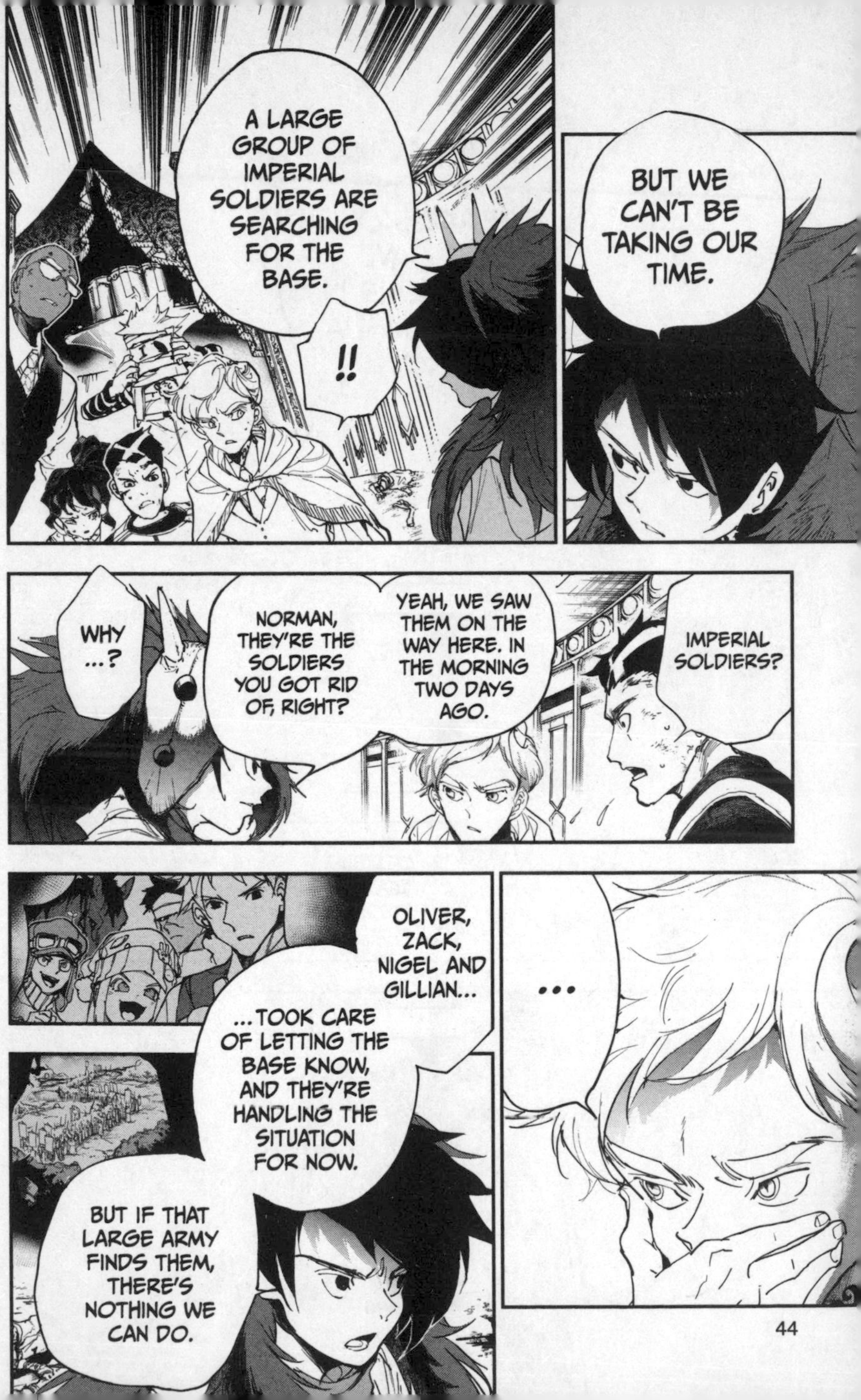
BUT WE CAN'T BE TAKING OUR TIME.
A LARGE GROUP OF IMPERIAL SOLDIERS ARE SEARCHING FOR THE BASE.
!!
IMPERIAL SOLDIERS?
YEAH, WE SAW THEM ON THE WAY HERE. IN THE MORNING TWO DAYS AGO.
NORMAN, THEY'RE THE SOLDIERS YOU GOT RID OF, RIGHT?
WHY ...?
...
OLIVER, ZACK, NIGEL AND GILLIAN...
...TOOK CARE OF LETTING THE BASE KNOW, AND THEY'RE HANDLING THE SITUATION FOR NOW.
BUT IF THAT LARGE ARMY FINDS THEM, THERE'S NOTHING WE CAN DO.

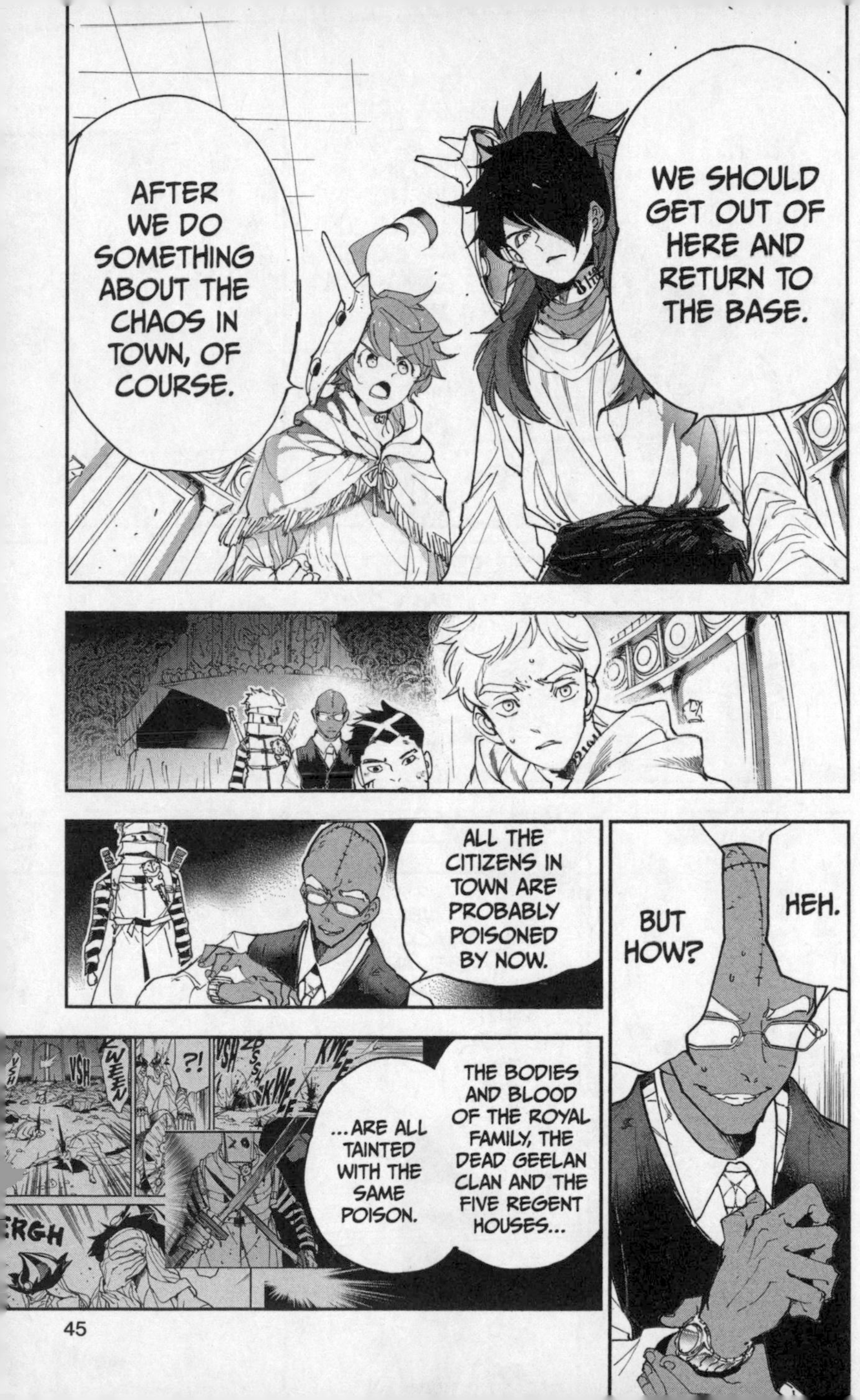
WE SHOULD GET OUT OF HERE AND RETURN TO THE BASE.
AFTER WE DO SOMETHING ABOUT THE CHAOS IN TOWN, OF COURSE.
HEH.
BUT HOW?
ALL THE CITIZENS IN TOWN ARE PROBABLY POISONED BY NOW.
THE BODIES AND BLOOD OF THE ROYAL FAMILY, THE DEAD GEELAN CLAN AND THE FIVE REGENT HOUSES...
...ARE ALL TAINTED WITH THE SAME POISON.
KWEE
KWEE
ZSSH
VSH
?!
WEEN
VSH
VSH
ERGH

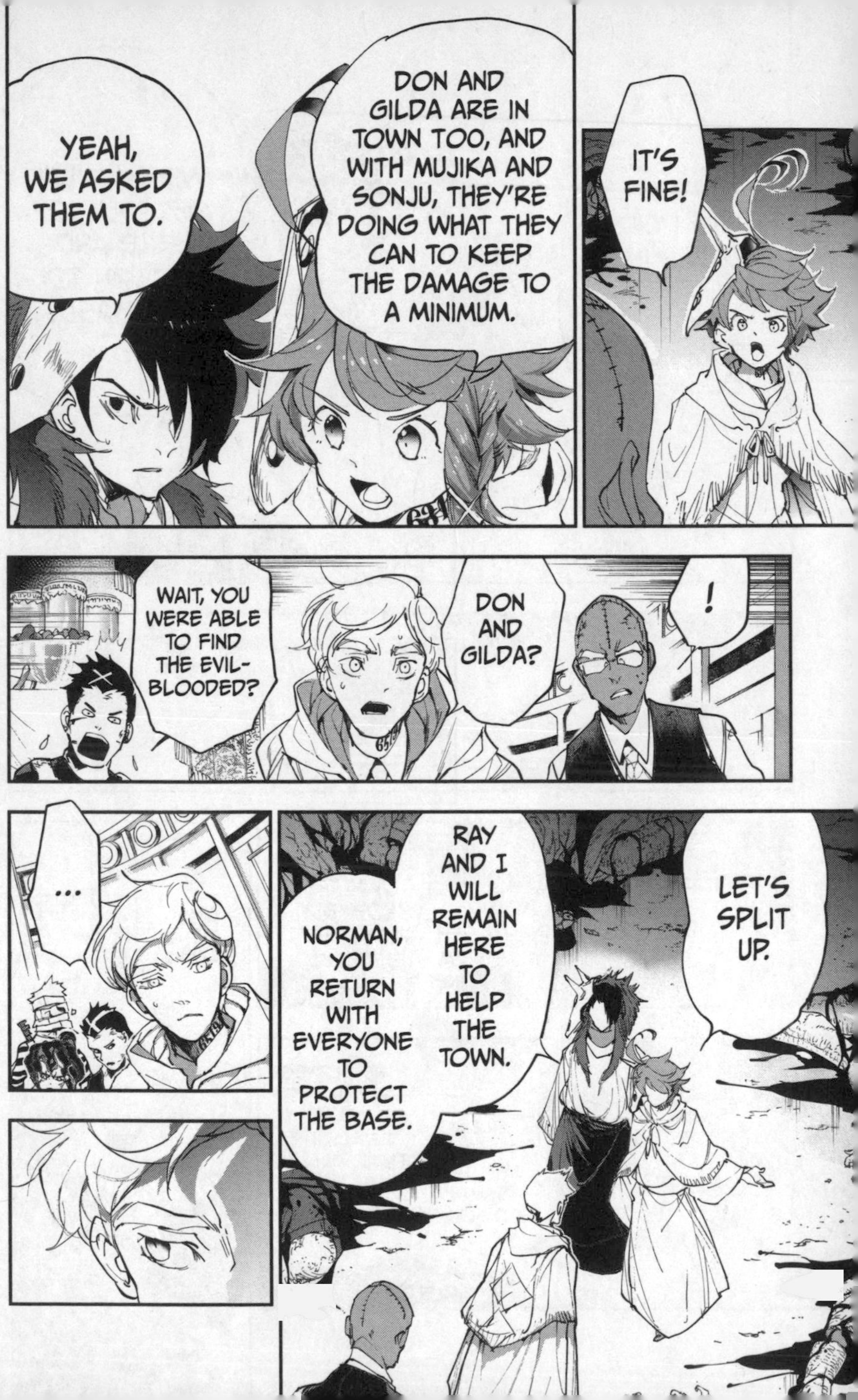
IT'S FINE!
DON AND GILDA ARE IN TOWN TOO, AND WITH MUJIKA AND SONJU, THEY'RE DOING WHAT THEY CAN TO KEEP THE DAMAGE TO A MINIMUM.
YEAH, WE ASKED THEM TO.
!
DON AND GILDA?
WAIT, YOU WERE ABLE TO FIND THE EVIL-BLOODED?
LET'S SPLIT UP.
RAY AND I WILL REMAIN HERE TO HELP THE TOWN.
NORMAN, YOU RETURN WITH EVERYONE TO PROTECT THE BASE.
...

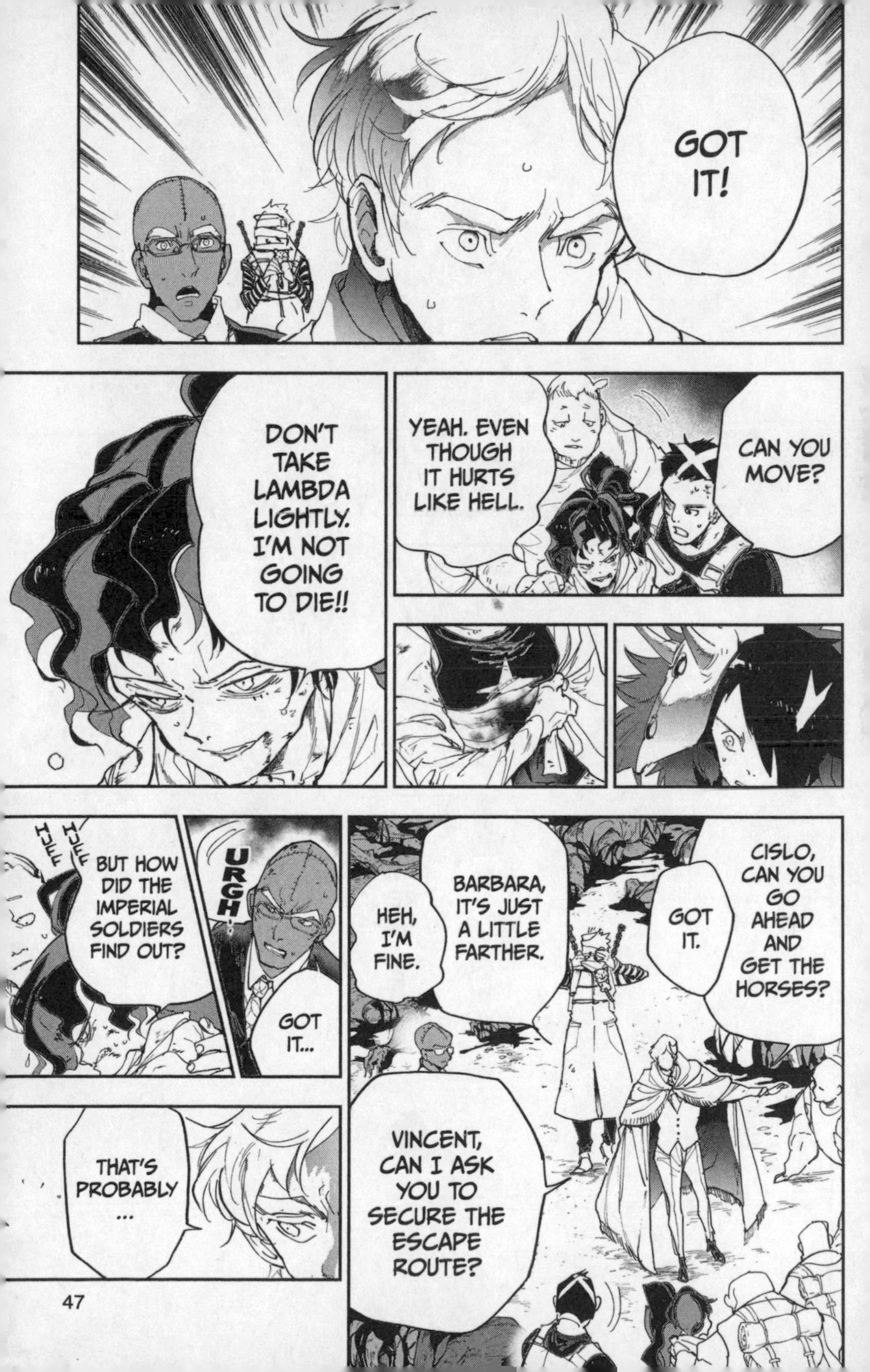
GOT IT!
CAN YOU MOVE?
YEAH. EVEN THOUGH IT HURTS LIKE HELL.
DON'T TAKE LAMBDA LIGHTLY. I'M NOT GOING TO DIE!!
CISLO, CAN YOU GO AHEAD AND GET THE HORSES?
GOT IT.
BARBARA, IT'S JUST A LITTLE FARTHER.
HEH, I'M FINE.
VINCENT, CAN I ASK YOU TO SECURE THE ESCAPE ROUTE?
URGH!
HUFF HUFF
BUT HOW DID THE IMPERIAL SOLDIERS FIND OUT?
GOT IT...
THAT'S PROBABLY...

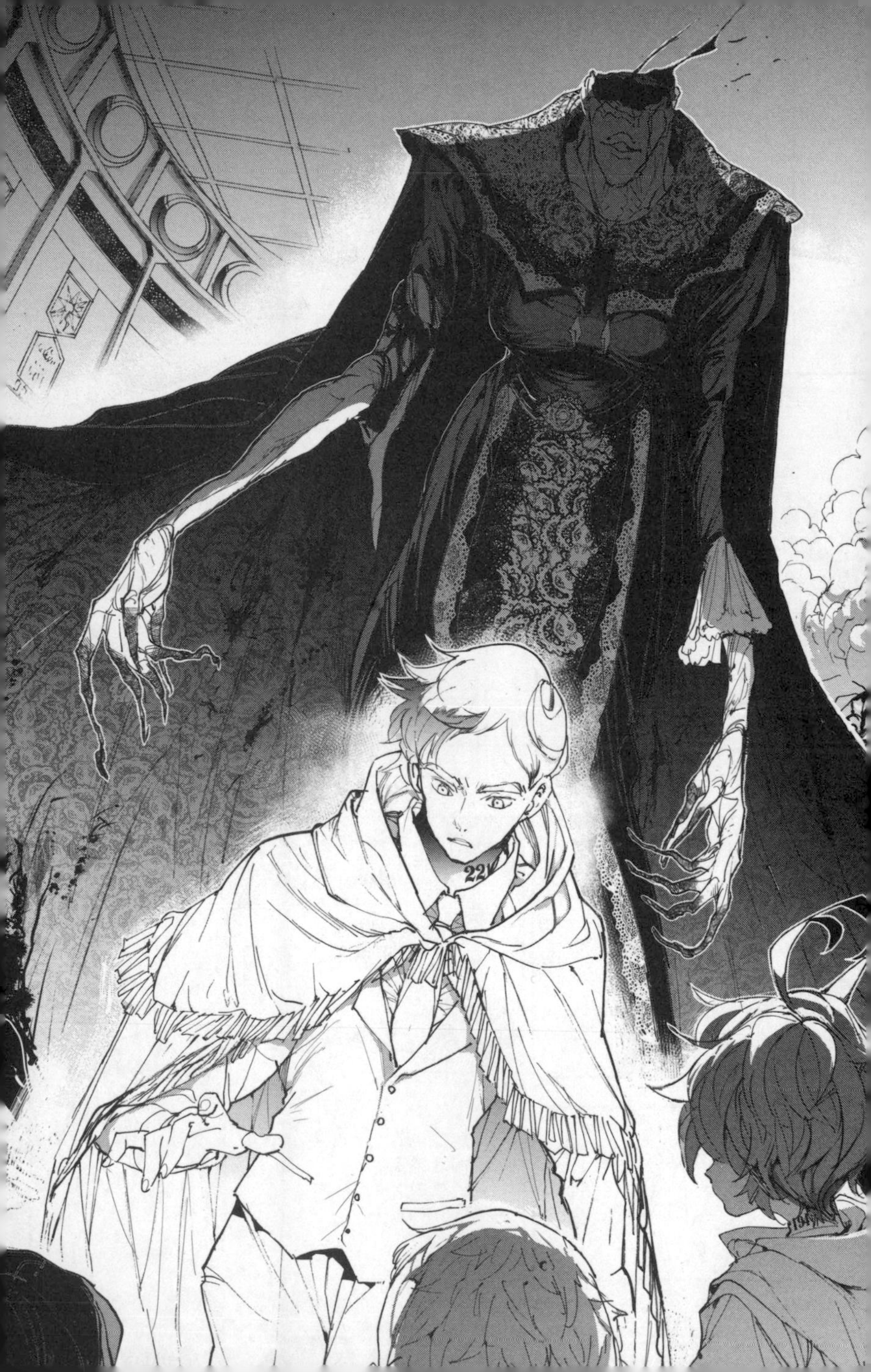

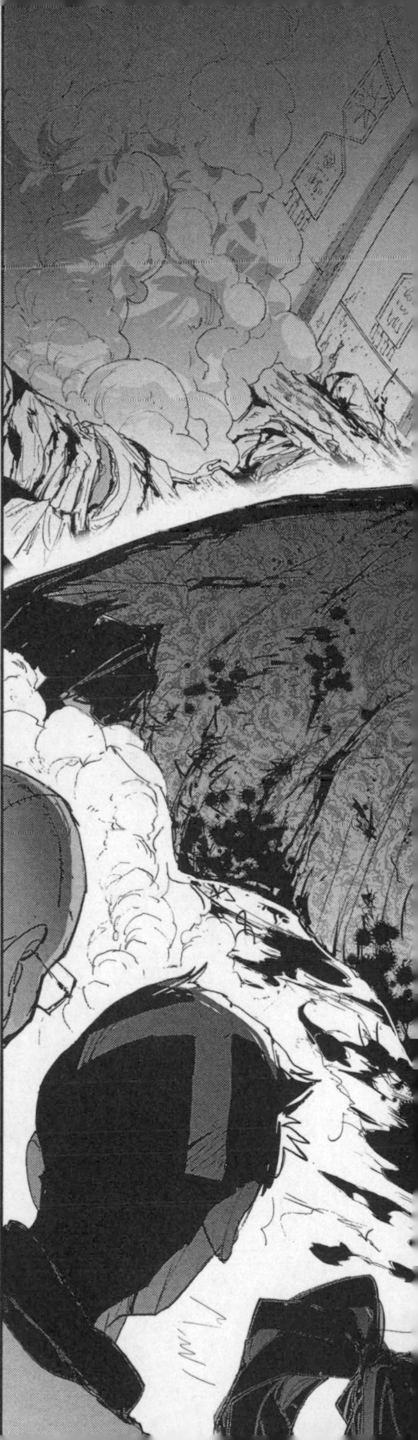

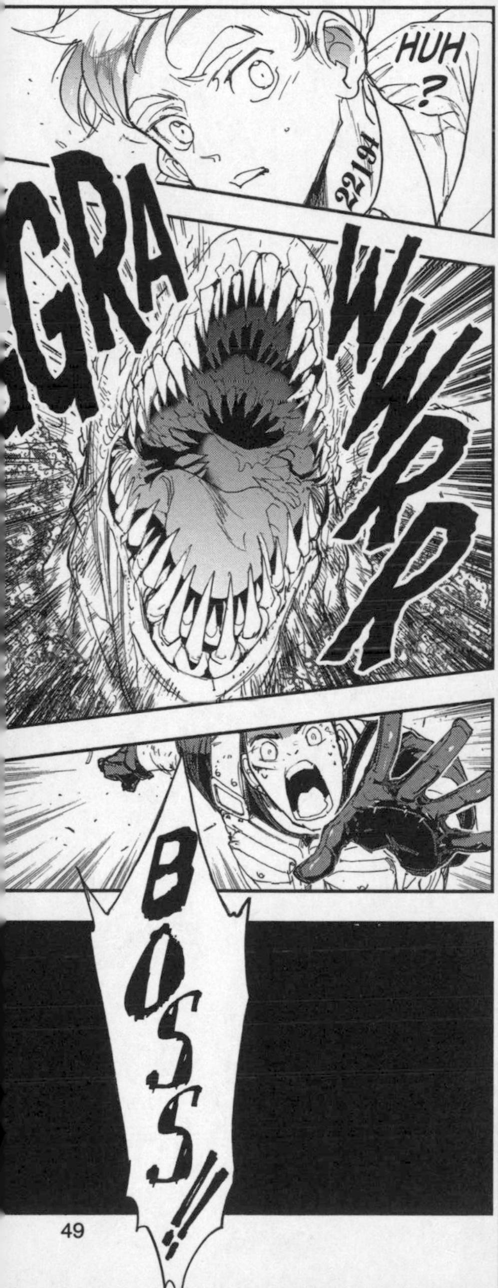
HUH ?
22194
GRAWWRR
BOSS!!

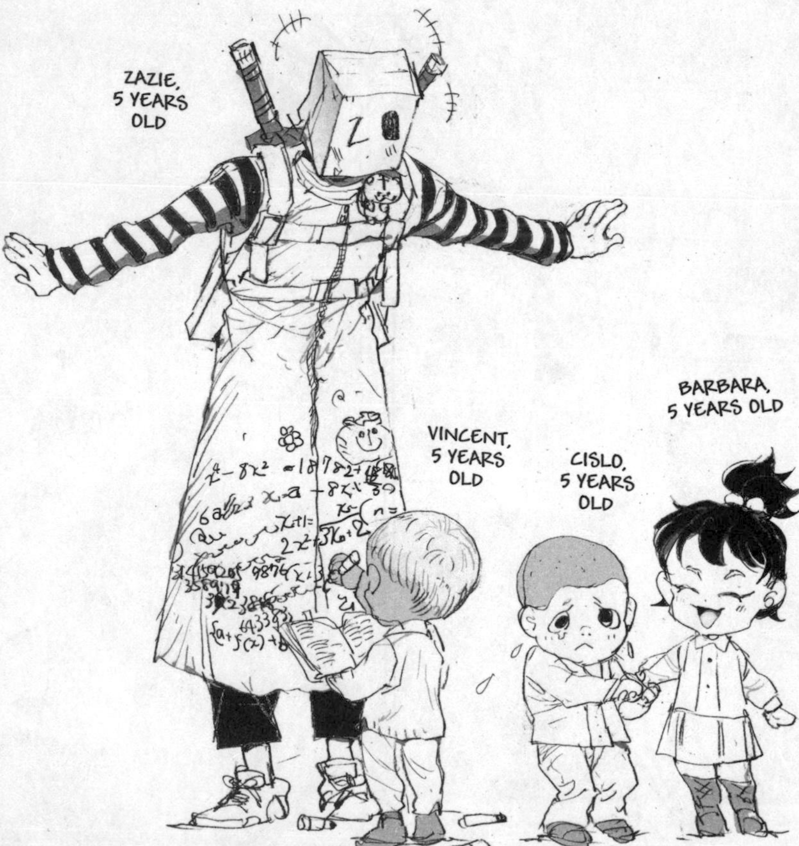
BARBARA, 5 YEARS OLD
CISLO, 5 YEARS OLD
VINCENT, 5 YEARS OLD
ZAZIE, 5 YEARS OLD

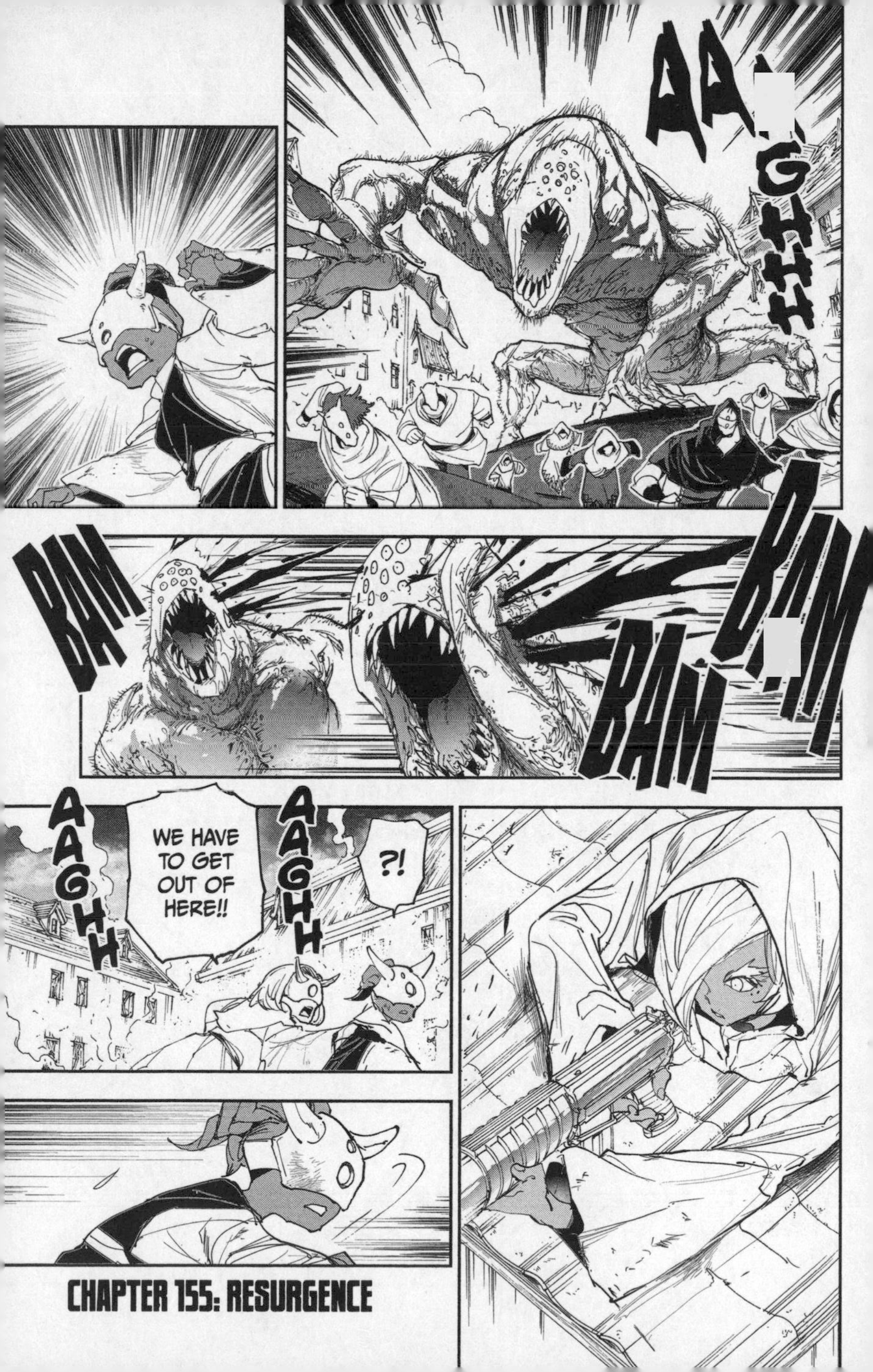
AA
GHHHH
BAM
BAM
BAM
?!
AAGHH
WE HAVE TO GET OUT OF HERE!!
AAGHH

CHAPTER 155: RESURGENCE

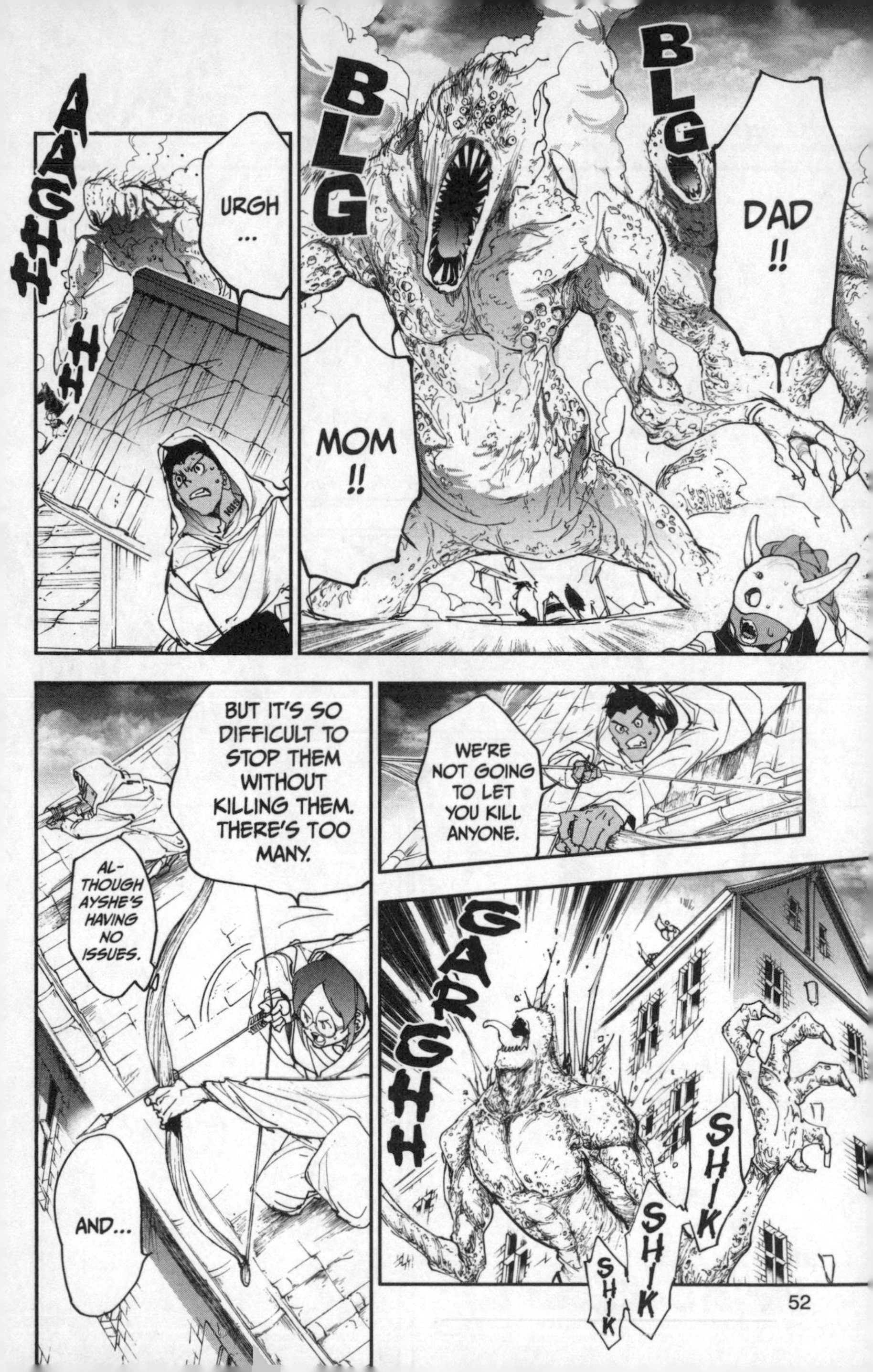
BLG
DAD !!
BLG
MOM !!
URGH ...
AAGHHHH
WE'RE NOT GOING TO LET YOU KILL ANYONE.
GARGHHH
SHIK
SHIK
SHIK
BUT IT'S SO DIFFICULT TO STOP THEM WITHOUT KILLING THEM. THERE'S TOO MANY.
AL-THOUGH AYSHE'S HAVING NO ISSUES.
AND...

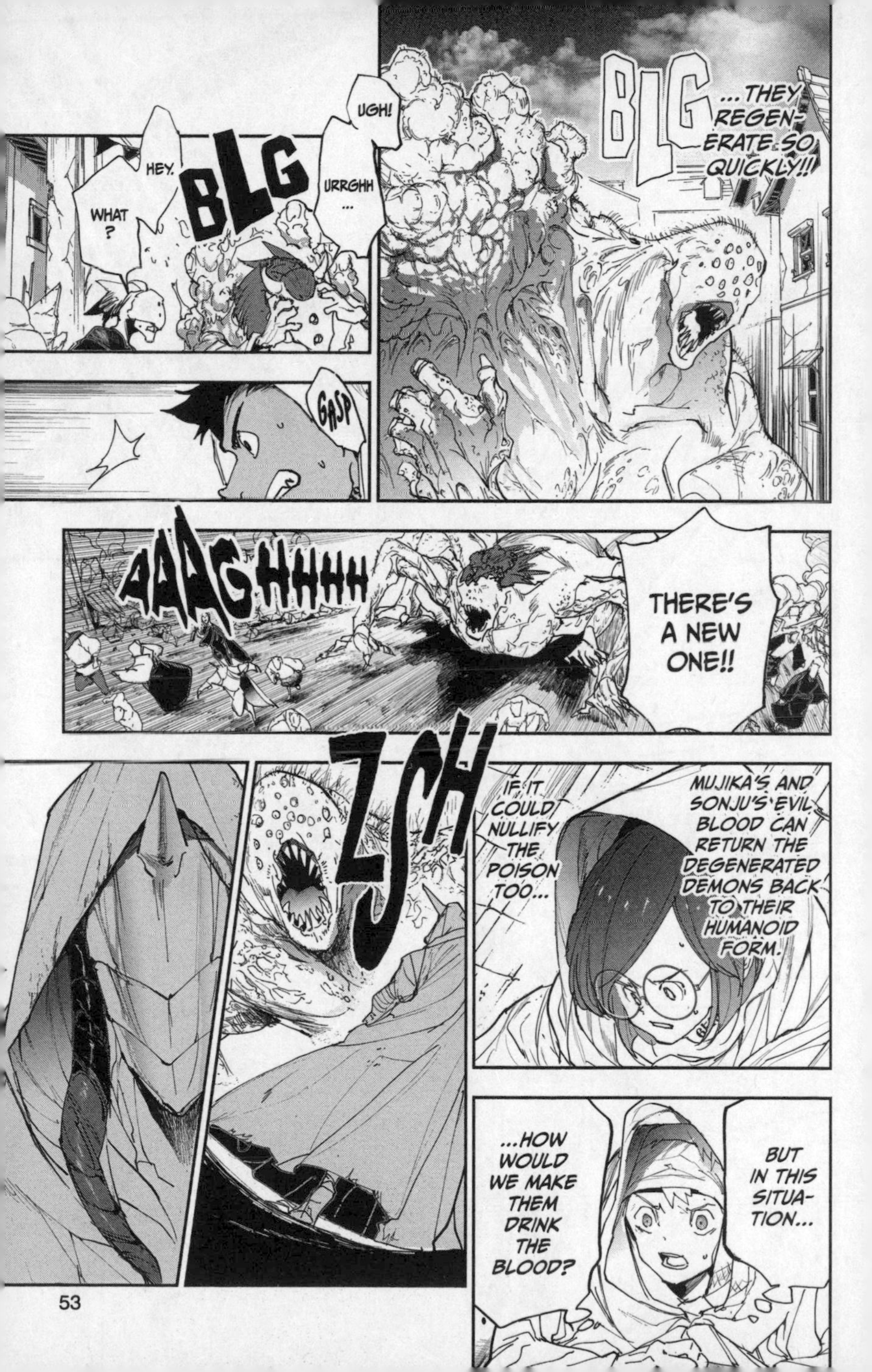
BLG
...THEY REGENERATE SO QUICKLY!!
UGH!
URRGHH ...
BLG
HEY.
WHAT ?
GASP
THERE'S A NEW ONE!!
AAAGHHHH
MUJIKA'S AND SONJU'S EVIL BLOOD CAN RETURN THE DEGENERATED DEMONS BACK TO THEIR HUMANOID FORM.
IF IT COULD NULLIFY THE POISON TOO...
BUT IN THIS SITUATION...
...HOW WOULD WE MAKE THEM DRINK THE BLOOD?
ZSH

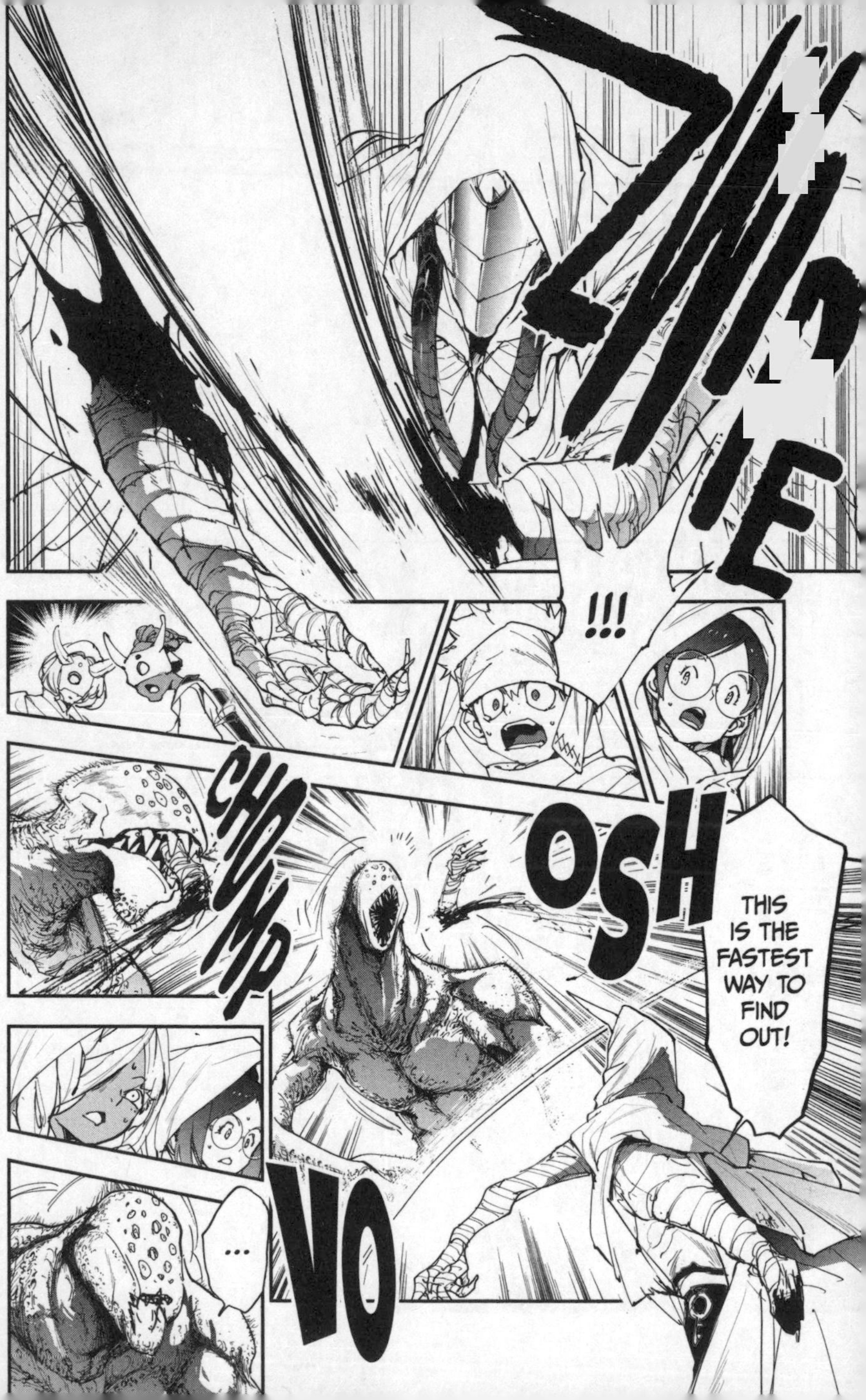
!!!
THIS IS THE FASTEST WAY TO FIND OUT!
OSH
CHOMP
VO
...

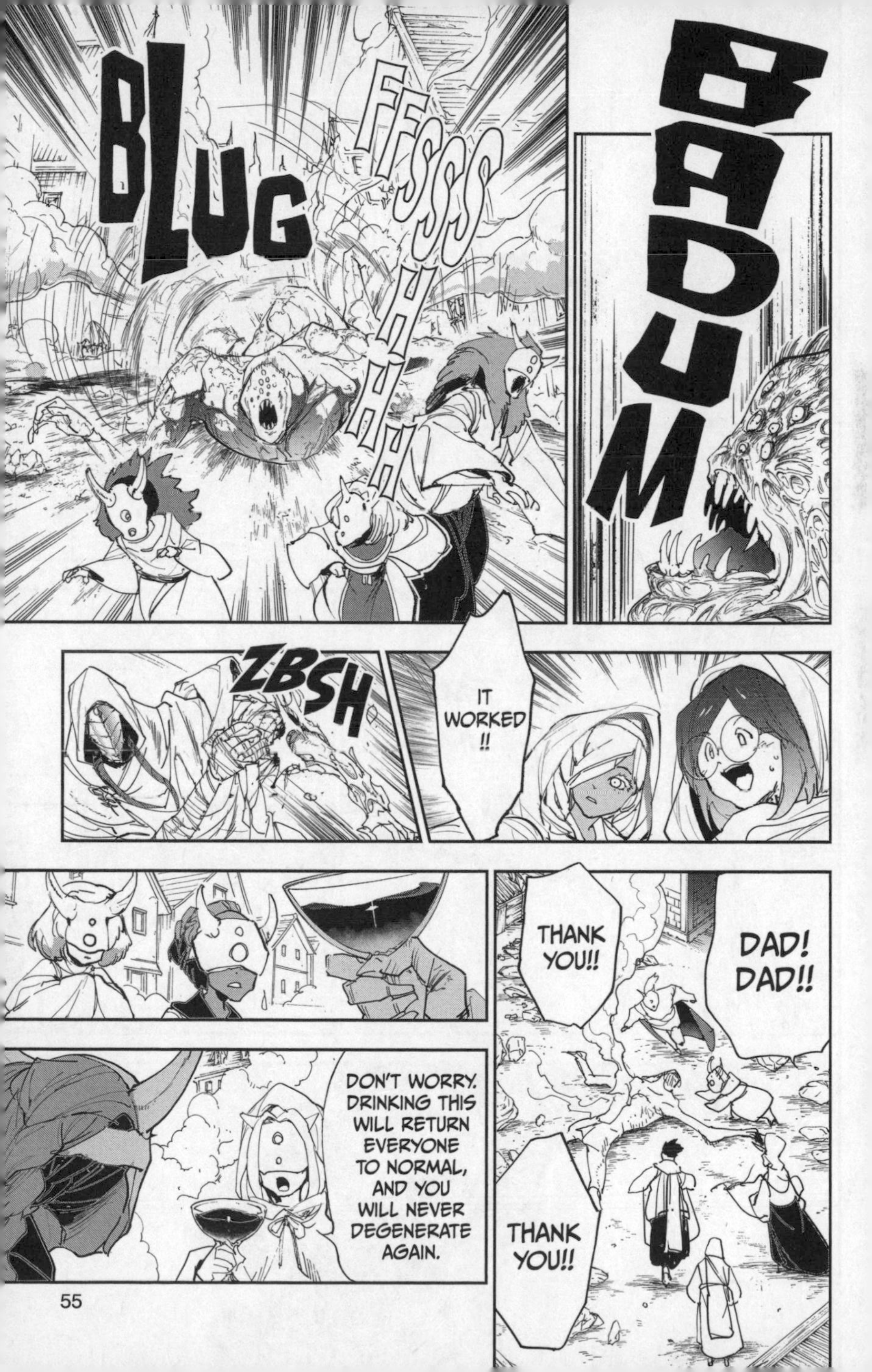
BADUM
BLUG
FFSSSHHHHH
IT WORKED!!
ZBSH
DAD! DAD!!
THANK YOU!!
THANK YOU!!
DON'T WORRY. DRINKING THIS WILL RETURN EVERYONE TO NORMAL, AND YOU WILL NEVER DEGENERATE AGAIN.

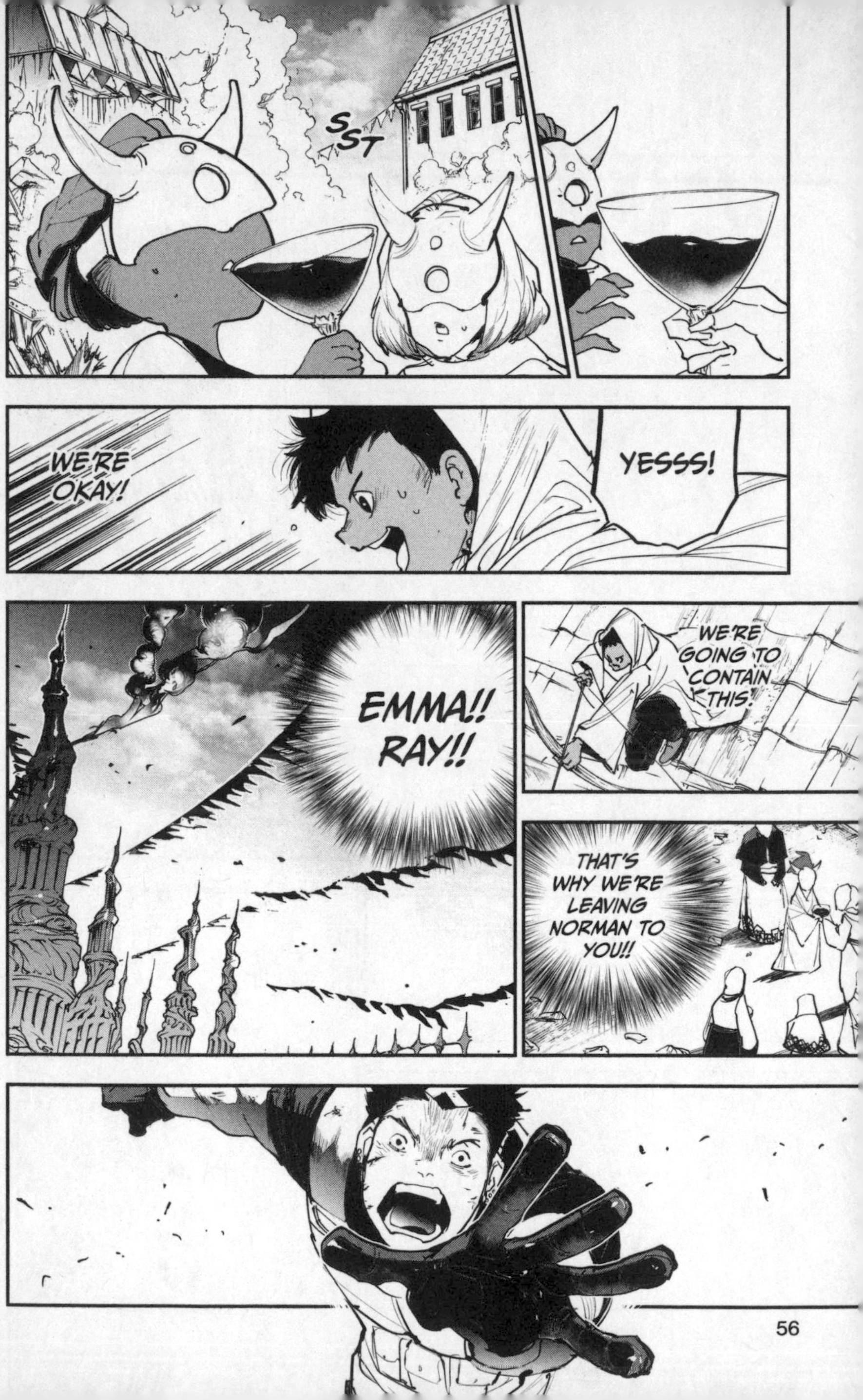
SST
YESSS!
WE'RE OKAY!
WE'RE GOING TO CONTAIN THIS.
THAT'S WHY WE'RE LEAVING NORMAN TO YOU!!
EMMA!! RAY!!

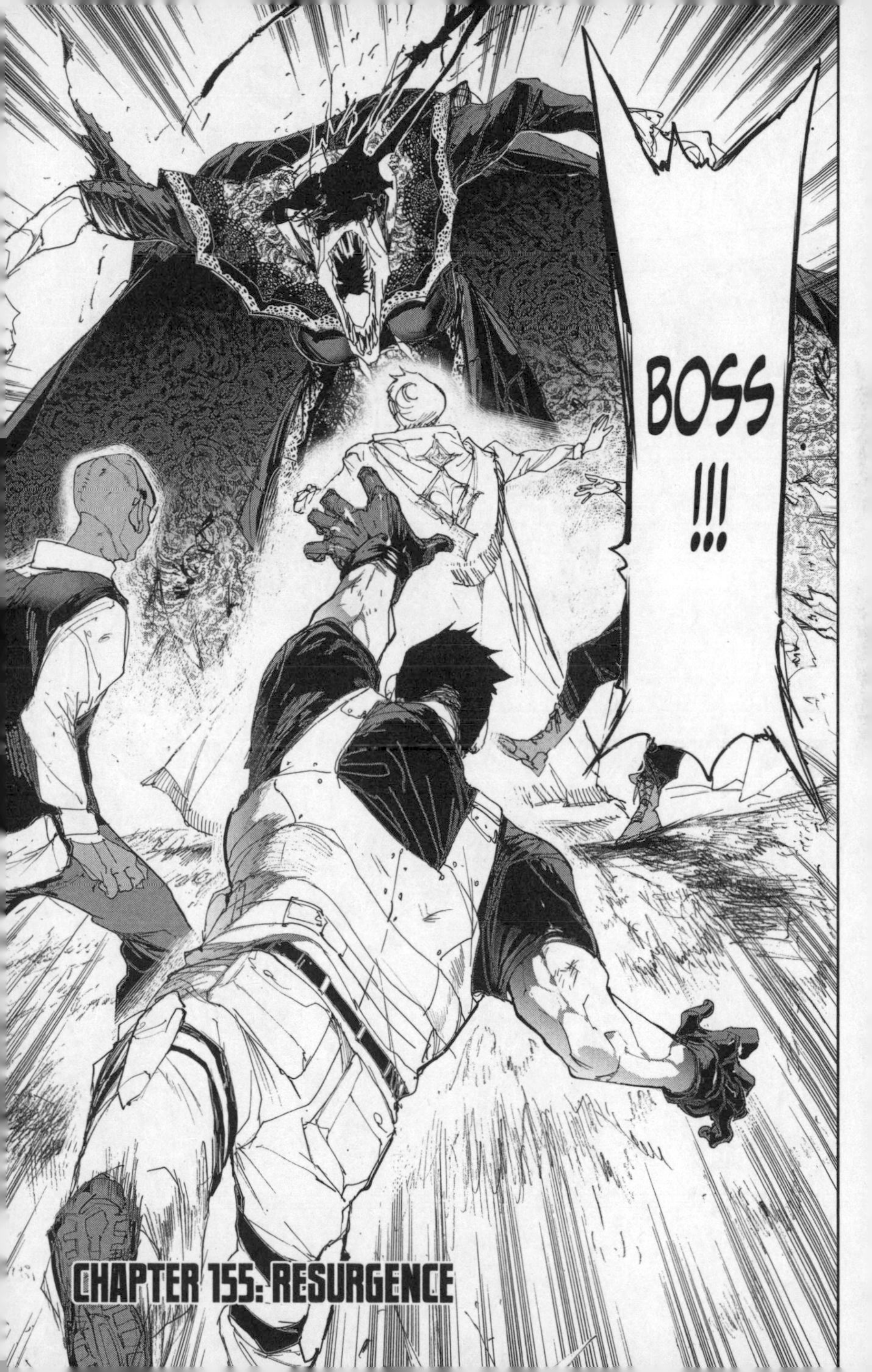
BOSS
!!!
CHAPTER 155: RESURGENCE

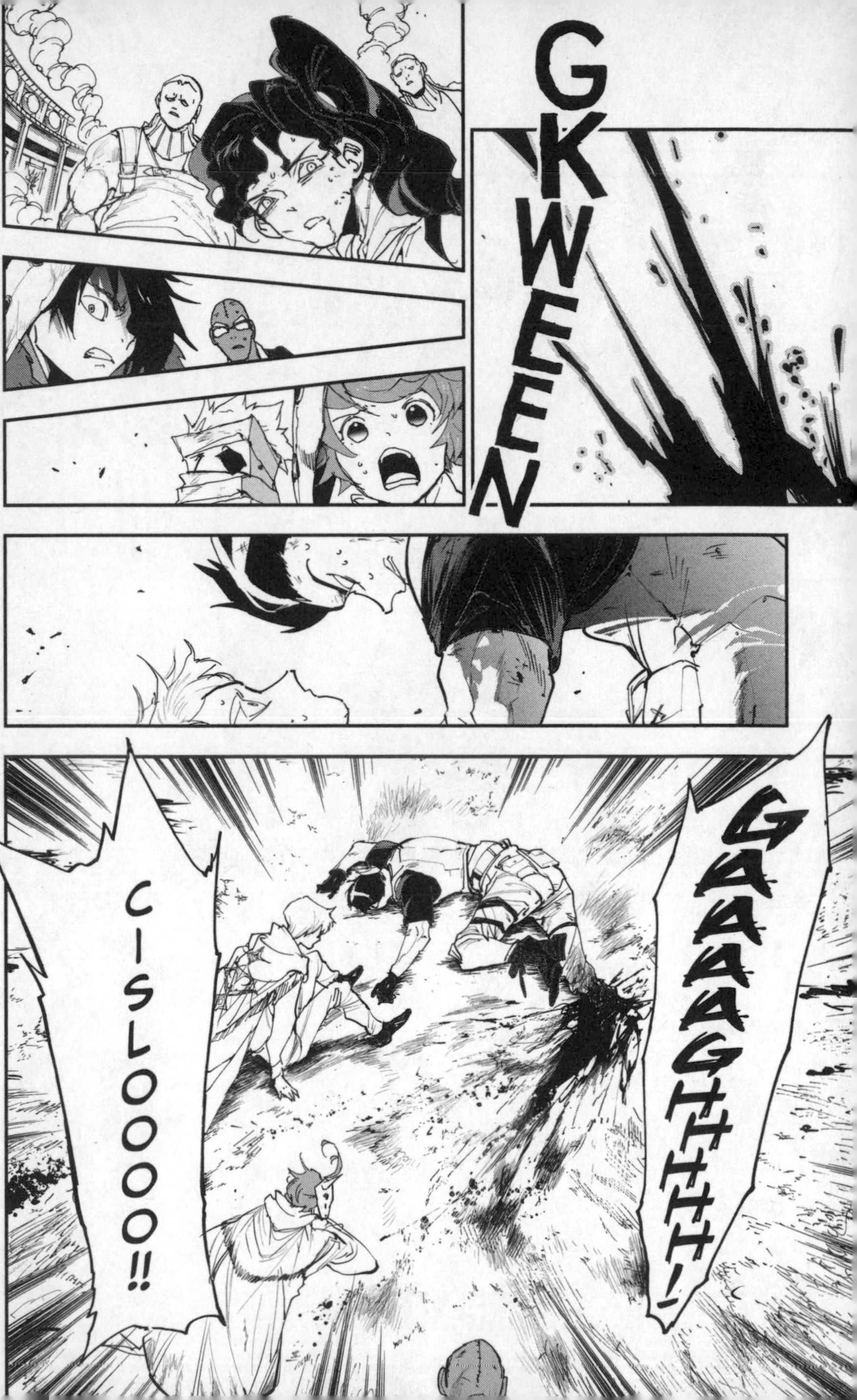
GKWEEN
GAAAAGHHHHH!
CISLOOOO!!

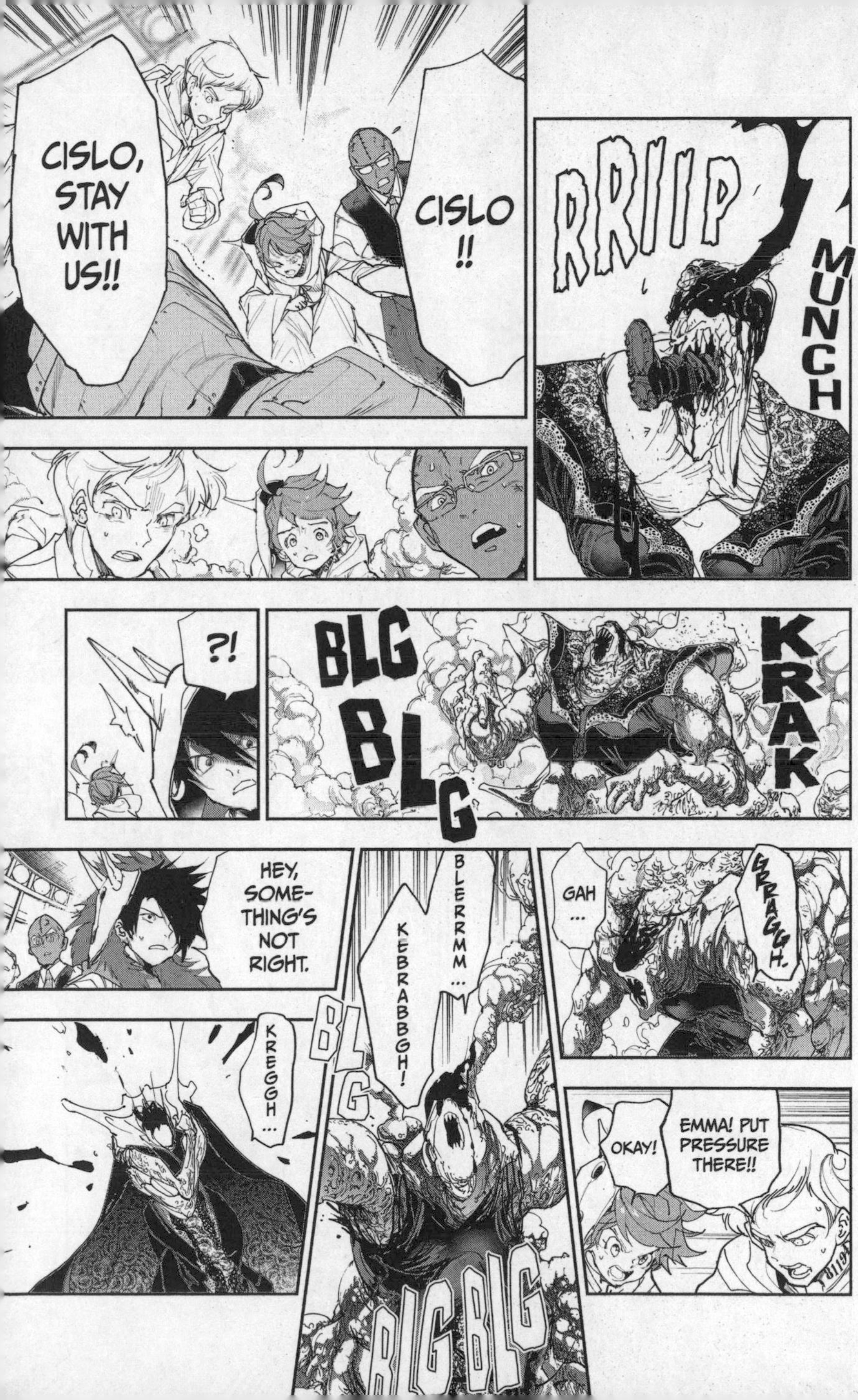
RRIIP
MUNCH
CISLO !!
CISLO, STAY WITH US!!
KRAK
BLG BLG BLG
?!
GRRAGGH.
GAH ...
EMMA! PUT PRESSURE THERE!!
OKAY!
BLERRMM ...
KEBRABBGH!
BLG
BLG BLG
HEY, SOMETHING'S NOT RIGHT.
KREGGH ...

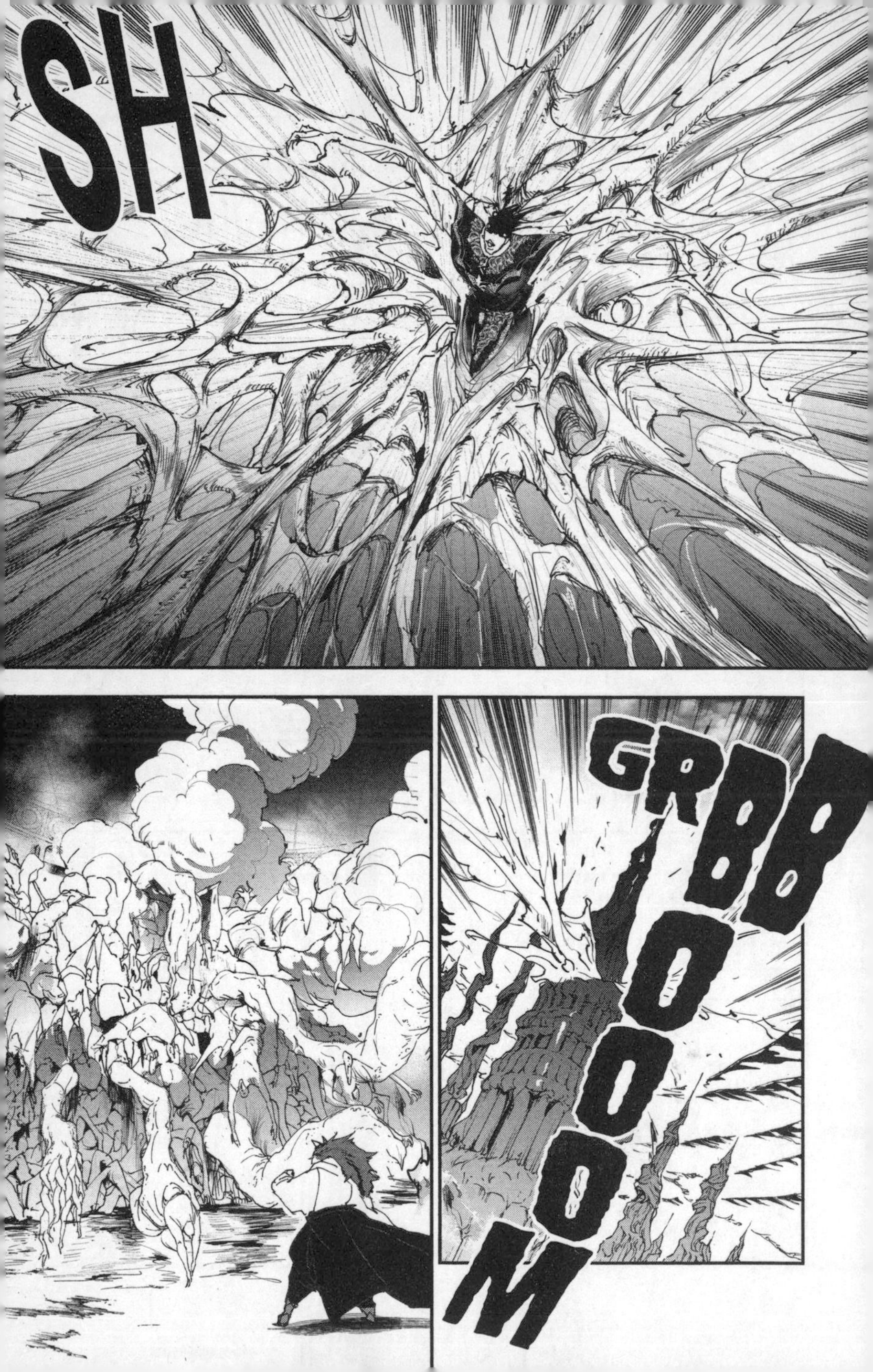
SH
GRBBOOOOM

ZWWOOOO

AAAGH!!

SHE'S EATING THEM...

WATCH OUT!!

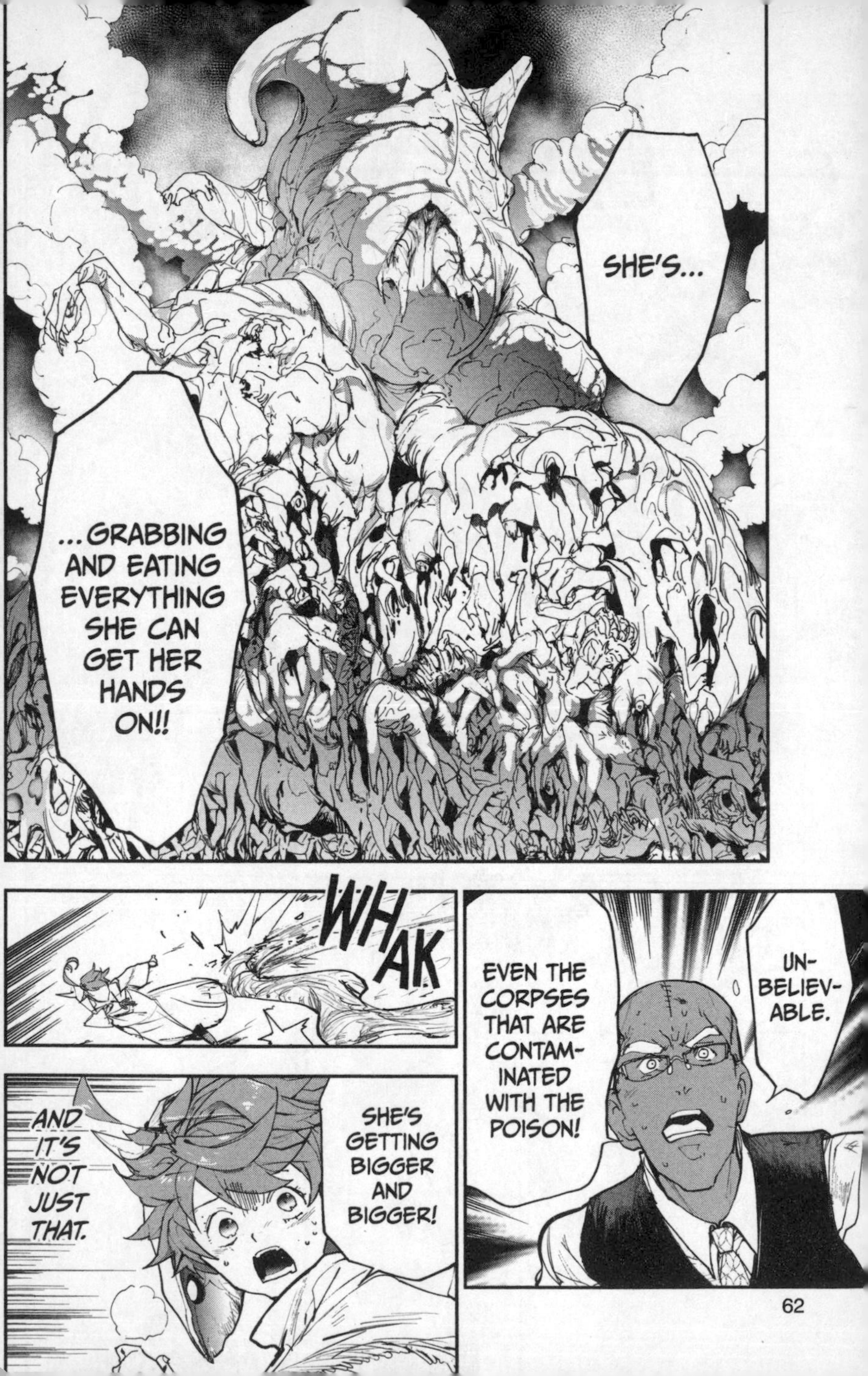
SHE'S...
...GRABBING AND EATING EVERYTHING SHE CAN GET HER HANDS ON!!
UN-BELIEV-ABLE.
EVEN THE CORPSES THAT ARE CONTAM-INATED WITH THE POISON!
WHAK
SHE'S GETTING BIGGER AND BIGGER!
AND IT'S NOT JUST THAT.

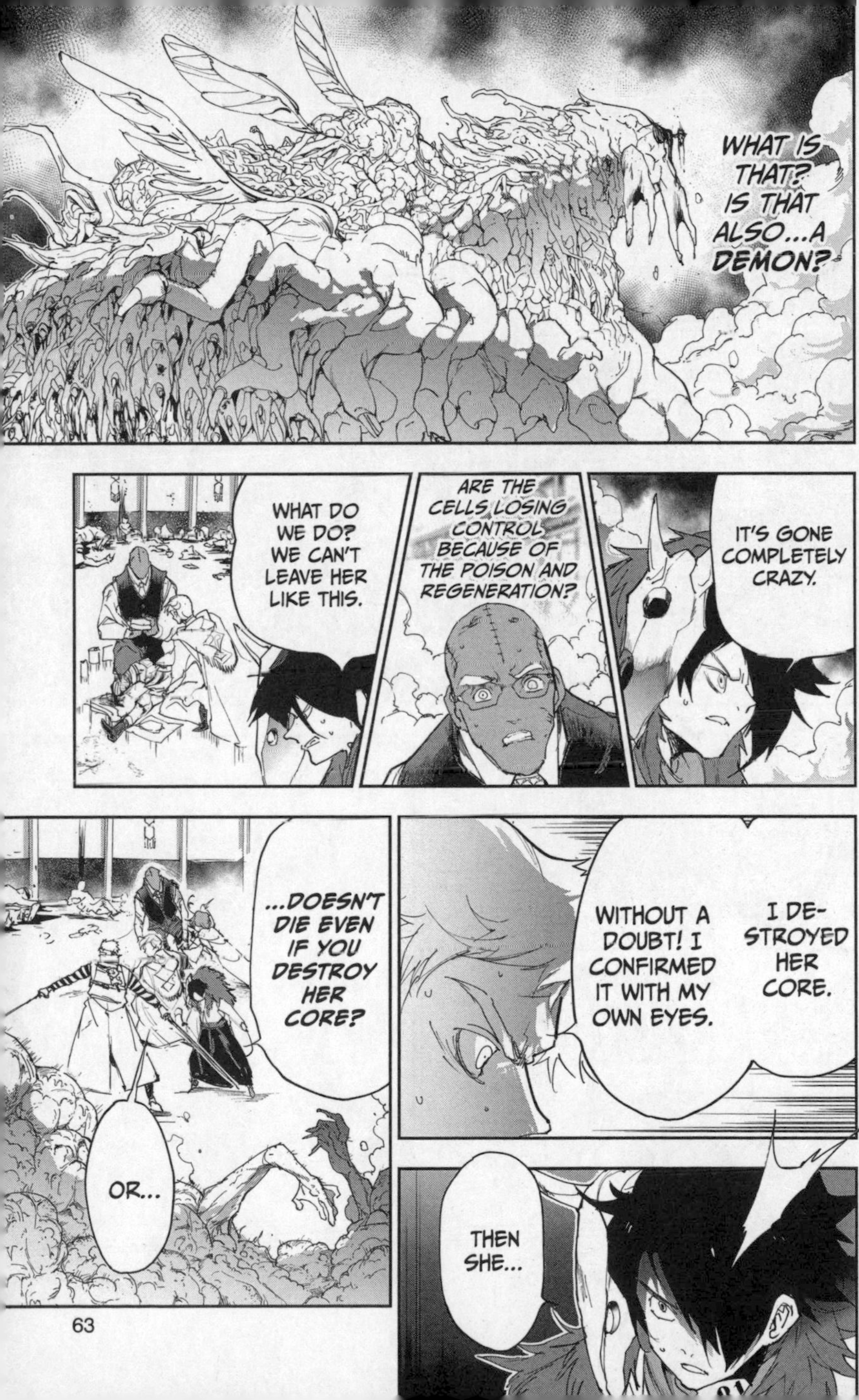
WHAT IS THAT? IS THAT ALSO...A DEMON?
IT'S GONE COMPLETELY CRAZY.
ARE THE CELLS LOSING CONTROL BECAUSE OF THE POISON AND REGENERATION?
WHAT DO WE DO? WE CAN'T LEAVE HER LIKE THIS.
I DE-STROYED HER CORE.
WITHOUT A DOUBT! I CONFIRMED IT WITH MY OWN EYES.
THEN SHE...
...DOESN'T DIE EVEN IF YOU DESTROY HER CORE?
OR...

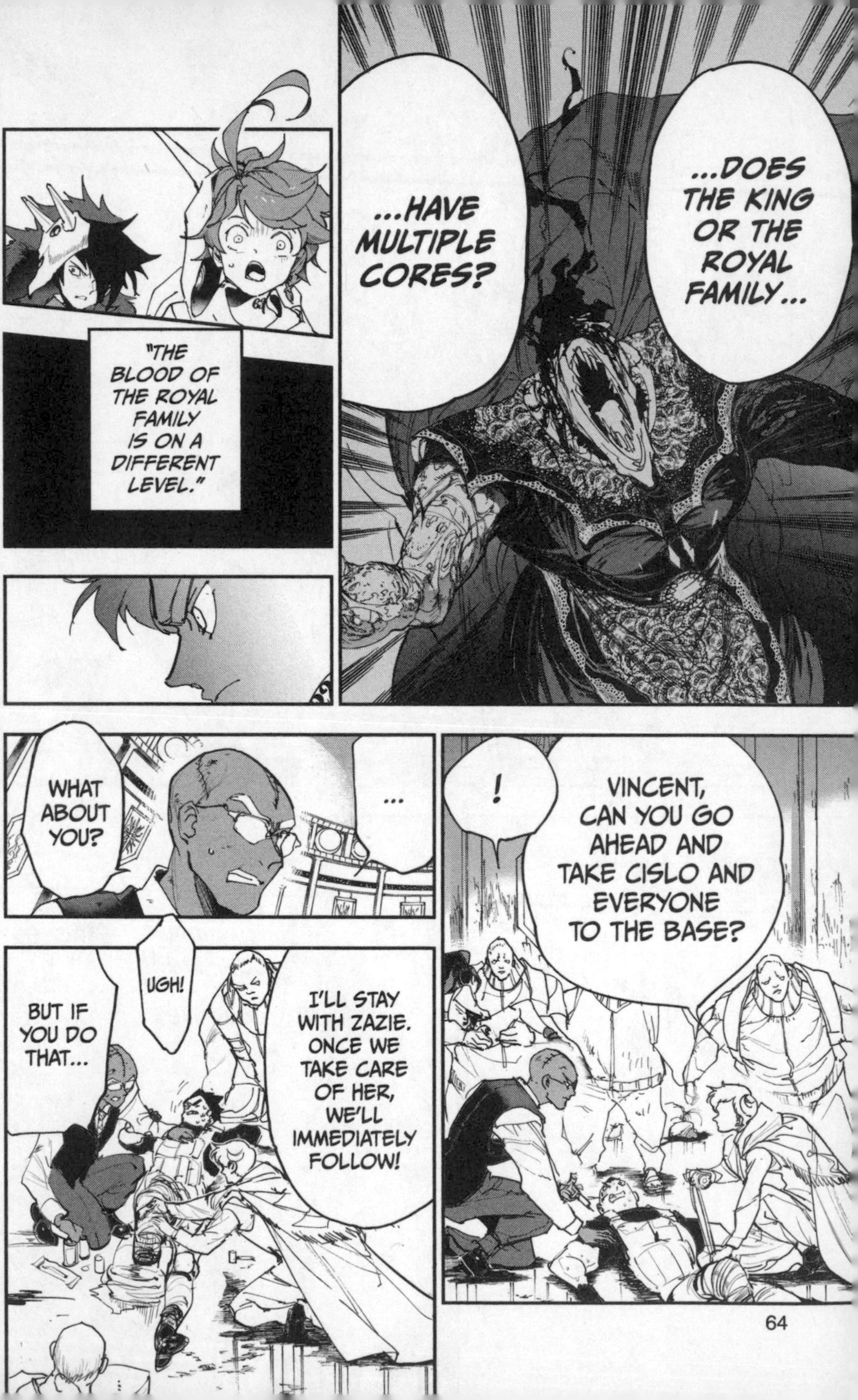
...DOES THE KING OR THE ROYAL FAMILY...
...HAVE MULTIPLE CORES?
"THE BLOOD OF THE ROYAL FAMILY IS ON A DIFFERENT LEVEL."
VINCENT, CAN YOU GO AHEAD AND TAKE CISLO AND EVERYONE TO THE BASE?
!
...
WHAT ABOUT YOU?
I'LL STAY WITH ZAZIE. ONCE WE TAKE CARE OF HER, WE'LL IMMEDIATELY FOLLOW!
UGH!
BUT IF YOU DO THAT...

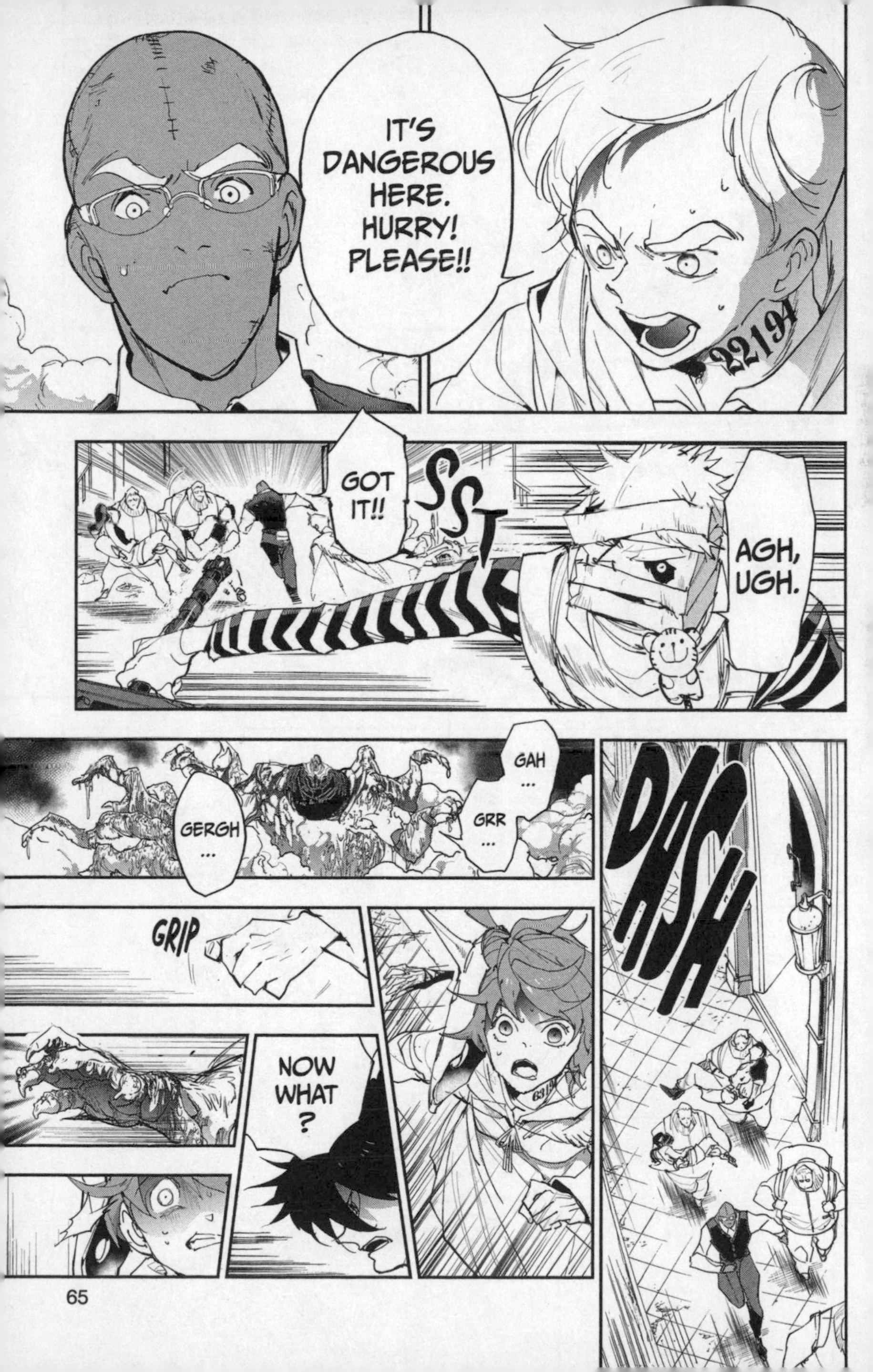
IT'S DANGEROUS HERE. HURRY! PLEASE!!
22194
AGH, UGH.
SST
GOT IT!!
DASH
GAH ...
GRR ...
GERGH ...
GRIP
NOW WHAT ?

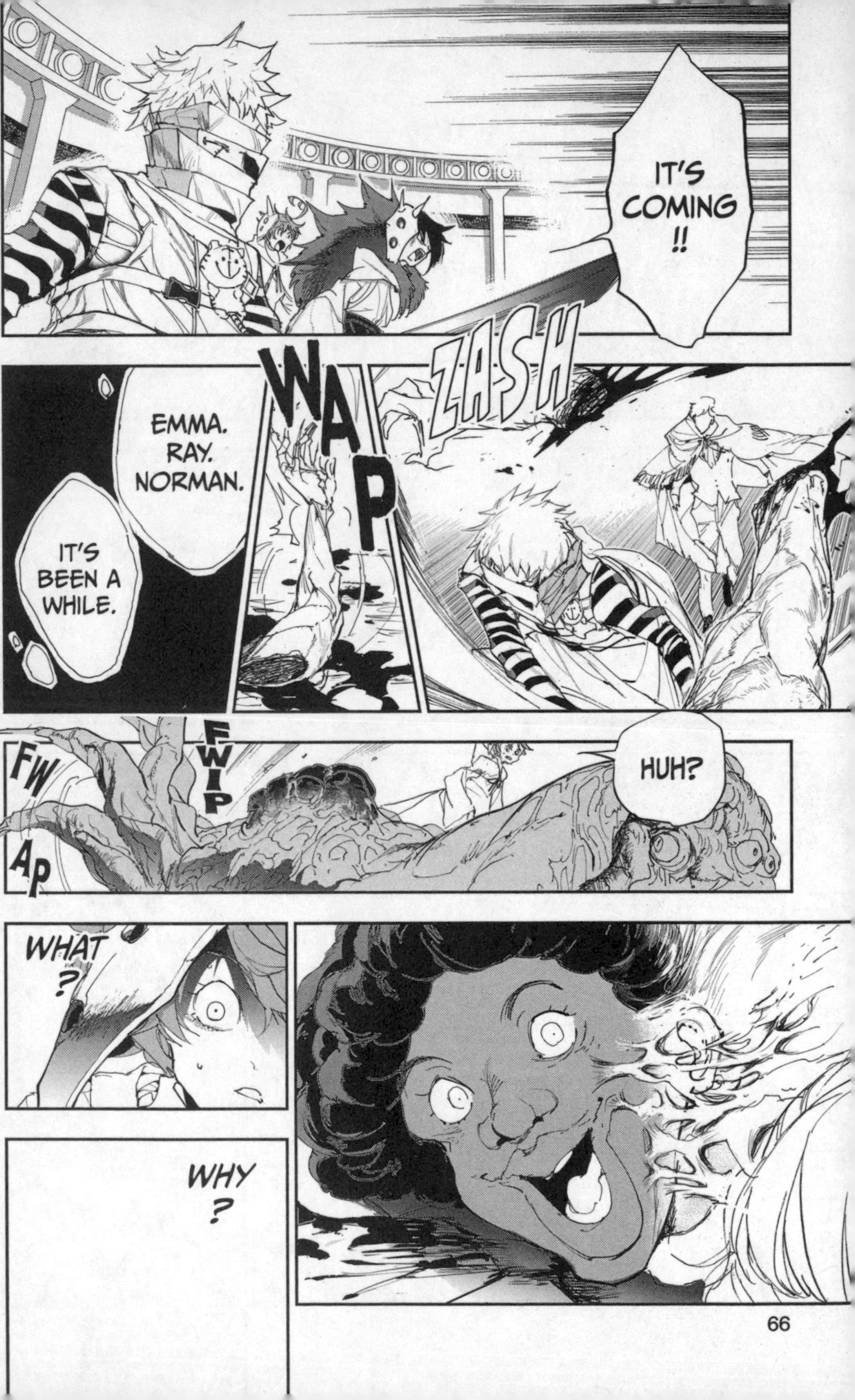
IT'S COMING !!
ZASH
WAP
EMMA. RAY. NORMAN.
IT'S BEEN A WHILE.
HUH?
FWIP
FWAP
WHAT?
WHY?

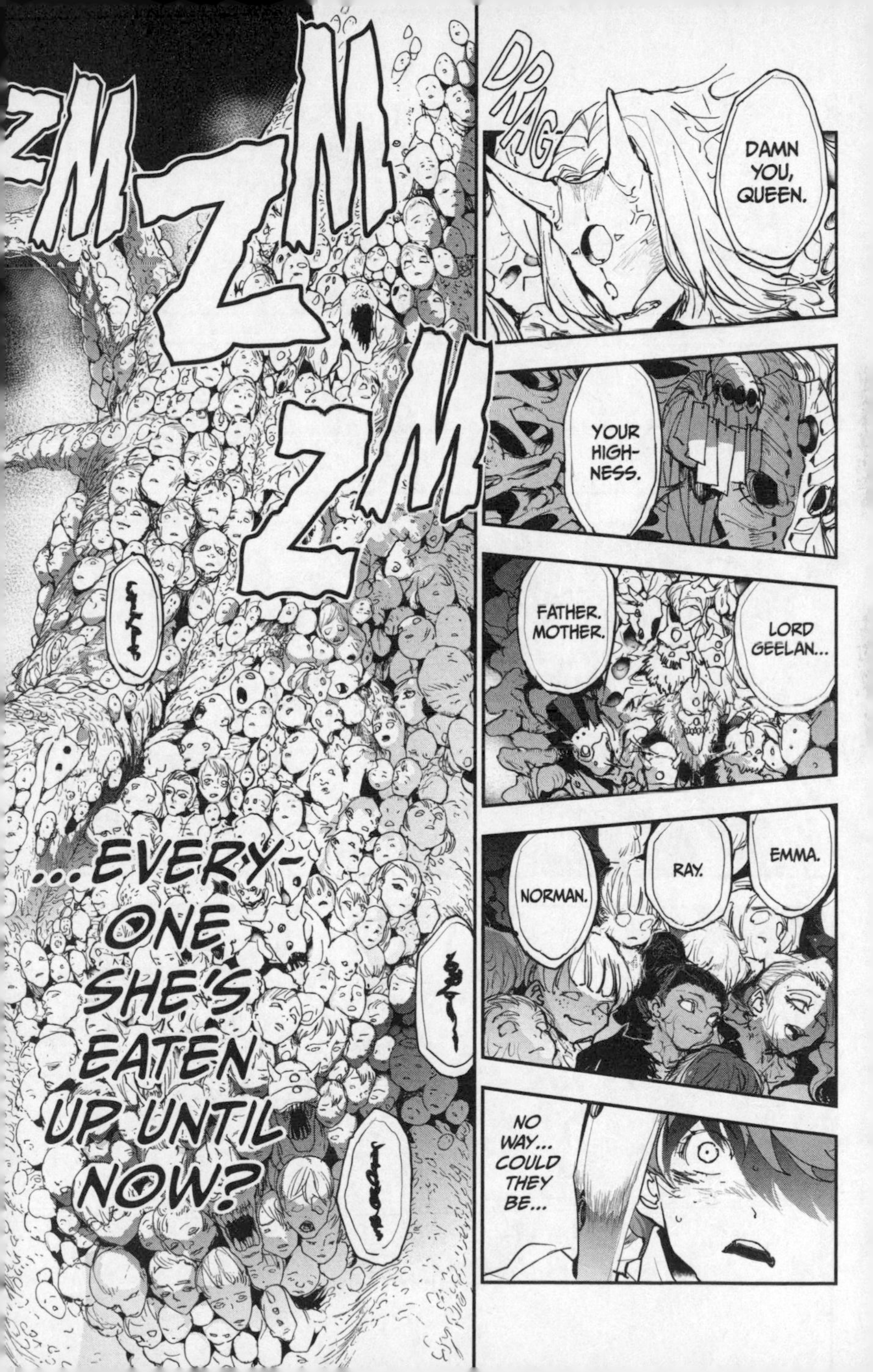
DRAG-
DAMN YOU, QUEEN.
YOUR HIGHNESS.
LORD GEELAN...
FATHER. MOTHER.
EMMA.
RAY.
NORMAN.
NO WAY... COULD THEY BE...
ZM ZM
ZM
...EVERYONE SHE'S EATEN UP UNTIL NOW?

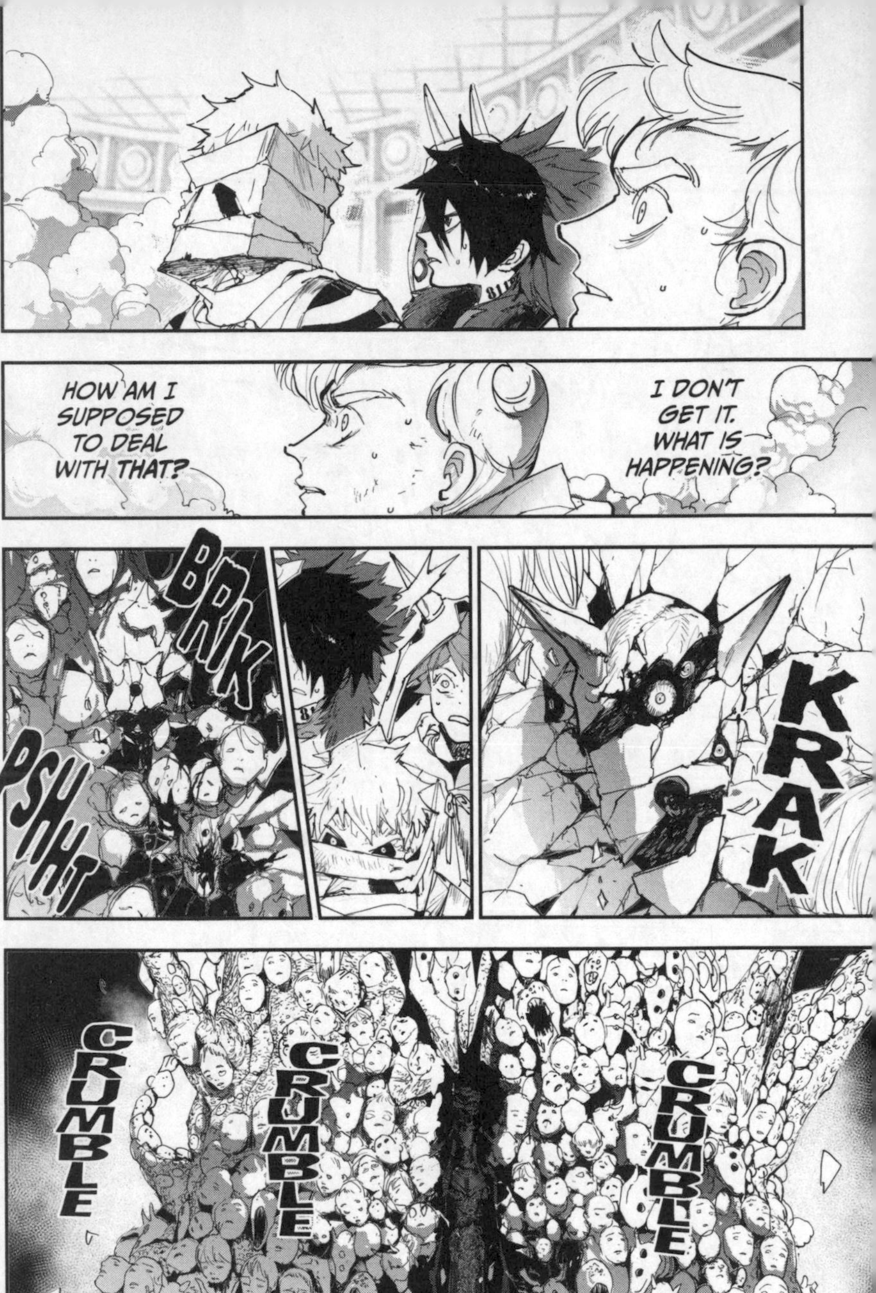
I DON'T GET IT. WHAT IS HAPPENING?
HOW AM I SUPPOSED TO DEAL WITH THAT?
KRAK
BRIK
PSHHT
CRUMBLE
CRUMBLE
CRUMBLE

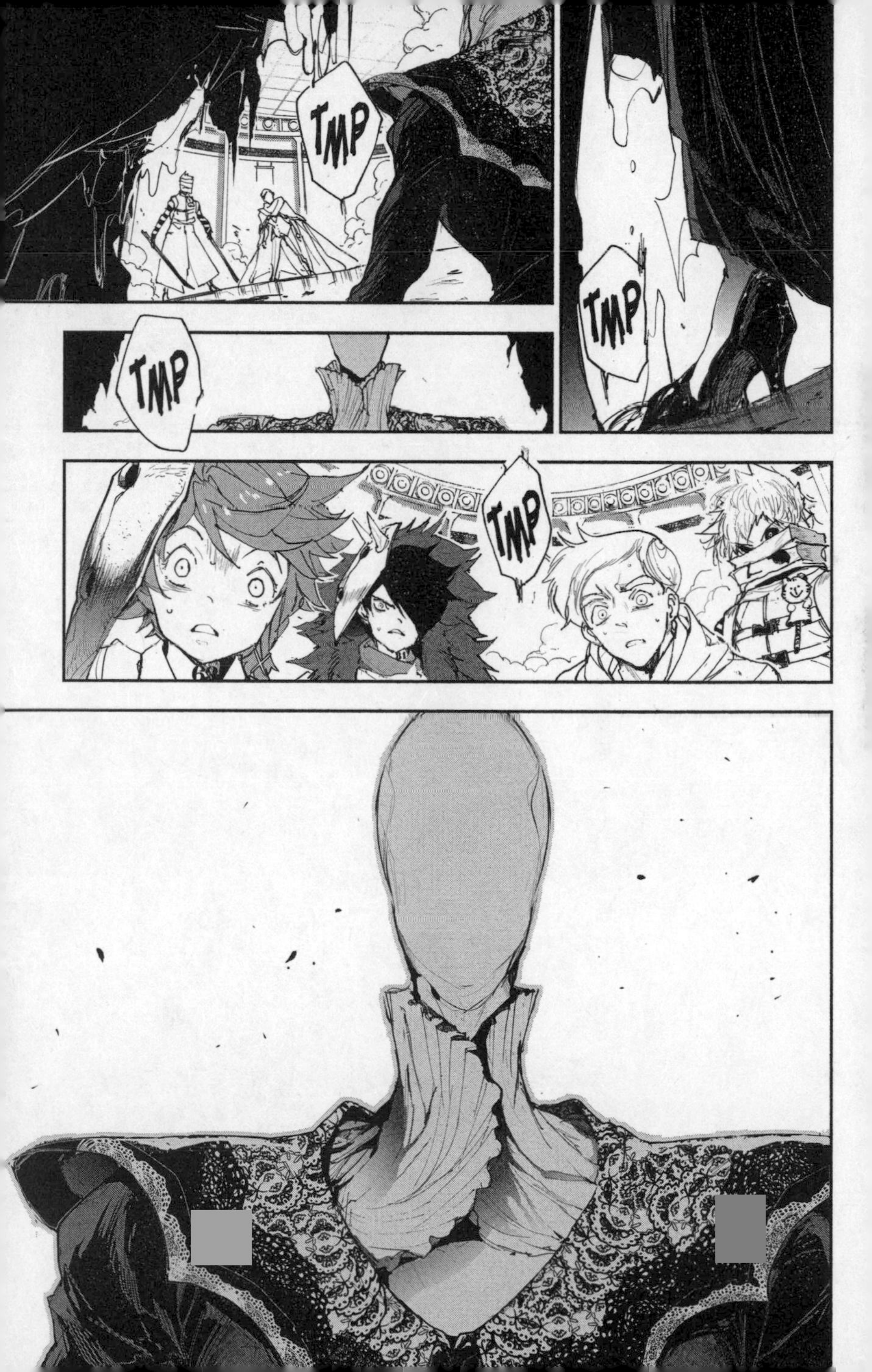
TMP
TMP
TMP
TMP

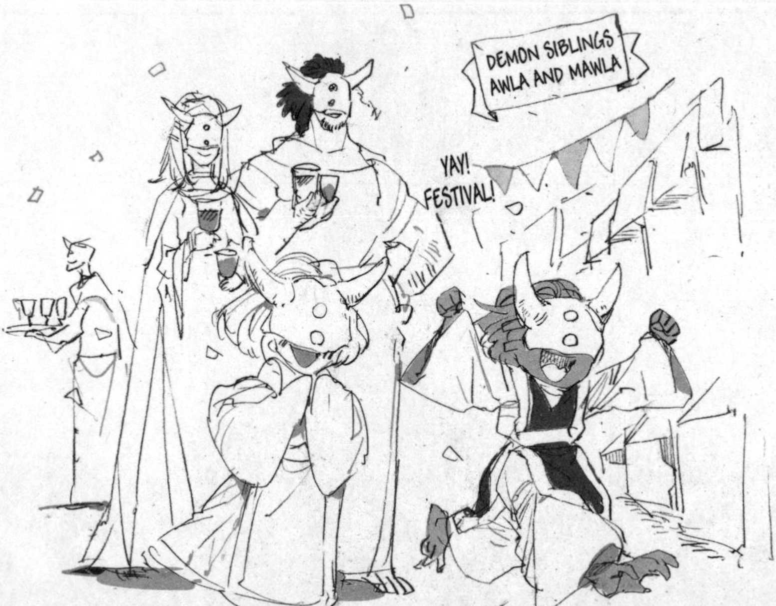
DEMON SIBLINGS
AWLA AND MAWLA
YAY!
FESTIVAL!

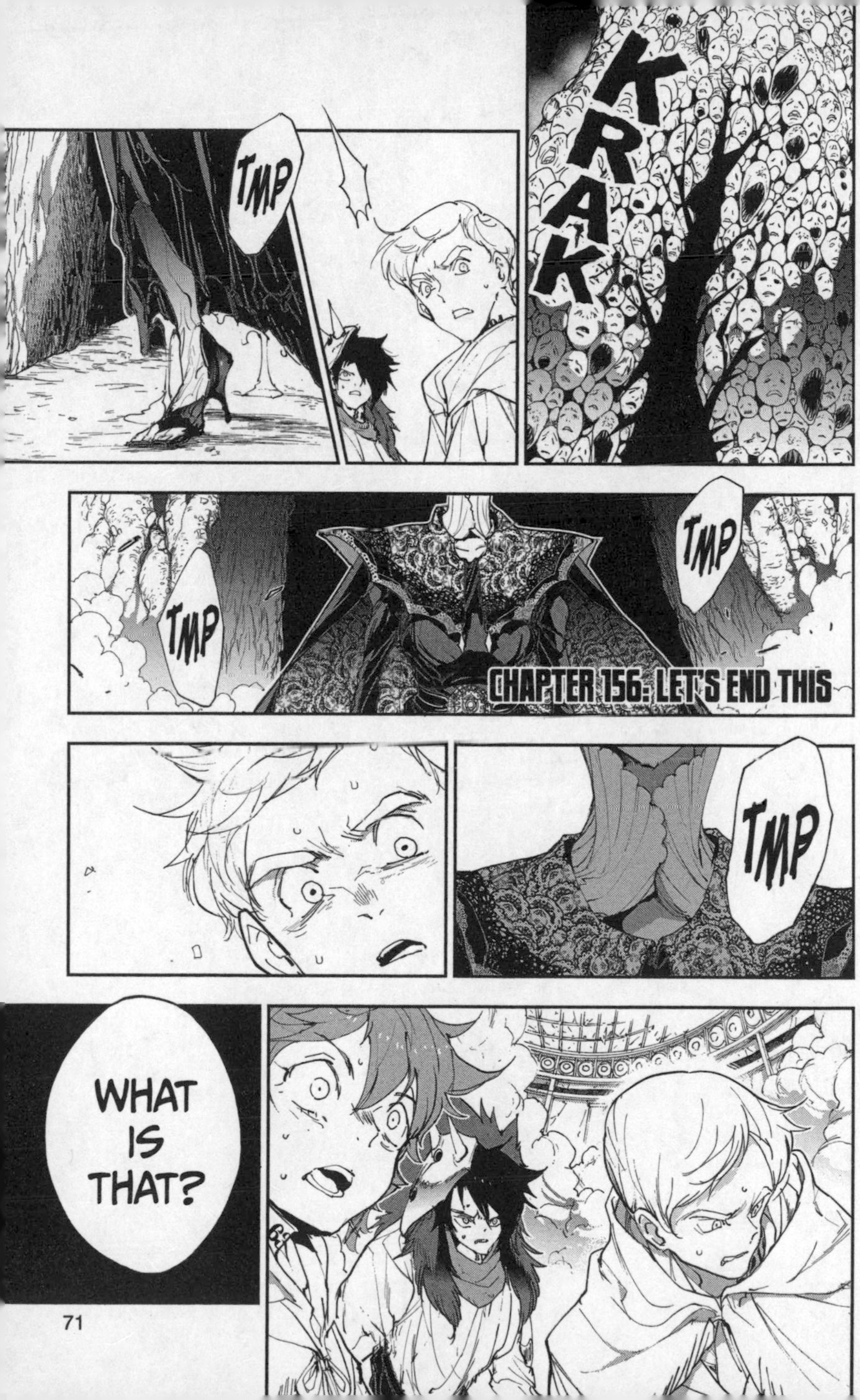
KRAK
TMP
TMP
CHAPTER 156: LET'S END THIS
TMP
TMP
WHAT IS THAT?

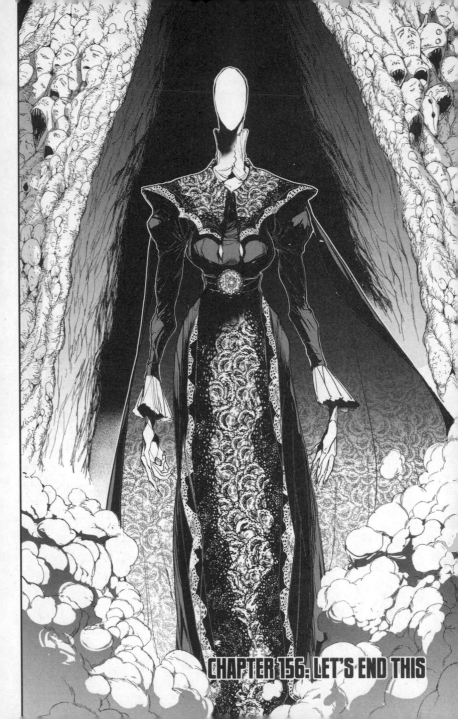

CHAPTER 156: LET'S END THIS

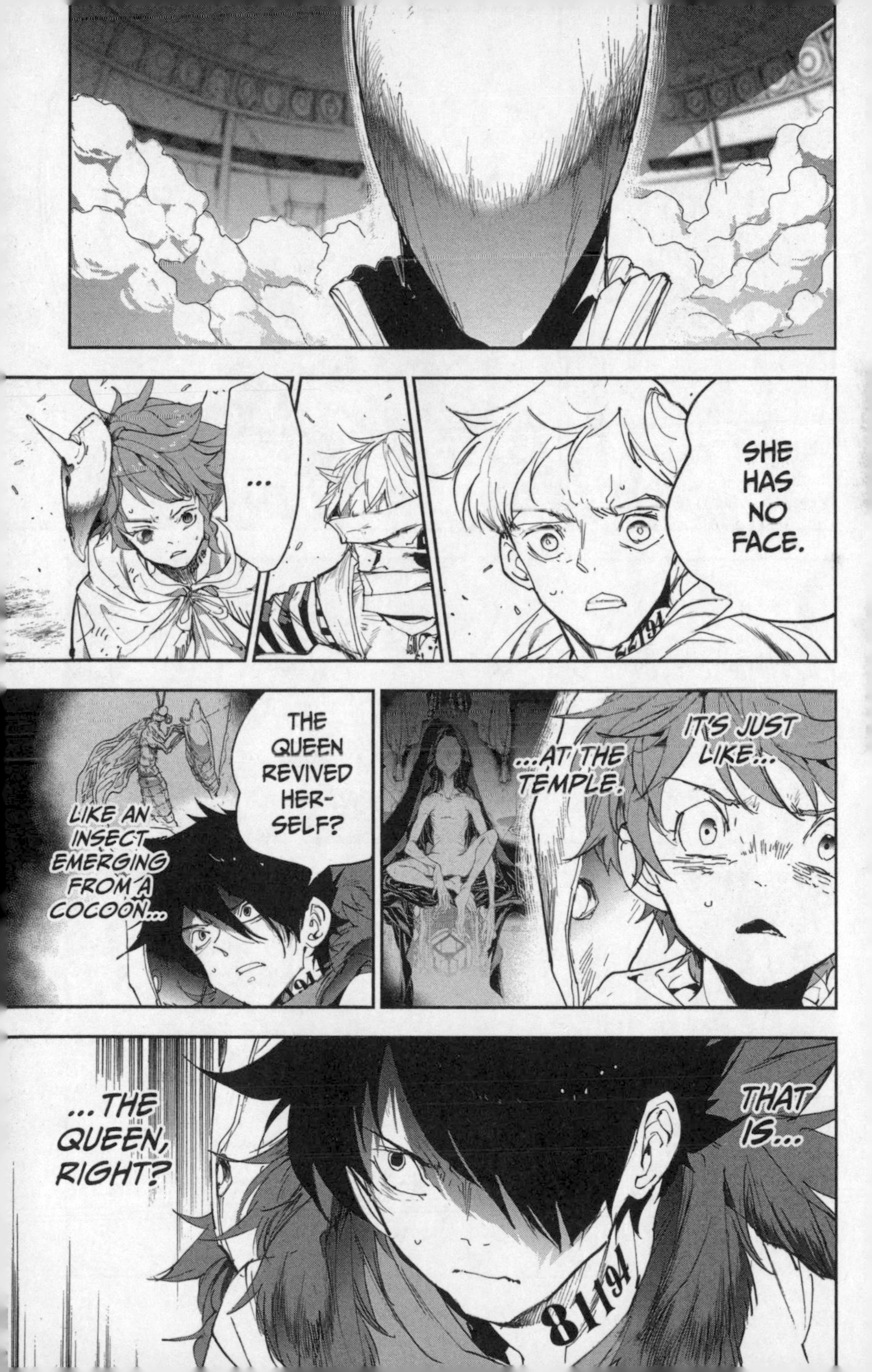
SHE HAS NO FACE.
...
IT'S JUST LIKE...
...AT THE TEMPLE.
THE QUEEN REVIVED HER-SELF?
LIKE AN INSECT EMERGING FROM A COCOON...
THAT IS...
...THE QUEEN, RIGHT?

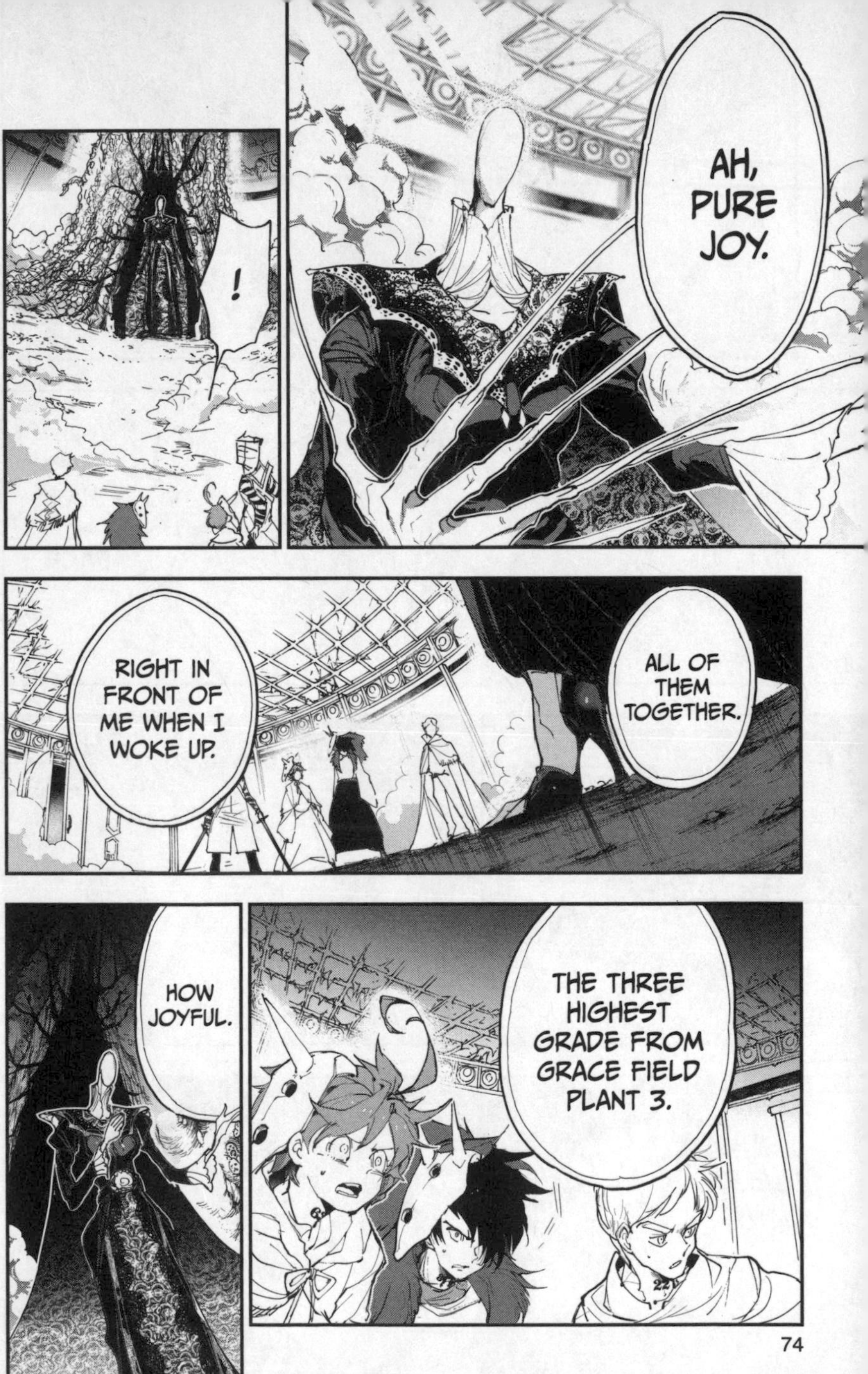
AH, PURE JOY.
!
ALL OF THEM TOGETHER.
RIGHT IN FRONT OF ME WHEN I WOKE UP.
THE THREE HIGHEST GRADE FROM GRACE FIELD PLANT 3.
HOW JOYFUL.

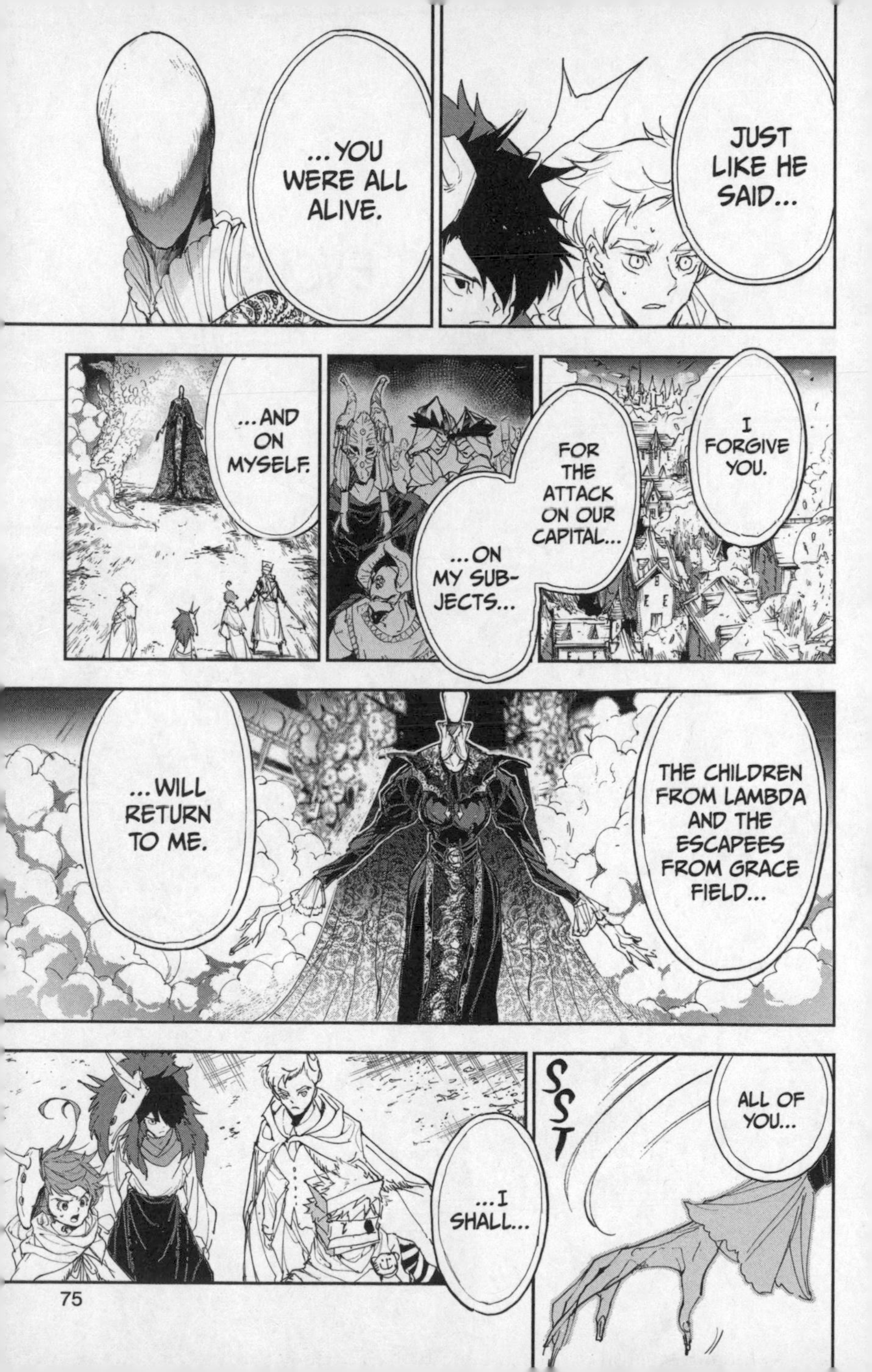
JUST LIKE HE SAID...
...YOU WERE ALL ALIVE.
I FORGIVE YOU.
FOR THE ATTACK ON OUR CAPITAL...
...ON MY SUB-JECTS...
...AND ON MYSELF.
THE CHILDREN FROM LAMBDA AND THE ESCAPEES FROM GRACE FIELD...
...WILL RETURN TO ME.
SST
ALL OF YOU...
...I SHALL...

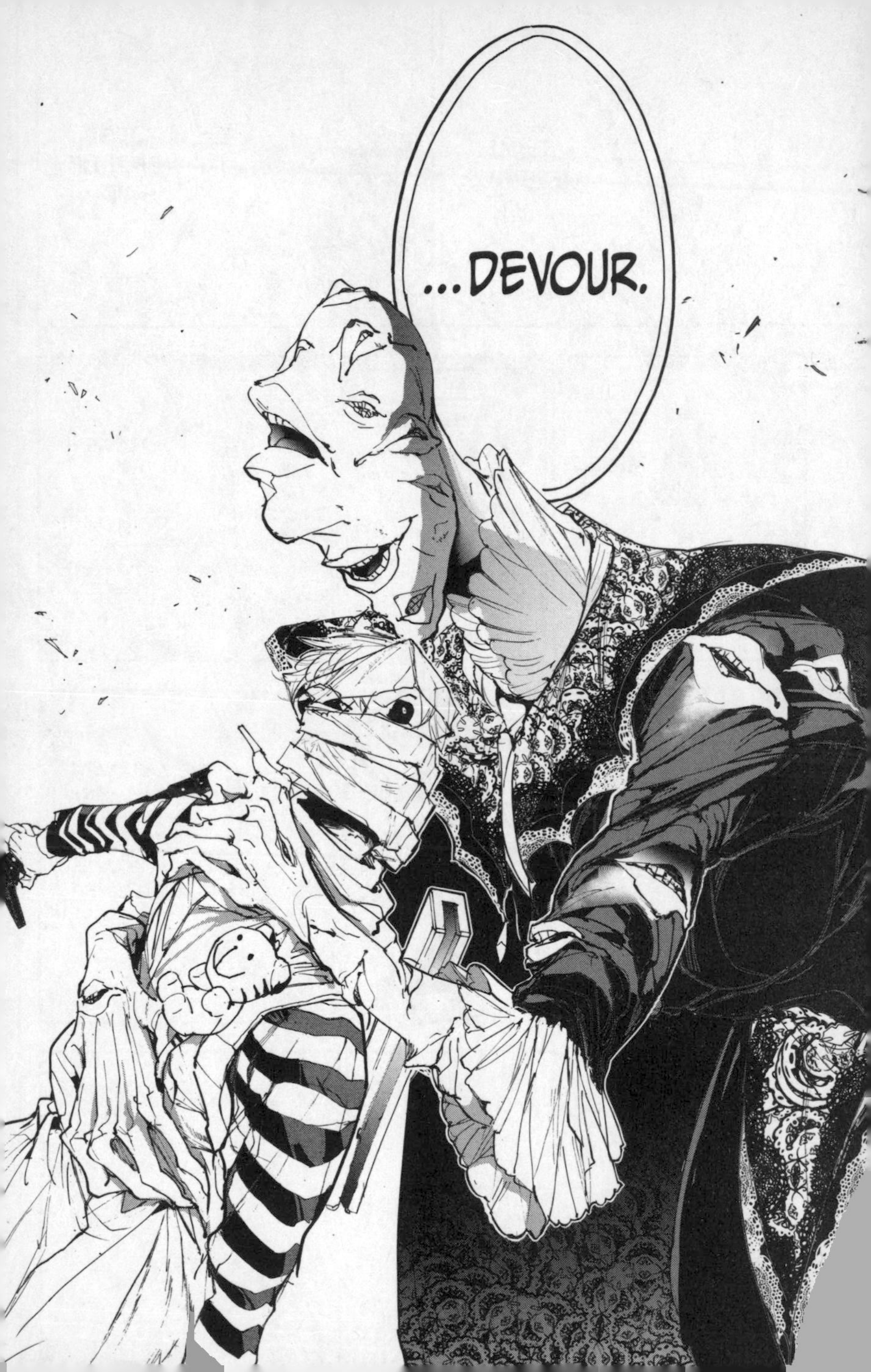
...DEVOUR.

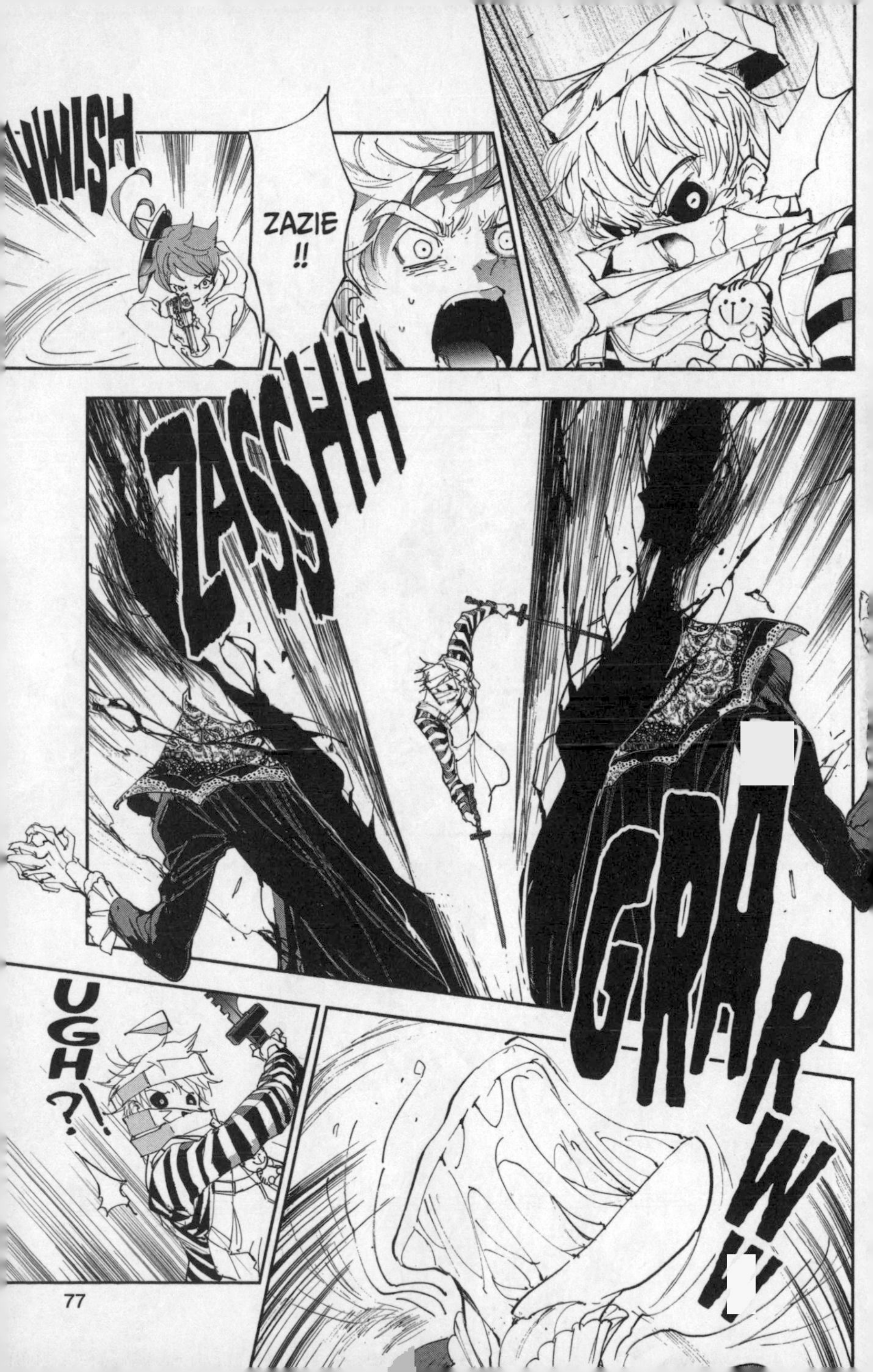
ZAZIE !!
VWISH
ZASSHH
GRARWW
UGH?!

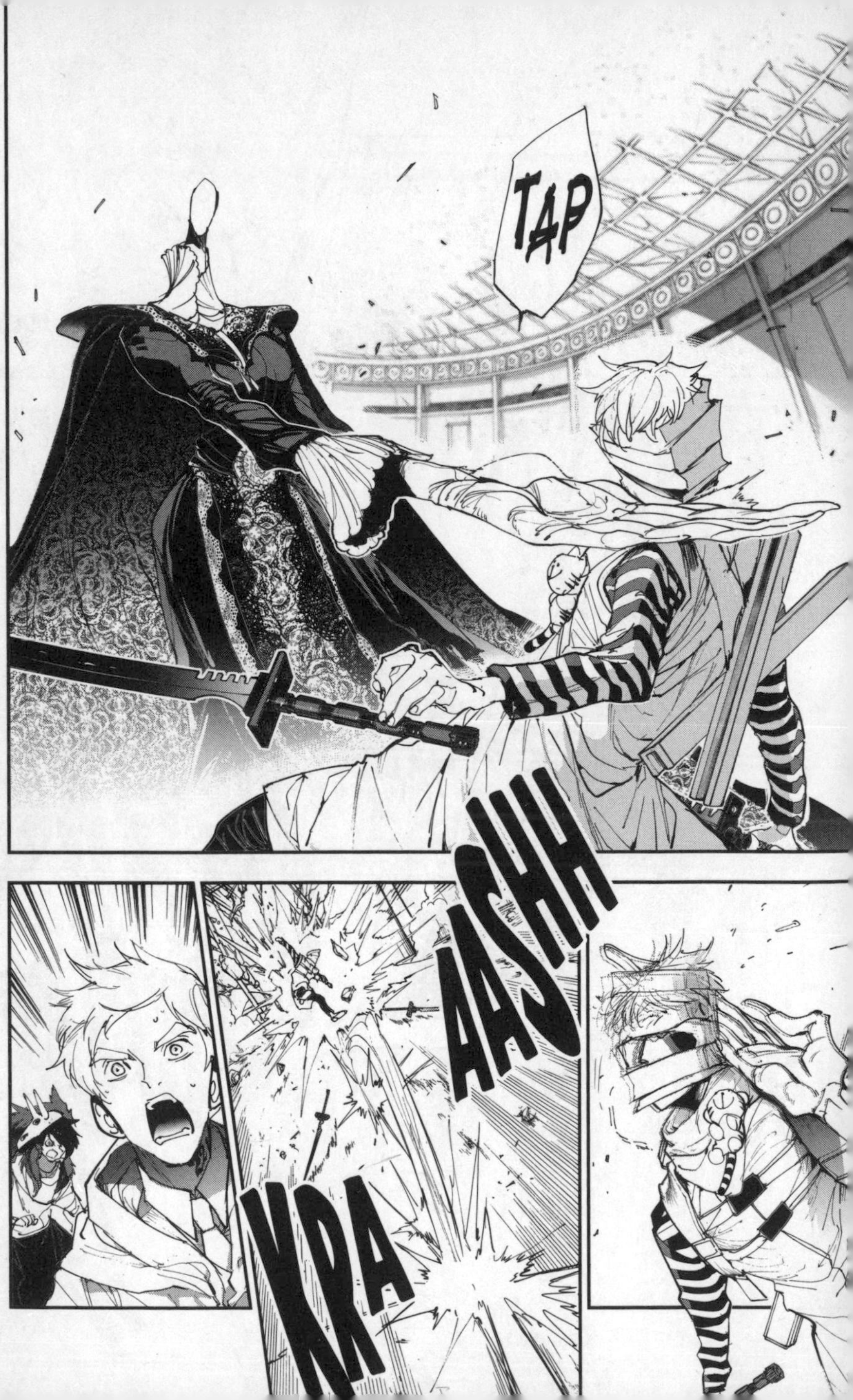
TAP
KRA
AASHH

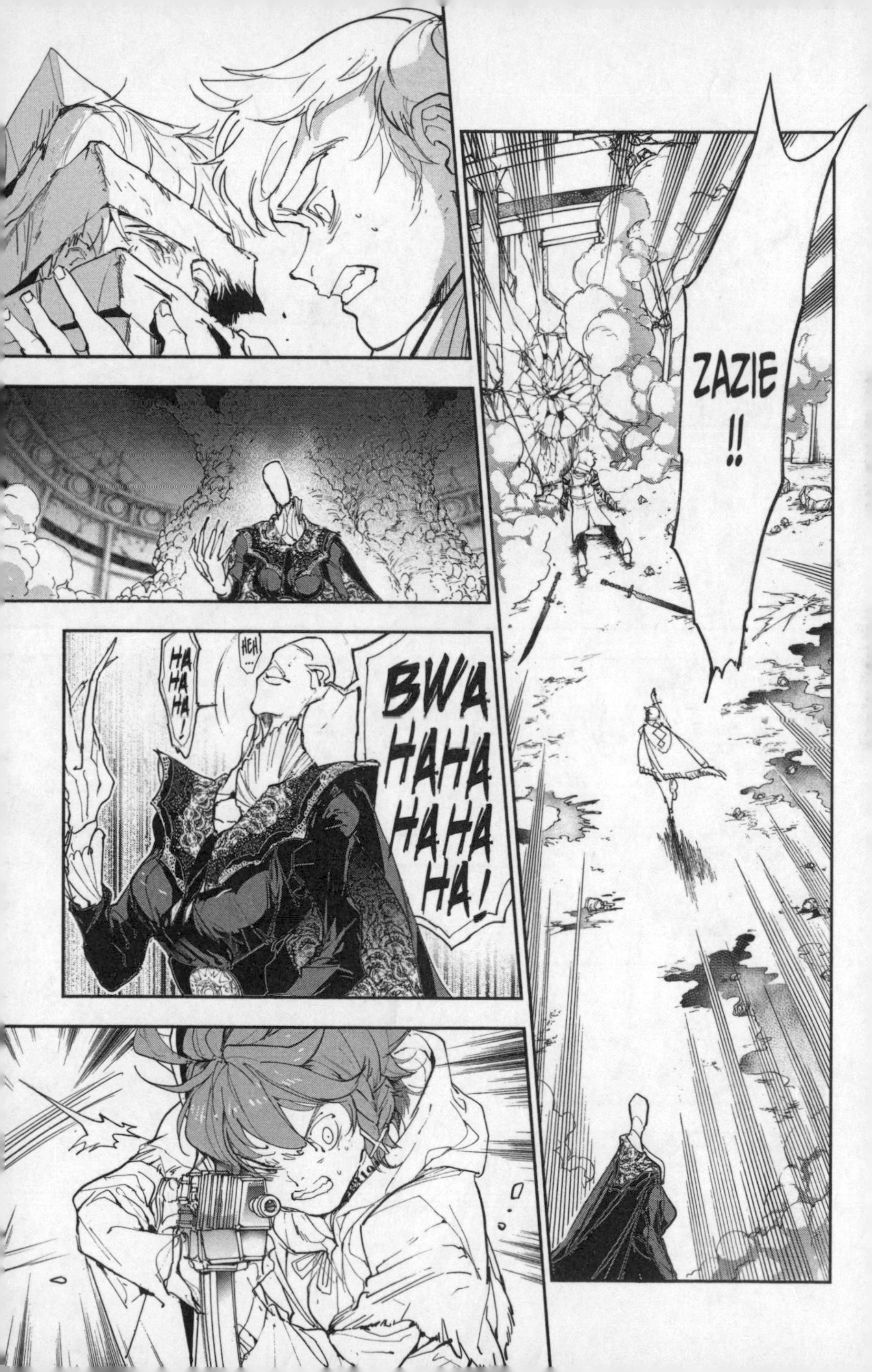
ZAZIE !!
BWA HAHA HAHA HA!
HEH...
HA HA HA HA!

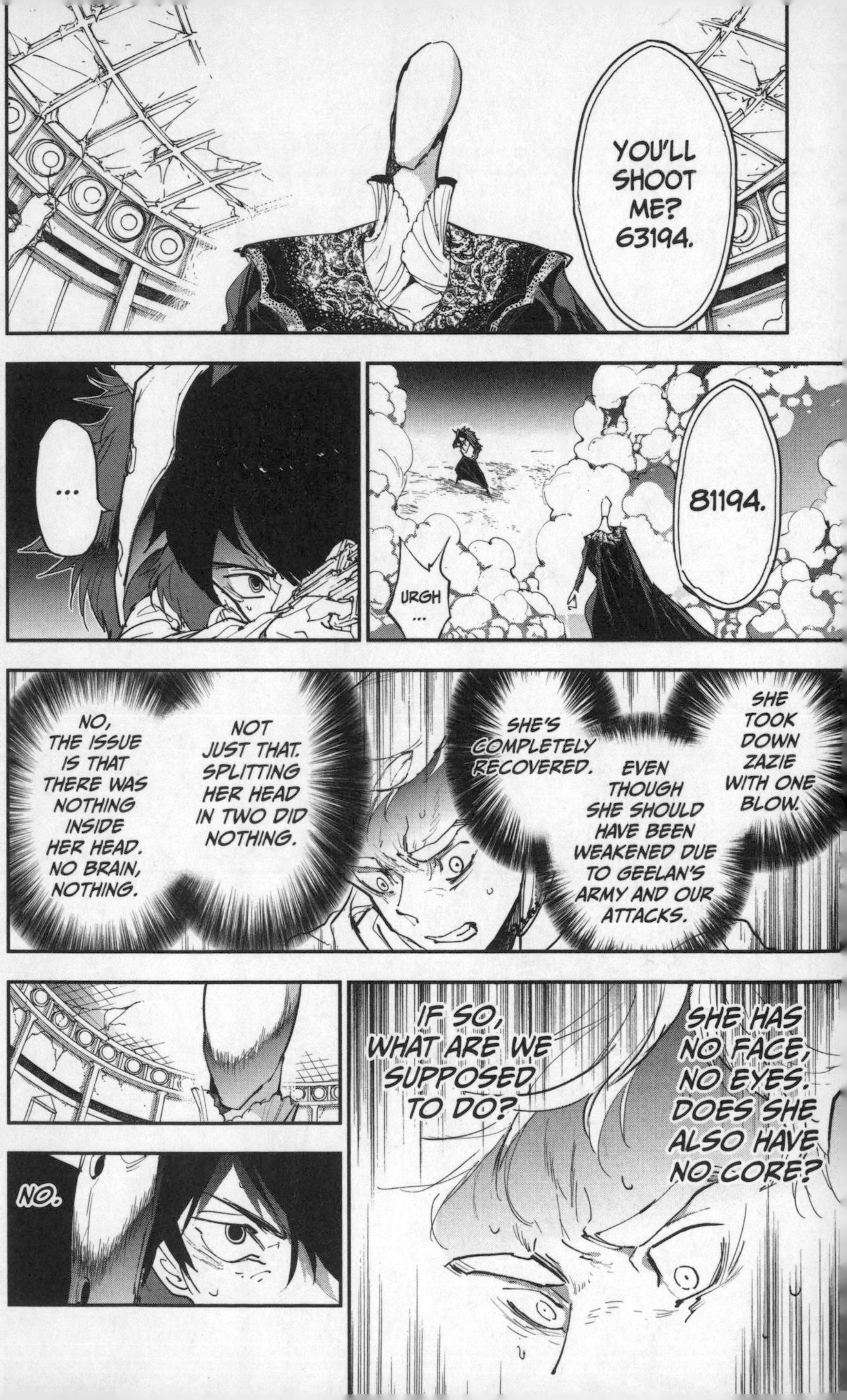
YOU'LL SHOOT ME? 63194.
81194.
URGH ...
...
SHE TOOK DOWN ZAZIE WITH ONE BLOW.
SHE'S COMPLETELY RECOVERED.
EVEN THOUGH SHE SHOULD HAVE BEEN WEAKENED DUE TO GEELAN'S ARMY AND OUR ATTACKS.
NOT JUST THAT. SPLITTING HER HEAD IN TWO DID NOTHING.
NO, THE ISSUE IS THAT THERE WAS NOTHING INSIDE HER HEAD. NO BRAIN, NOTHING.
SHE HAS NO FACE, NO EYES. DOES SHE ALSO HAVE NO CORE?
IF SO, WHAT ARE WE SUPPOSED TO DO?
NO.

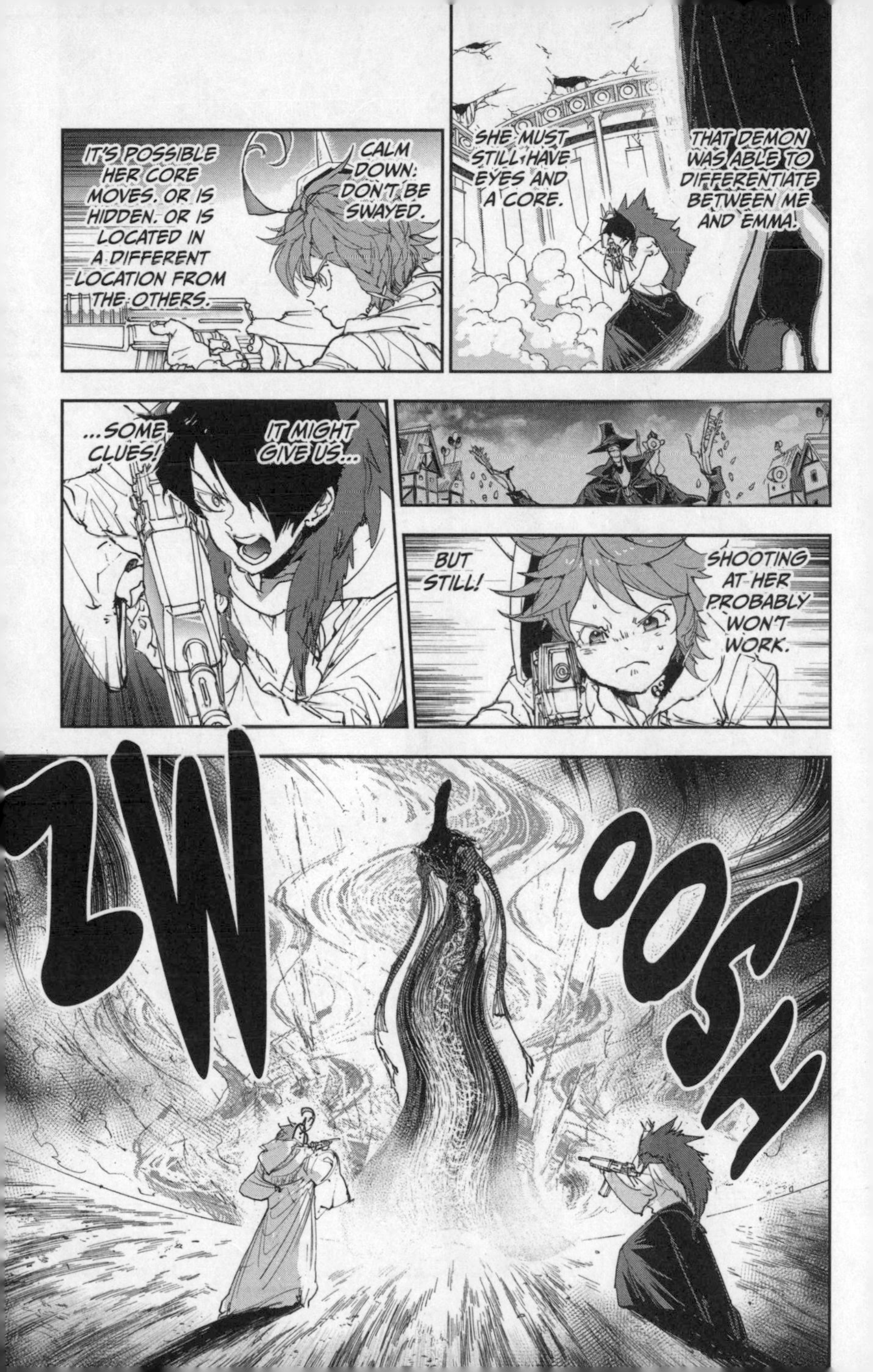
THAT DEMON WAS ABLE TO DIFFERENTIATE BETWEEN ME AND EMMA.
SHE MUST STILL HAVE EYES AND A CORE.
CALM DOWN: DON'T BE SWAYED.
IT'S POSSIBLE HER CORE MOVES. OR IS HIDDEN. OR IS LOCATED IN A DIFFERENT LOCATION FROM THE OTHERS.
SHOOTING AT HER PROBABLY WON'T WORK.
BUT STILL!
IT MIGHT GIVE US...
...SOME CLUES!
ZWOOSH

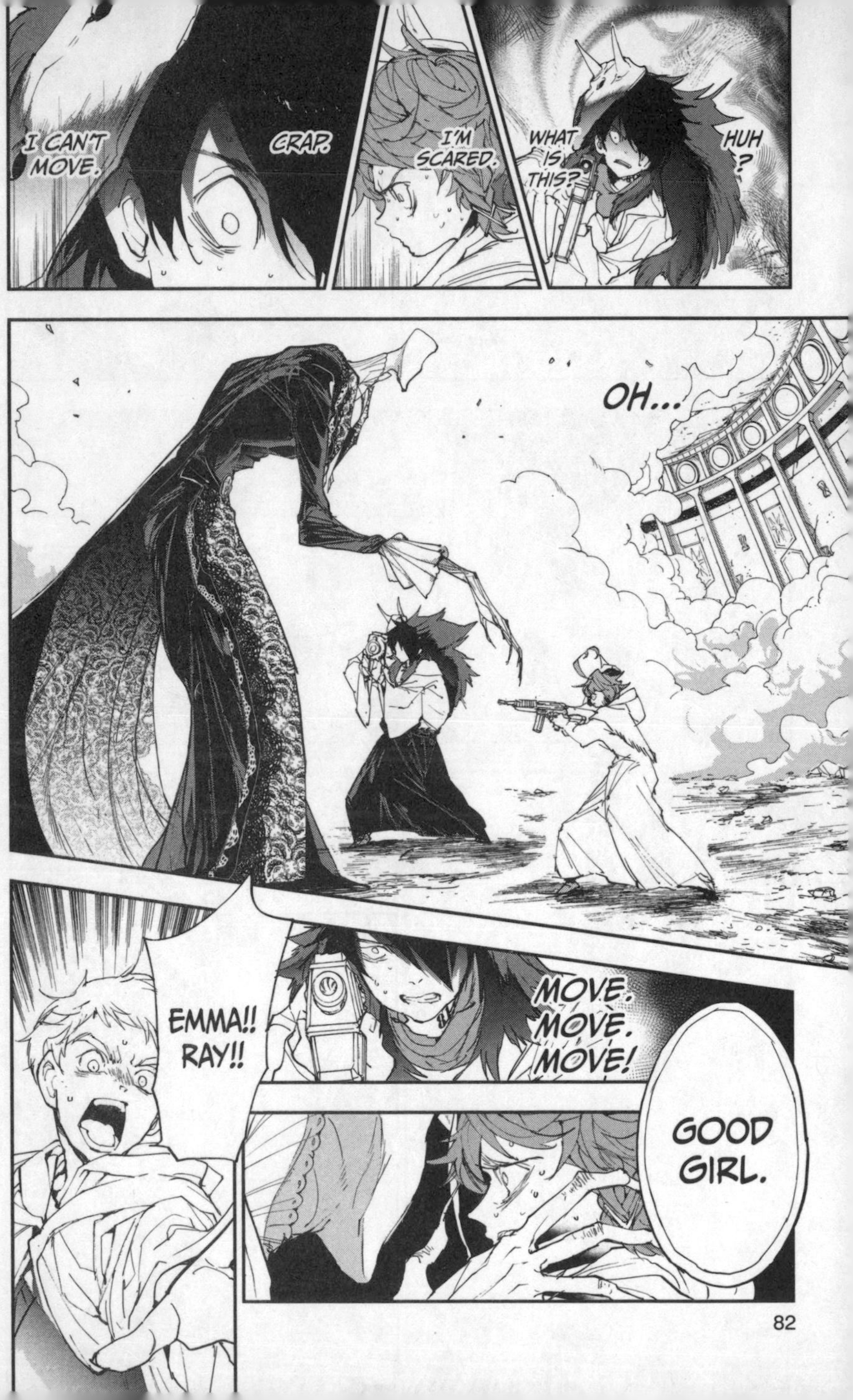

HUH?
WHAT IS THIS?
I'M SCARED.
CRAP.
I CAN'T MOVE.
OH...
MOVE. MOVE. MOVE!
GOOD GIRL.
EMMA!! RAY!!

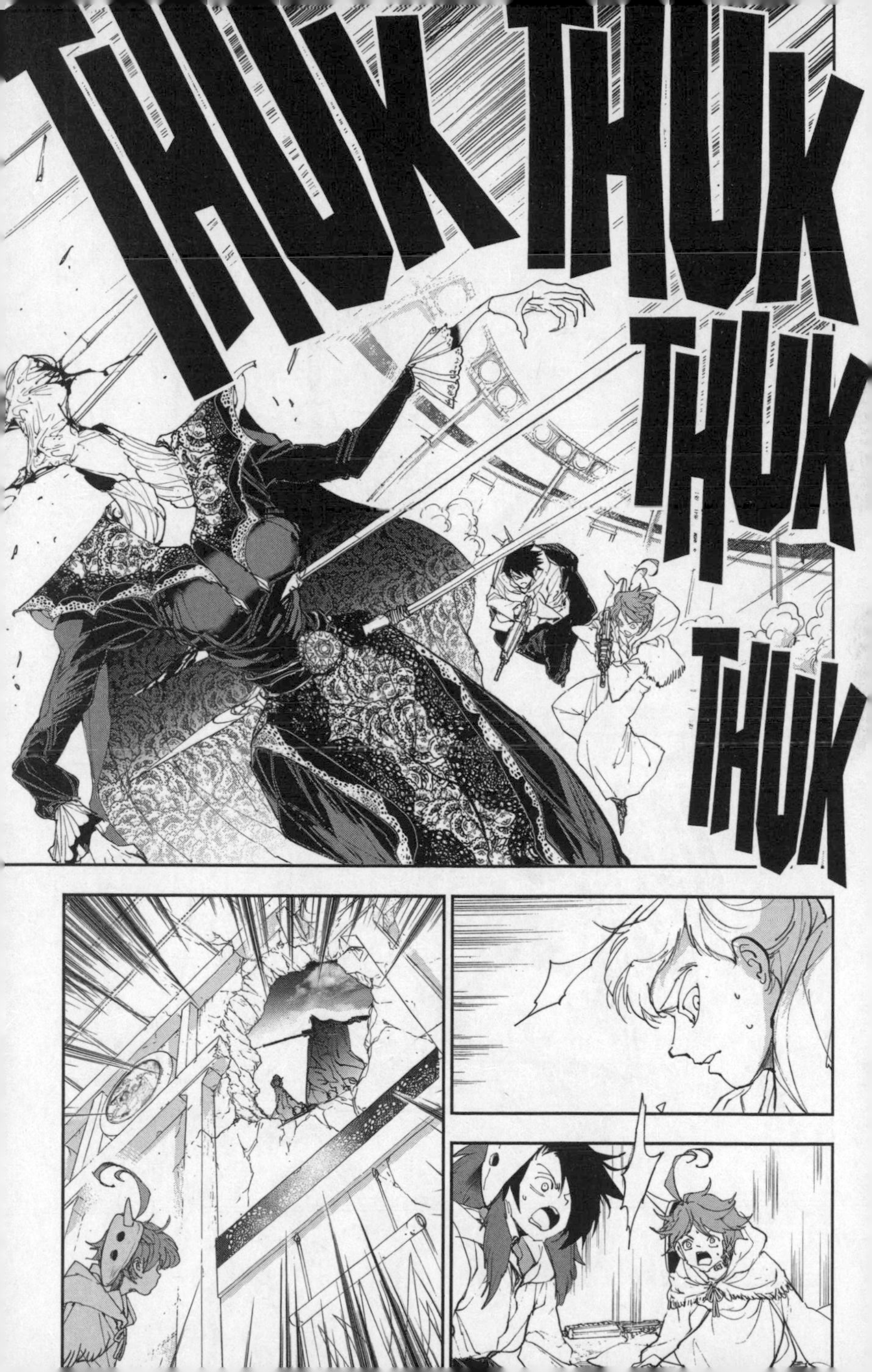
THUK THUK
THUK
THUK

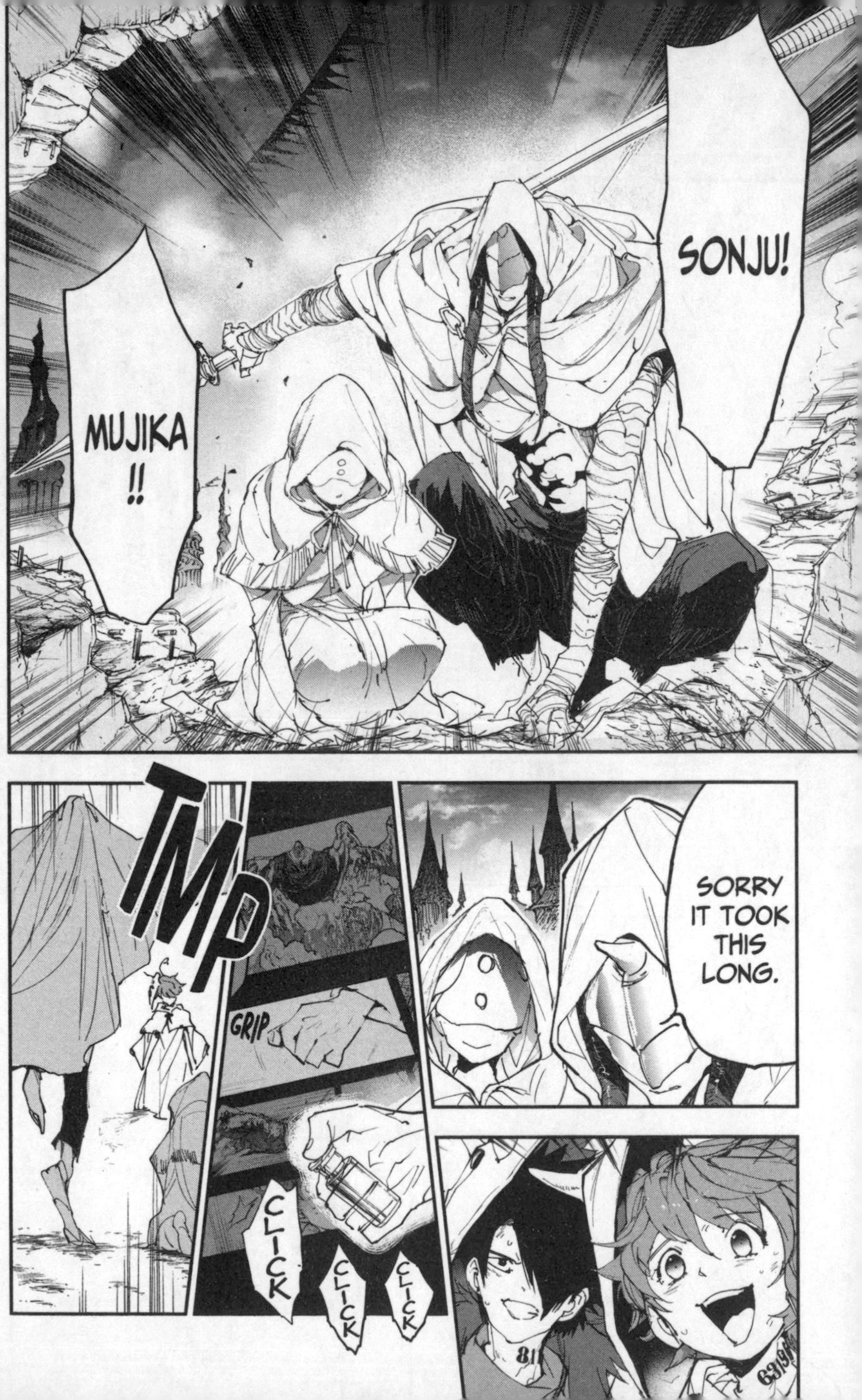
SONJU!
MUJIKA !!
SORRY IT TOOK THIS LONG.
TMP
GRIP
CLICK
CLICK
CLICK

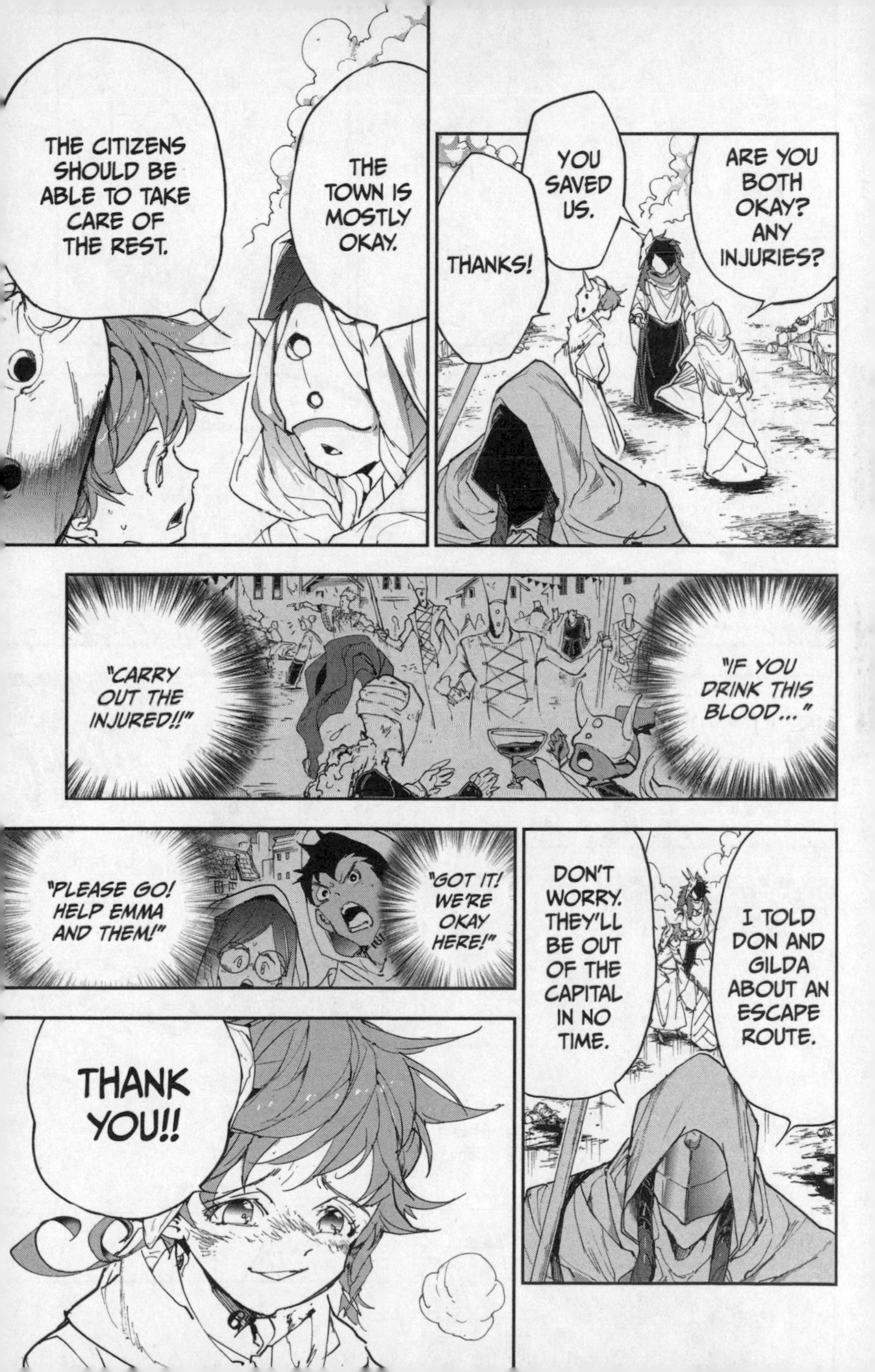
ARE YOU BOTH OKAY? ANY INJURIES?
YOU SAVED US.
THANKS!
THE TOWN IS MOSTLY OKAY.
THE CITIZENS SHOULD BE ABLE TO TAKE CARE OF THE REST.
"IF YOU DRINK THIS BLOOD..."
"CARRY OUT THE INJURED!!"
I TOLD DON AND GILDA ABOUT AN ESCAPE ROUTE.
DON'T WORRY. THEY'LL BE OUT OF THE CAPITAL IN NO TIME.
"GOT IT! WE'RE OKAY HERE!"
"PLEASE GO! HELP EMMA AND THEM!"
THANK YOU!!

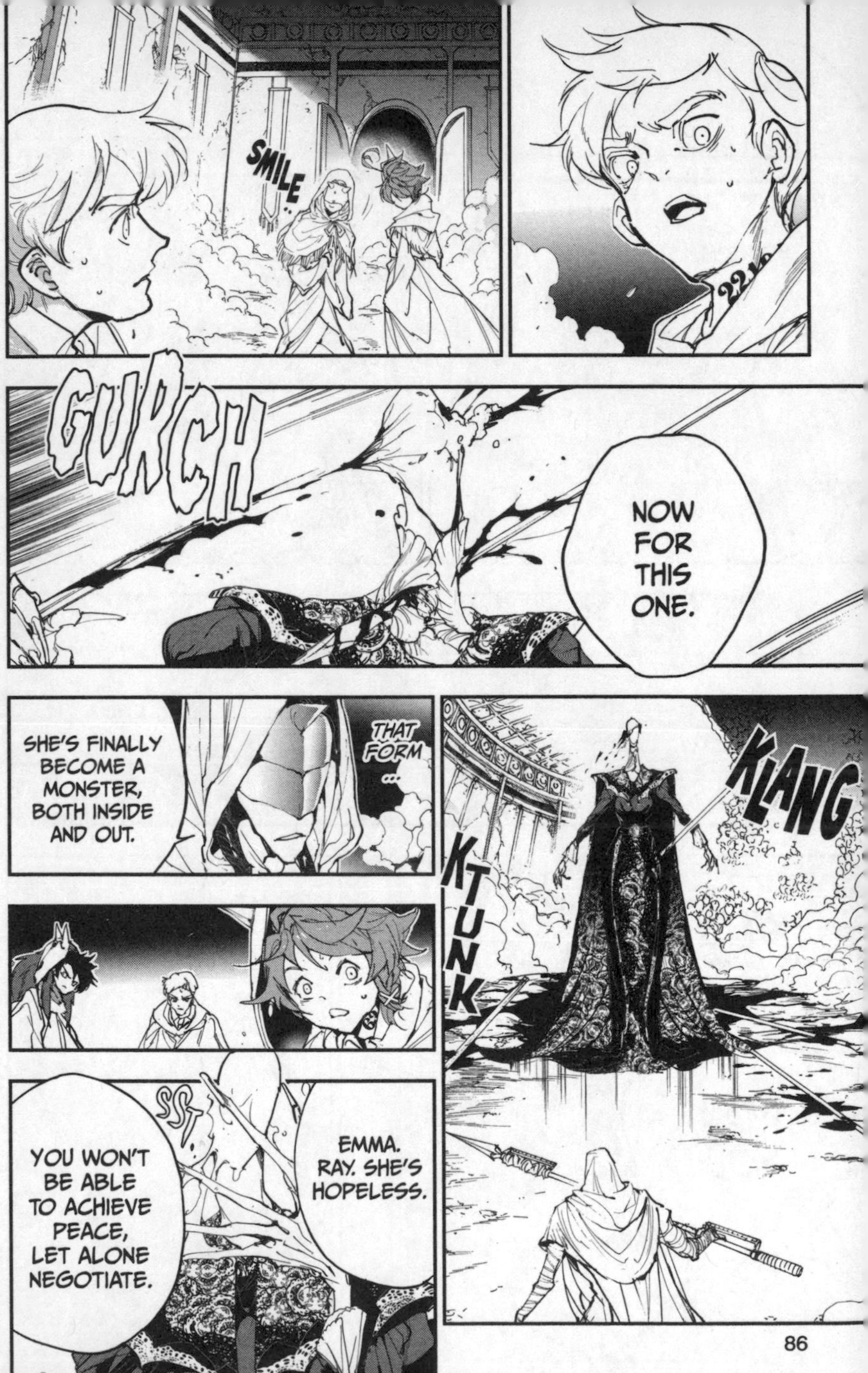
SMILE
GURCH
NOW FOR THIS ONE.
KLANG
KTUNK
THAT FORM...
SHE'S FINALLY BECOME A MONSTER, BOTH INSIDE AND OUT.
EMMA. RAY. SHE'S HOPELESS.
SSt
YOU WON'T BE ABLE TO ACHIEVE PEACE, LET ALONE NEGOTIATE.

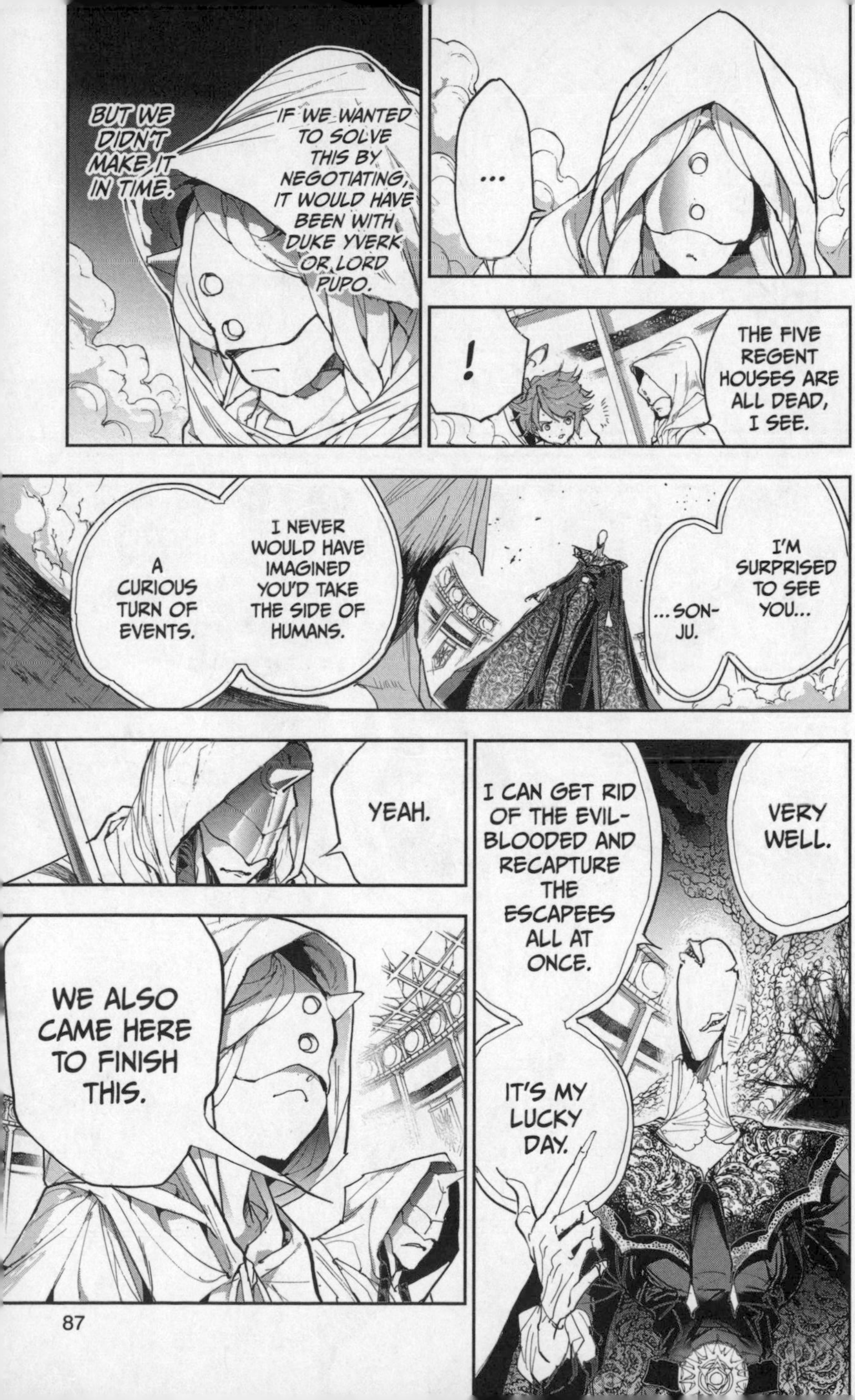
...
!
THE FIVE REGENT HOUSES ARE ALL DEAD, I SEE.
IF WE WANTED TO SOLVE THIS BY NEGOTIATING, IT WOULD HAVE BEEN WITH DUKE YVERK OR LORD PUPO.
BUT WE DIDN'T MAKE IT IN TIME.
I'M SURPRISED TO SEE YOU... ...SON-JU.
I NEVER WOULD HAVE IMAGINED YOU'D TAKE THE SIDE OF HUMANS.
A CURIOUS TURN OF EVENTS.
VERY WELL.
I CAN GET RID OF THE EVIL-BLOODED AND RECAPTURE THE ESCAPEES ALL AT ONCE.
IT'S MY LUCKY DAY.
YEAH.
WE ALSO CAME HERE TO FINISH THIS.

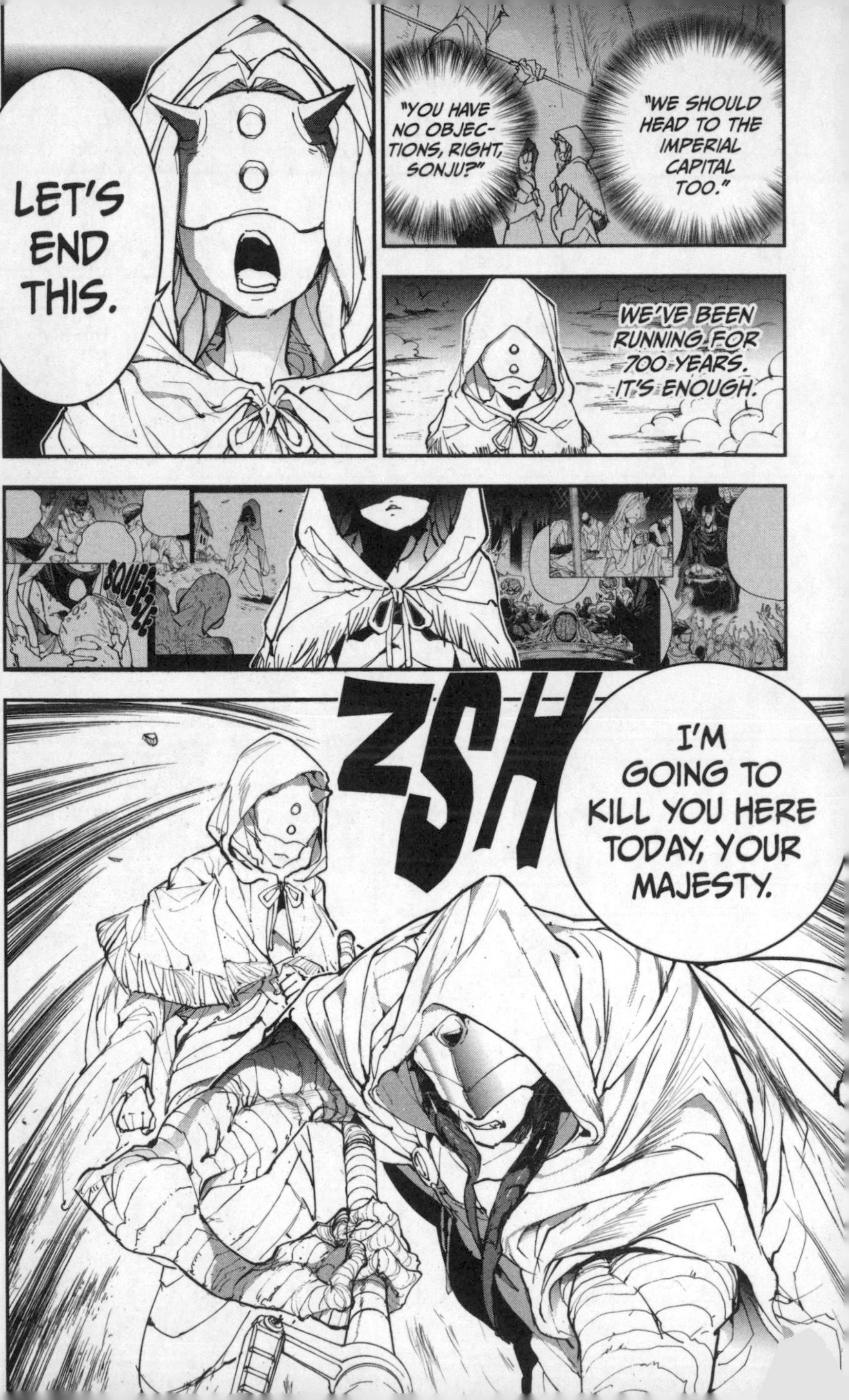
"WE SHOULD HEAD TO THE IMPERIAL CAPITAL TOO."
"YOU HAVE NO OBJECTIONS, RIGHT, SONJU?"
WE'VE BEEN RUNNING FOR 700 YEARS. IT'S ENOUGH.
LET'S END THIS.
SQUEEZE
I'M GOING TO KILL YOU HERE TODAY, YOUR MAJESTY.
ZSH

KILL?

YOU? WILL KILL ME?

SMIRK

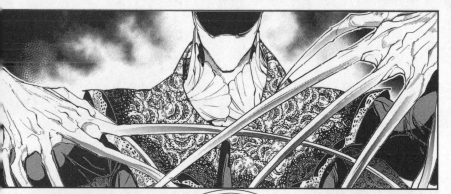

A TRUE FOOL YOU ARE, YOUNGER BROTHER.

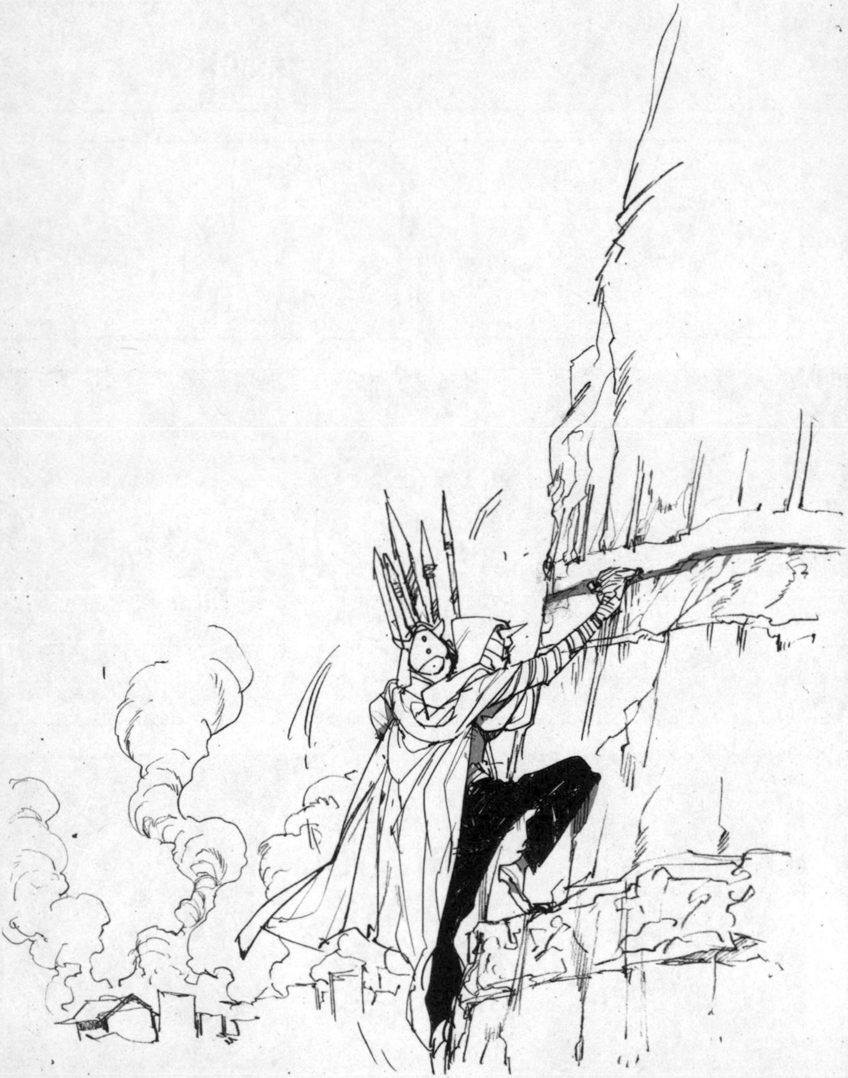

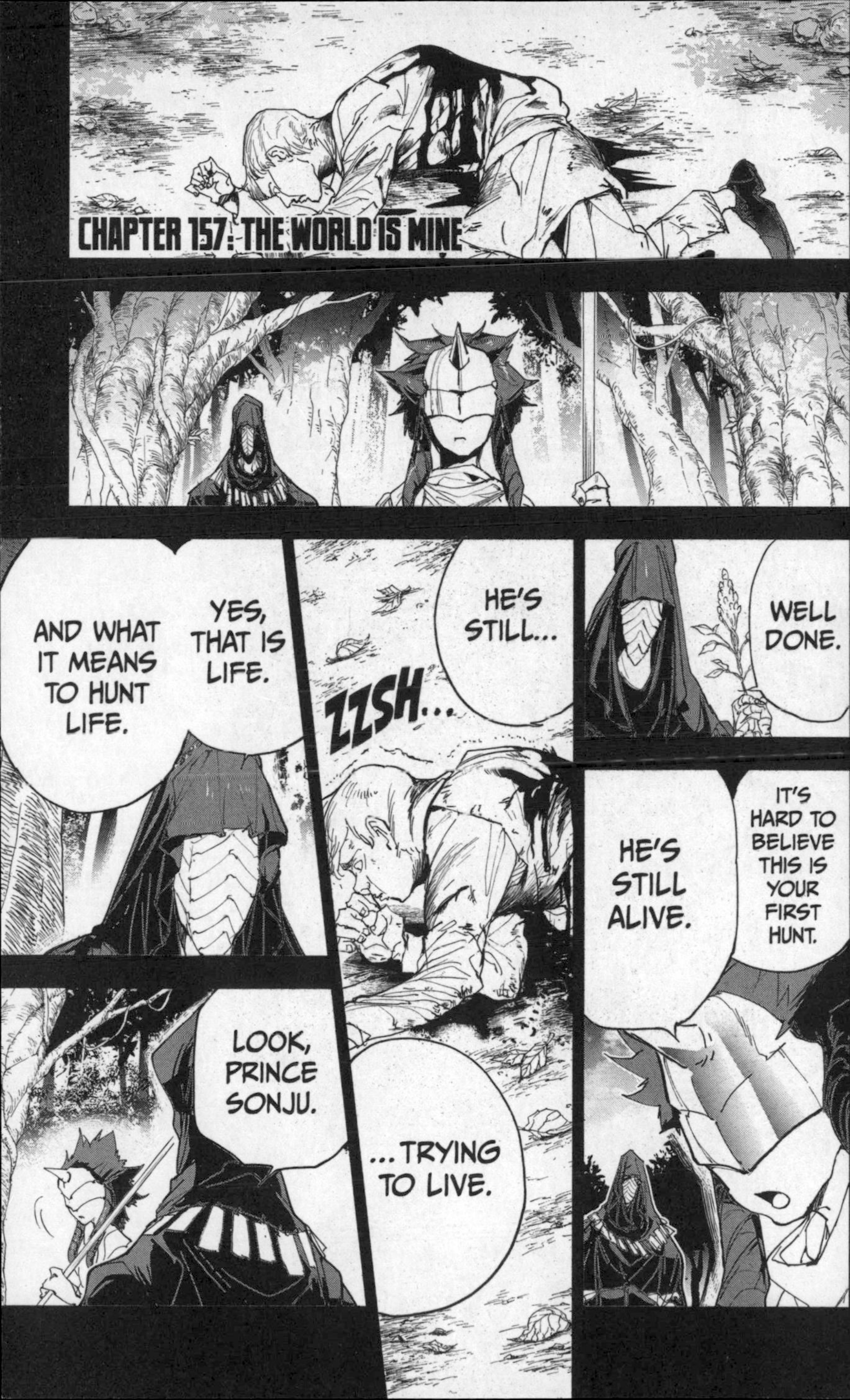

CHAPTER 157: THE WORLD IS MINE
WELL DONE.
IT'S HARD TO BELIEVE THIS IS YOUR FIRST HUNT.
HE'S STILL ALIVE.
HE'S STILL...
ZZSH...
...TRYING TO LIVE.
YES, THAT IS LIFE.
AND WHAT IT MEANS TO HUNT LIFE.
LOOK, PRINCE SONJU.

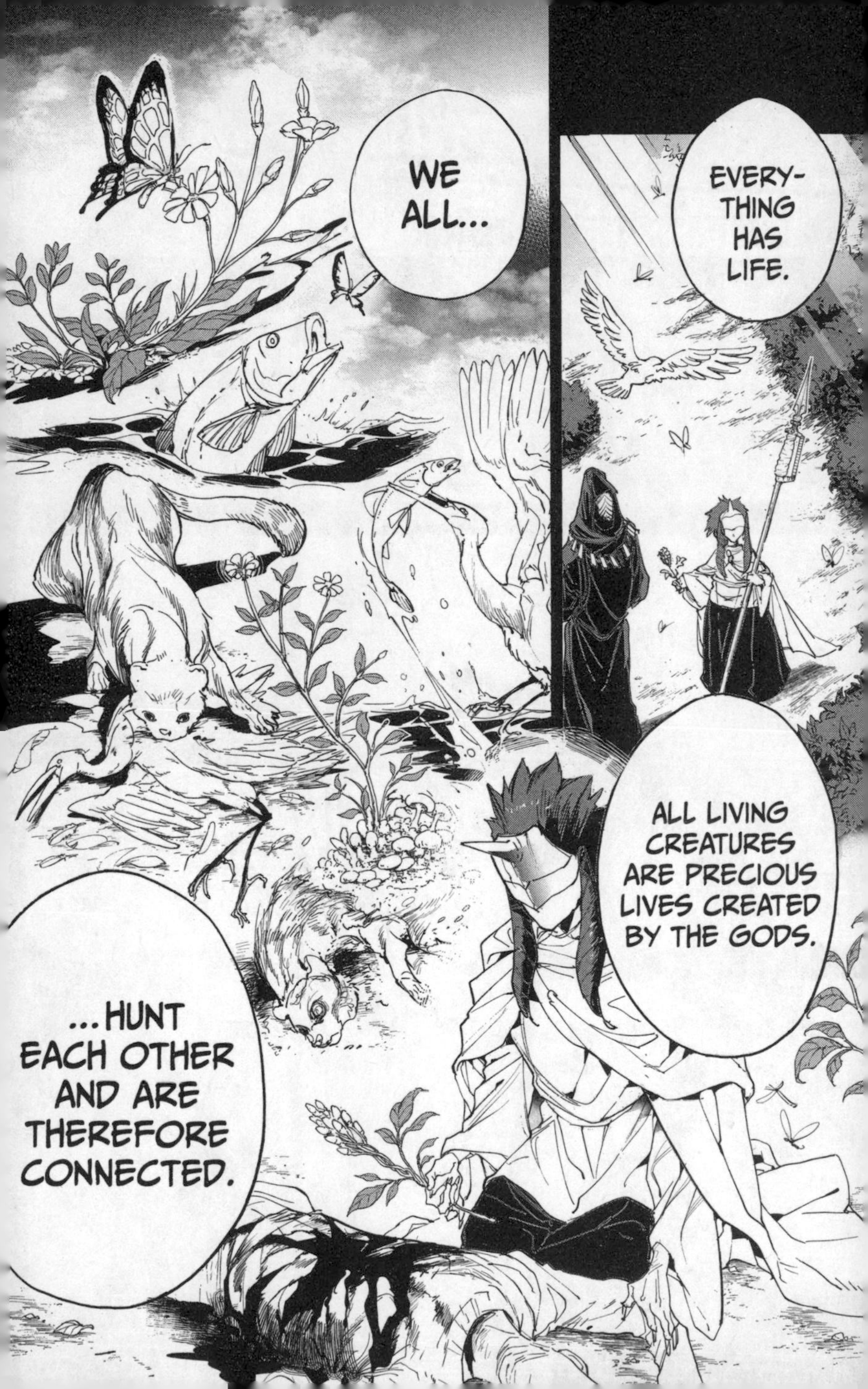
EVERY-THING HAS LIFE.
ALL LIVING CREATURES ARE PRECIOUS LIVES CREATED BY THE GODS.
WE ALL...
...HUNT EACH OTHER AND ARE THEREFORE CONNECTED.

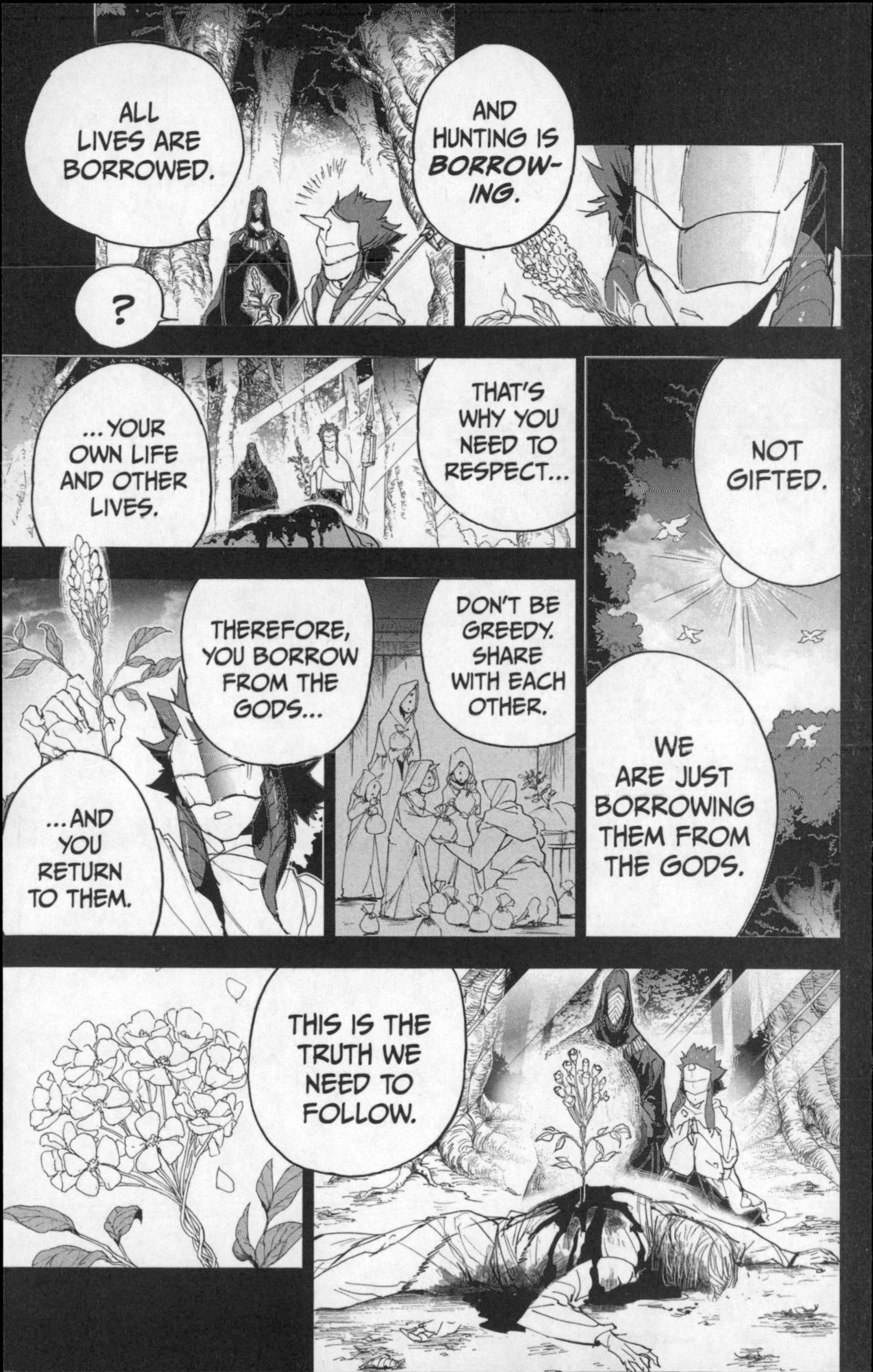
AND HUNTING IS BORROWING.
ALL LIVES ARE BORROWED.
?
NOT GIFTED.
WE ARE JUST BORROWING THEM FROM THE GODS.
THAT'S WHY YOU NEED TO RESPECT...
...YOUR OWN LIFE AND OTHER LIVES.
DON'T BE GREEDY. SHARE WITH EACH OTHER.
THEREFORE, YOU BORROW FROM THE GODS...
...AND YOU RETURN TO THEM.
THIS IS THE TRUTH WE NEED TO FOLLOW.

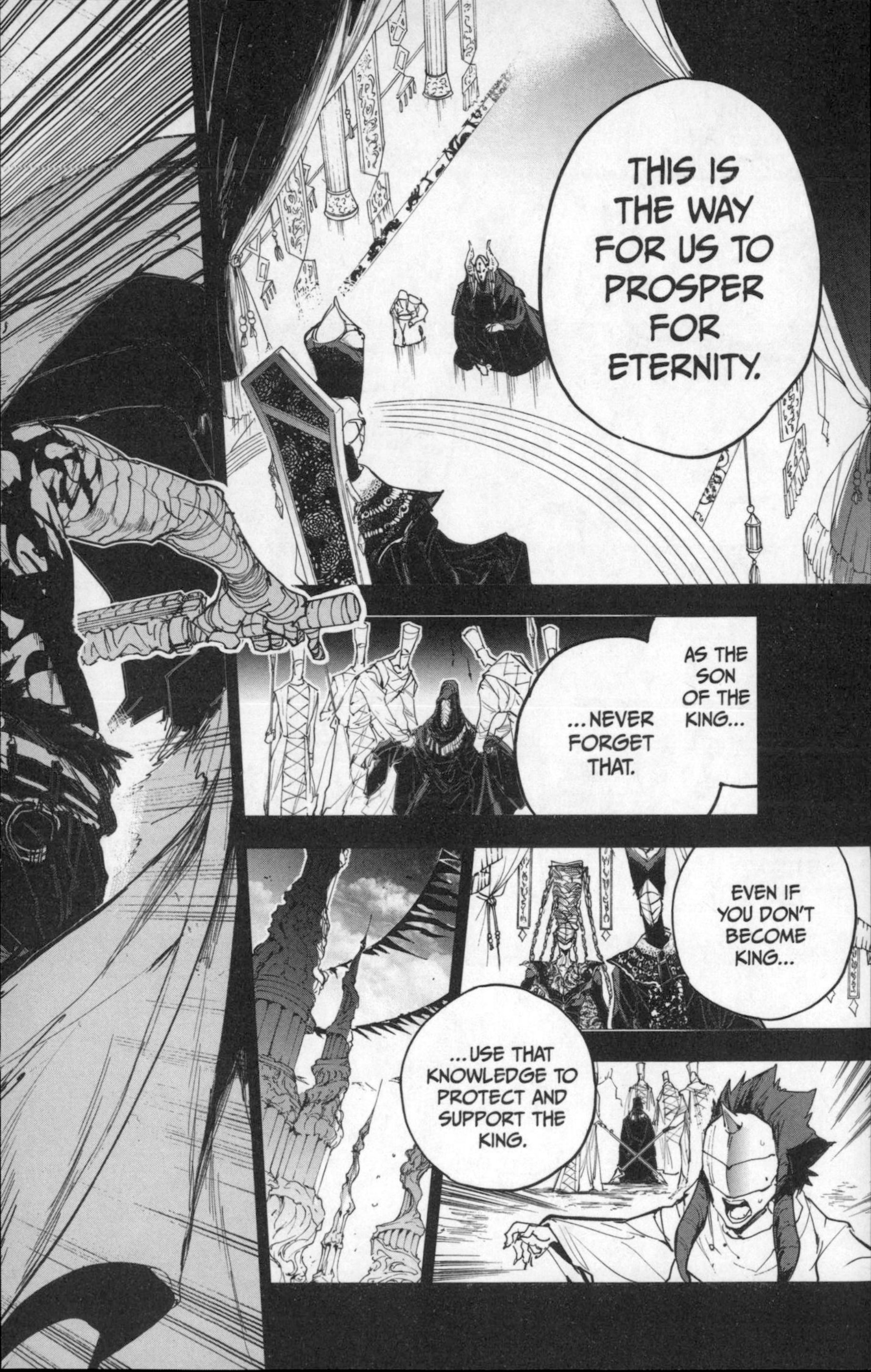
THIS IS THE WAY FOR US TO PROSPER FOR ETERNITY.
AS THE SON OF THE KING...
...NEVER FORGET THAT.
EVEN IF YOU DON'T BECOME KING...
...USE THAT KNOWLEDGE TO PROTECT AND SUPPORT THE KING.

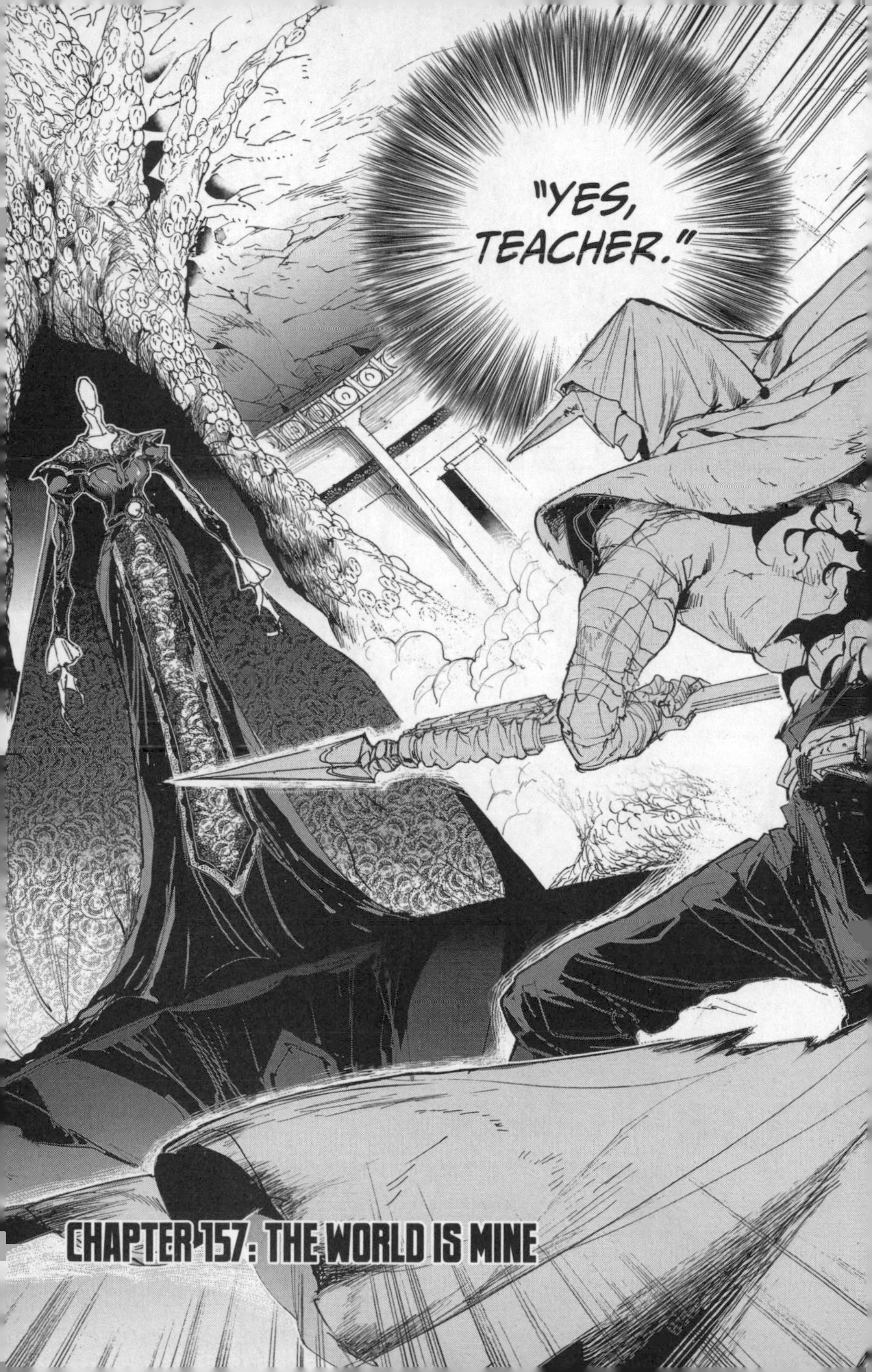
"YES, TEACHER."
CHAPTER 157: THE WORLD IS MINE

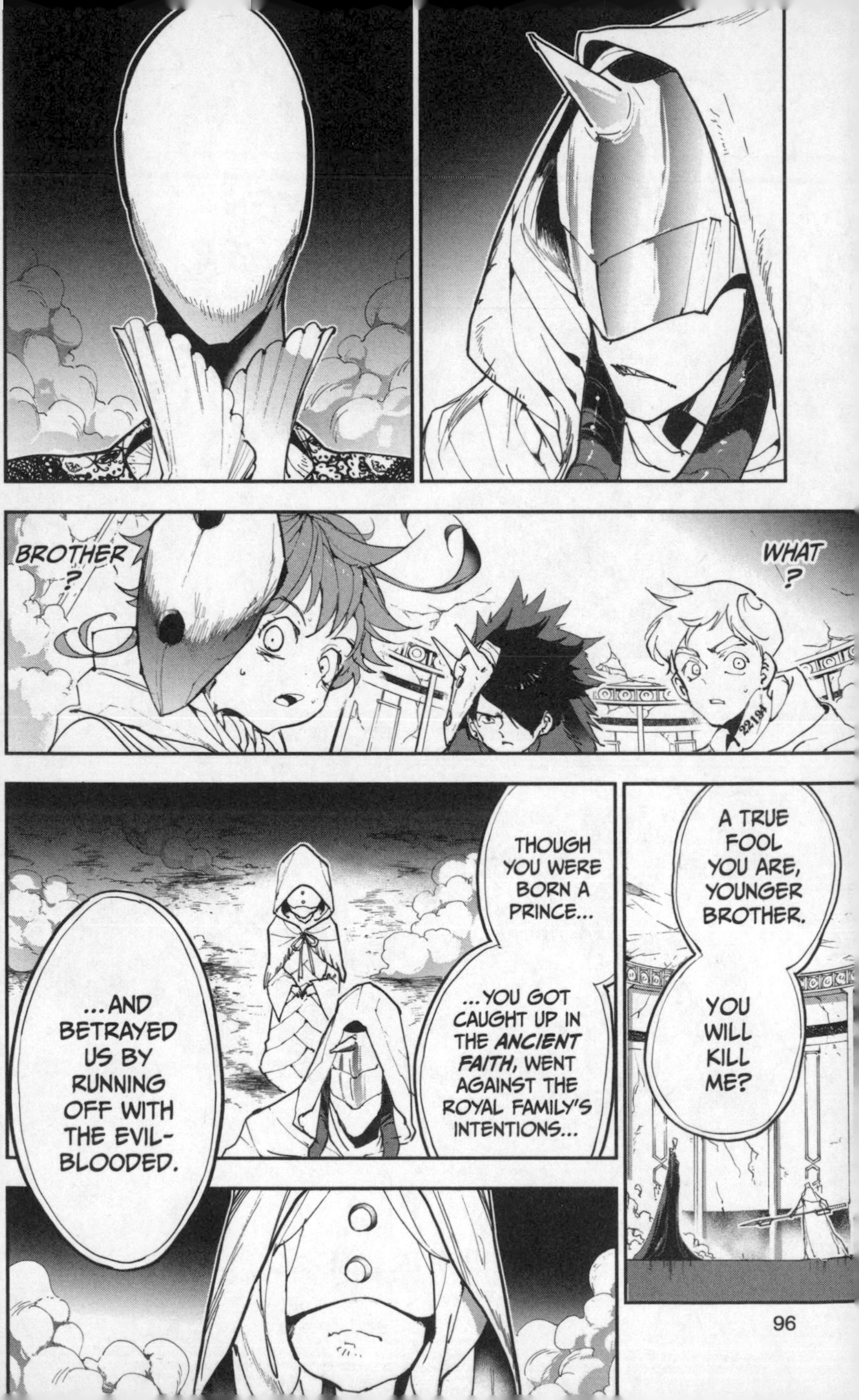
WHAT?
BROTHER?
A TRUE FOOL YOU ARE, YOUNGER BROTHER.
YOU WILL KILL ME?
THOUGH YOU WERE BORN A PRINCE...
...YOU GOT CAUGHT UP IN THE *ANCIENT FAITH*, WENT AGAINST THE ROYAL FAMILY'S INTENTIONS...
...AND BETRAYED US BY RUNNING OFF WITH THE EVIL-BLOODED.

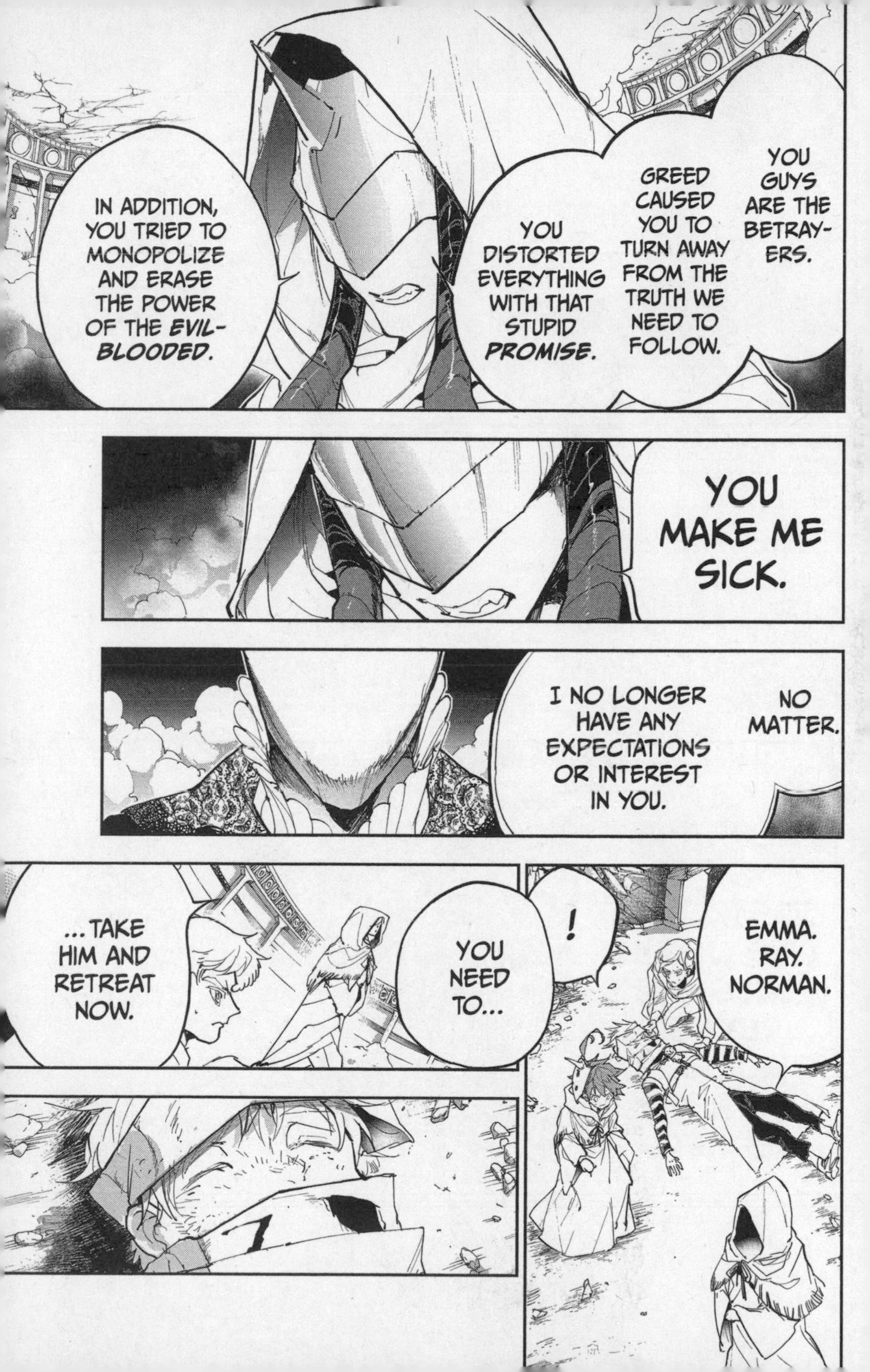
YOU GUYS ARE THE BETRAYERS.
GREED CAUSED YOU TO TURN AWAY FROM THE TRUTH WE NEED TO FOLLOW.
YOU DISTORTED EVERYTHING WITH THAT STUPID *PROMISE*.
IN ADDITION, YOU TRIED TO MONOPOLIZE AND ERASE THE POWER OF THE *EVIL-BLOODED*.
YOU MAKE ME SICK.
NO MATTER.
I NO LONGER HAVE ANY EXPECTATIONS OR INTEREST IN YOU.
EMMA. RAY. NORMAN.
!
YOU NEED TO...
...TAKE HIM AND RETREAT NOW.

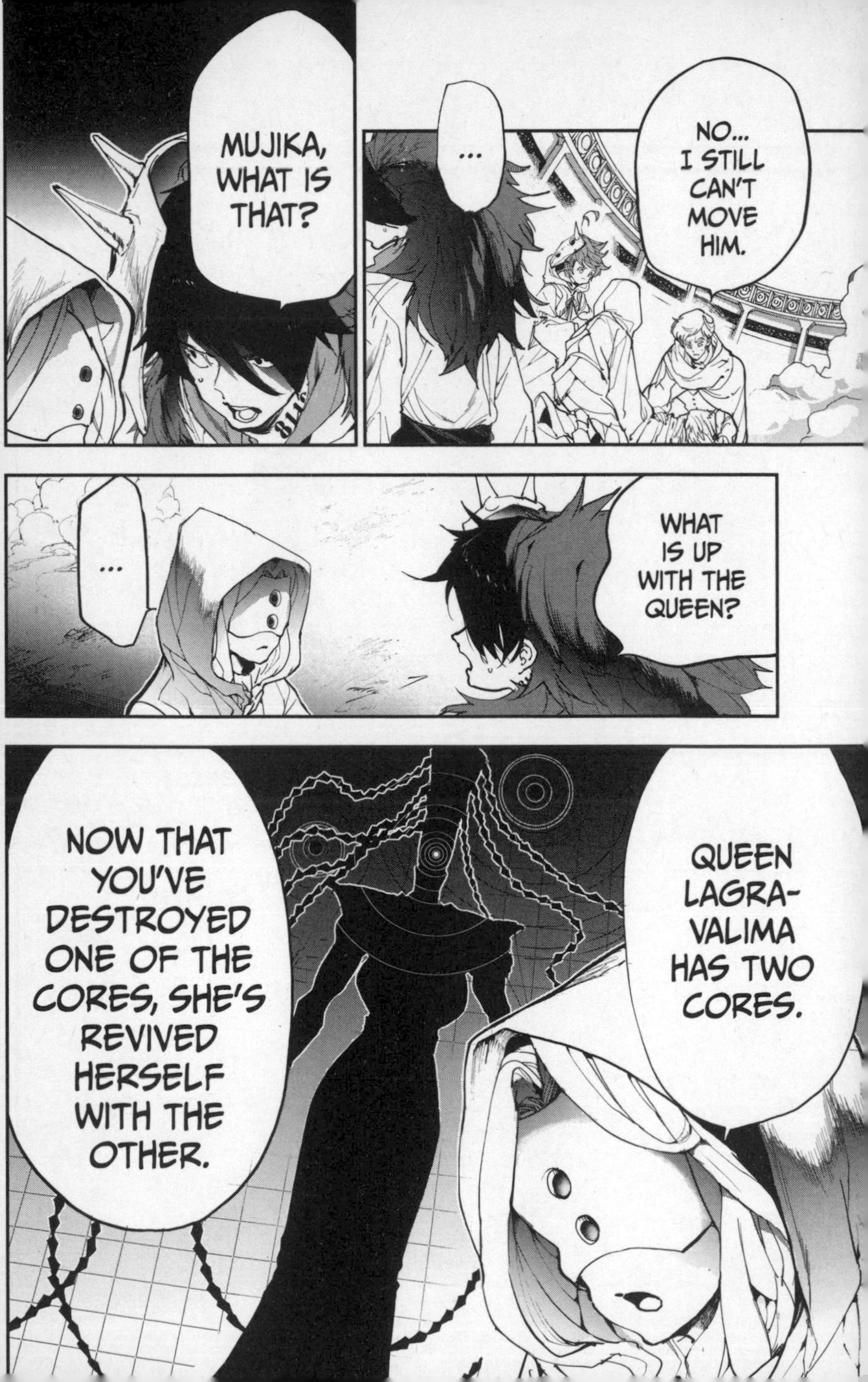
NO... I STILL CAN'T MOVE HIM.
...
MUJIKA, WHAT IS THAT?
WHAT IS UP WITH THE QUEEN?
...
QUEEN LAGRA-VALIMA HAS TWO CORES.
NOW THAT YOU'VE DESTROYED ONE OF THE CORES, SHE'S REVIVED HERSELF WITH THE OTHER.

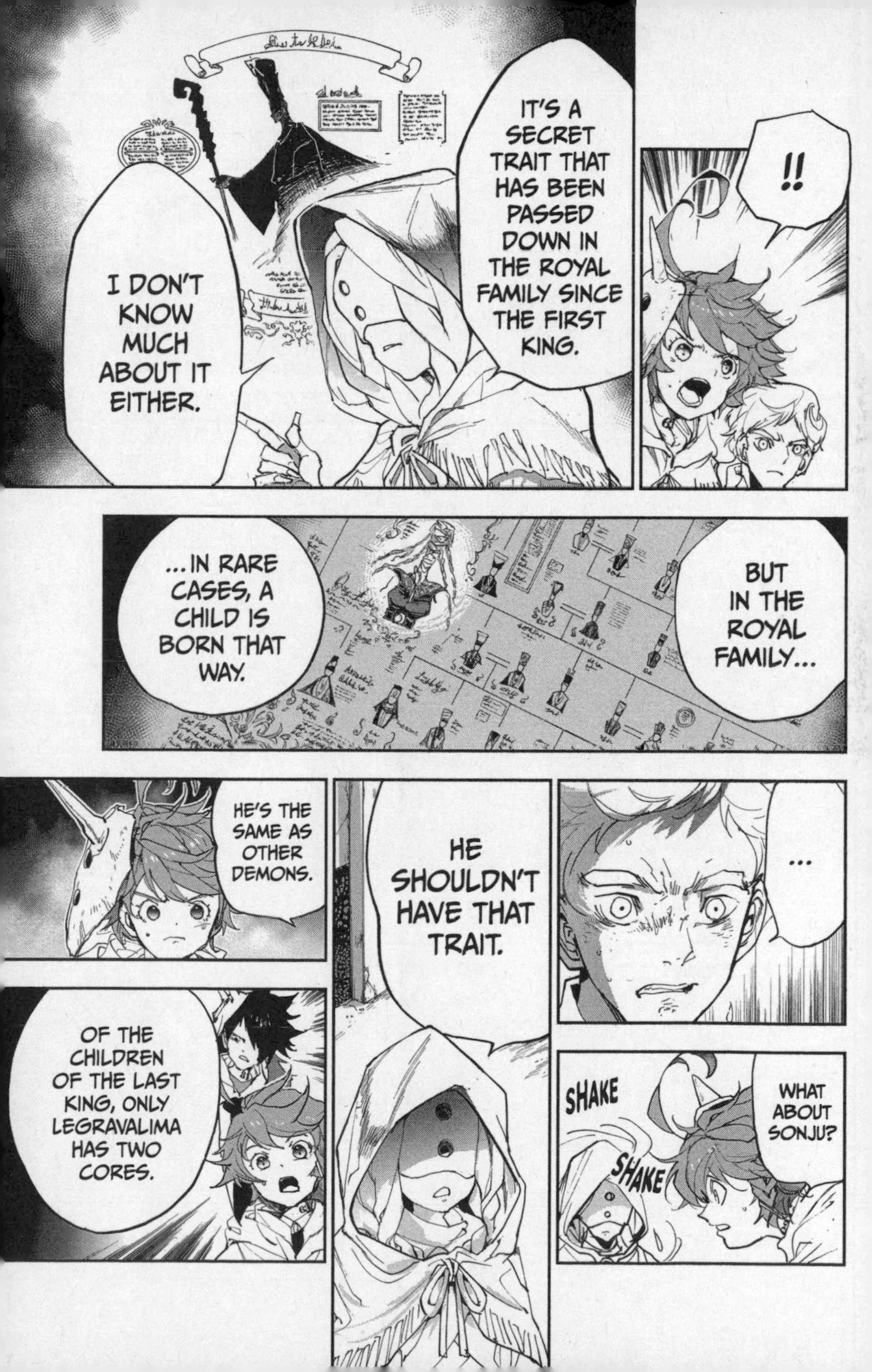
!!
IT'S A SECRET TRAIT THAT HAS BEEN PASSED DOWN IN THE ROYAL FAMILY SINCE THE FIRST KING.
I DON'T KNOW MUCH ABOUT IT EITHER.
BUT IN THE ROYAL FAMILY...
...IN RARE CASES, A CHILD IS BORN THAT WAY.
...
SHAKE
SHAKE
WHAT ABOUT SONJU?
HE SHOULDN'T HAVE THAT TRAIT.
HE'S THE SAME AS OTHER DEMONS.
OF THE CHILDREN OF THE LAST KING, ONLY LEGRAVALIMA HAS TWO CORES.

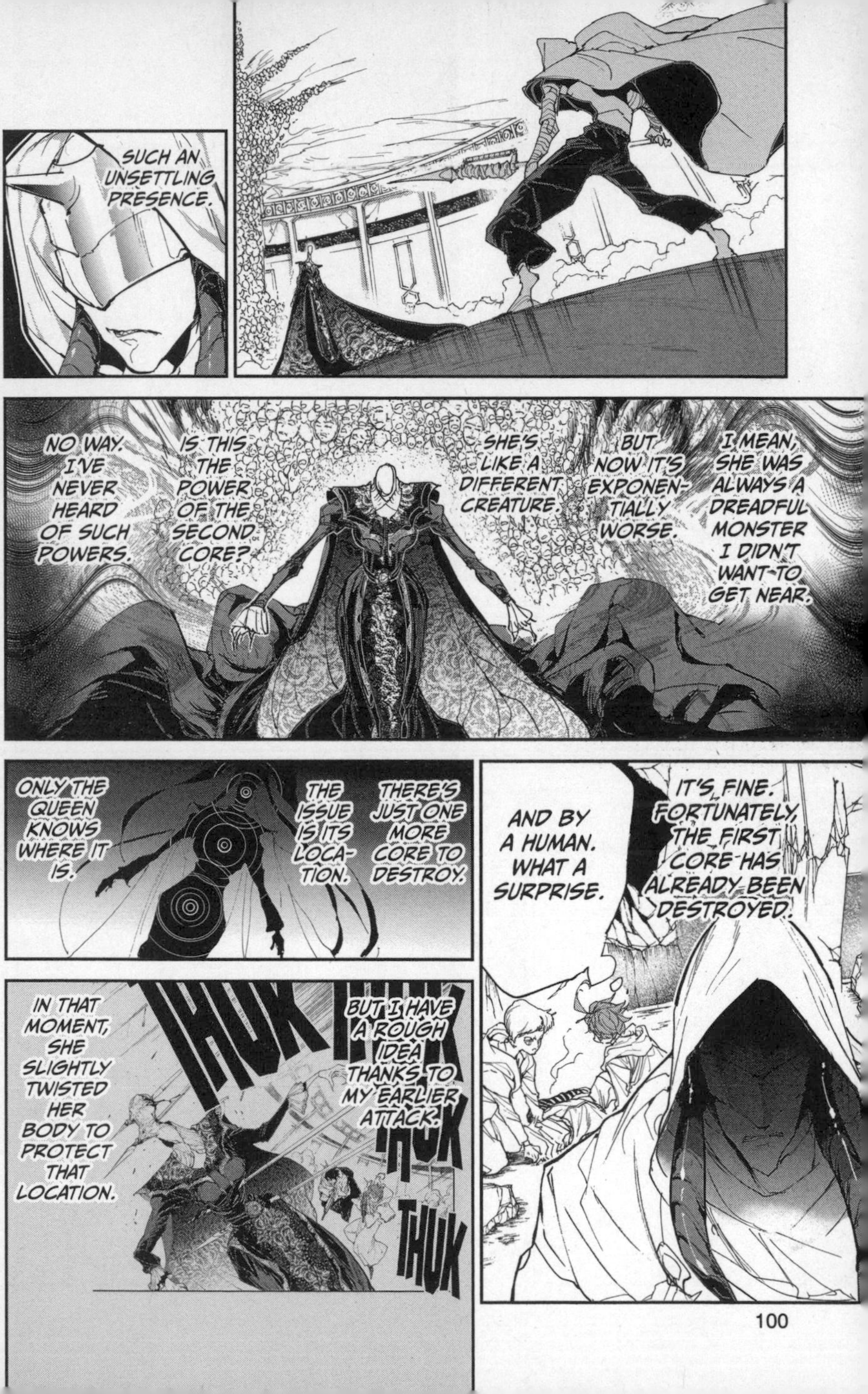
SUCH AN UNSETTLING PRESENCE.
I MEAN, SHE WAS ALWAYS A DREADFUL MONSTER I DIDN'T WANT TO GET NEAR.
BUT NOW IT'S EXPONENTIALLY WORSE.
SHE'S LIKE A DIFFERENT CREATURE.
IS THIS THE POWER OF THE SECOND CORE?
NO WAY. I'VE NEVER HEARD OF SUCH POWERS.
IT'S FINE. FORTUNATELY, THE FIRST CORE HAS ALREADY BEEN DESTROYED.
AND BY A HUMAN. WHAT A SURPRISE.
THERE'S JUST ONE MORE CORE TO DESTROY.
THE ISSUE IS ITS LOCATION.
ONLY THE QUEEN KNOWS WHERE IT IS.
BUT I HAVE A ROUGH IDEA THANKS TO MY EARLIER ATTACK.
THUK
THUK
THUK
IN THAT MOMENT, SHE SLIGHTLY TWISTED HER BODY TO PROTECT THAT LOCATION.

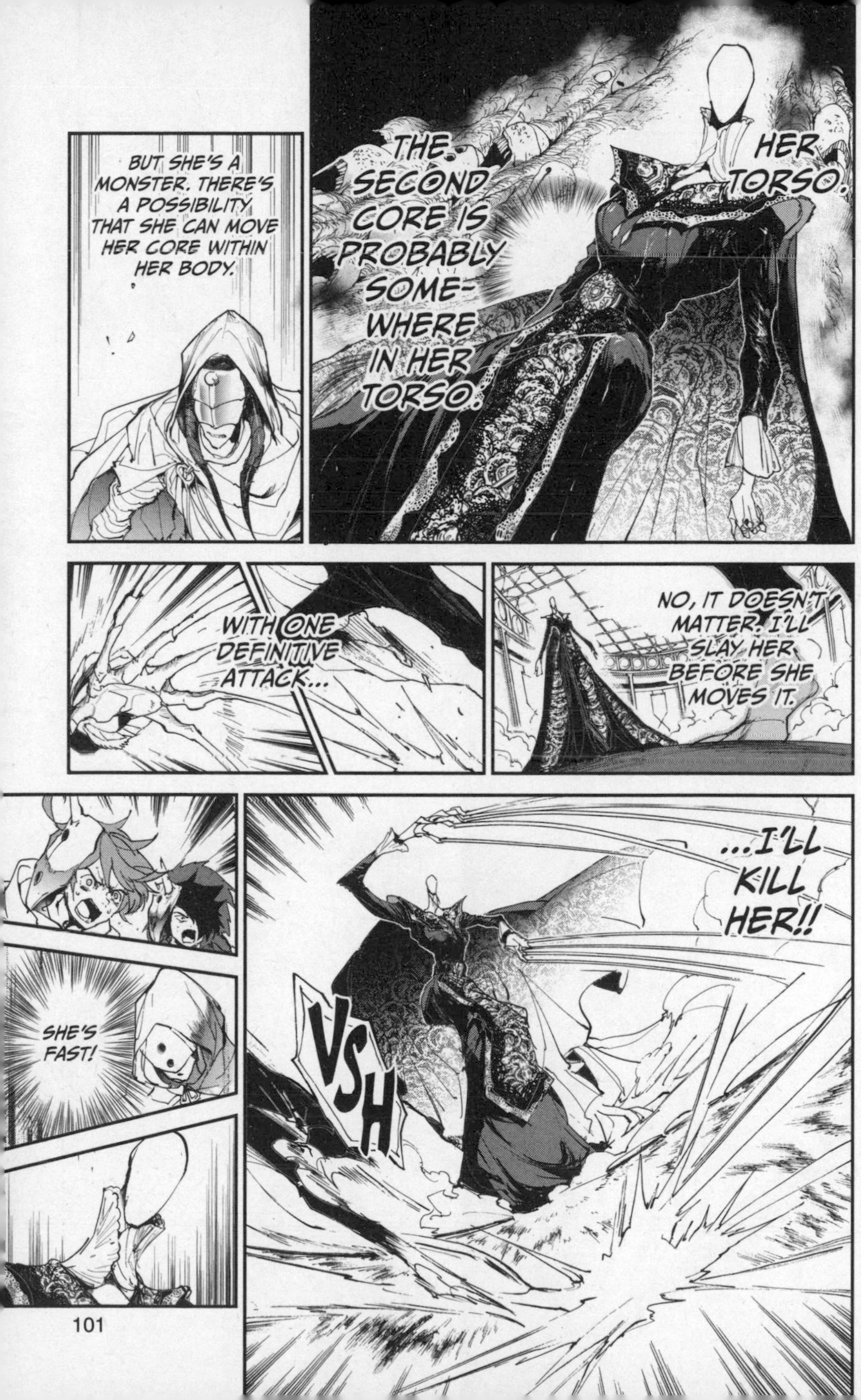
HER TORSO.
THE SECOND CORE IS PROBABLY SOME-WHERE IN HER TORSO.
BUT SHE'S A MONSTER. THERE'S A POSSIBILITY THAT SHE CAN MOVE HER CORE WITHIN HER BODY.
NO, IT DOESN'T MATTER. I'LL SLAY HER BEFORE SHE MOVES IT.
WITH ONE DEFINITIVE ATTACK...
...I'LL KILL HER!!
VSH
SHE'S FAST!

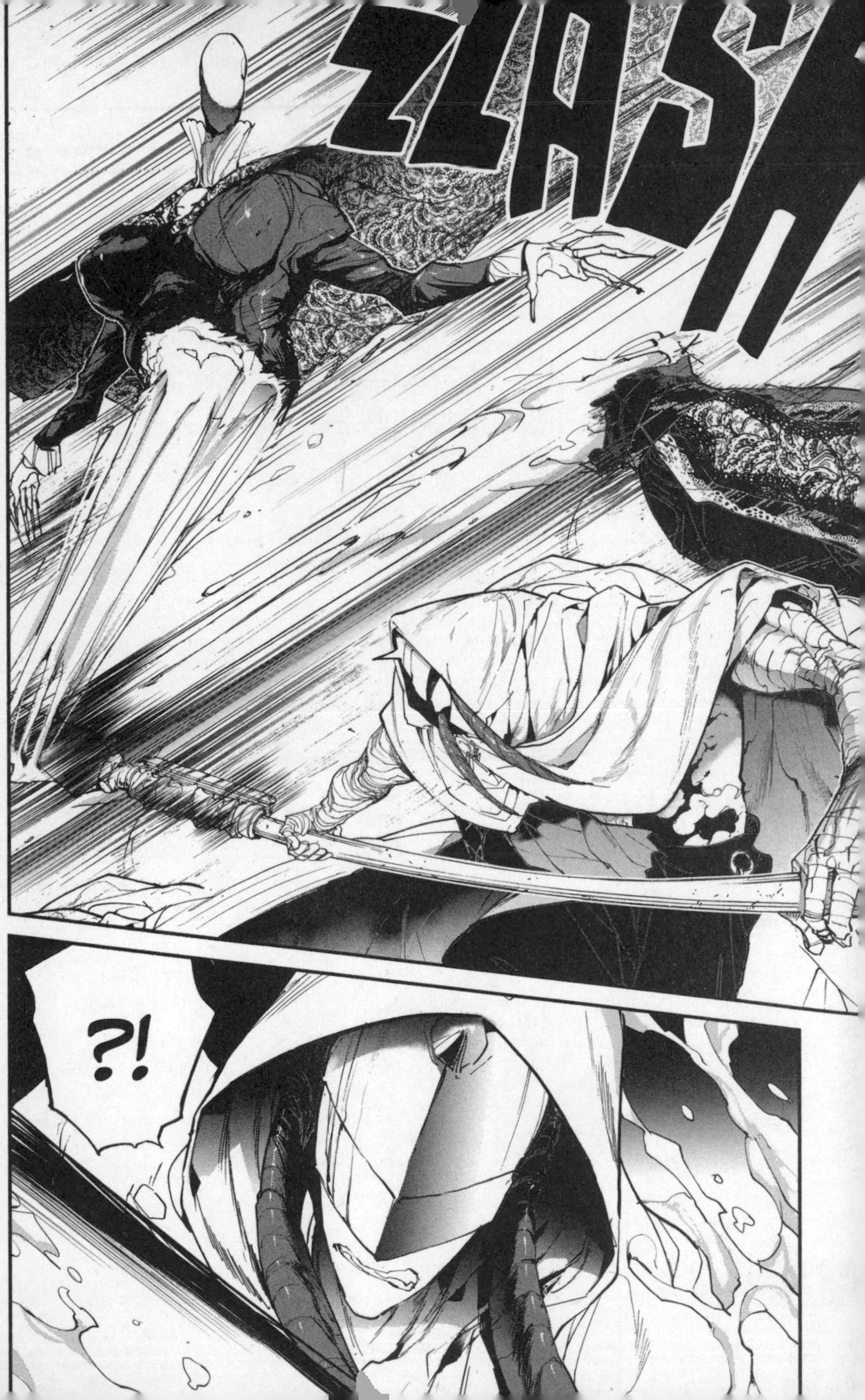
ZZASH
?!

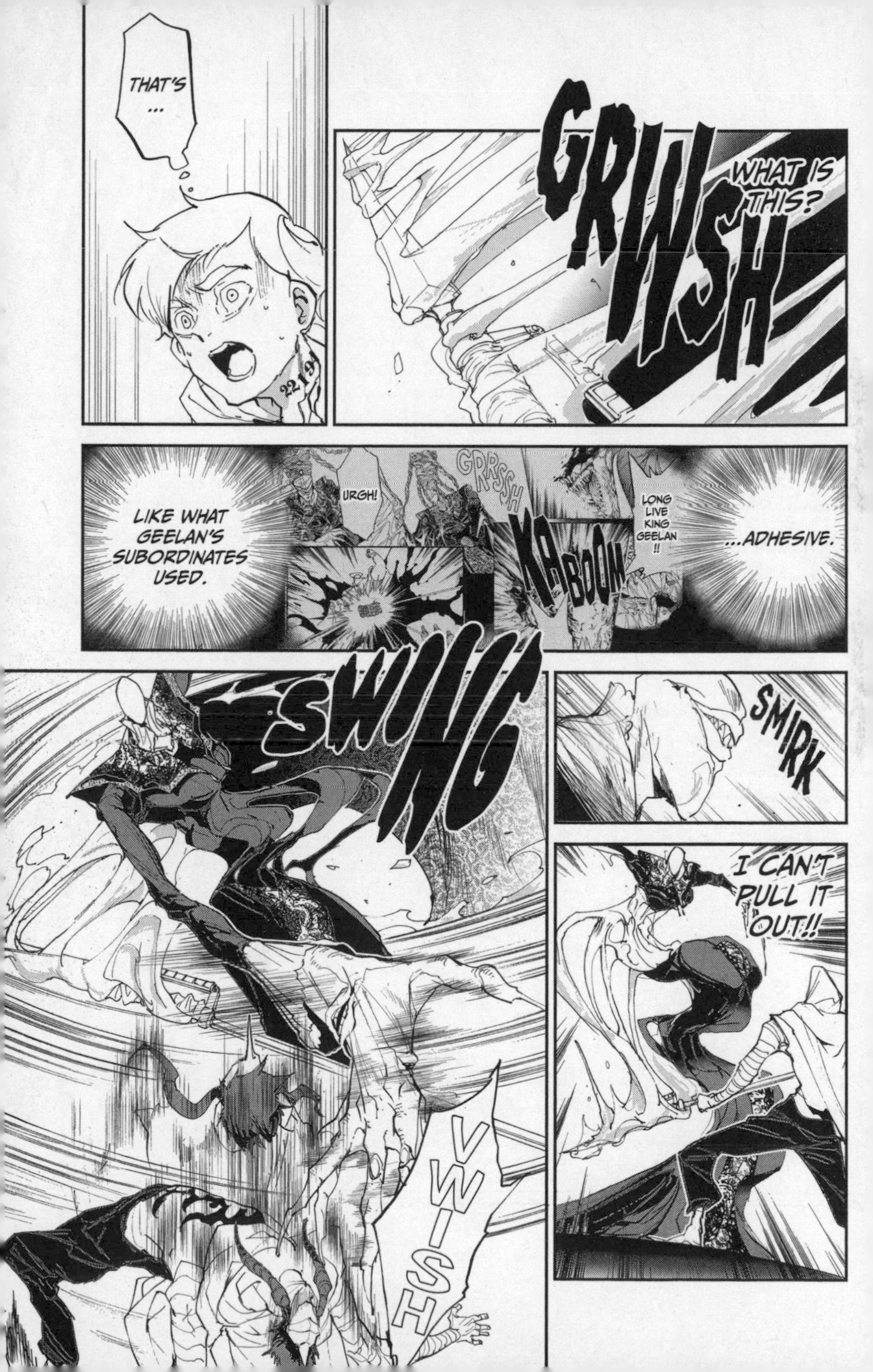

GRWSH
WHAT IS THIS?
THAT'S ...
...ADHESIVE.
LONG LIVE KING GEELAN !!
KABOOM
GRRSSH
URGH!
LIKE WHAT GEELAN'S SUBORDINATES USED.
SMIRK
I CAN'T PULL IT OUT!!
SWING
VWISH

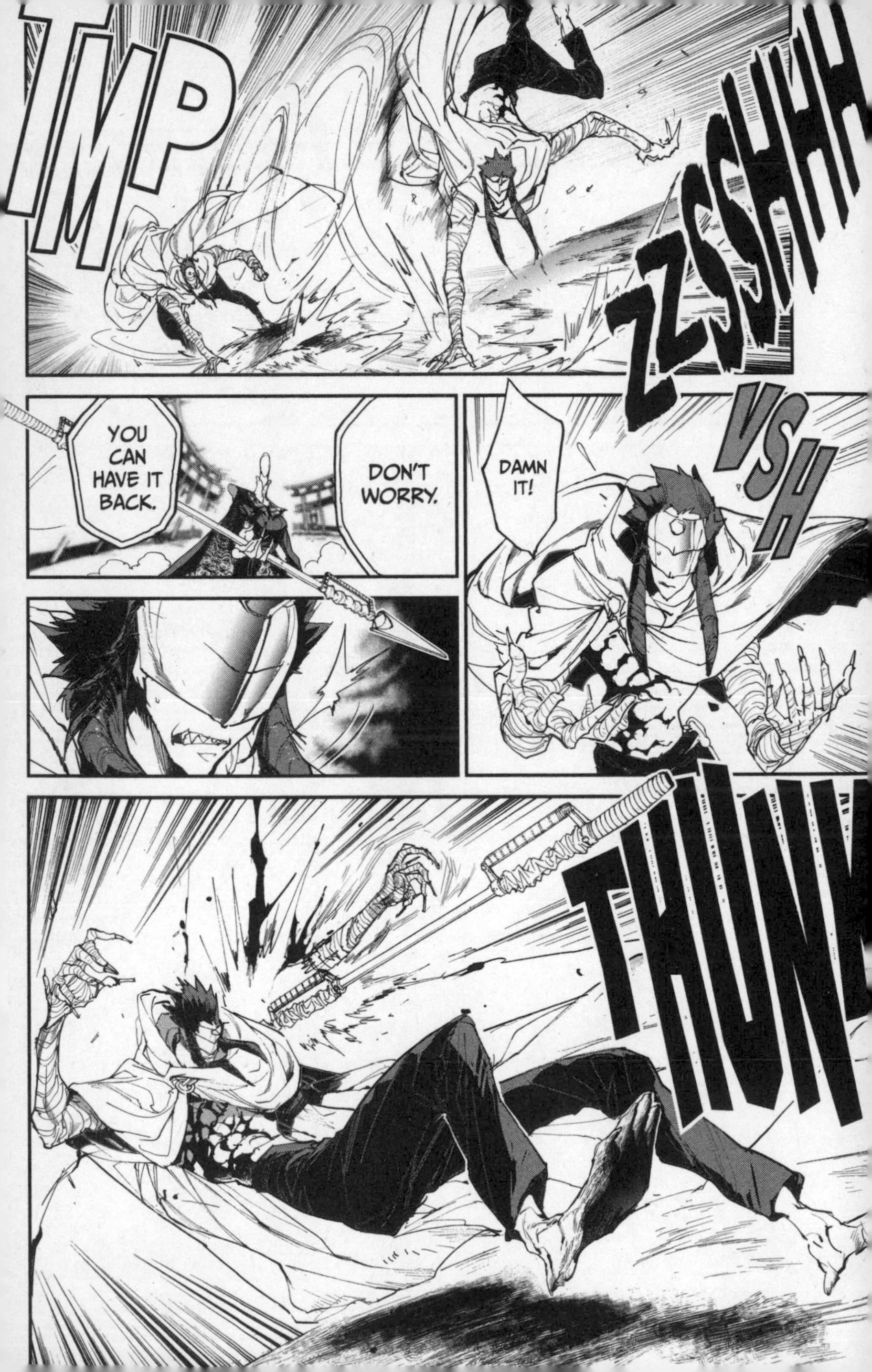
ZZSSHHH
TMP
VSH
DAMN IT!
DON'T WORRY.
YOU CAN HAVE IT BACK.
THUNK

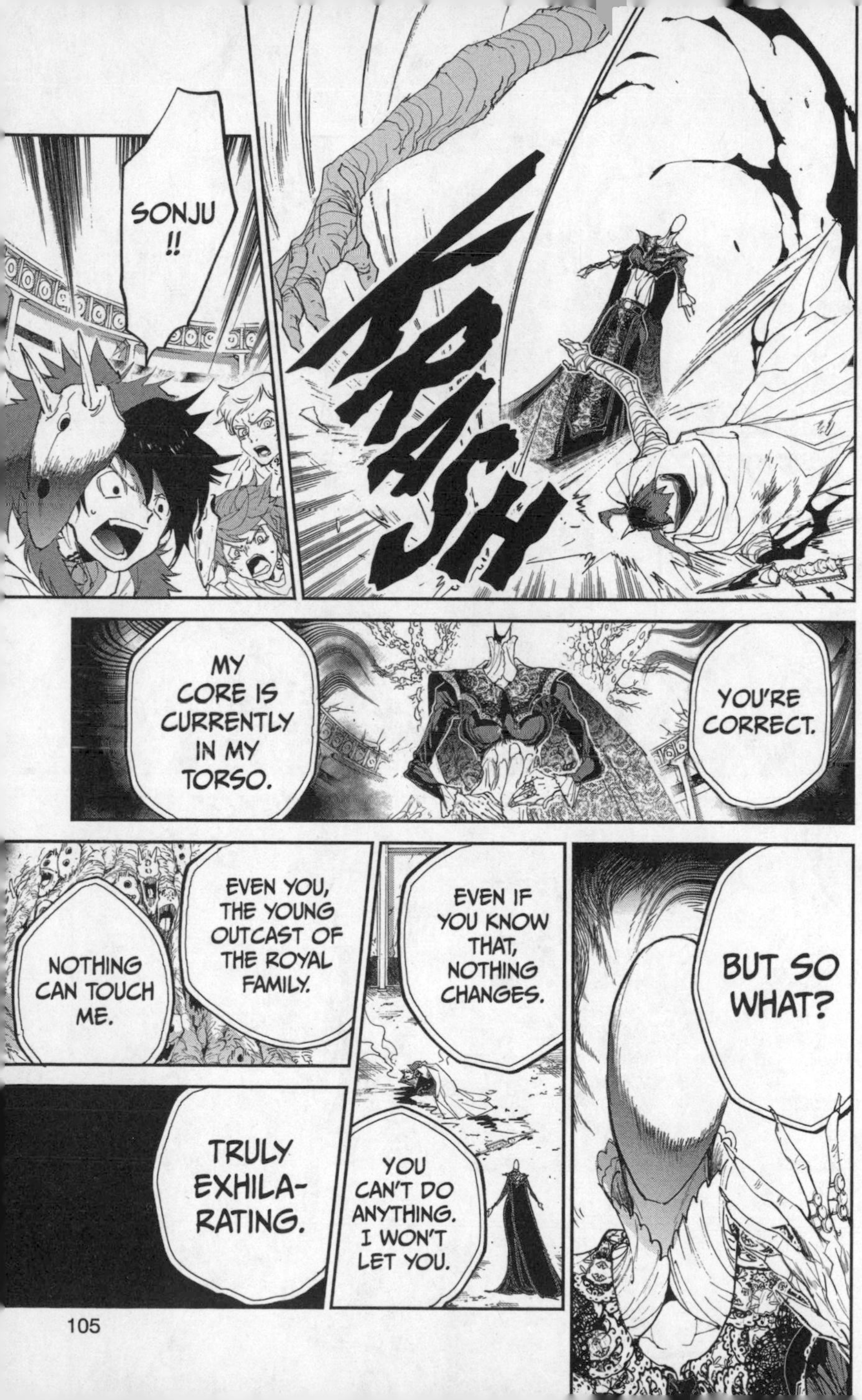
KRASH
SONJU !!
YOU'RE CORRECT.
MY CORE IS CURRENTLY IN MY TORSO.
BUT SO WHAT?
EVEN IF YOU KNOW THAT, NOTHING CHANGES.
YOU CAN'T DO ANYTHING. I WON'T LET YOU.
EVEN YOU, THE YOUNG OUTCAST OF THE ROYAL FAMILY.
NOTHING CAN TOUCH ME.
TRULY EXHILA- RATING.

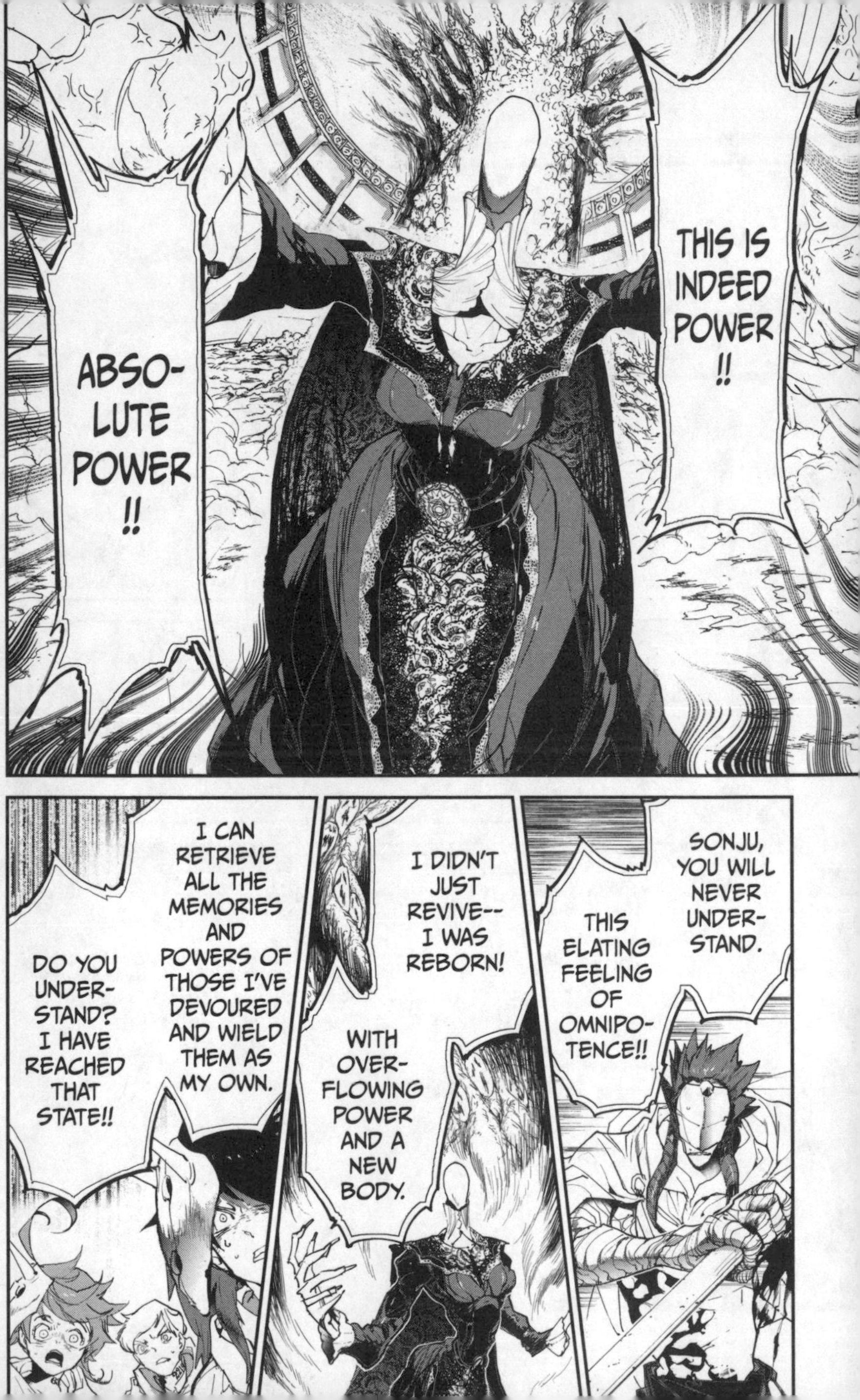
THIS IS INDEED POWER !!
ABSOLUTE POWER !!
SONJU, YOU WILL NEVER UNDERSTAND.
THIS ELATING FEELING OF OMNIPOTENCE!!
I DIDN'T JUST REVIVE-- I WAS REBORN!
WITH OVERFLOWING POWER AND A NEW BODY.
I CAN RETRIEVE ALL THE MEMORIES AND POWERS OF THOSE I'VE DEVOURED AND WIELD THEM AS MY OWN.
DO YOU UNDERSTAND? I HAVE REACHED THAT STATE!!

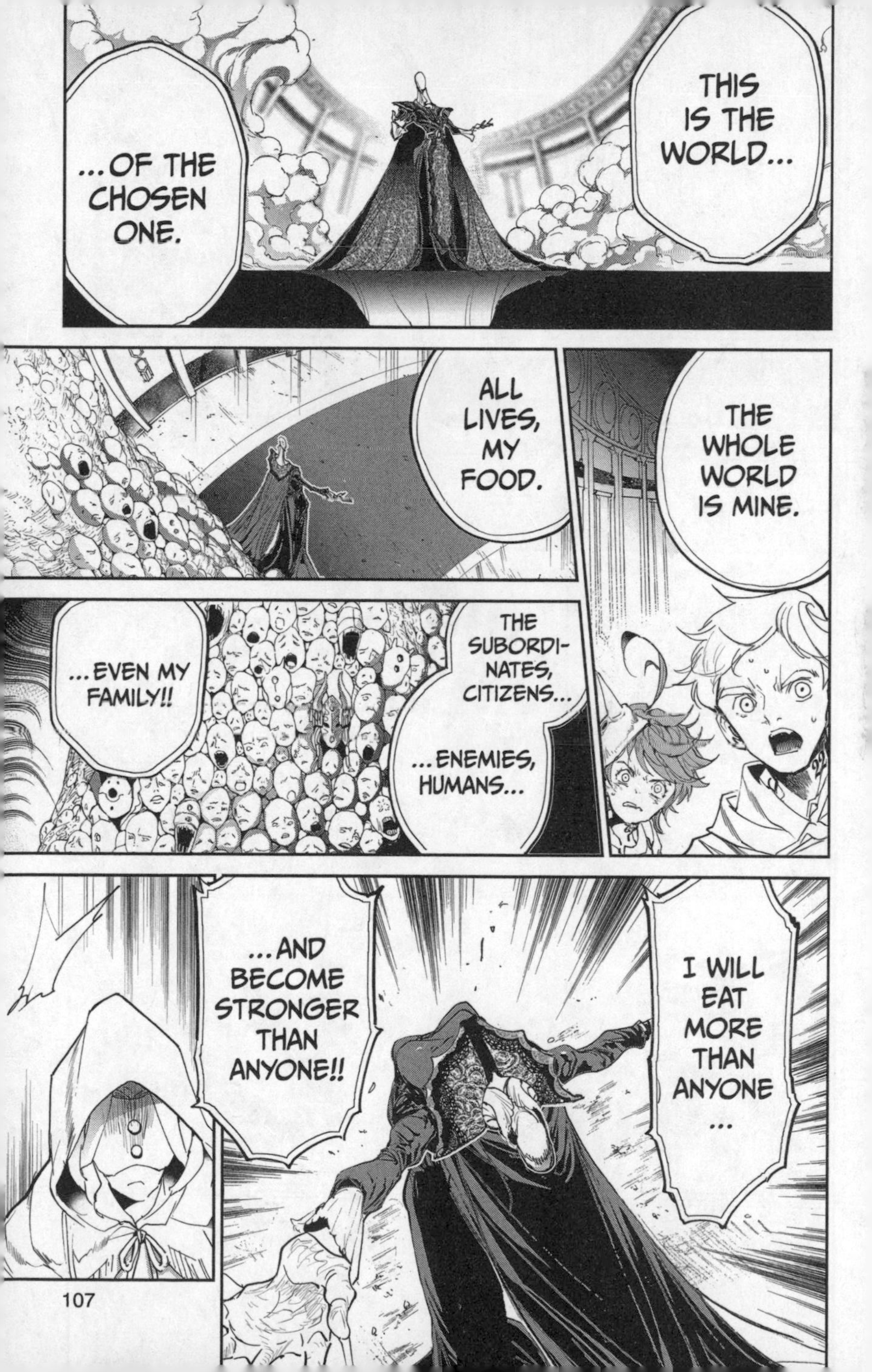
THIS IS THE WORLD...
...OF THE CHOSEN ONE.
THE WHOLE WORLD IS MINE.
ALL LIVES, MY FOOD.
THE SUBORDI-NATES, CITIZENS...
...ENEMIES, HUMANS...
...EVEN MY FAMILY!!
I WILL EAT MORE THAN ANYONE ...
...AND BECOME STRONGER THAN ANYONE!!

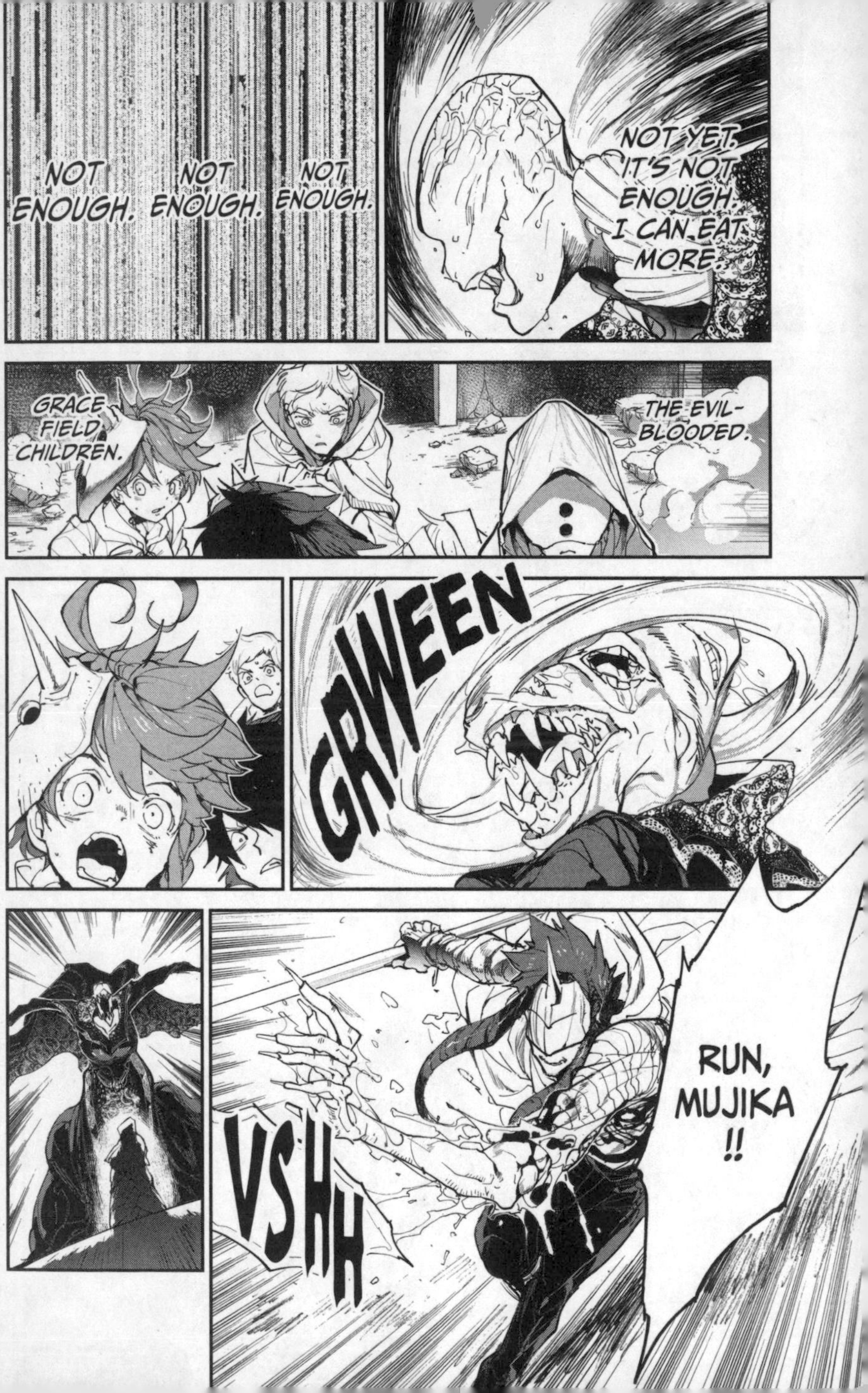
NOT YET. IT'S NOT ENOUGH. I CAN EAT MORE.
NOT ENOUGH.
NOT ENOUGH.
NOT ENOUGH.
THE EVIL-BLOODED.
GRACE FIELD CHILDREN.
GRWEEN
RUN, MUJIKA!!
VSHH

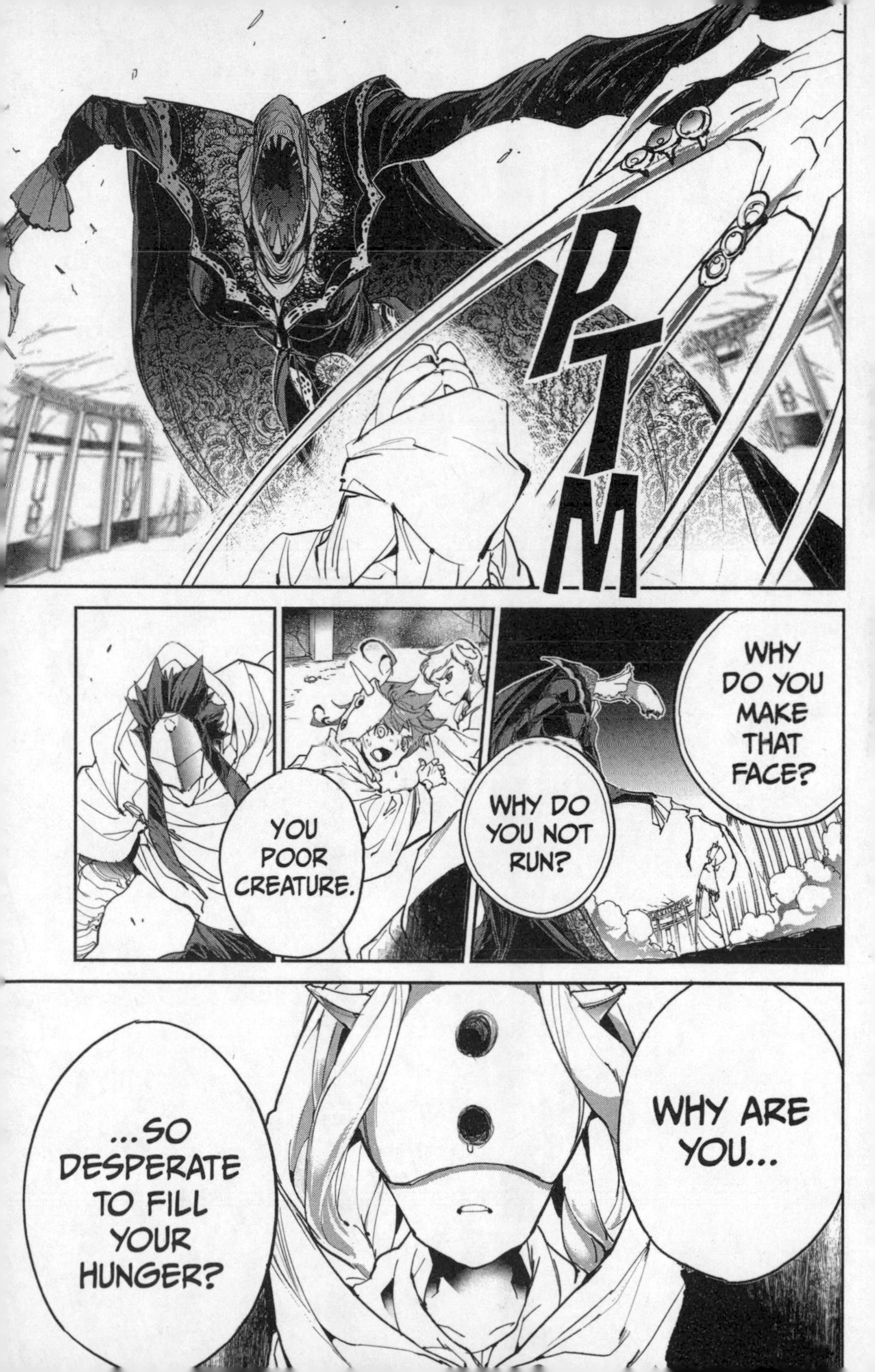
PTM
WHY DO YOU MAKE THAT FACE?
WHY DO YOU NOT RUN?
YOU POOR CREATURE.
WHY ARE YOU...
...SO DESPERATE TO FILL YOUR HUNGER?

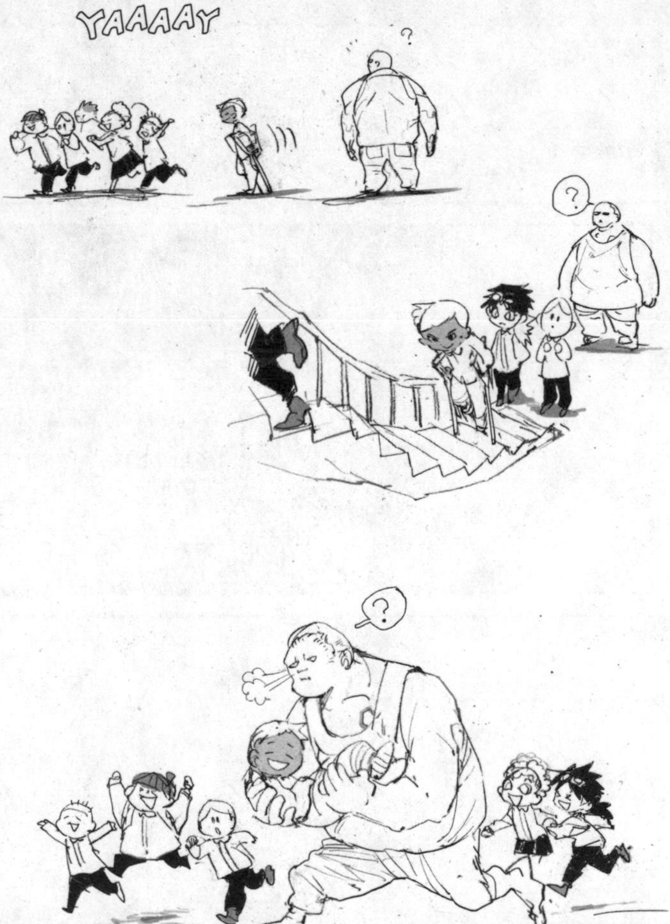
YAAAAY
?
?
?

CHAPTER 158: THE REASON I WAS BORN

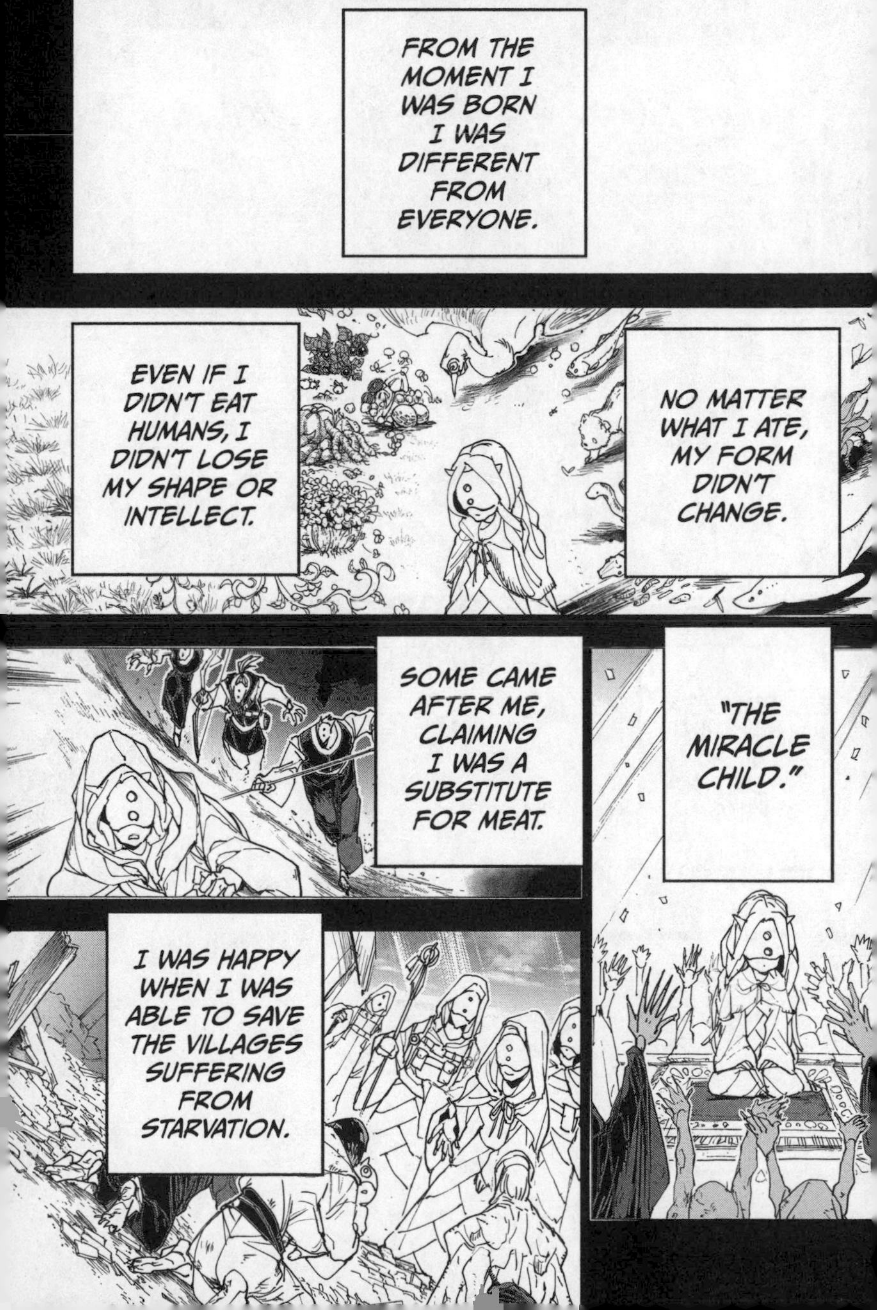
FROM THE MOMENT I WAS BORN I WAS DIFFERENT FROM EVERYONE.
NO MATTER WHAT I ATE, MY FORM DIDN'T CHANGE.
EVEN IF I DIDN'T EAT HUMANS, I DIDN'T LOSE MY SHAPE OR INTELLECT.
"THE MIRACLE CHILD."
SOME CAME AFTER ME, CLAIMING I WAS A SUBSTITUTE FOR MEAT.
I WAS HAPPY WHEN I WAS ABLE TO SAVE THE VILLAGES SUFFERING FROM STARVATION.

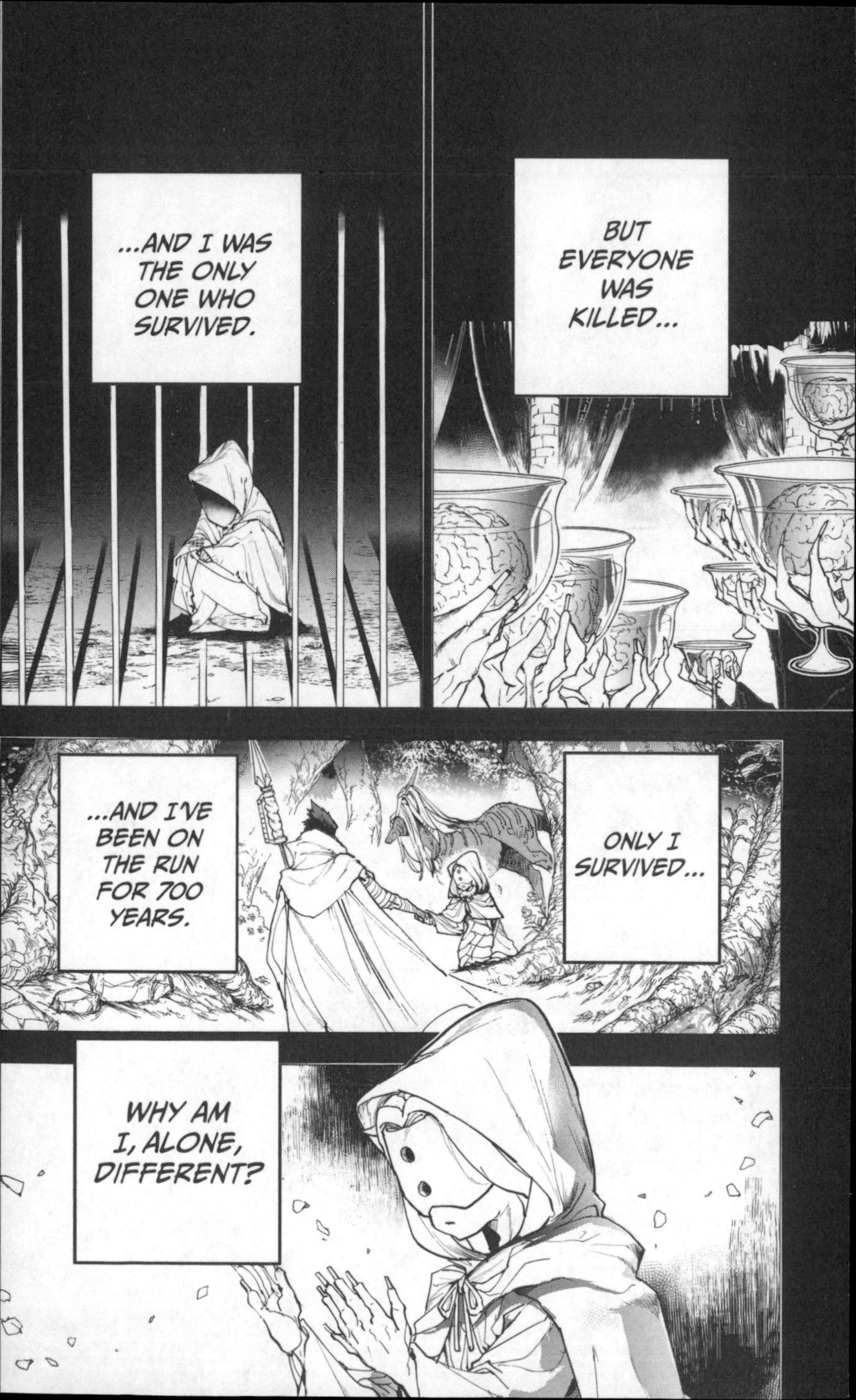
BUT EVERYONE WAS KILLED...
...AND I WAS THE ONLY ONE WHO SURVIVED.
ONLY I SURVIVED...
...AND I'VE BEEN ON THE RUN FOR 700 YEARS.
WHY AM I, ALONE, DIFFERENT?

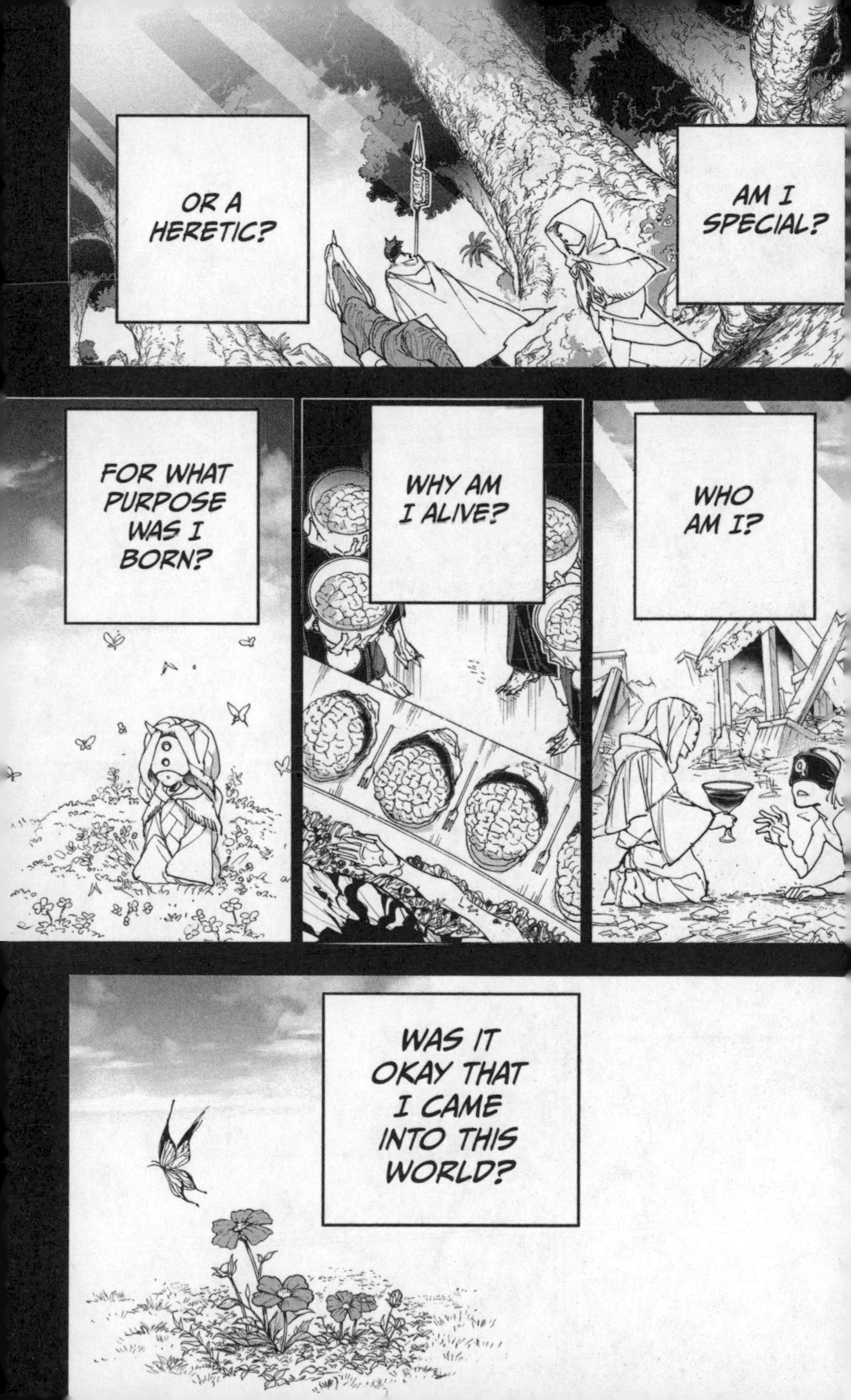
AM I SPECIAL?
OR A HERETIC?
WHO AM I?
WHY AM I ALIVE?
FOR WHAT PURPOSE WAS I BORN?
WAS IT OKAY THAT I CAME INTO THIS WORLD?

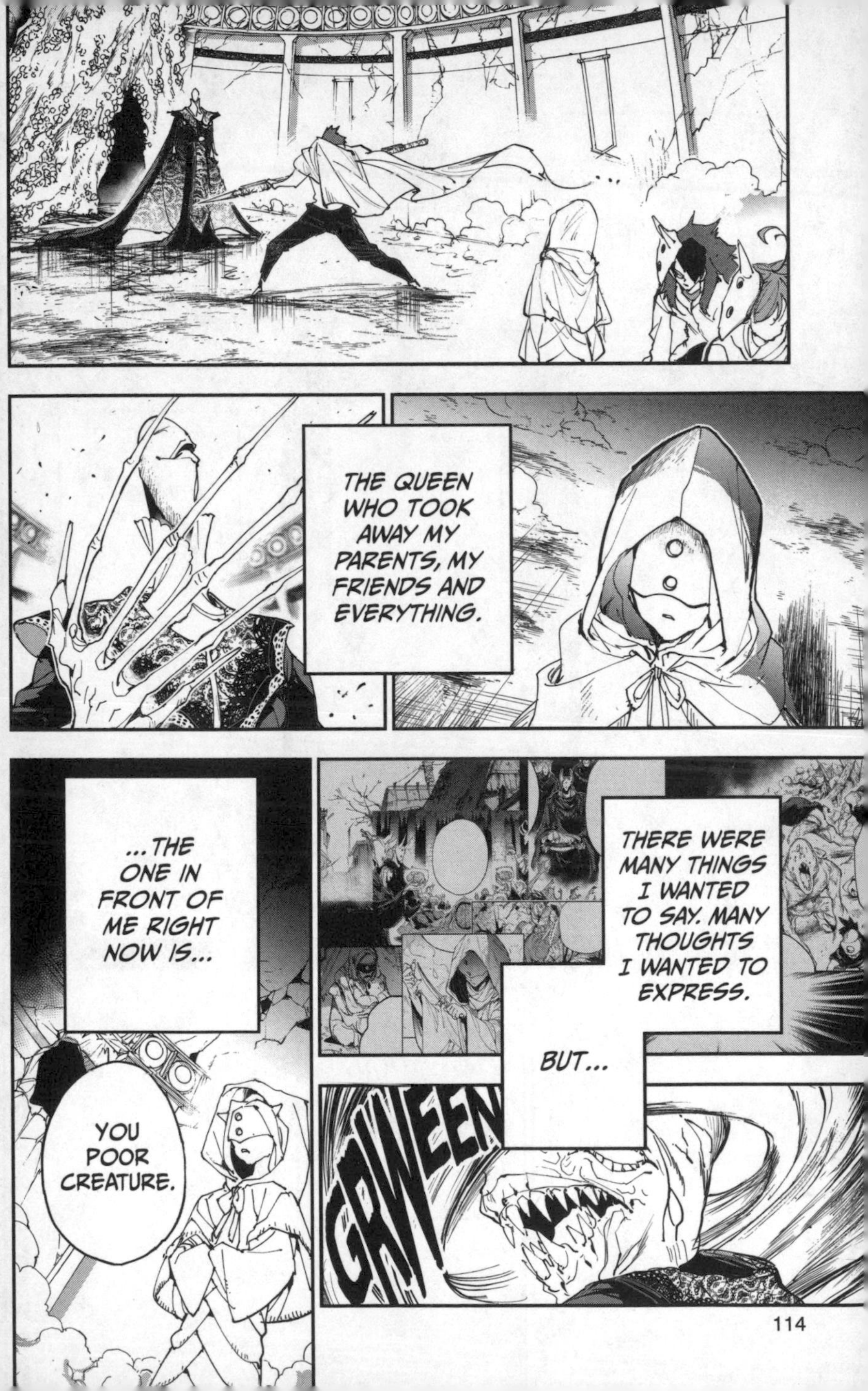
THE QUEEN WHO TOOK AWAY MY PARENTS, MY FRIENDS AND EVERYTHING.
THERE WERE MANY THINGS I WANTED TO SAY. MANY THOUGHTS I WANTED TO EXPRESS.
BUT...
GRWEEN
...THE ONE IN FRONT OF ME RIGHT NOW IS...
YOU POOR CREATURE.

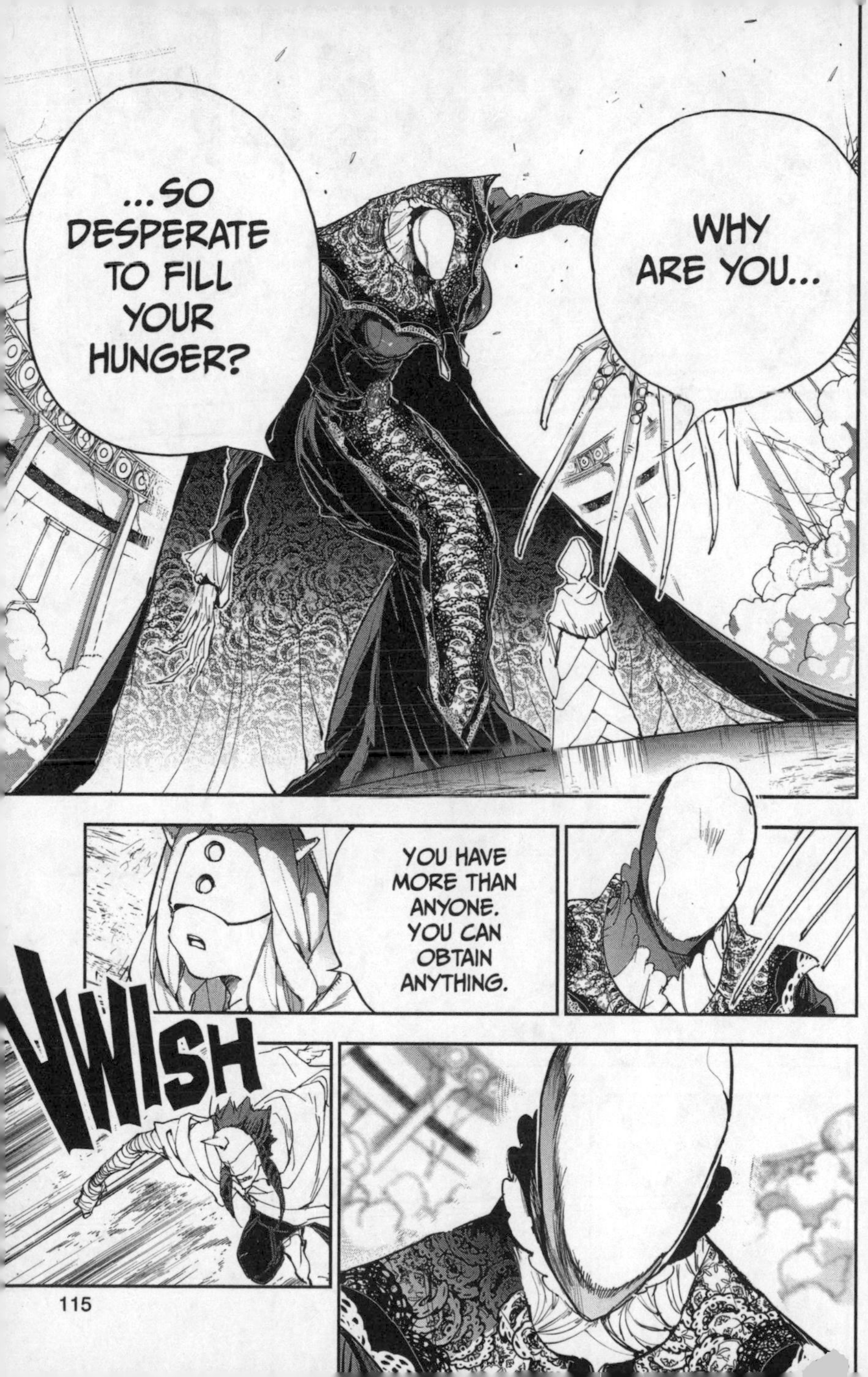
WHY ARE YOU...
...SO DESPERATE TO FILL YOUR HUNGER?
YOU HAVE MORE THAN ANYONE. YOU CAN OBTAIN ANYTHING.
VWISH

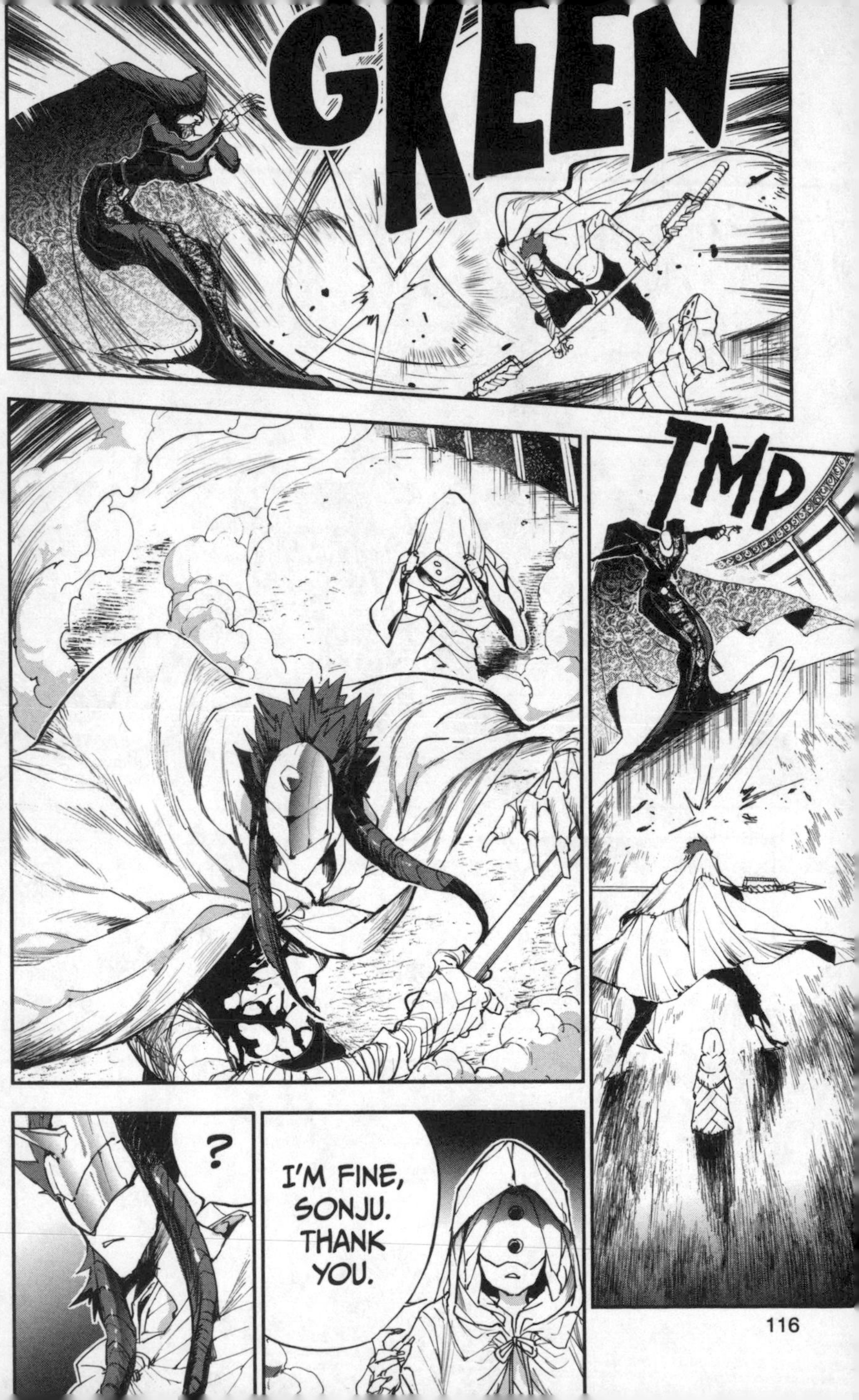
GKEEN
TMP
I'M FINE, SONJU. THANK YOU.
?

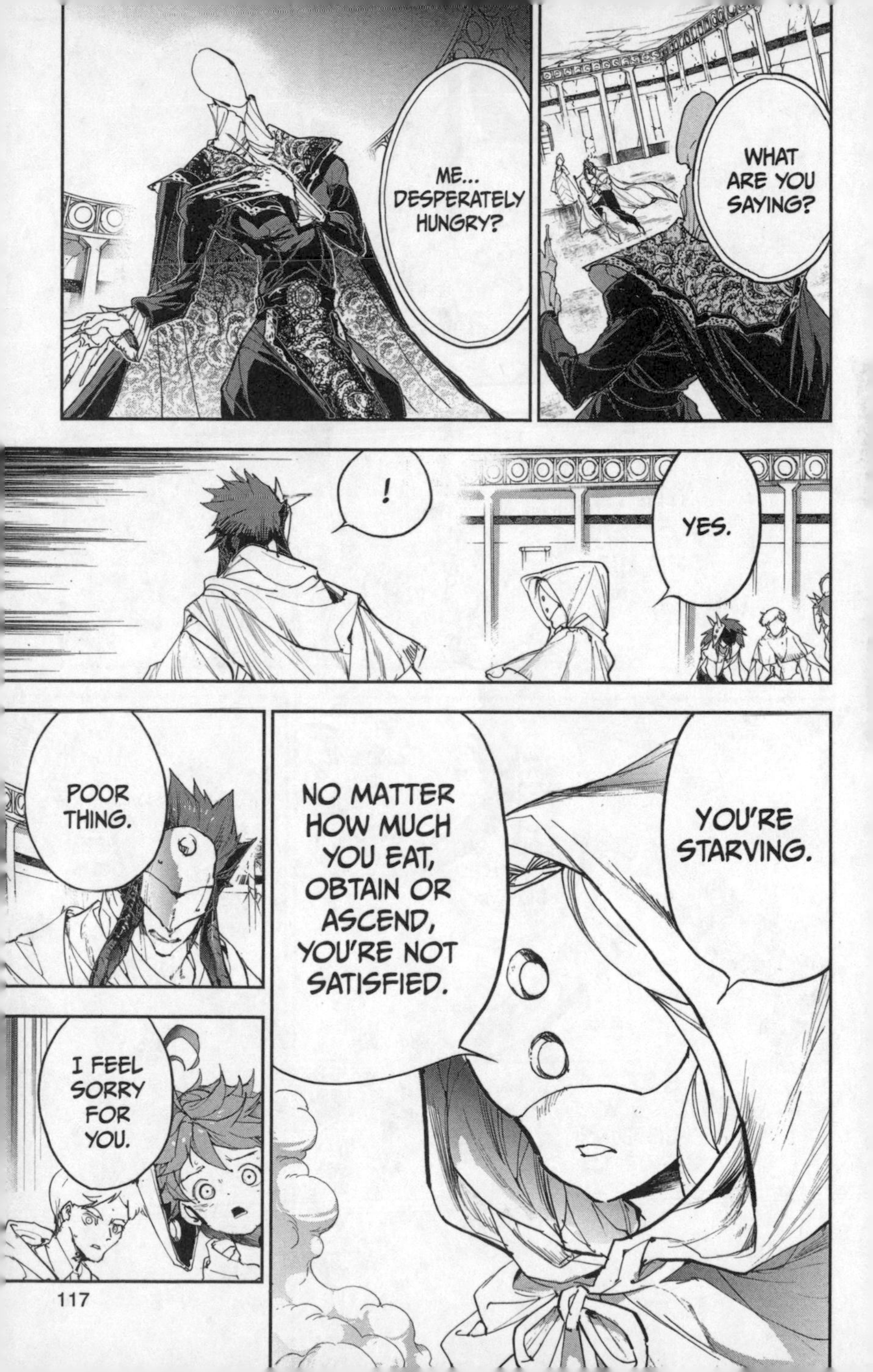
WHAT ARE YOU SAYING?
ME... DESPERATELY HUNGRY?
YES.
!
YOU'RE STARVING.
NO MATTER HOW MUCH YOU EAT, OBTAIN OR ASCEND, YOU'RE NOT SATISFIED.
POOR THING.
I FEEL SORRY FOR YOU.

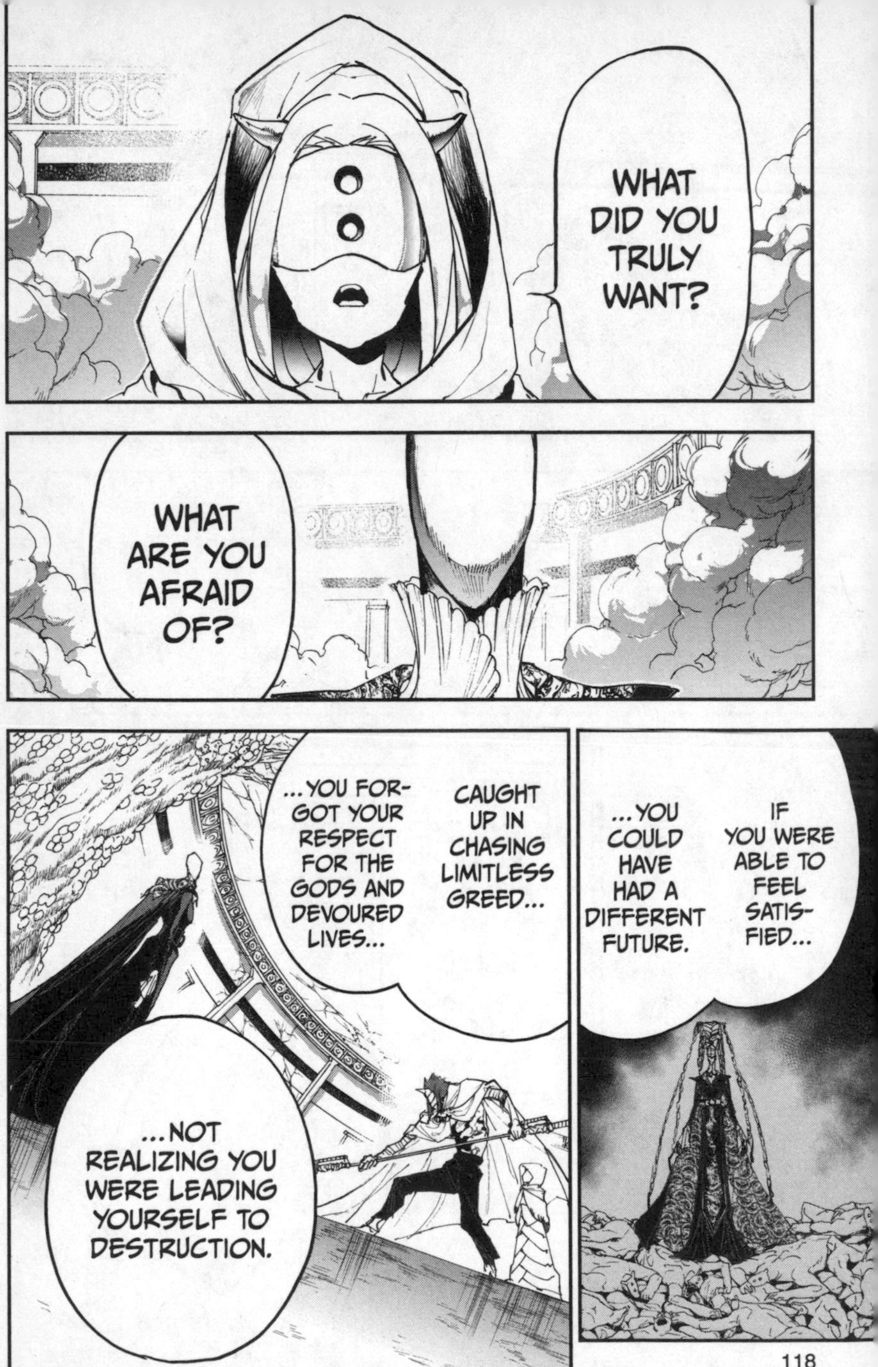
WHAT DID YOU TRULY WANT?
WHAT ARE YOU AFRAID OF?
IF YOU WERE ABLE TO FEEL SATIS-FIED...
...YOU COULD HAVE HAD A DIFFERENT FUTURE.
CAUGHT UP IN CHASING LIMITLESS GREED...
...YOU FOR-GOT YOUR RESPECT FOR THE GODS AND DEVOURED LIVES...
...NOT REALIZING YOU WERE LEADING YOURSELF TO DESTRUCTION.

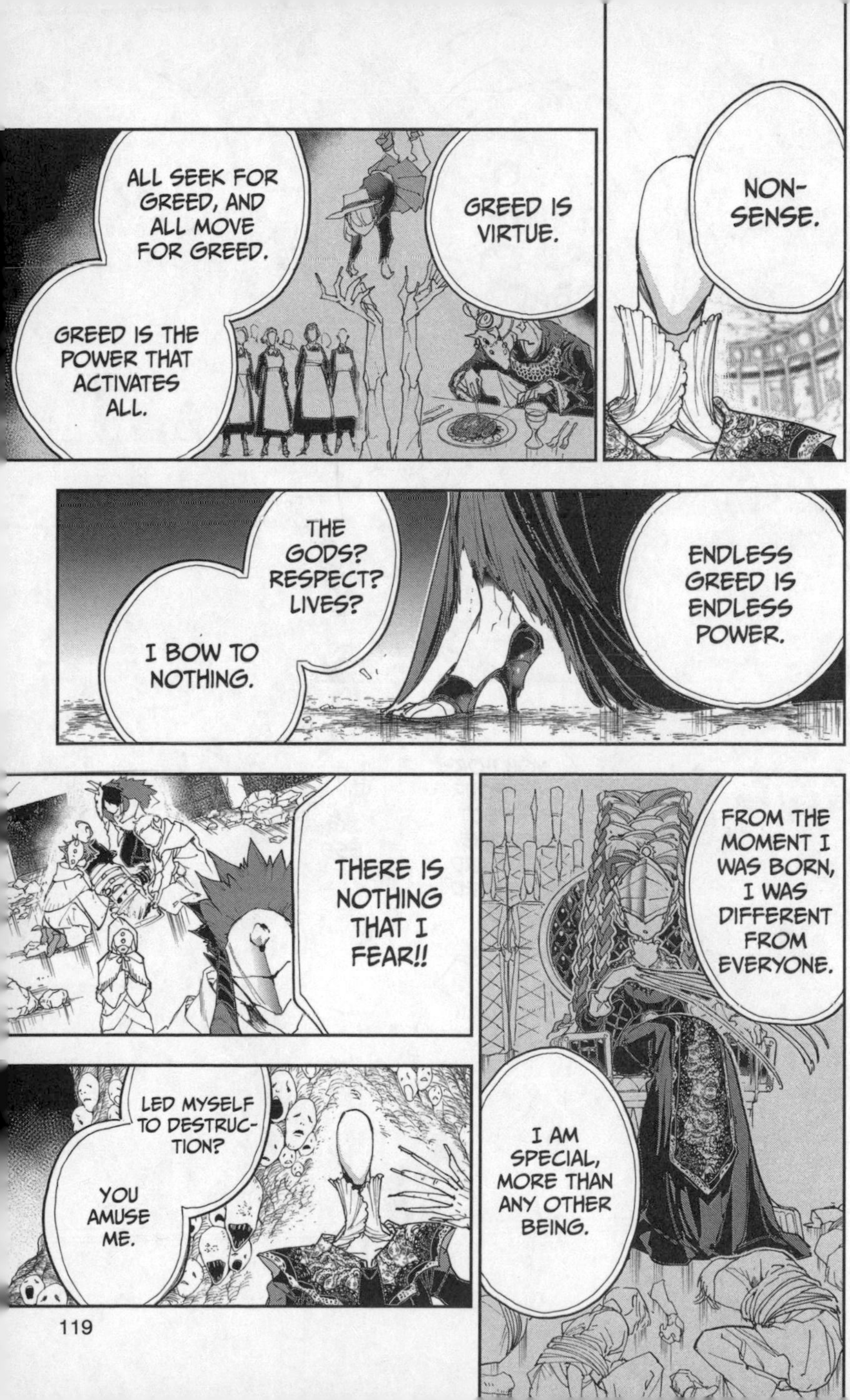
NON-SENSE.
GREED IS VIRTUE.
ALL SEEK FOR GREED, AND ALL MOVE FOR GREED.
GREED IS THE POWER THAT ACTIVATES ALL.
ENDLESS GREED IS ENDLESS POWER.
THE GODS? RESPECT? LIVES?
I BOW TO NOTHING.
FROM THE MOMENT I WAS BORN, I WAS DIFFERENT FROM EVERYONE.
I AM SPECIAL, MORE THAN ANY OTHER BEING.
THERE IS NOTHING THAT I FEAR!!
LED MYSELF TO DESTRUC-TION?
YOU AMUSE ME.

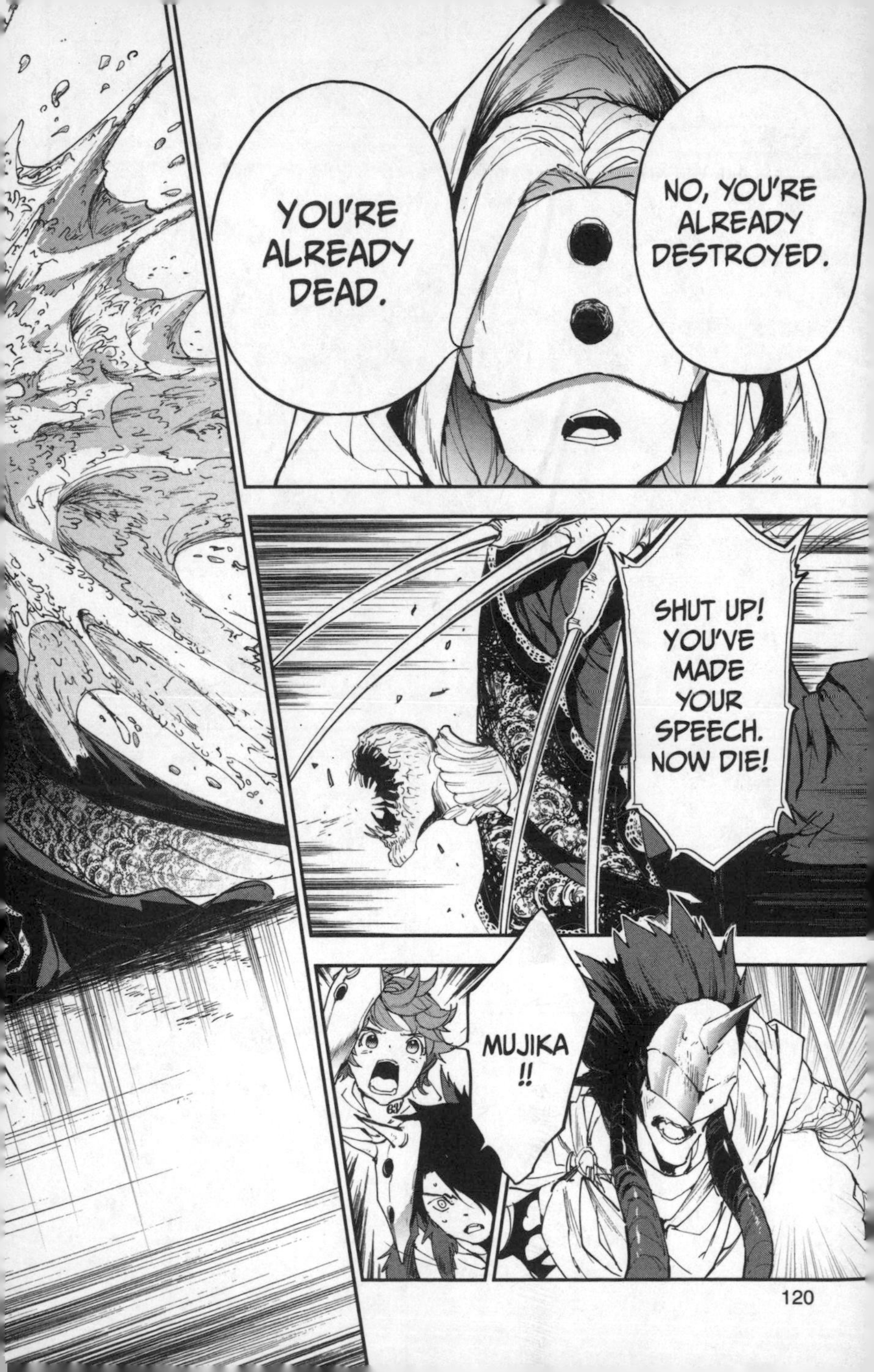
NO, YOU'RE ALREADY DESTROYED.
YOU'RE ALREADY DEAD.
SHUT UP! YOU'VE MADE YOUR SPEECH. NOW DIE!
MUJIKA !!

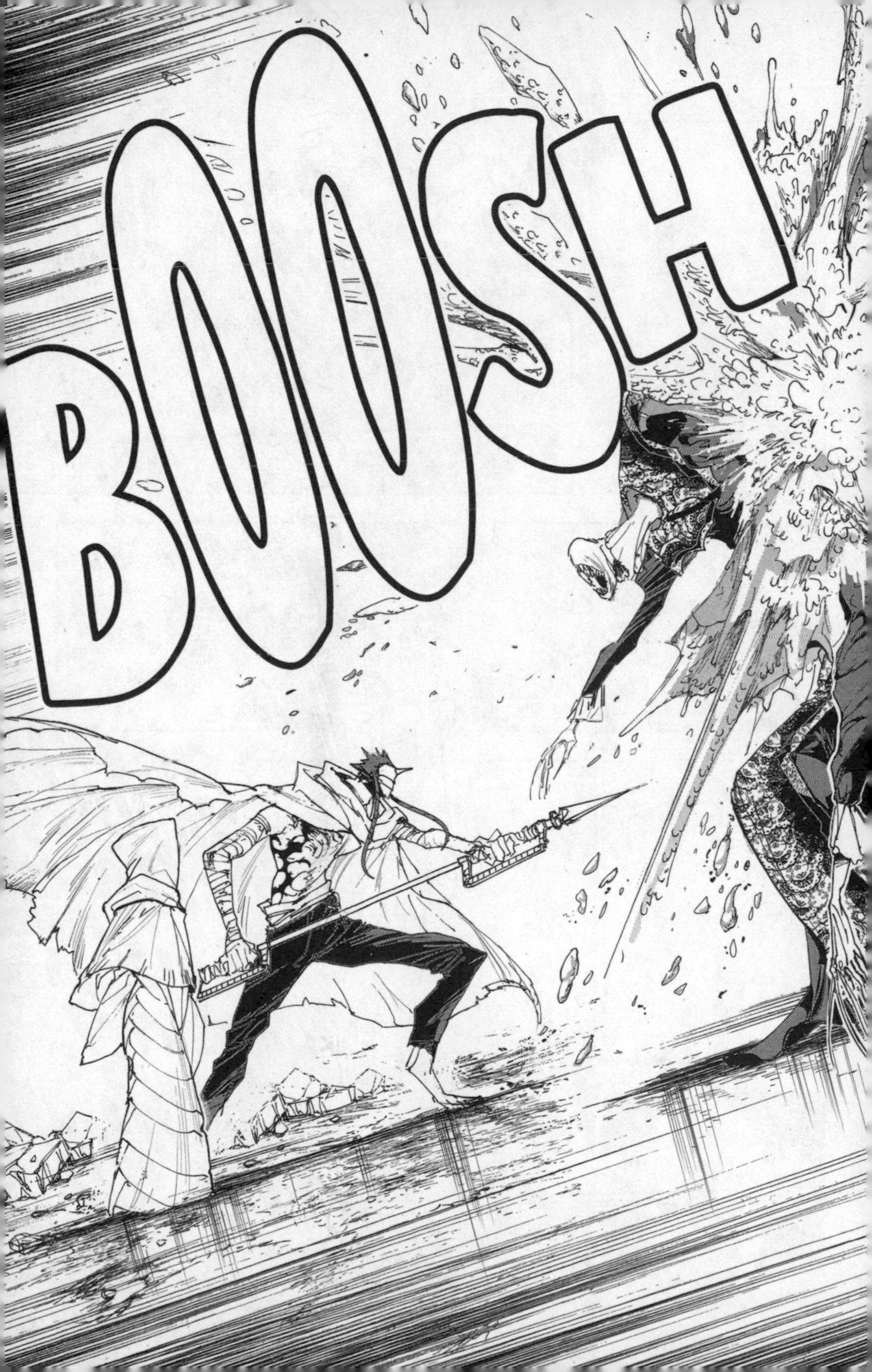
BOOSH

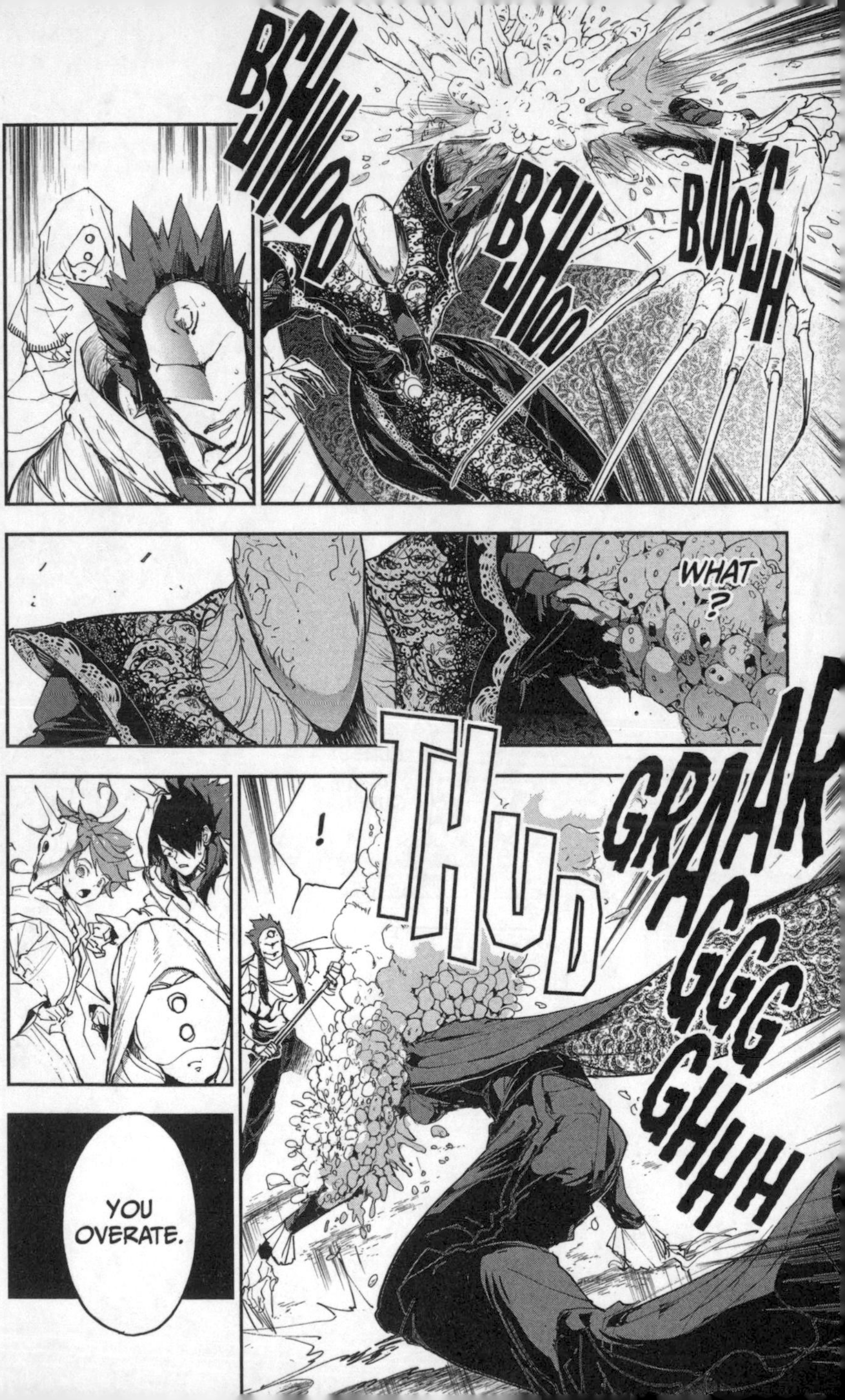
BOOSH
BSHOO
BSHWOO
WHAT?
GRAAKAGGGGHHH
THUD
!
YOU OVERATE.

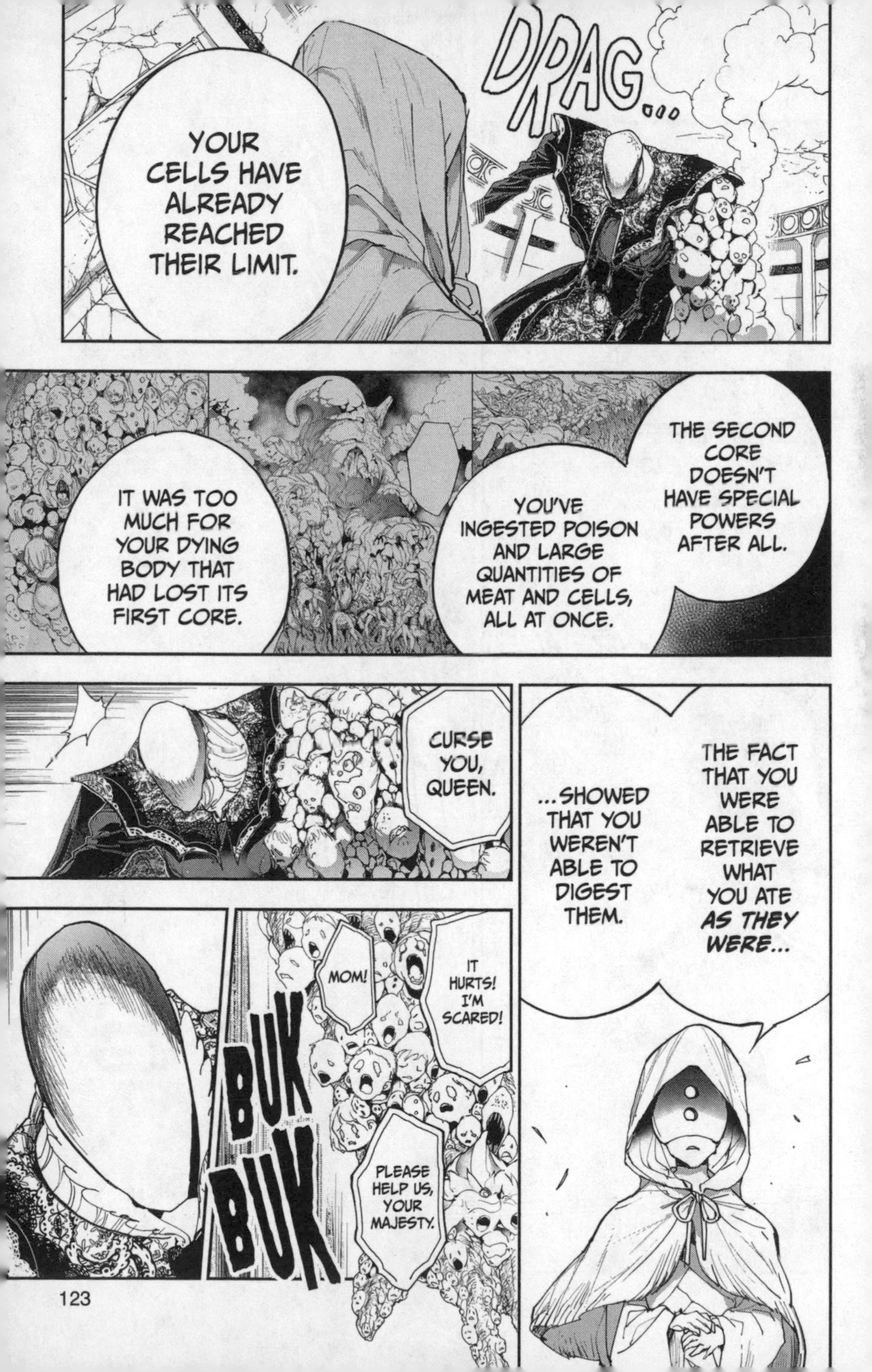
DRAG...
YOUR CELLS HAVE ALREADY REACHED THEIR LIMIT.
THE SECOND CORE DOESN'T HAVE SPECIAL POWERS AFTER ALL.
YOU'VE INGESTED POISON AND LARGE QUANTITIES OF MEAT AND CELLS, ALL AT ONCE.
IT WAS TOO MUCH FOR YOUR DYING BODY THAT HAD LOST ITS FIRST CORE.
THE FACT THAT YOU WERE ABLE TO RETRIEVE WHAT YOU ATE *AS THEY WERE...*
...SHOWED THAT YOU WEREN'T ABLE TO DIGEST THEM.
CURSE YOU, QUEEN.
IT HURTS! I'M SCARED!
MOM!
BUK BUK
PLEASE HELP US, YOUR MAJESTY.

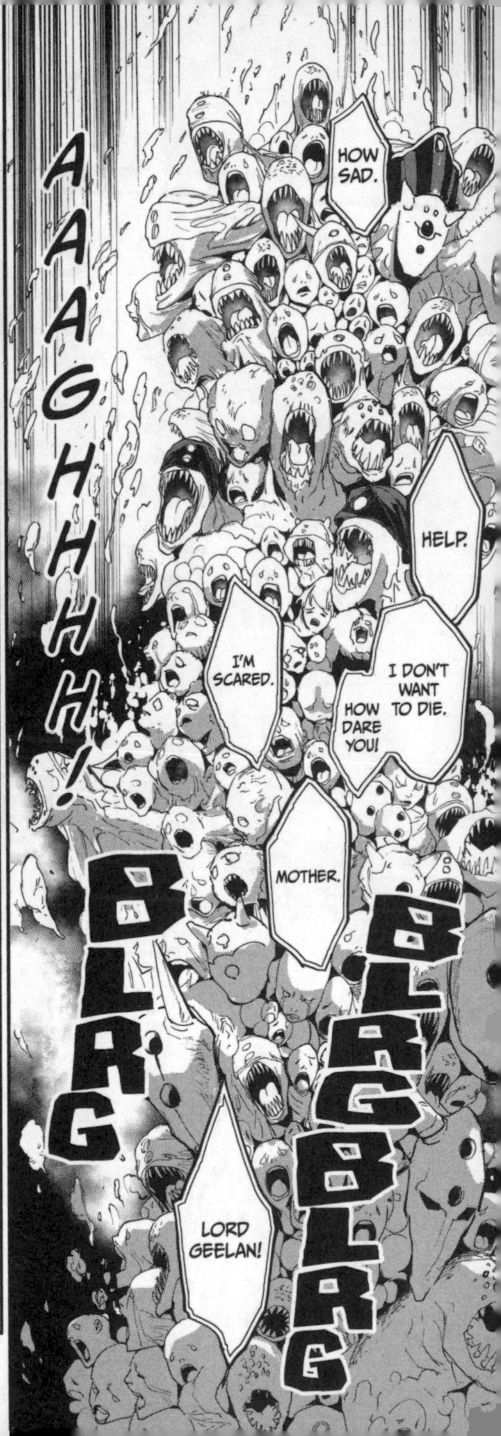
HOW SAD.
HELP.
I DON'T WANT TO DIE.
HOW DARE YOU!
I'M SCARED.
AAAGHHHH!
MOTHER.
BLRG BLRG
BLRG
LORD GEELAN!
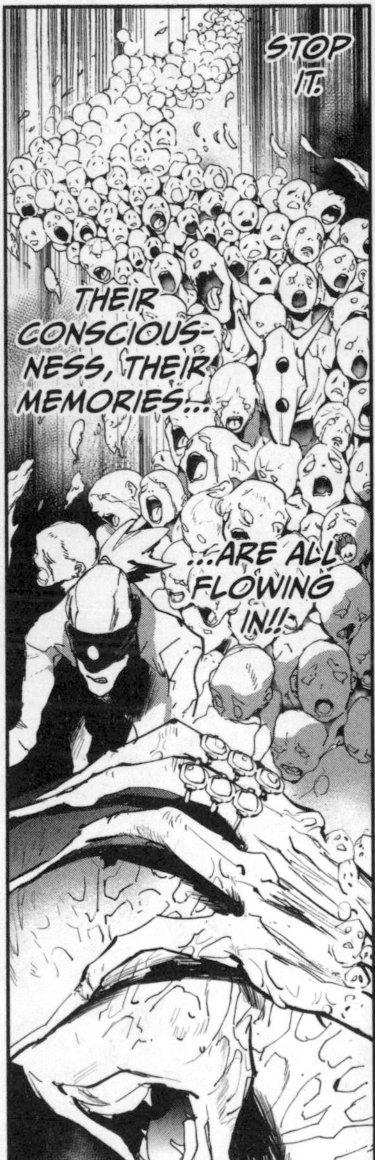
STOP IT.
THEIR CONSCIOUS-NESS, THEIR MEMORIES...
...ARE ALL FLOWING IN!!

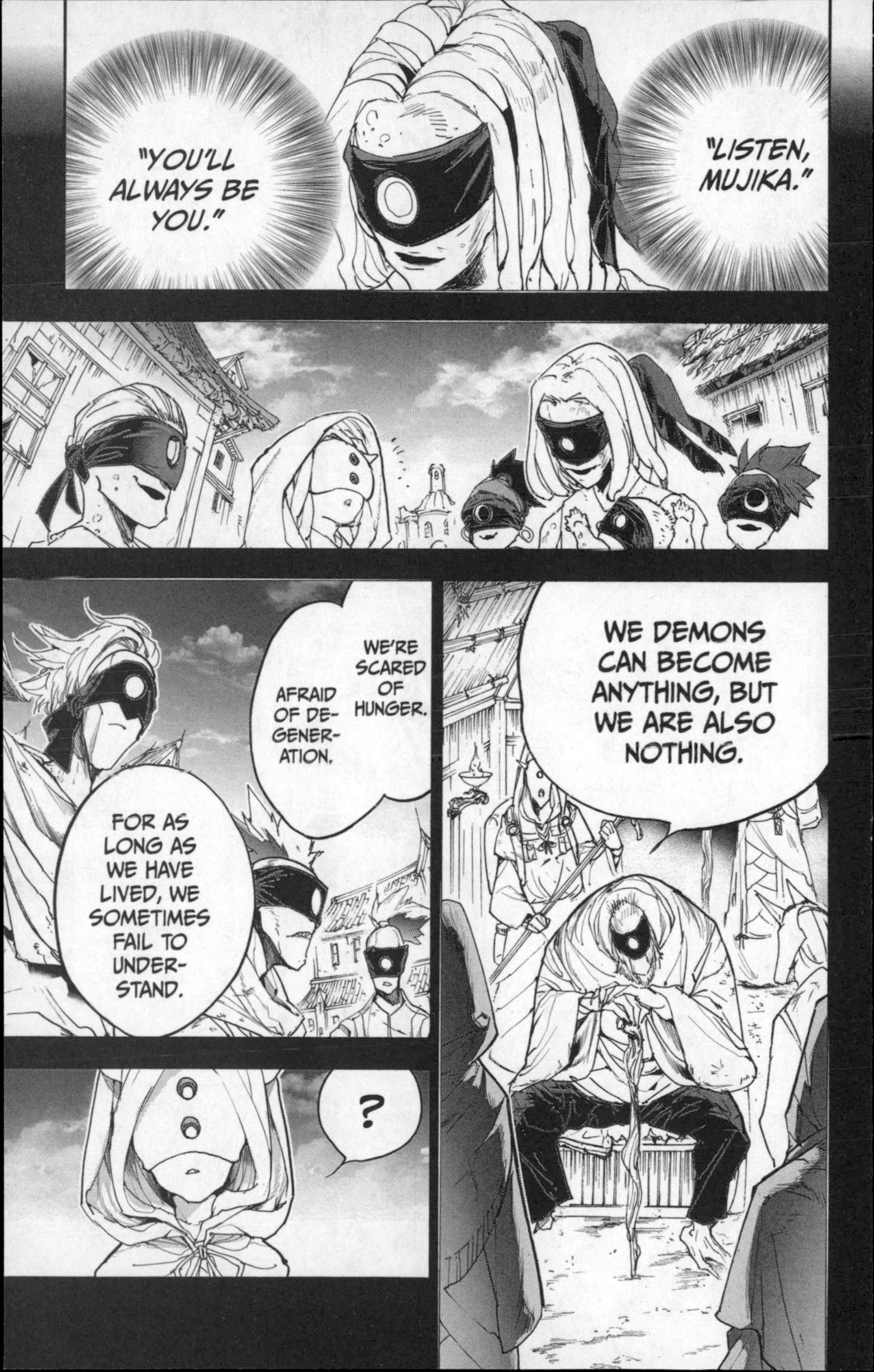
"LISTEN, MUJIKA."
"YOU'LL ALWAYS BE YOU."
WE DEMONS CAN BECOME ANYTHING, BUT WE ARE ALSO NOTHING.
WE'RE SCARED OF HUNGER.
AFRAID OF DE-GENER-ATION.
FOR AS LONG AS WE HAVE LIVED, WE SOMETIMES FAIL TO UNDER-STAND.
?

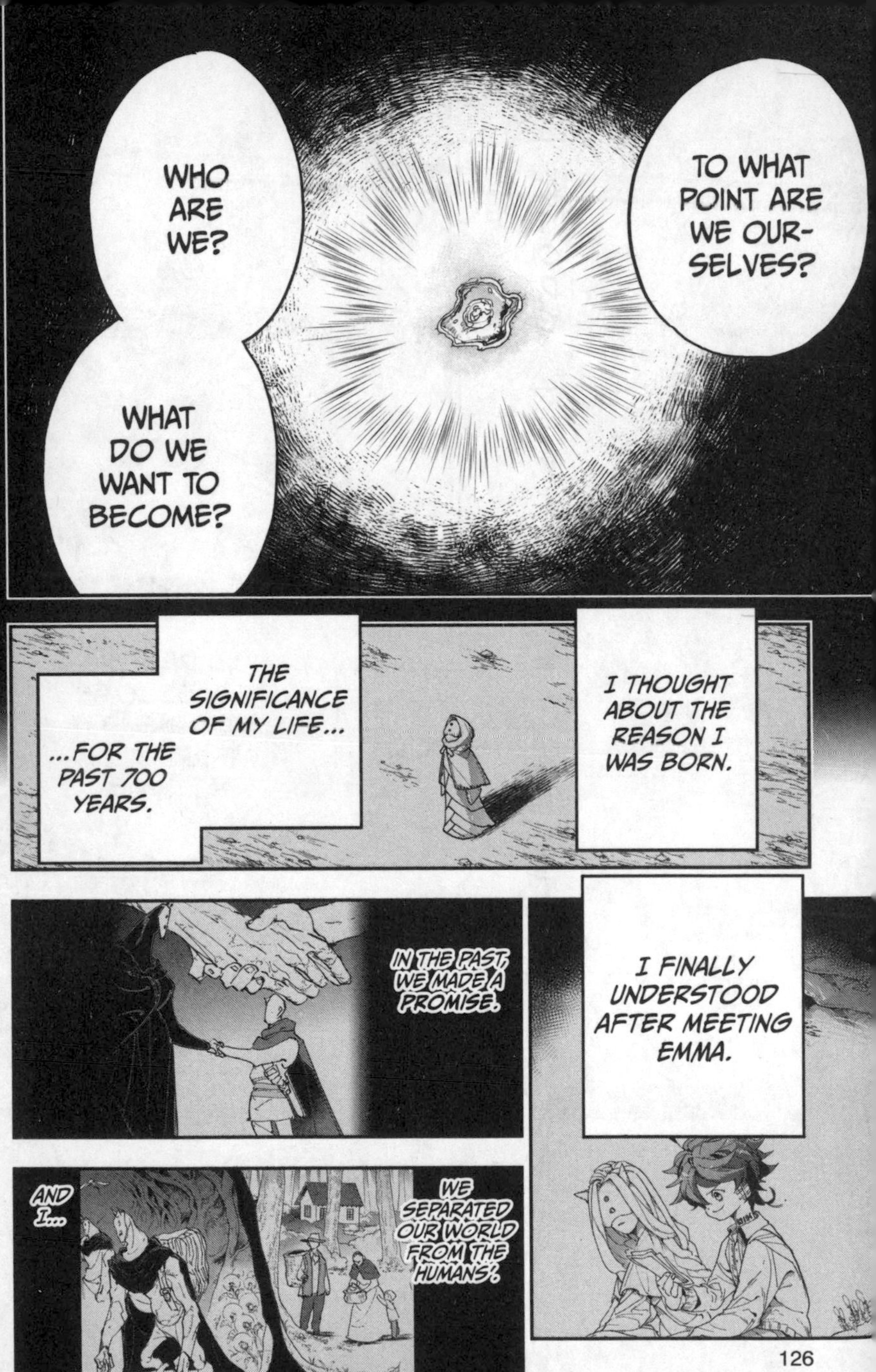
TO WHAT POINT ARE WE OUR-SELVES?
WHO ARE WE?
WHAT DO WE WANT TO BECOME?
I THOUGHT ABOUT THE REASON I WAS BORN.
THE SIGNIFICANCE OF MY LIFE...
...FOR THE PAST 700 YEARS.
I FINALLY UNDERSTOOD AFTER MEETING EMMA.
IN THE PAST, WE MADE A PROMISE.
WE SEPARATED OUR WORLD FROM THE HUMANS.
AND I...

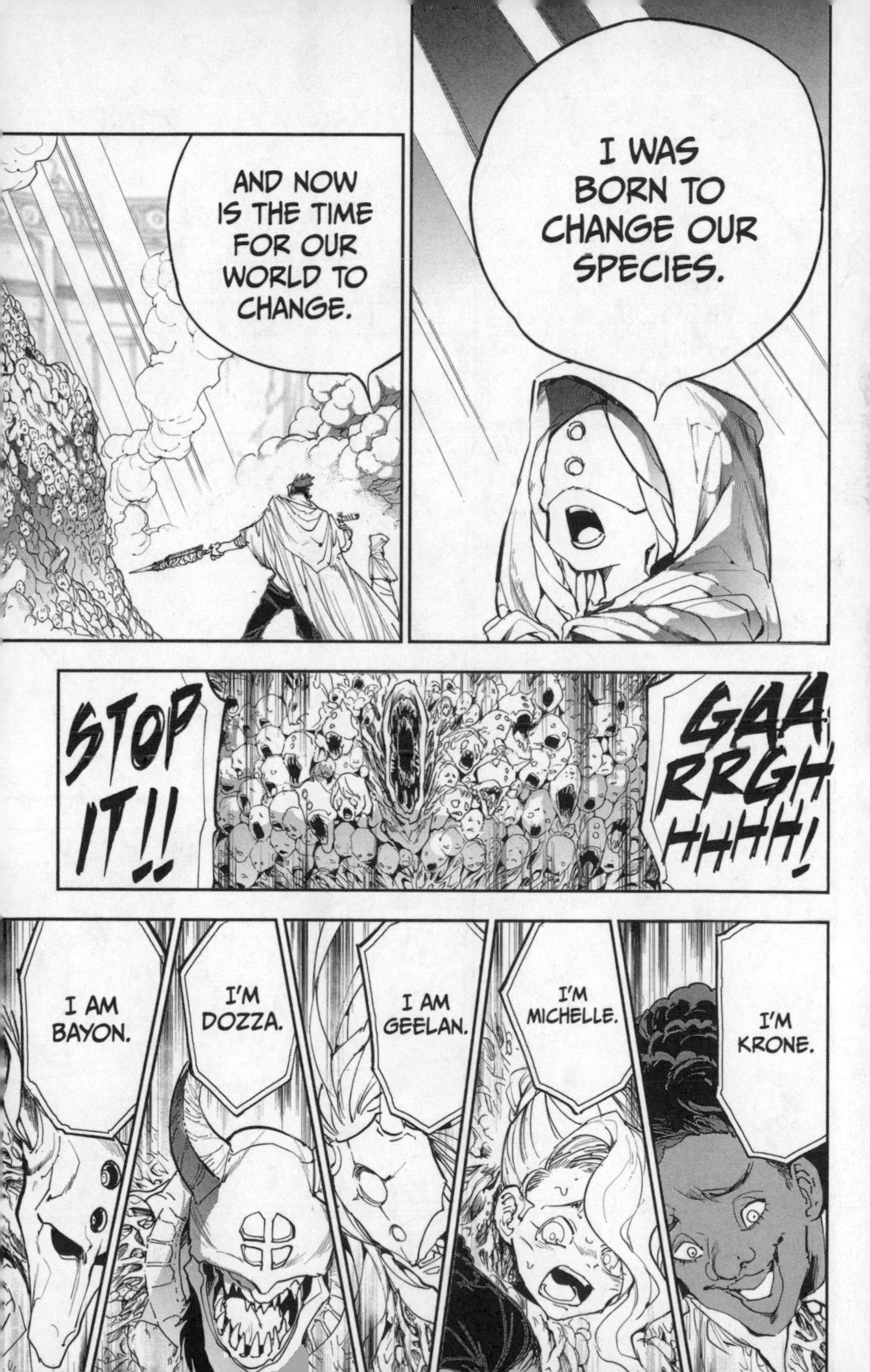
I WAS BORN TO CHANGE OUR SPECIES.
AND NOW IS THE TIME FOR OUR WORLD TO CHANGE.
GAARRGHHHHH!
STOP IT!!
I'M KRONE.
I'M MICHELLE.
I AM GEELAN.
I'M DOZZA.
I AM BAYON.

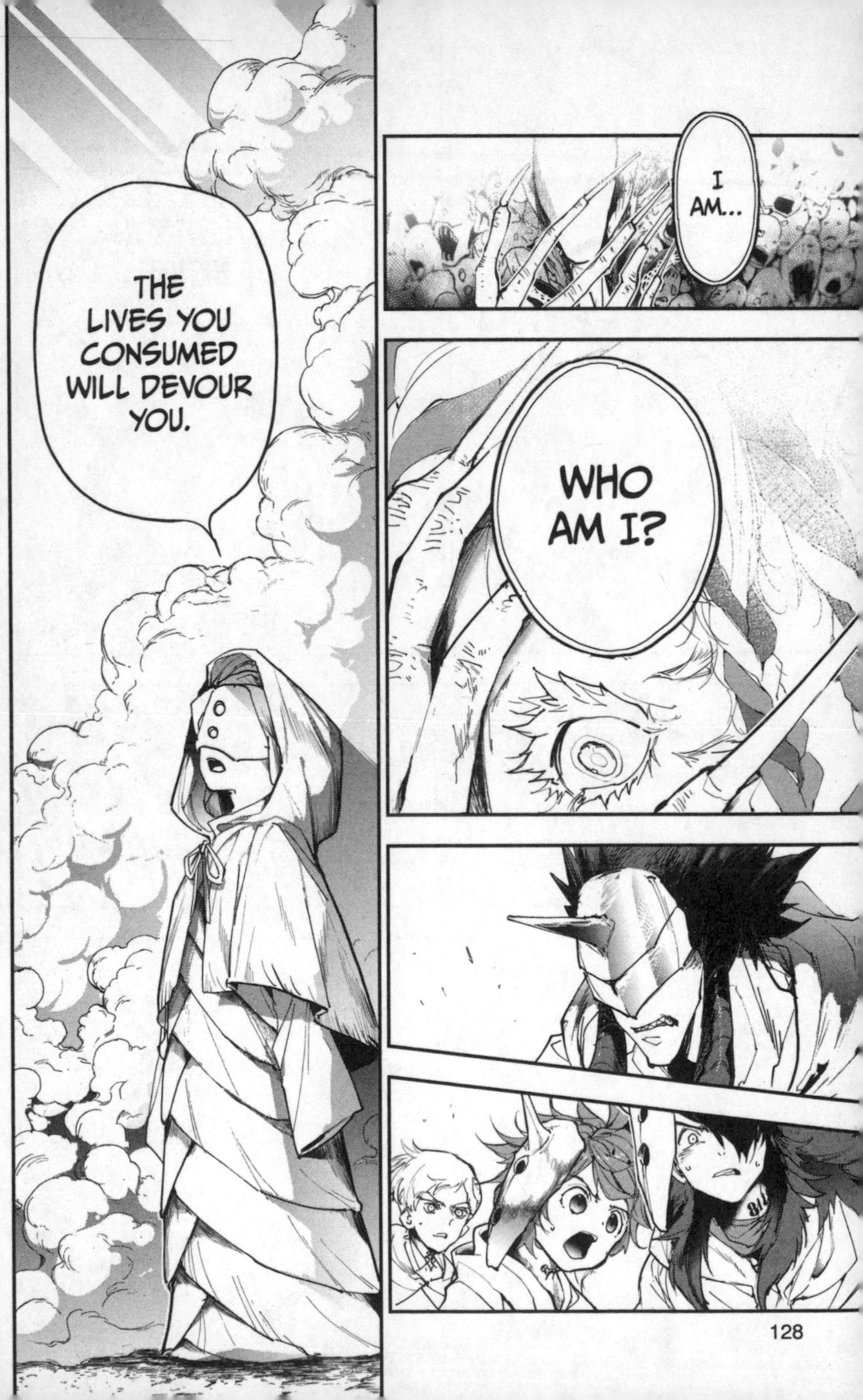
I AM...
WHO AM I?
THE LIVES YOU CONSUMED WILL DEVOUR YOU.

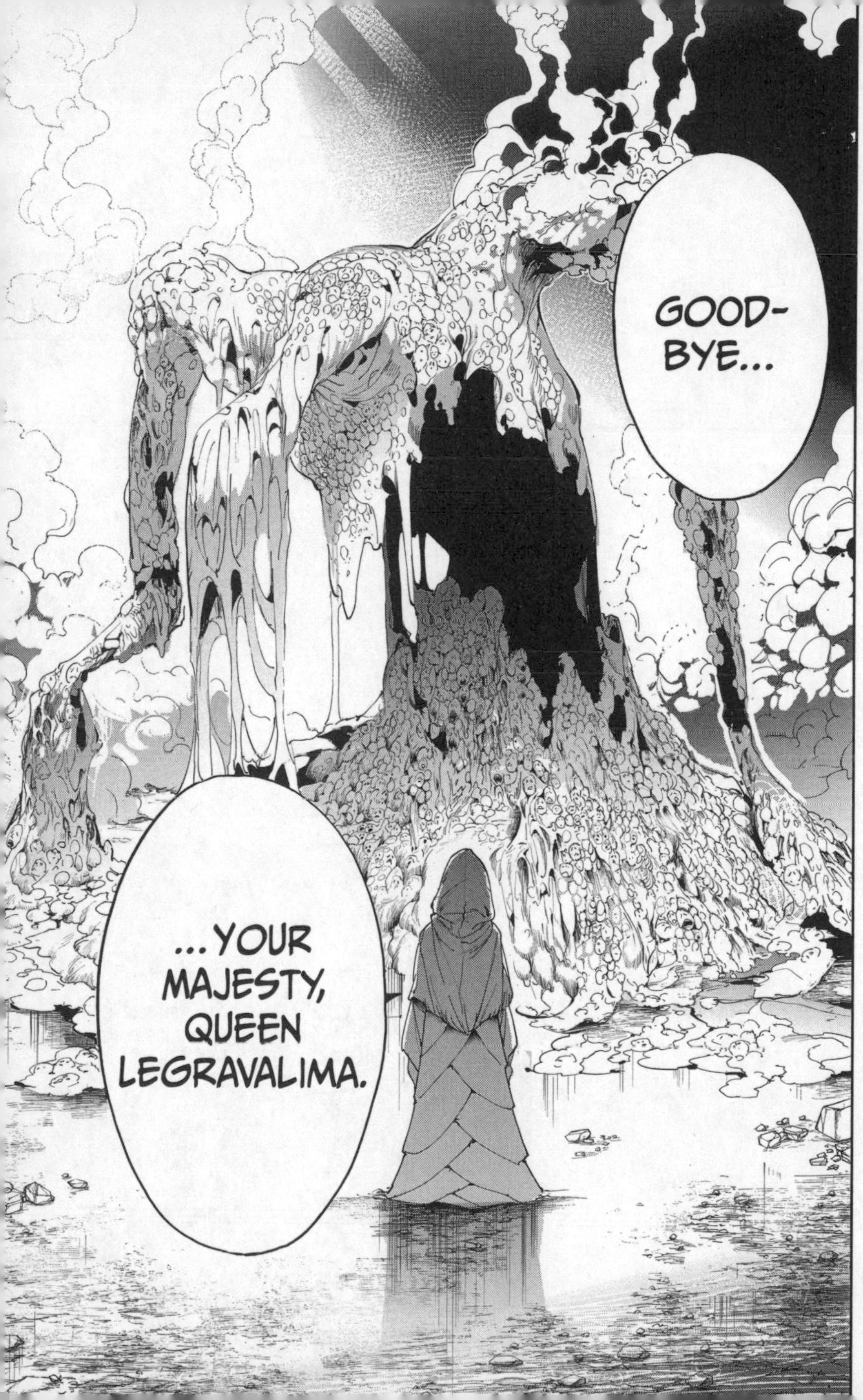
GOOD-BYE...
...YOUR MAJESTY, QUEEN LEGRAVALIMA.

MICHELLE

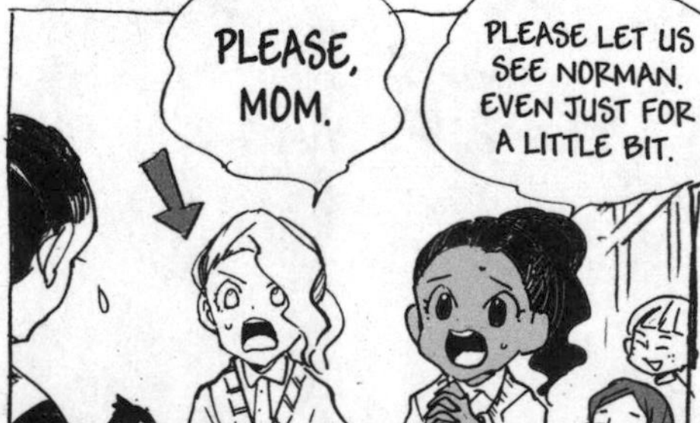
PLEASE LET US SEE NORMAN. EVEN JUST FOR A LITTLE BIT.
PLEASE, MOM.

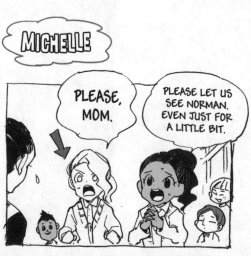

SHE ALSO APPEARS IN VOLUME 3, CHAPTER 17.

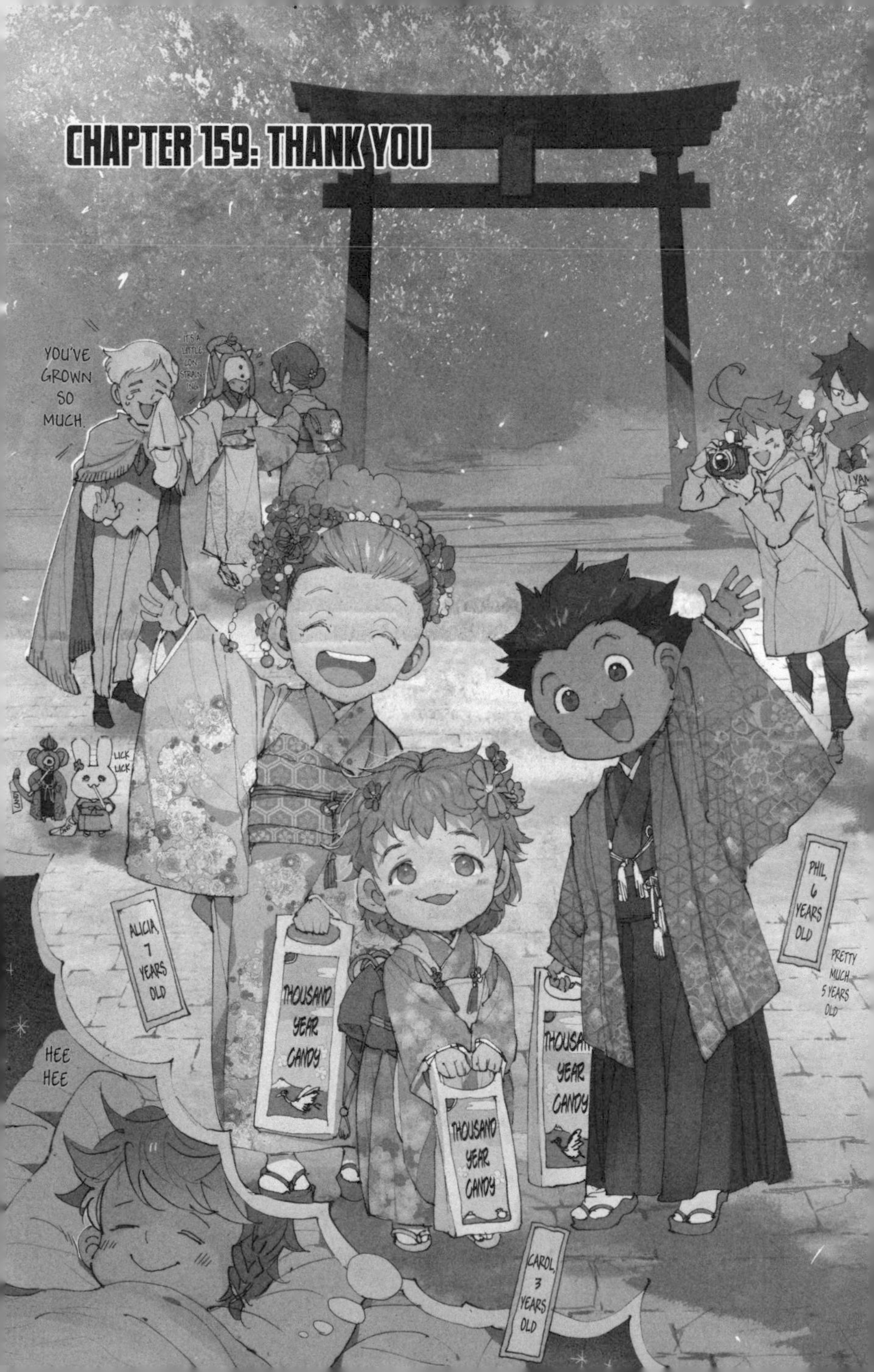
CHAPTER 159: THANK YOU
PHIL, 6 YEARS OLD
PRETTY MUCH 5 YEARS OLD
IT'S A LITTLE CONSTRAINING.
YOU'VE GROWN SO MUCH.
LICK LICK
ALICIA, 7 YEARS OLD
THOUSAND YEAR CANDY
THOUSAND YEAR CANDY
THOUSAND YEAR CANDY
HEE HEE
CAROL, 3 YEARS OLD

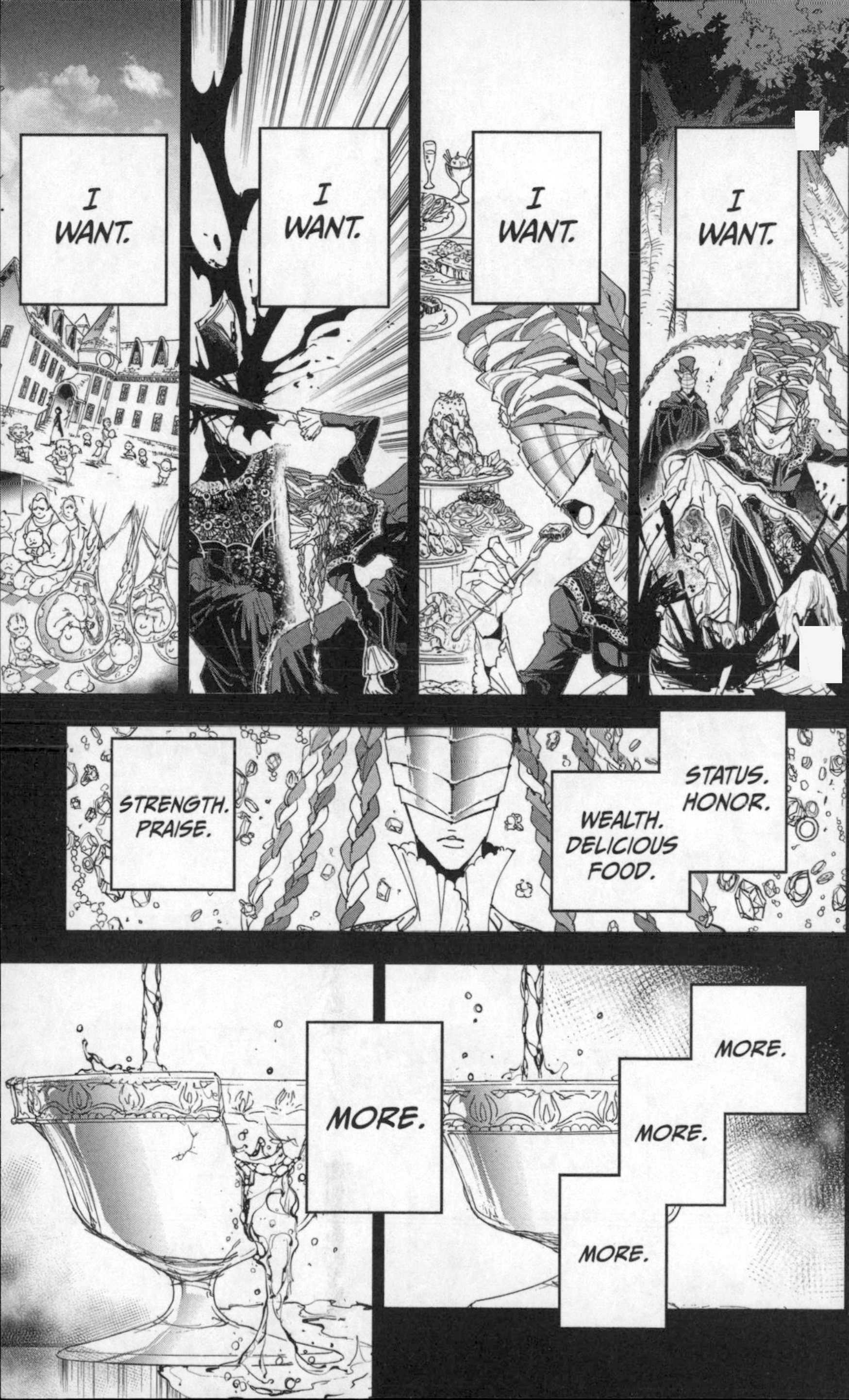
I WANT.
I WANT.
I WANT.
I WANT.
STATUS. HONOR.
WEALTH. DELICIOUS FOOD.
STRENGTH. PRAISE.
MORE.
MORE.
MORE.
MORE.

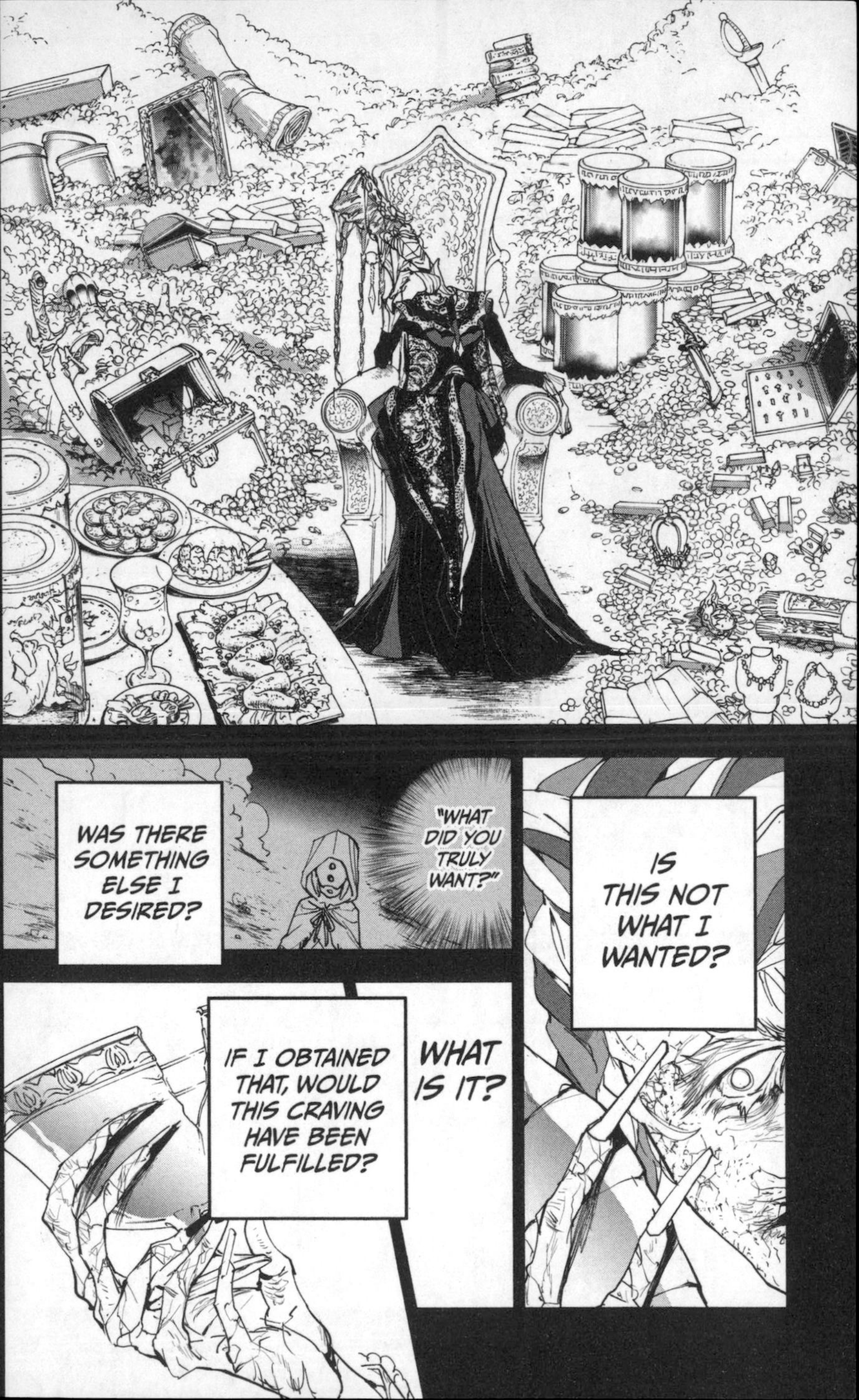
IS THIS NOT WHAT I WANTED?
"WHAT DID YOU TRULY WANT?"
WAS THERE SOMETHING ELSE I DESIRED?
WHAT IS IT?
IF I OBTAINED THAT, WOULD THIS CRAVING HAVE BEEN FULFILLED?

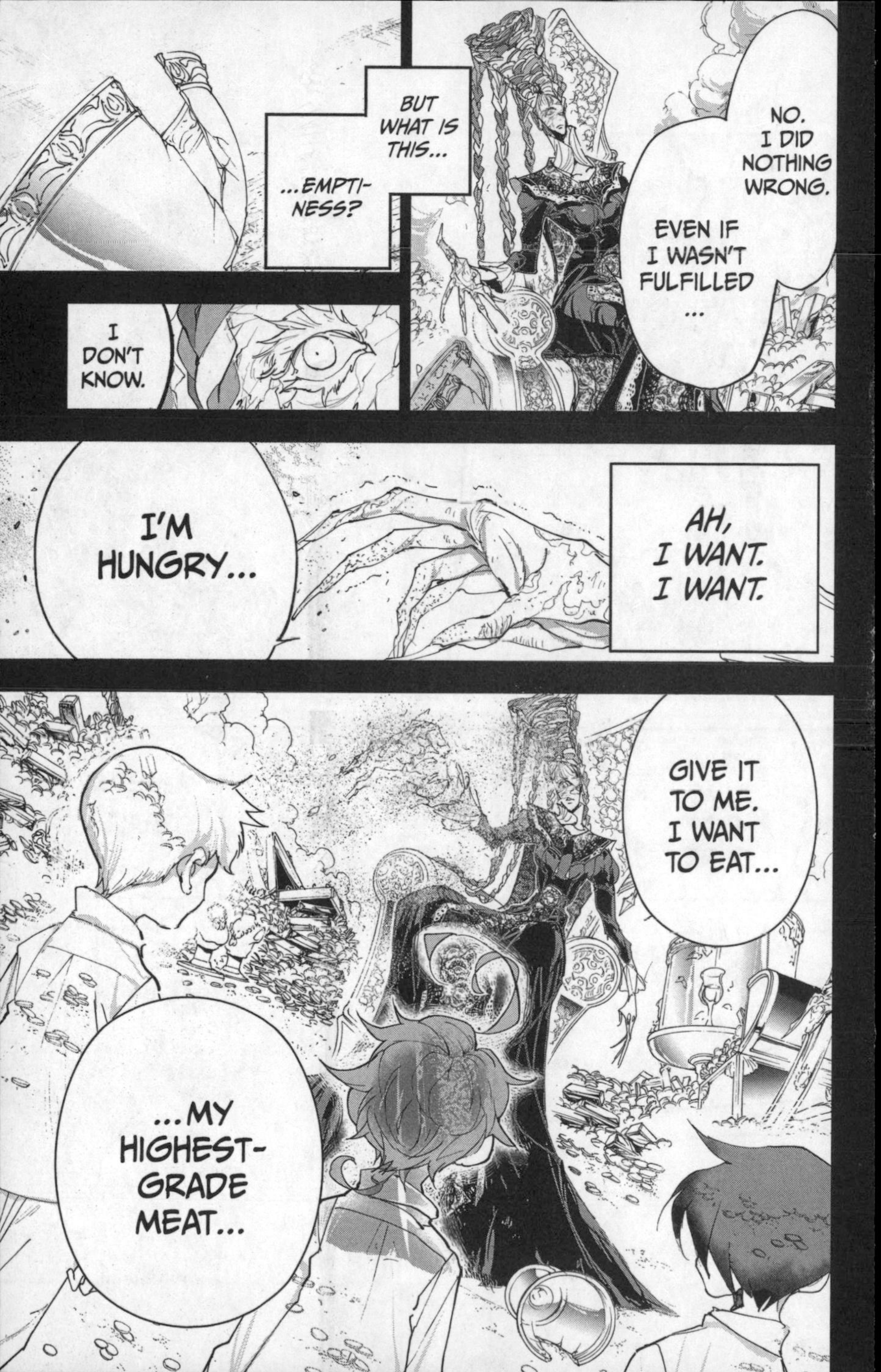
NO. I DID NOTHING WRONG.
EVEN IF I WASN'T FULFILLED ...
BUT WHAT IS THIS...
...EMPTI-NESS?
I DON'T KNOW.
AH, I WANT. I WANT.
I'M HUNGRY...
GIVE IT TO ME. I WANT TO EAT...
...MY HIGHEST-GRADE MEAT...

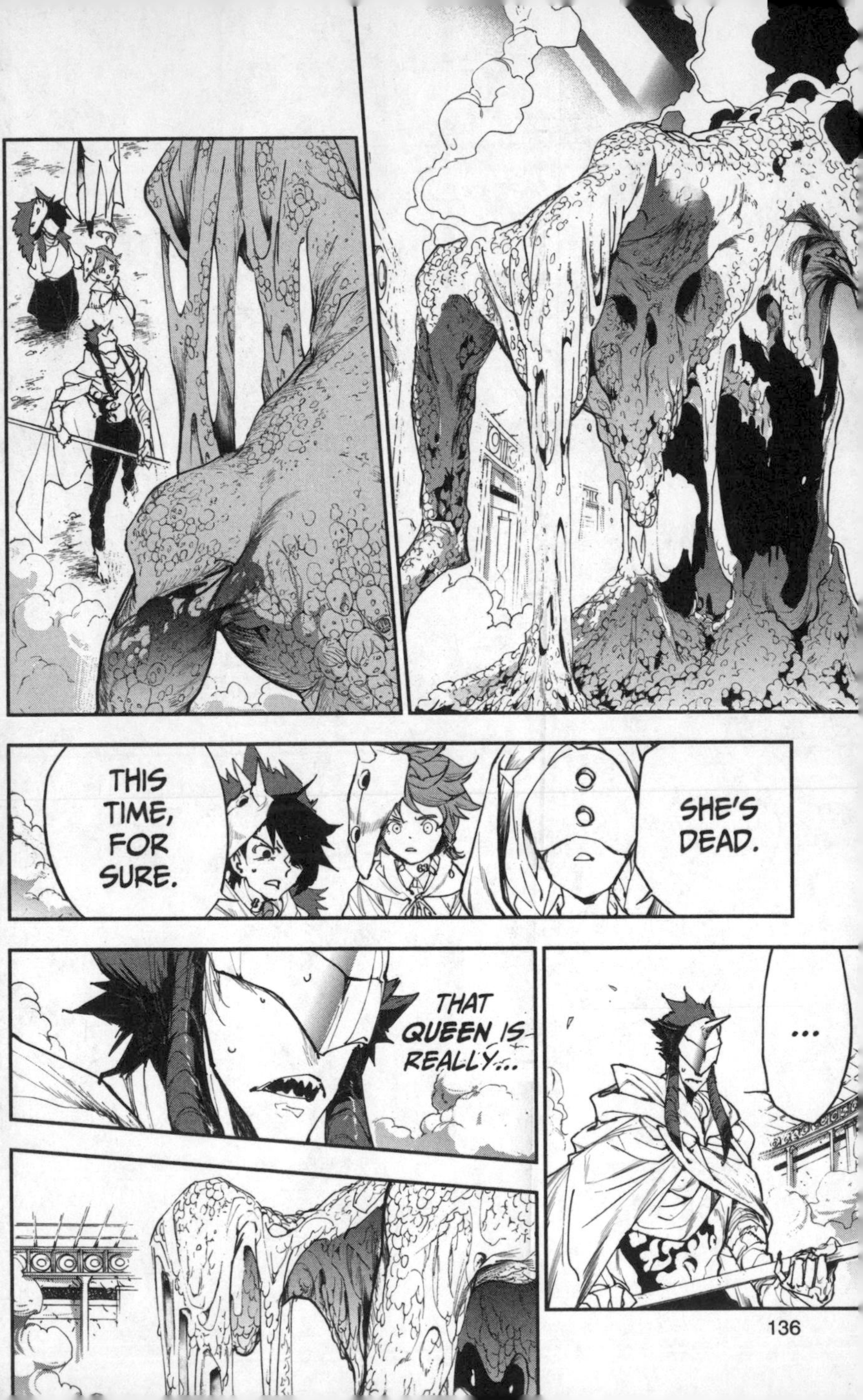
SHE'S DEAD.
THIS TIME, FOR SURE.
...
THAT QUEEN IS REALLY...

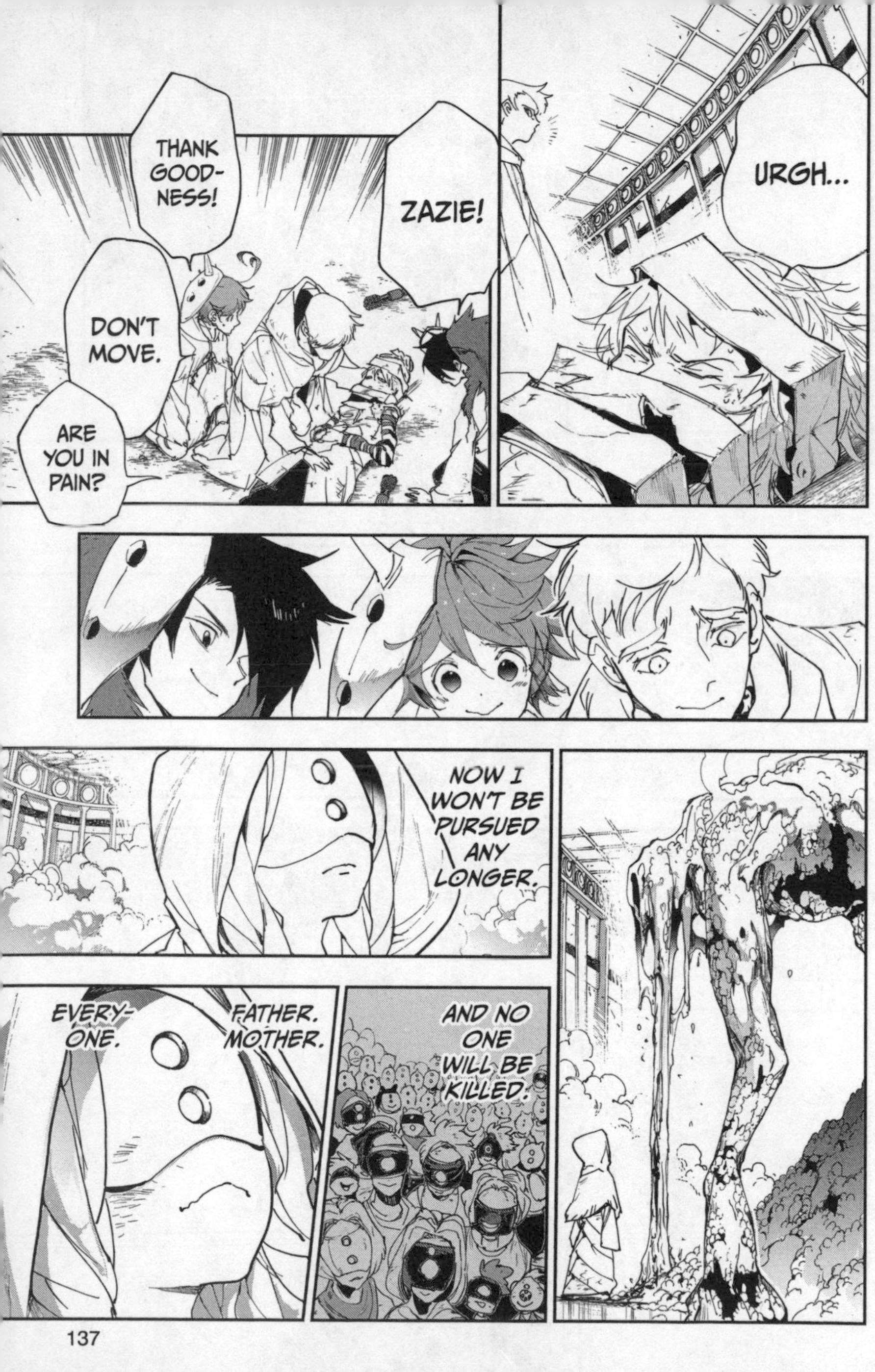
URGH...
ZAZIE!
THANK GOOD-NESS!
DON'T MOVE.
ARE YOU IN PAIN?
NOW I WON'T BE PURSUED ANY LONGER.
AND NO ONE WILL BE KILLED.
FATHER. MOTHER.
EVERY-ONE.

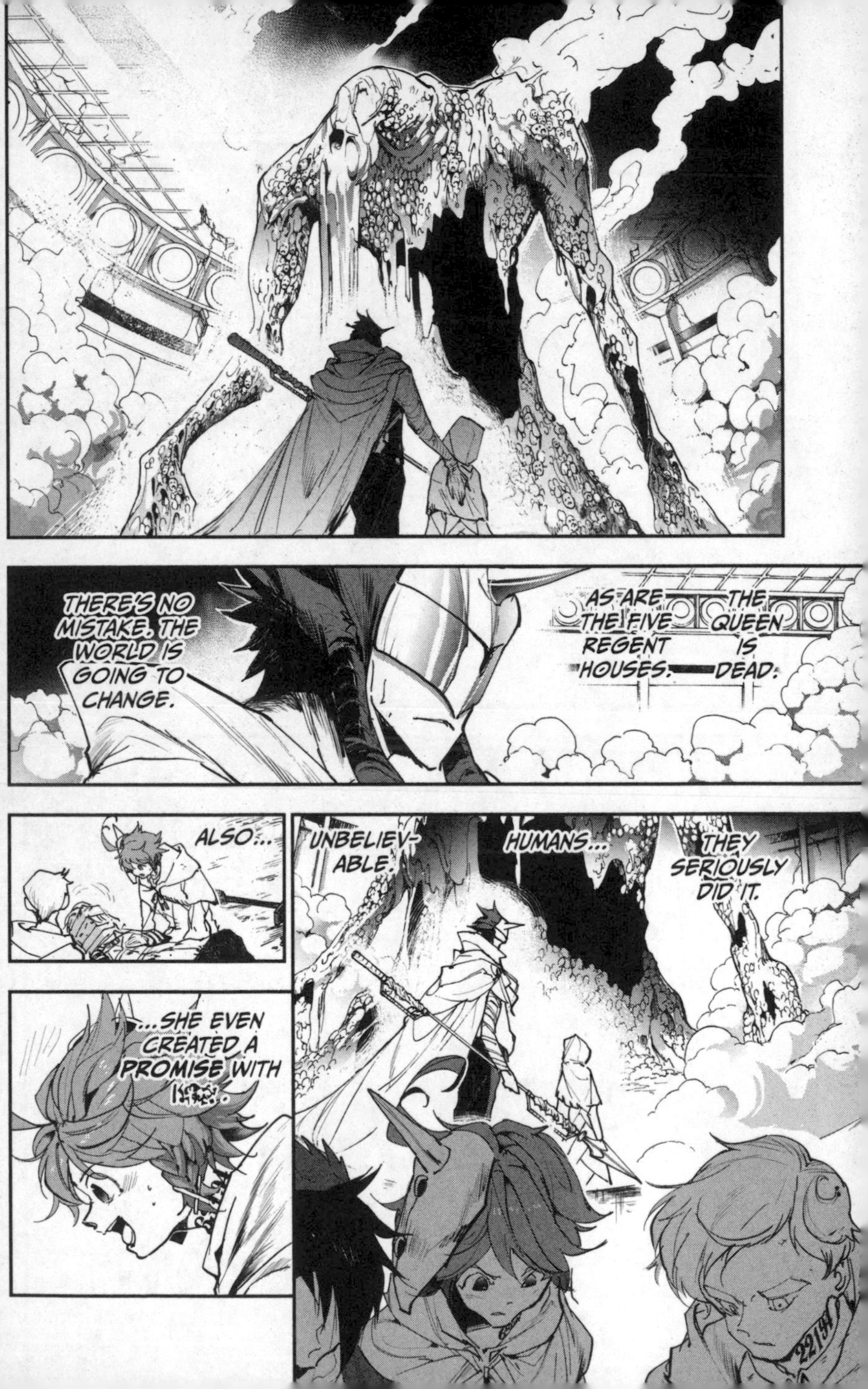
THE QUEEN IS DEAD.
AS ARE THE FIVE REGENT HOUSES.
THERE'S NO MISTAKE. THE WORLD IS GOING TO CHANGE.
THEY SERIOUSLY DID IT.
HUMANS...
UNBELIEV-ABLE.
ALSO...
...SHE EVEN CREATED A PROMISE WITH

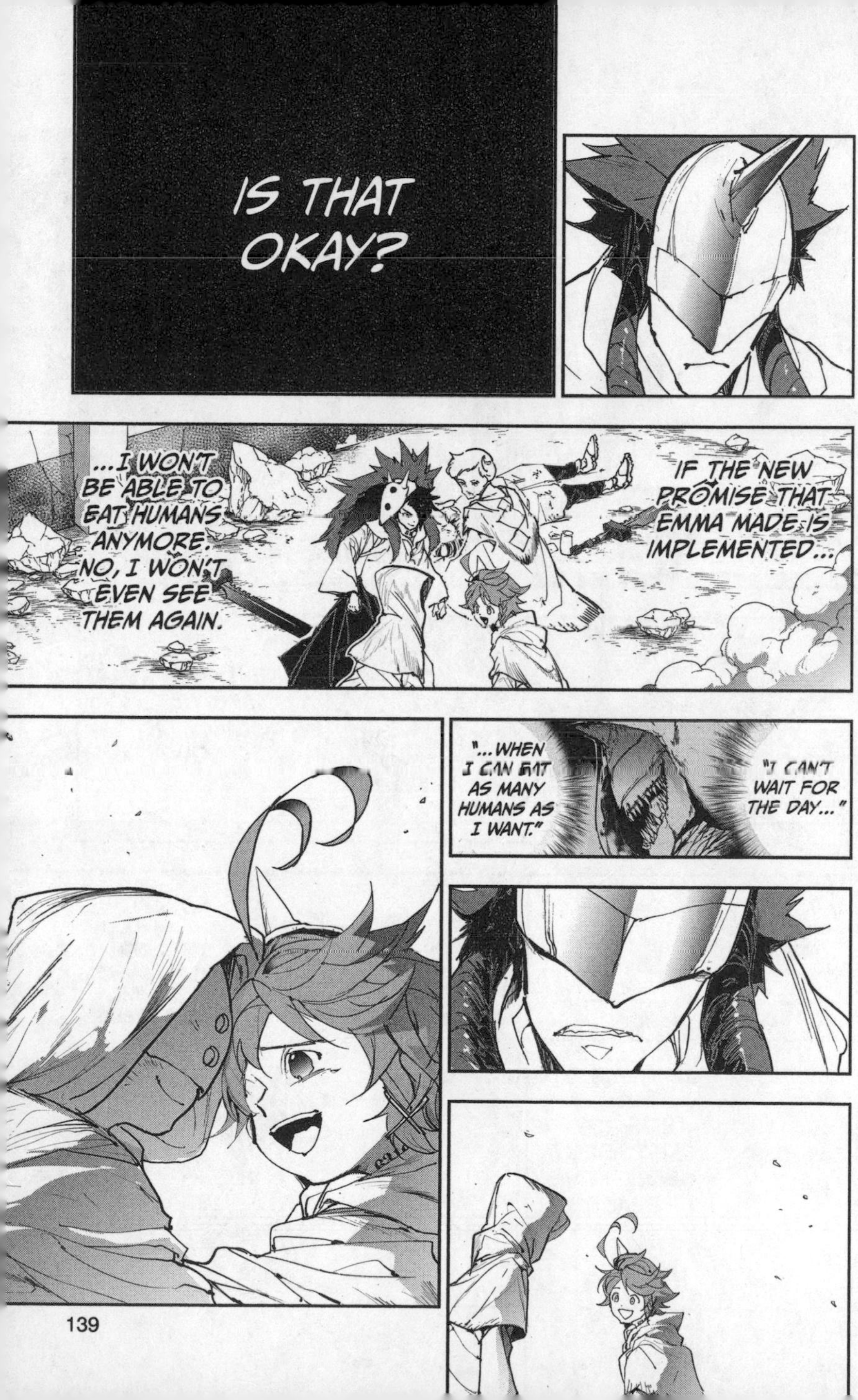
IS THAT OKAY?
IF THE NEW PROMISE THAT EMMA MADE IS IMPLEMENTED...
...I WON'T BE ABLE TO EAT HUMANS ANYMORE. NO, I WON'T EVEN SEE THEM AGAIN.
"I CAN'T WAIT FOR THE DAY..."
"...WHEN I CAN EAT AS MANY HUMANS AS I WANT."

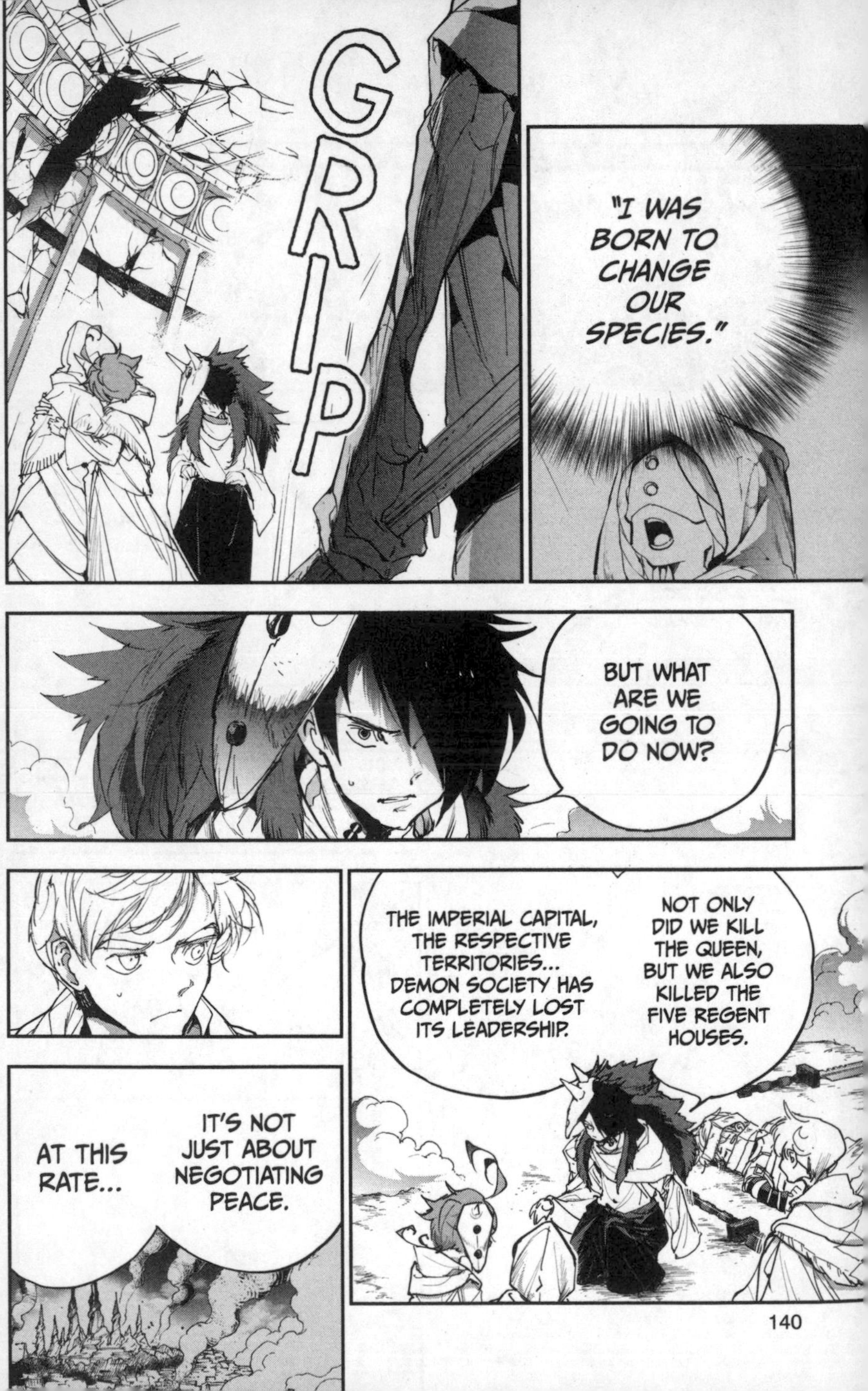
"I WAS BORN TO CHANGE OUR SPECIES."
GRIP
BUT WHAT ARE WE GOING TO DO NOW?
NOT ONLY DID WE KILL THE QUEEN, BUT WE ALSO KILLED THE FIVE REGENT HOUSES.
THE IMPERIAL CAPITAL, THE RESPECTIVE TERRITORIES... DEMON SOCIETY HAS COMPLETELY LOST ITS LEADERSHIP.
IT'S NOT JUST ABOUT NEGOTIATING PEACE.
AT THIS RATE...

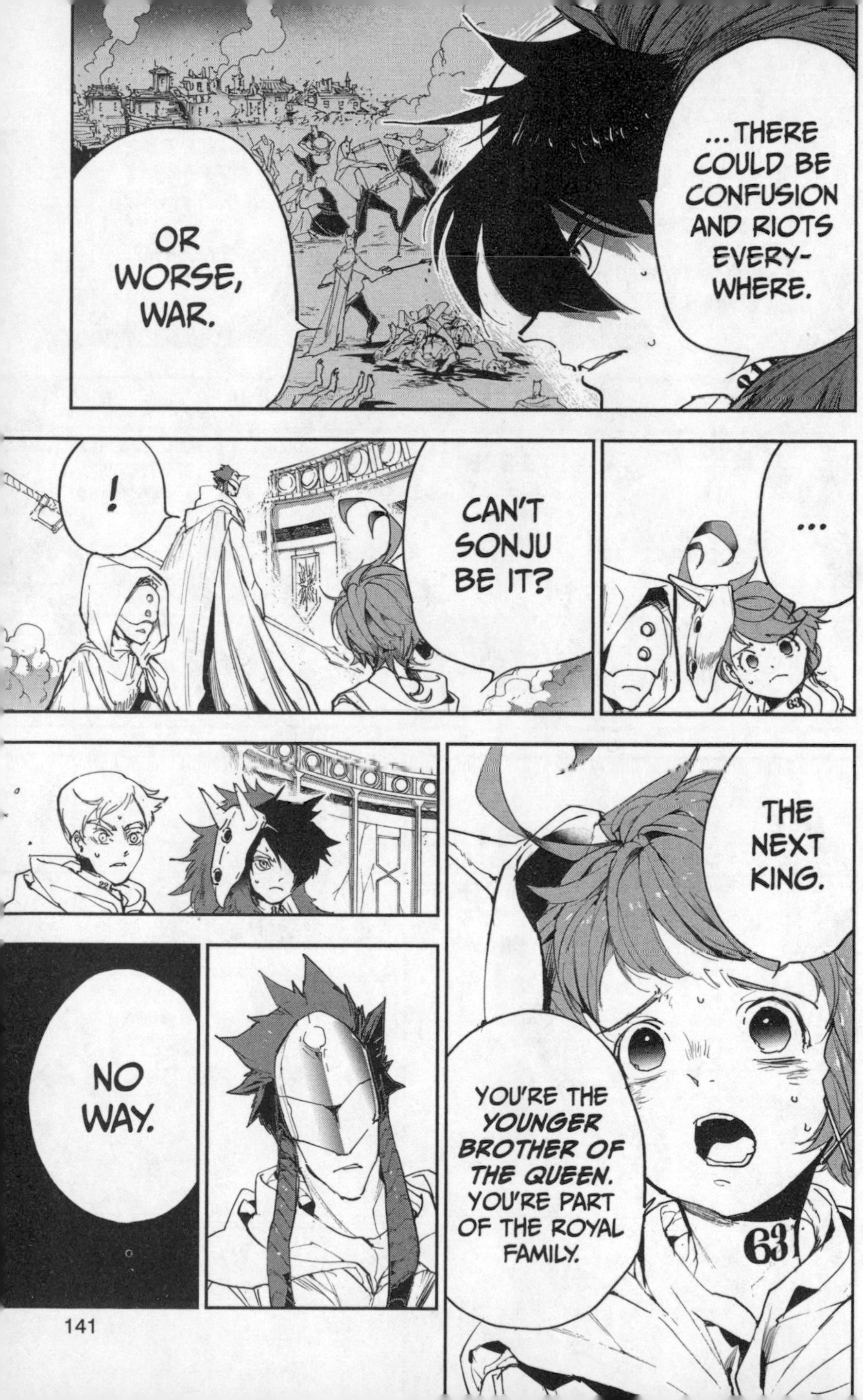
...THERE COULD BE CONFUSION AND RIOTS EVERY-WHERE.
OR WORSE, WAR.
...
CAN'T SONJU BE IT?
!
THE NEXT KING.
YOU'RE THE *YOUNGER BROTHER OF THE QUEEN*. YOU'RE PART OF THE ROYAL FAMILY.
NO WAY.

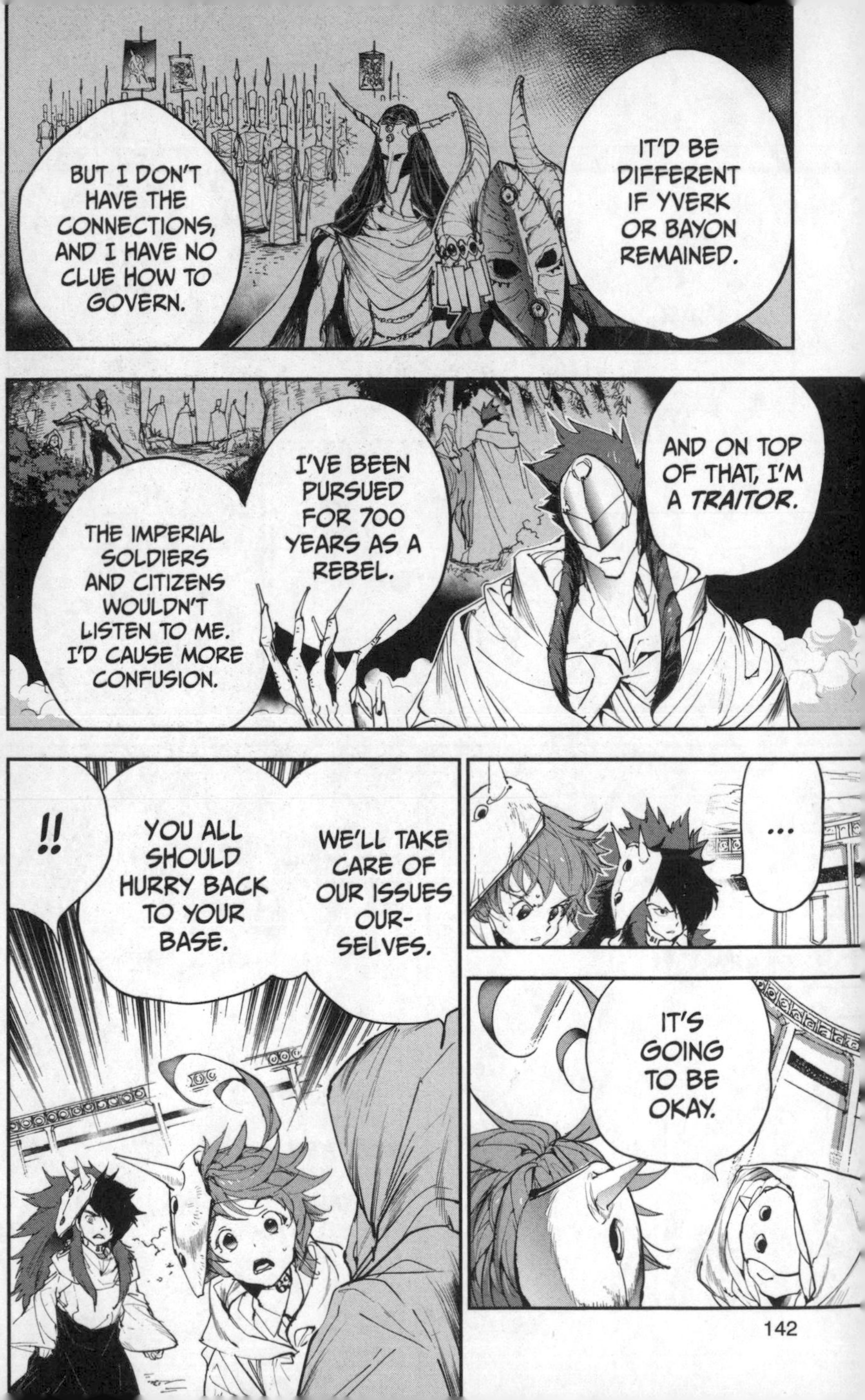
IT'D BE DIFFERENT IF YVERK OR BAYON REMAINED.
BUT I DON'T HAVE THE CONNECTIONS, AND I HAVE NO CLUE HOW TO GOVERN.
AND ON TOP OF THAT, I'M A *TRAITOR*.
I'VE BEEN PURSUED FOR 700 YEARS AS A REBEL.
THE IMPERIAL SOLDIERS AND CITIZENS WOULDN'T LISTEN TO ME. I'D CAUSE MORE CONFUSION.
...
IT'S GOING TO BE OKAY.
WE'LL TAKE CARE OF OUR ISSUES OUR-SELVES.
YOU ALL SHOULD HURRY BACK TO YOUR BASE.
!!

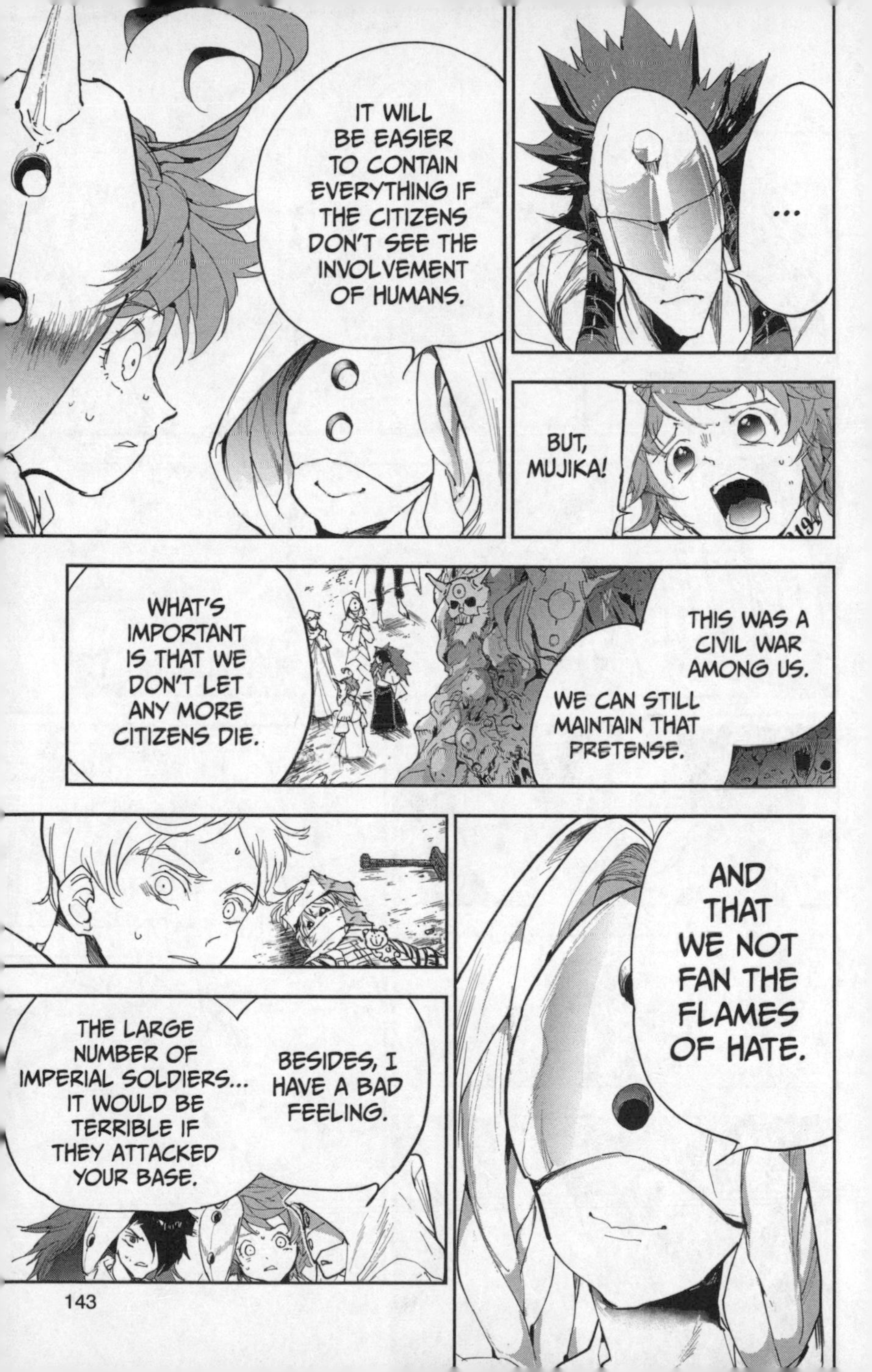
...
BUT, MUJIKA!
IT WILL BE EASIER TO CONTAIN EVERYTHING IF THE CITIZENS DON'T SEE THE INVOLVEMENT OF HUMANS.
THIS WAS A CIVIL WAR AMONG US.
WE CAN STILL MAINTAIN THAT PRETENSE.
WHAT'S IMPORTANT IS THAT WE DON'T LET ANY MORE CITIZENS DIE.
AND THAT WE NOT FAN THE FLAMES OF HATE.
BESIDES, I HAVE A BAD FEELING.
THE LARGE NUMBER OF IMPERIAL SOLDIERS... IT WOULD BE TERRIBLE IF THEY ATTACKED YOUR BASE.

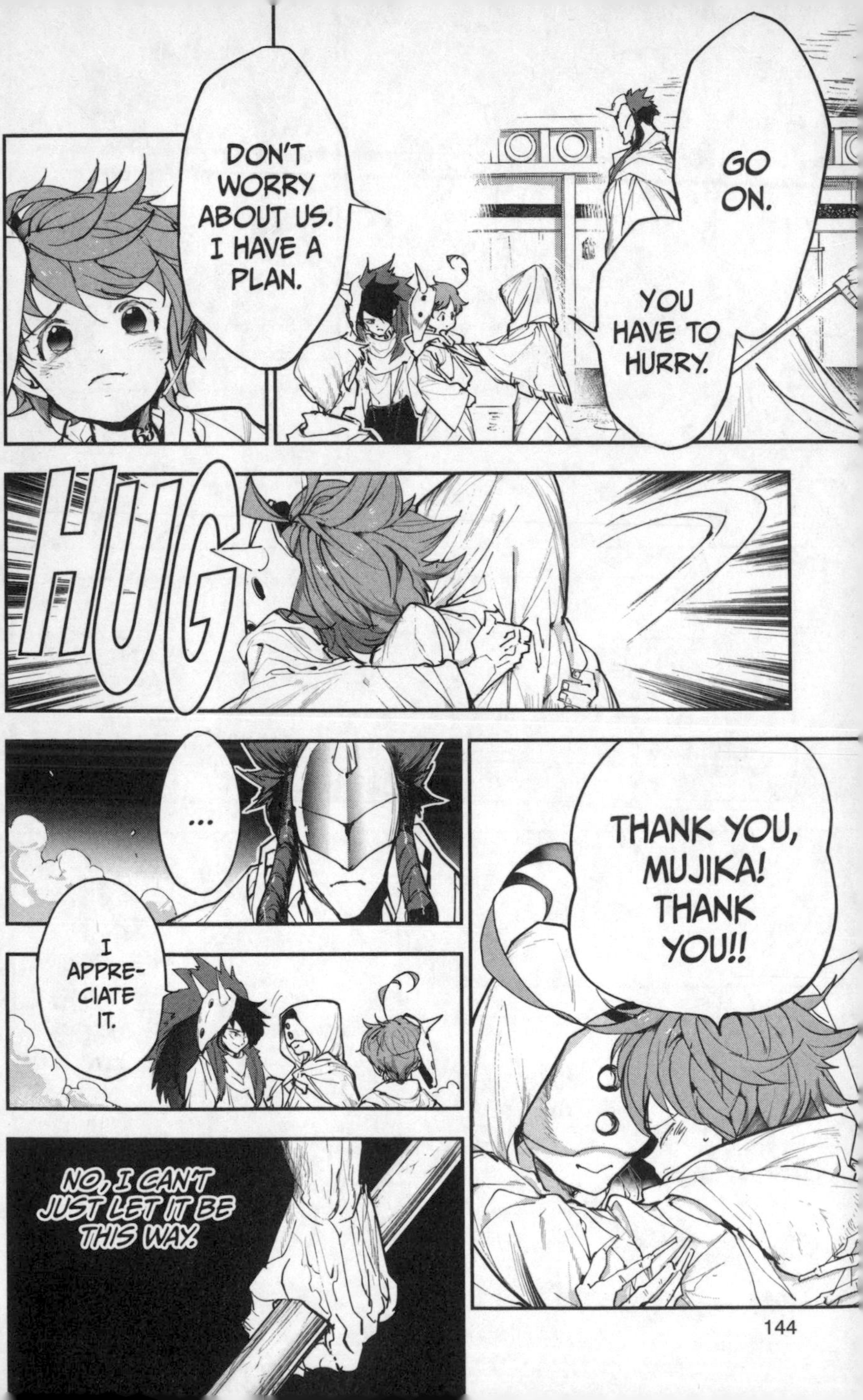
GO ON.
YOU HAVE TO HURRY.
DON'T WORRY ABOUT US. I HAVE A PLAN.
HUG
THANK YOU, MUJIKA! THANK YOU!!
...
I APPRE-CIATE IT.
NO, I CAN'T JUST LET IT BE THIS WAY.

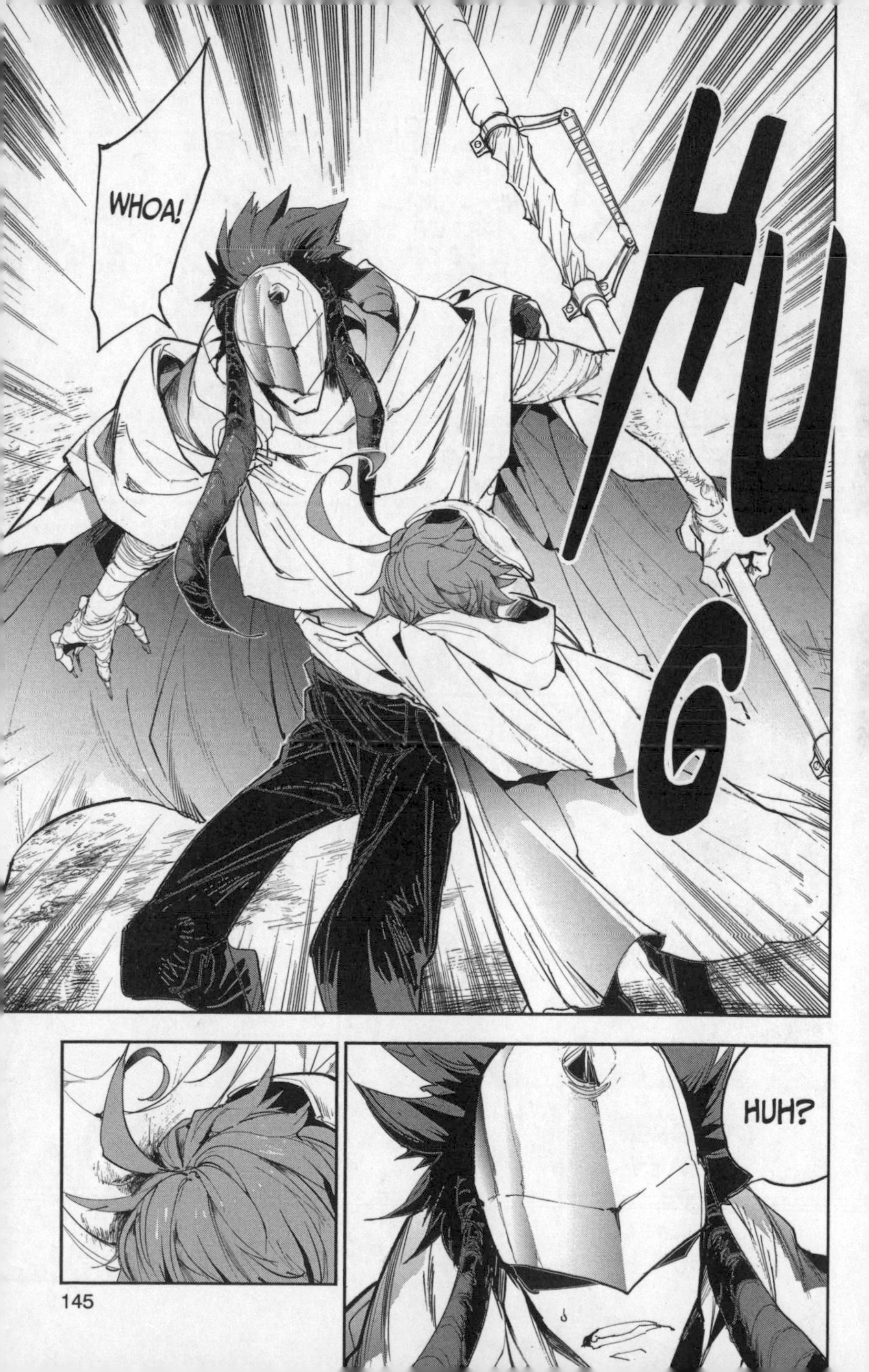
WHOA!
HUG
HUH?

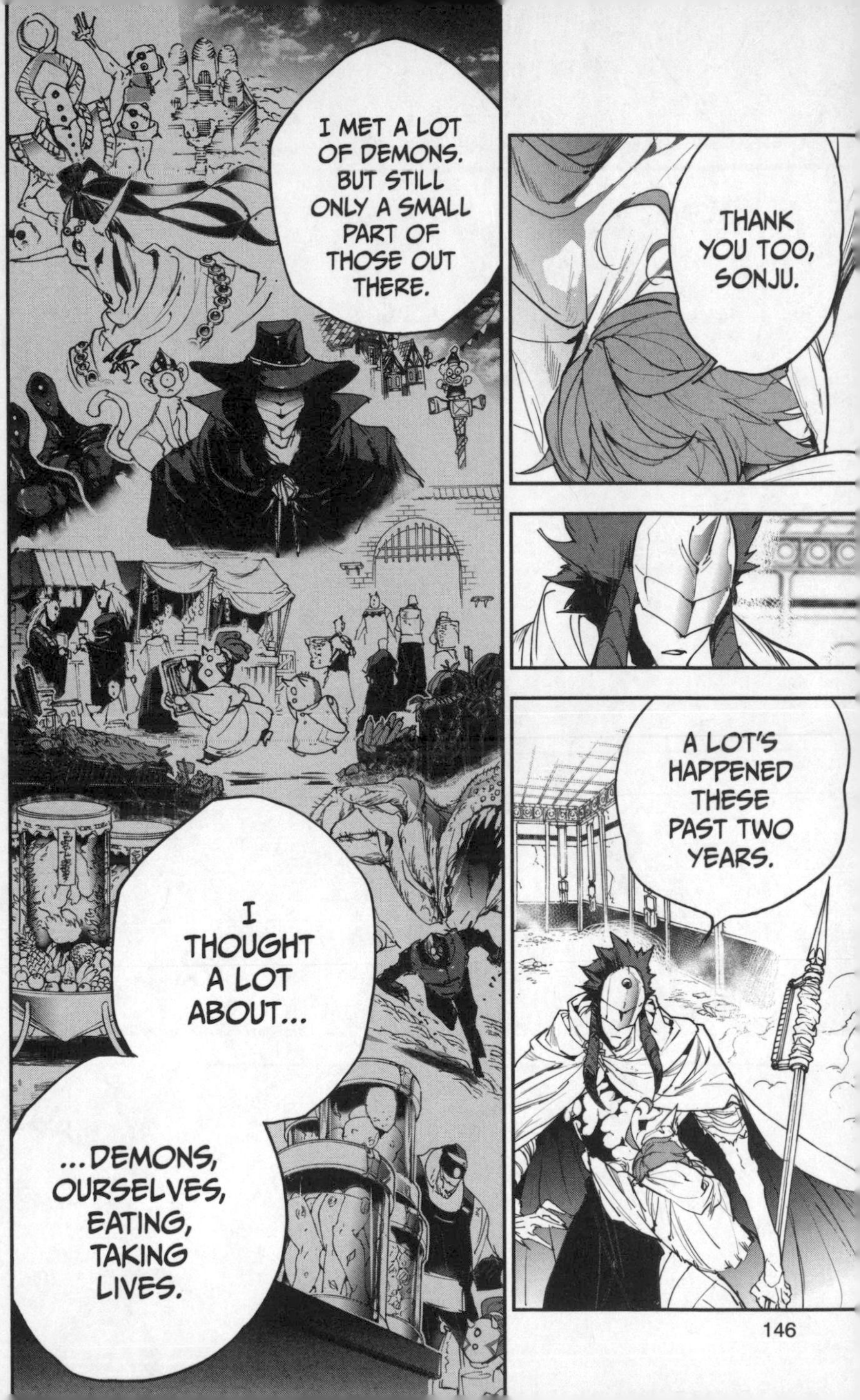
THANK YOU TOO, SONJU.
A LOT'S HAPPENED THESE PAST TWO YEARS.
I MET A LOT OF DEMONS. BUT STILL ONLY A SMALL PART OF THOSE OUT THERE.
I THOUGHT A LOT ABOUT...
...DEMONS, OURSELVES, EATING, TAKING LIVES.

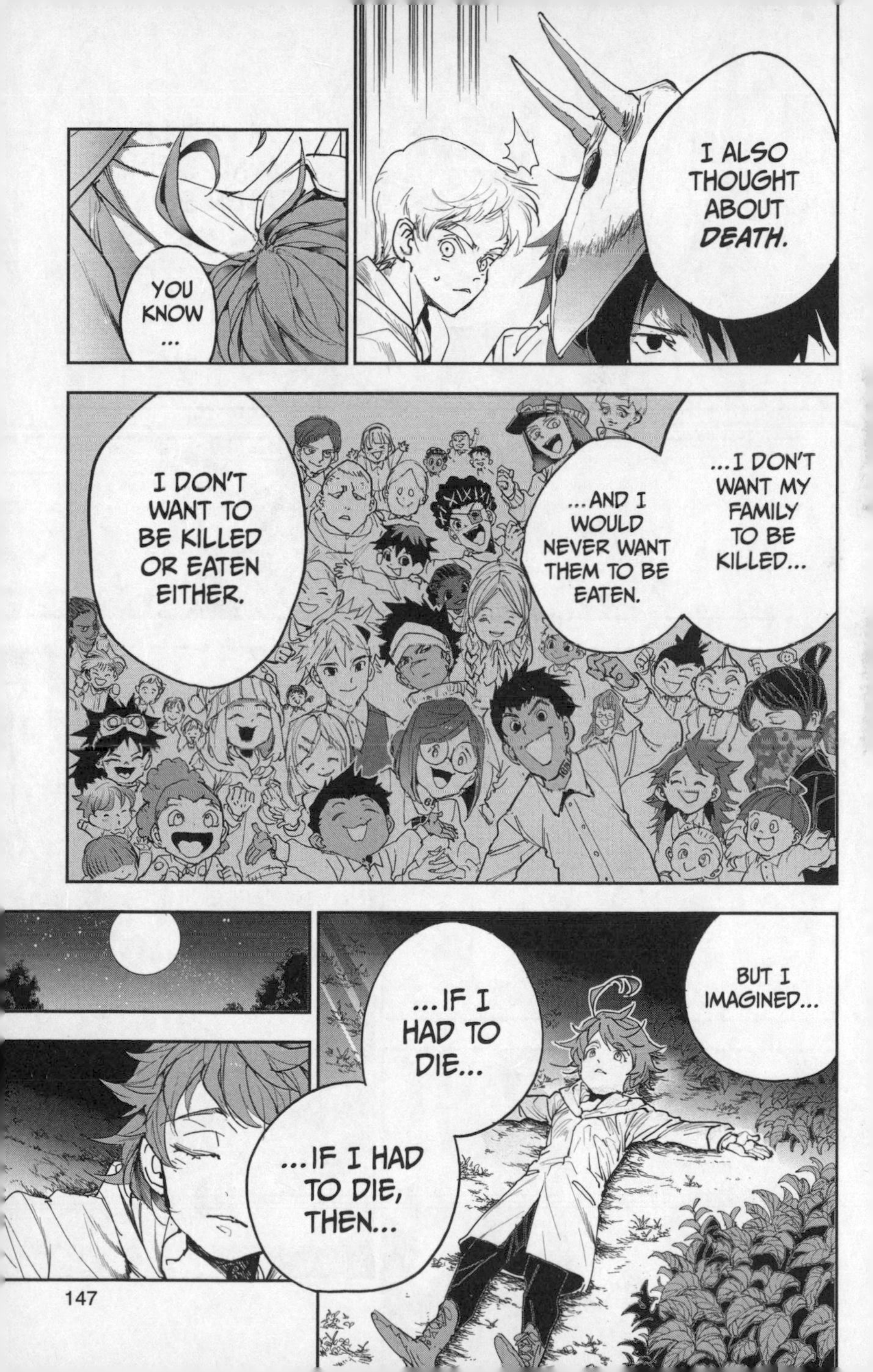
I ALSO THOUGHT ABOUT DEATH.
YOU KNOW ...
...I DON'T WANT MY FAMILY TO BE KILLED...
...AND I WOULD NEVER WANT THEM TO BE EATEN.
I DON'T WANT TO BE KILLED OR EATEN EITHER.
BUT I IMAGINED...
...IF I HAD TO DIE...
...IF I HAD TO DIE, THEN...

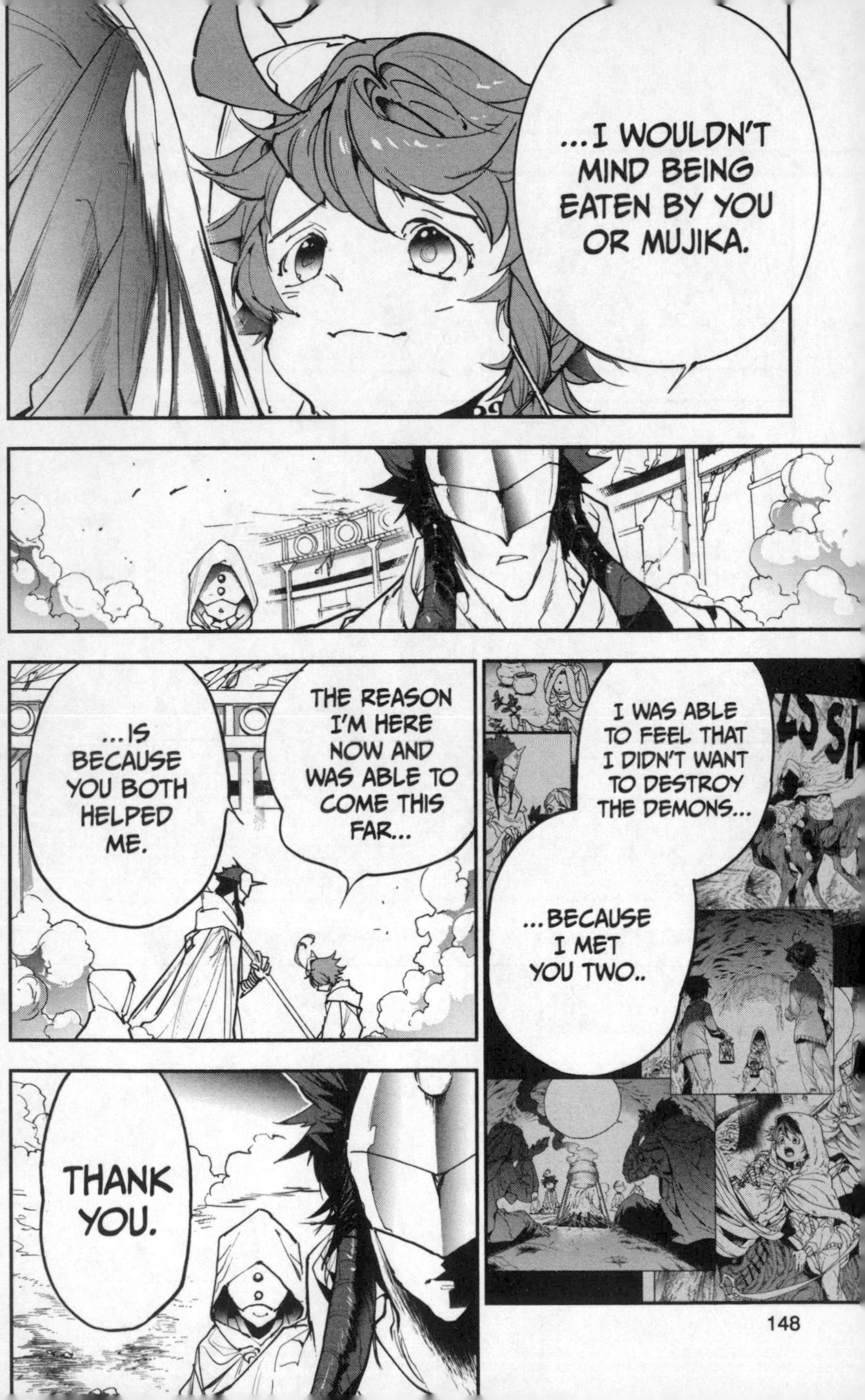
...I WOULDN'T MIND BEING EATEN BY YOU OR MUJIKA.
I WAS ABLE TO FEEL THAT I DIDN'T WANT TO DESTROY THE DEMONS...
...BECAUSE I MET YOU TWO..
THE REASON I'M HERE NOW AND WAS ABLE TO COME THIS FAR...
...IS BECAUSE YOU BOTH HELPED ME.
THANK YOU.

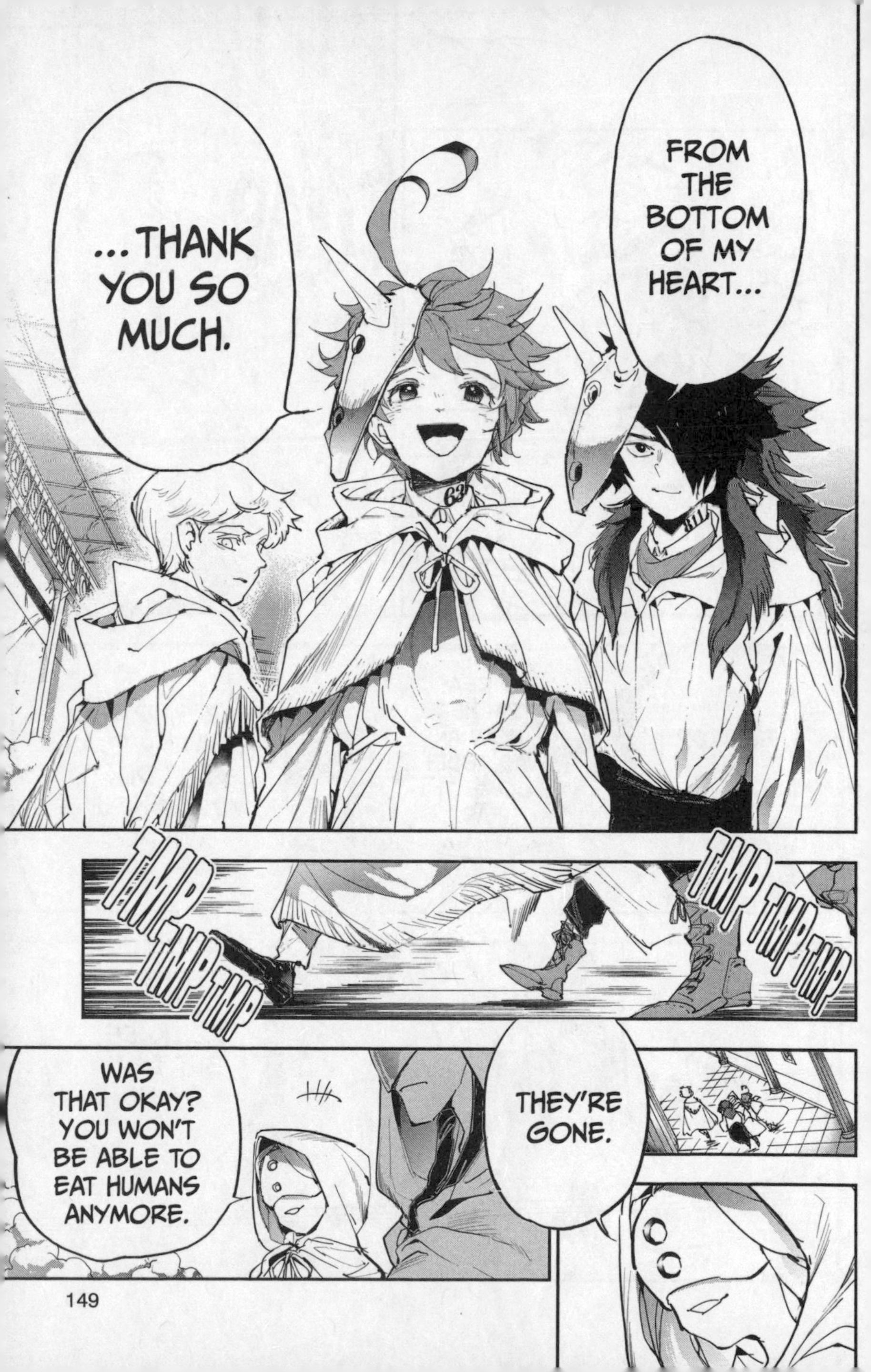
FROM THE BOTTOM OF MY HEART...
...THANK YOU SO MUCH.
TMP TMP TMP
TMP TMP TMP
THEY'RE GONE.
WAS THAT OKAY? YOU WON'T BE ABLE TO EAT HUMANS ANYMORE.

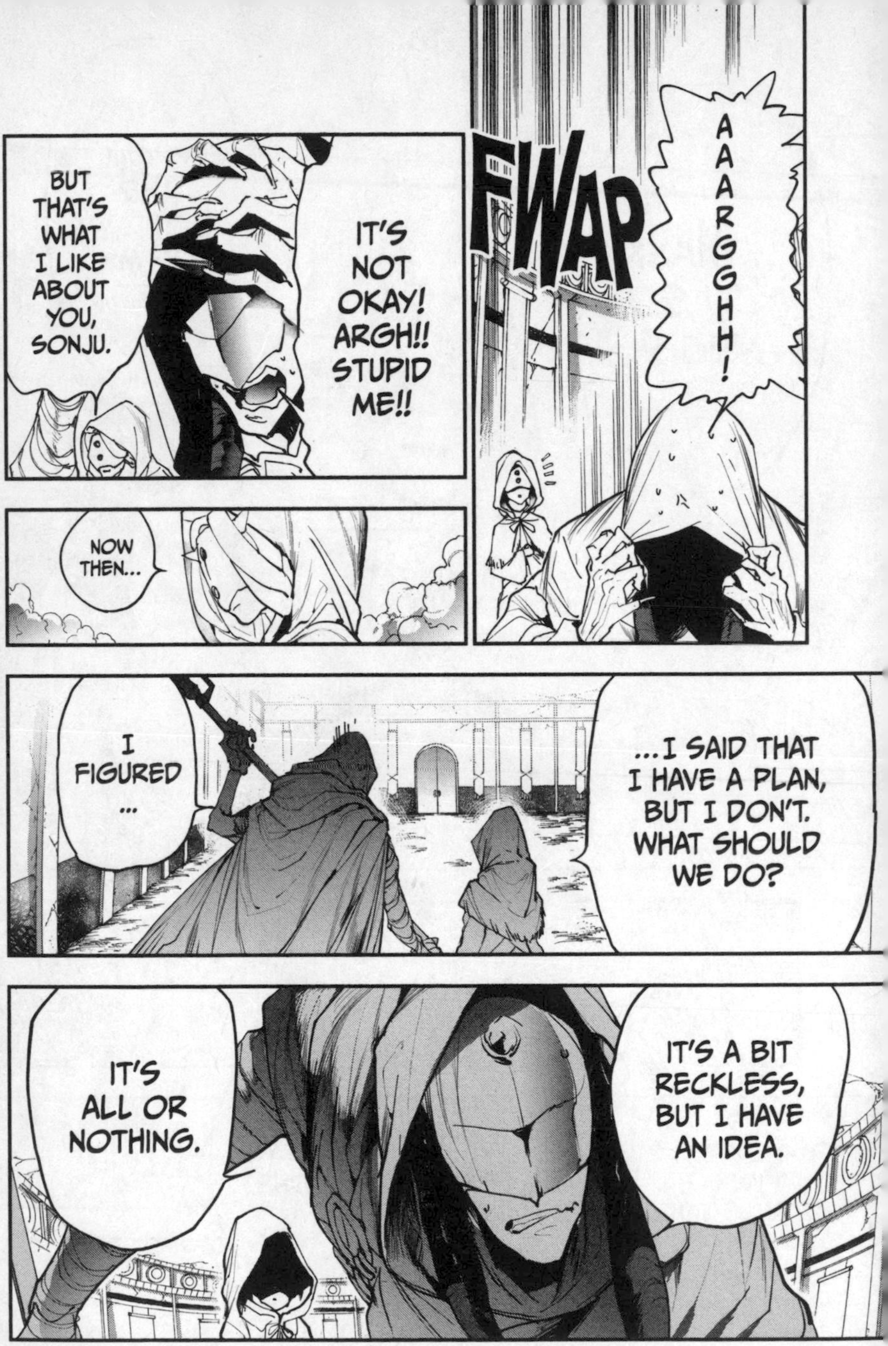
AAARGGHH!
FWAP
IT'S NOT OKAY! ARGH!! STUPID ME!!
BUT THAT'S WHAT I LIKE ABOUT YOU, SONJU.
NOW THEN...
...I SAID THAT I HAVE A PLAN, BUT I DON'T. WHAT SHOULD WE DO?
I FIGURED...
IT'S A BIT RECKLESS, BUT I HAVE AN IDEA.
IT'S ALL OR NOTHING.

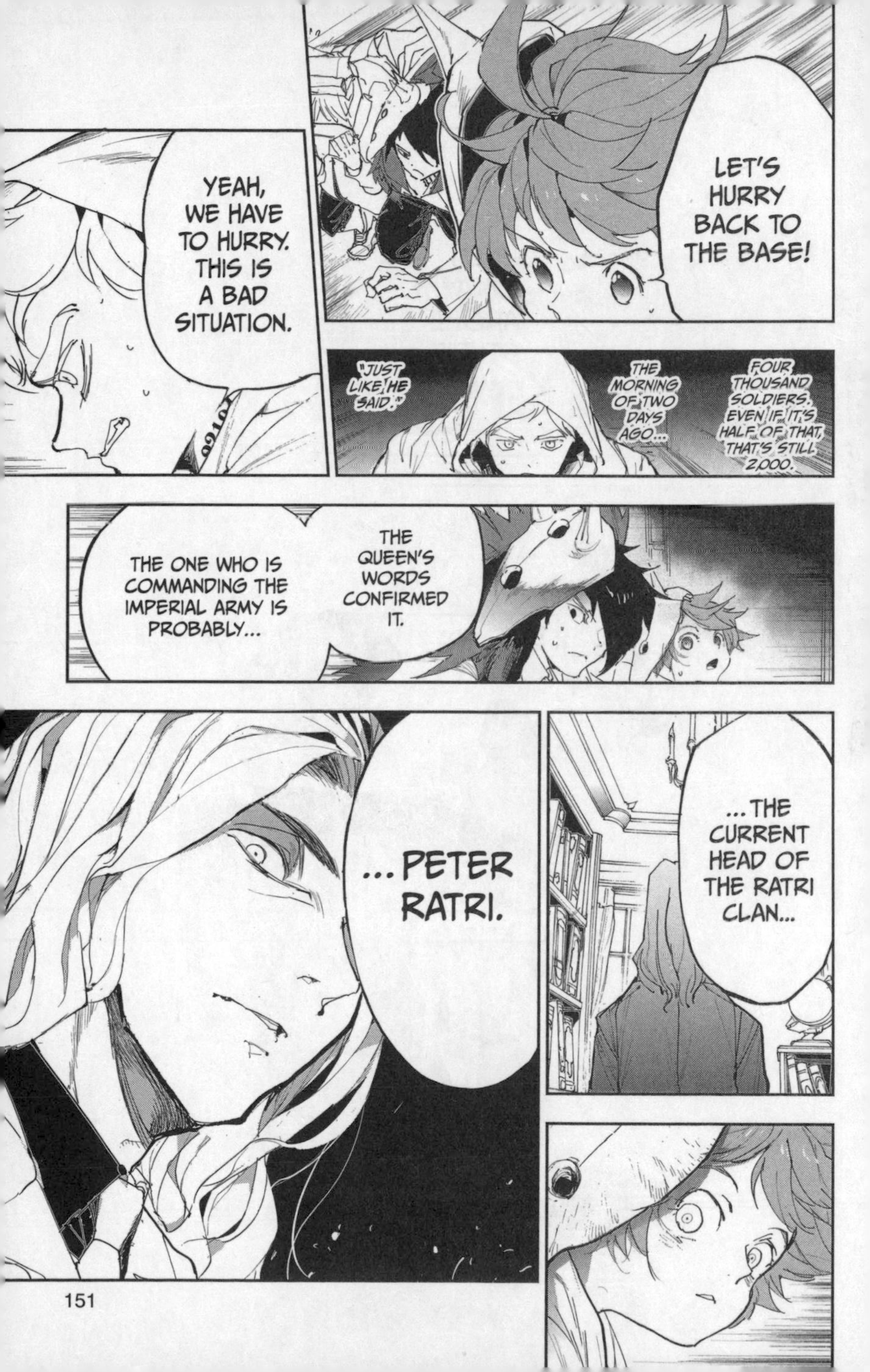
LET'S HURRY BACK TO THE BASE!
FOUR THOUSAND SOLDIERS. EVEN IF IT'S HALF OF THAT, THAT'S STILL 2,000.
THE MORNING OF TWO DAYS AGO...
"JUST LIKE HE SAID."
YEAH, WE HAVE TO HURRY. THIS IS A BAD SITUATION.
THE QUEEN'S WORDS CONFIRMED IT.
THE ONE WHO IS COMMANDING THE IMPERIAL ARMY IS PROBABLY...
...THE CURRENT HEAD OF THE RATRI CLAN...
...PETER RATRI.

"IF I HAD GIVEN UP
BACK THEN..."

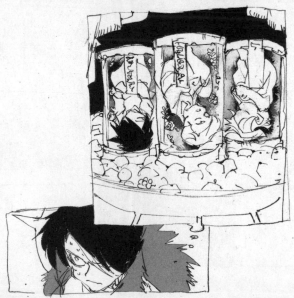

CHAPTER 160: SHACKLES

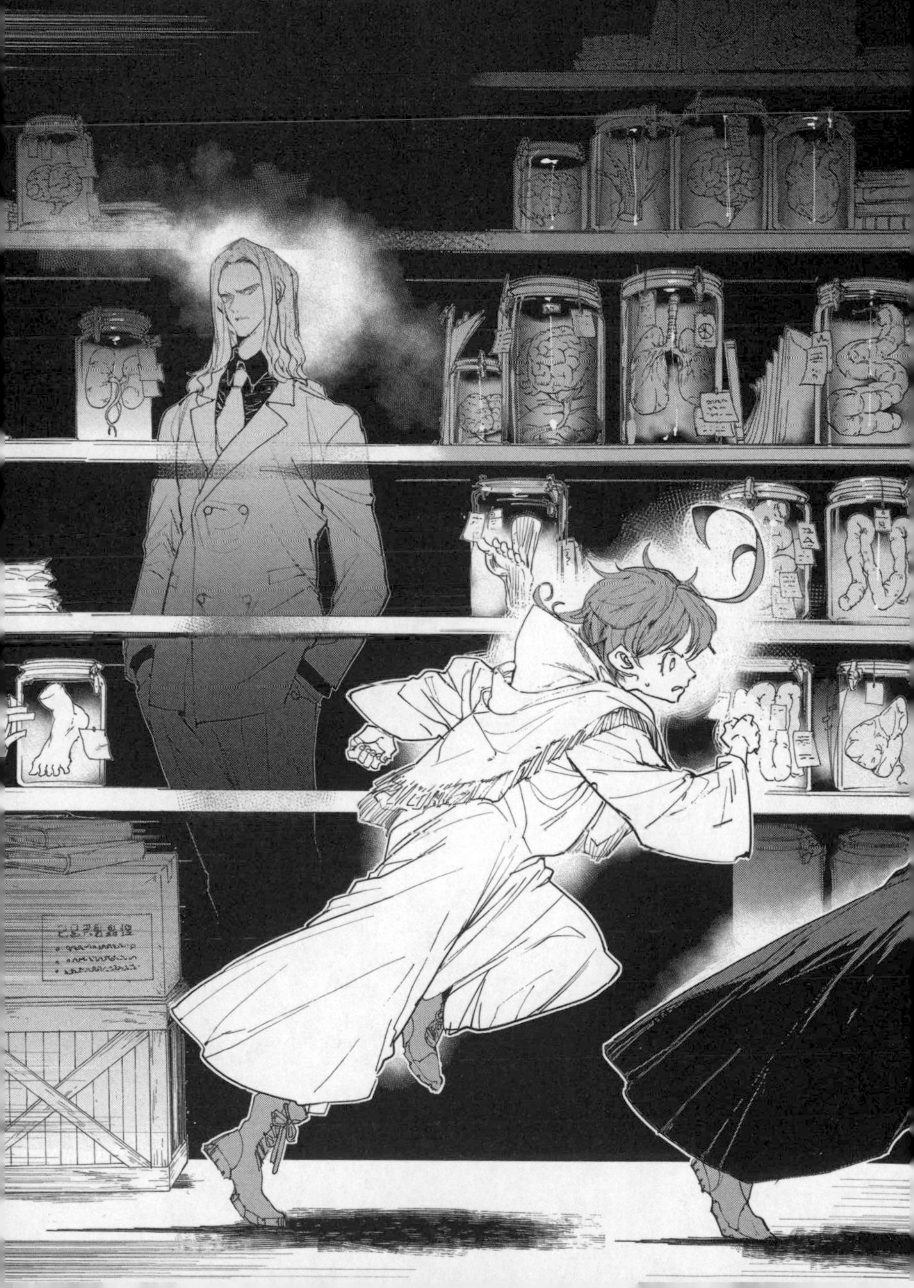

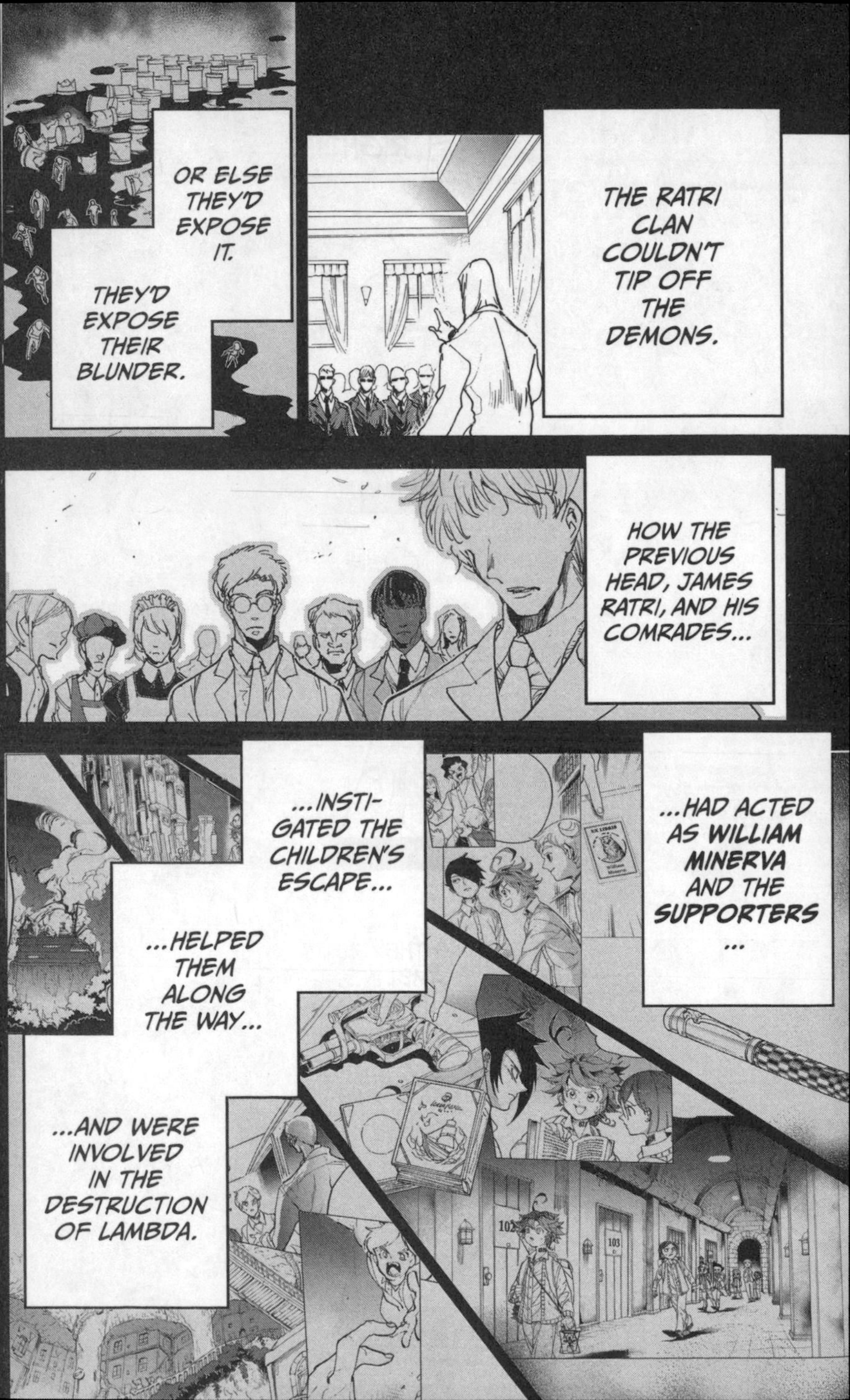
THE RATRI CLAN COULDN'T TIP OFF THE DEMONS.
OR ELSE THEY'D EXPOSE IT.
THEY'D EXPOSE THEIR BLUNDER.
HOW THE PREVIOUS HEAD, JAMES RATRI, AND HIS COMRADES...
...HAD ACTED AS WILLIAM MINERVA AND THE SUPPORTERS...
...INSTI-GATED THE CHILDREN'S ESCAPE...
...HELPED THEM ALONG THE WAY...
...AND WERE INVOLVED IN THE DESTRUCTION OF LAMBDA.

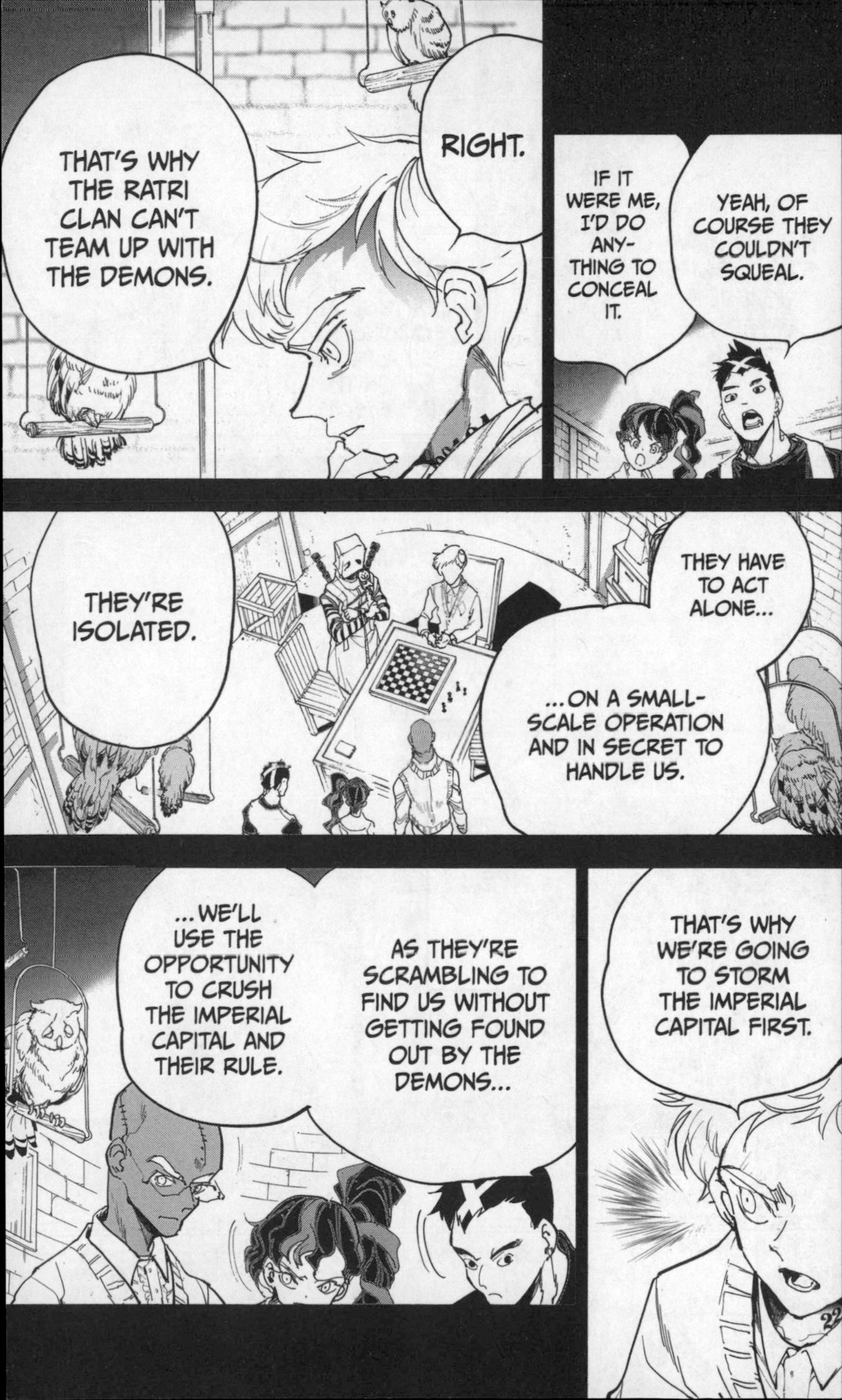
YEAH, OF COURSE THEY COULDN'T SQUEAL.
IF IT WERE ME, I'D DO ANY-THING TO CONCEAL IT.
RIGHT.
THAT'S WHY THE RATRI CLAN CAN'T TEAM UP WITH THE DEMONS.
THEY HAVE TO ACT ALONE...
...ON A SMALL-SCALE OPERATION AND IN SECRET TO HANDLE US.
THEY'RE ISOLATED.
THAT'S WHY WE'RE GOING TO STORM THE IMPERIAL CAPITAL FIRST.
AS THEY'RE SCRAMBLING TO FIND US WITHOUT GETTING FOUND OUT BY THE DEMONS...
...WE'LL USE THE OPPORTUNITY TO CRUSH THE IMPERIAL CAPITAL AND THEIR RULE.

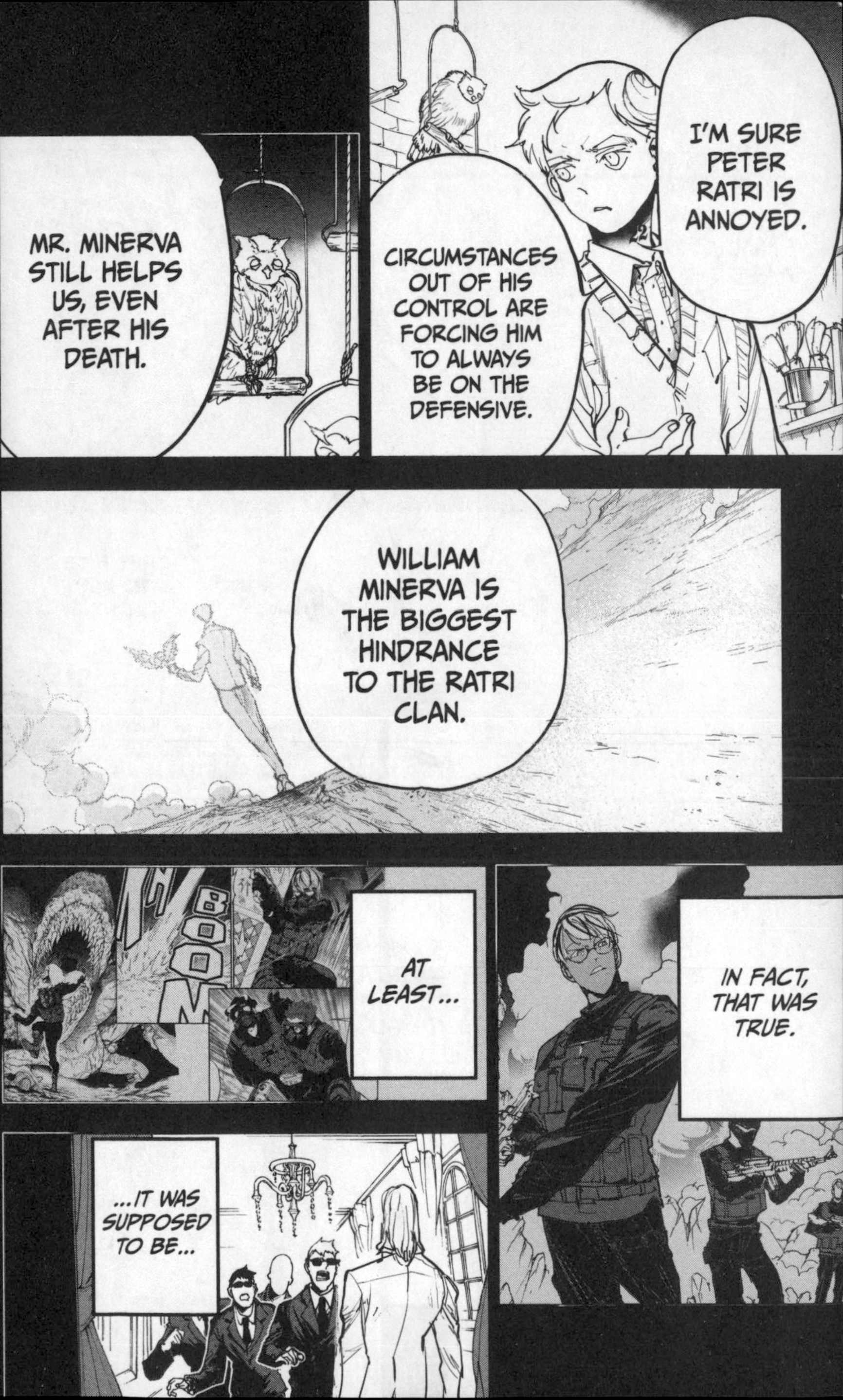
I'M SURE PETER RATRI IS ANNOYED.
CIRCUMSTANCES OUT OF HIS CONTROL ARE FORCING HIM TO ALWAYS BE ON THE DEFENSIVE.
MR. MINERVA STILL HELPS US, EVEN AFTER HIS DEATH.
WILLIAM MINERVA IS THE BIGGEST HINDRANCE TO THE RATRI CLAN.
IN FACT, THAT WAS TRUE.
AT LEAST...
BOOM
...IT WAS SUPPOSED TO BE...

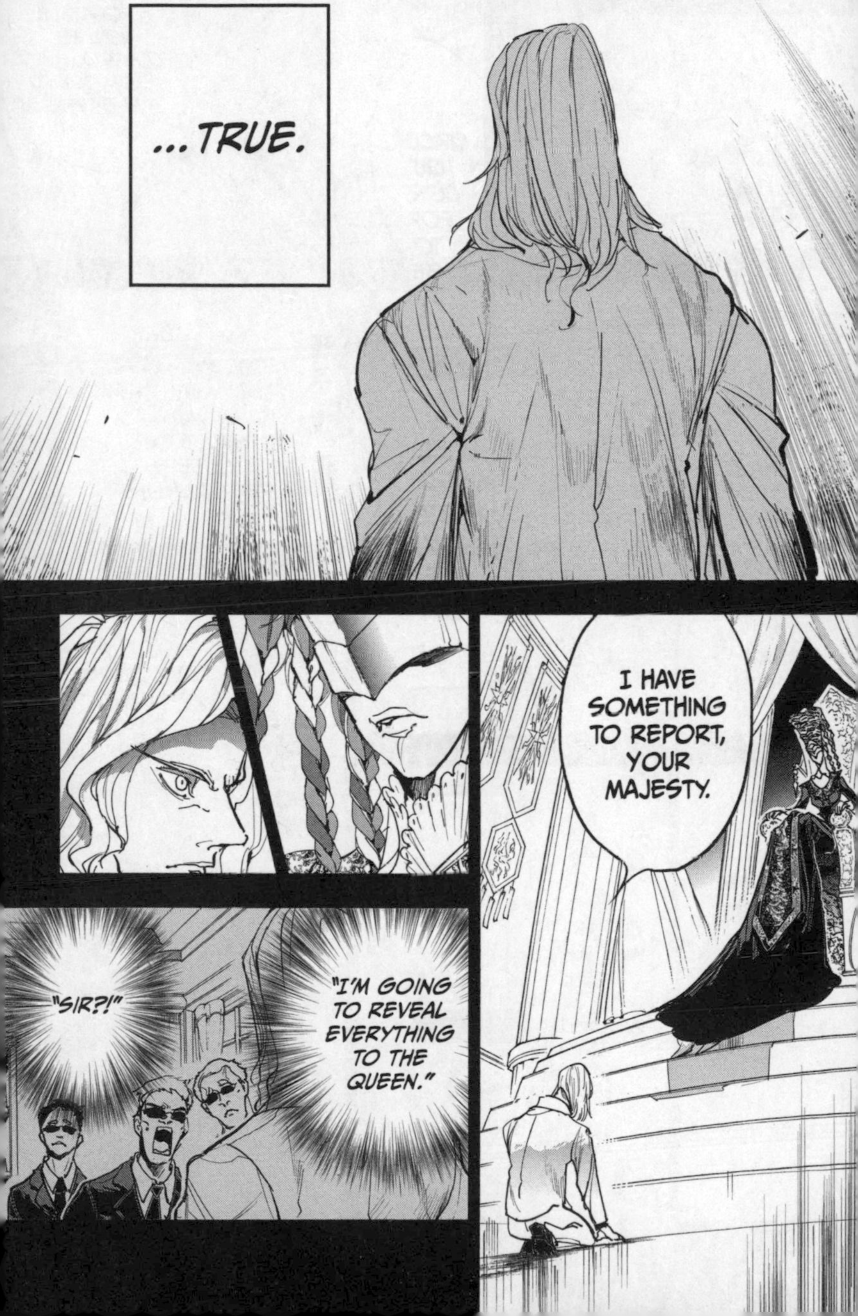
...TRUE.
I HAVE SOMETHING TO REPORT, YOUR MAJESTY.
"I'M GOING TO REVEAL EVERYTHING TO THE QUEEN."
"SIR?!"

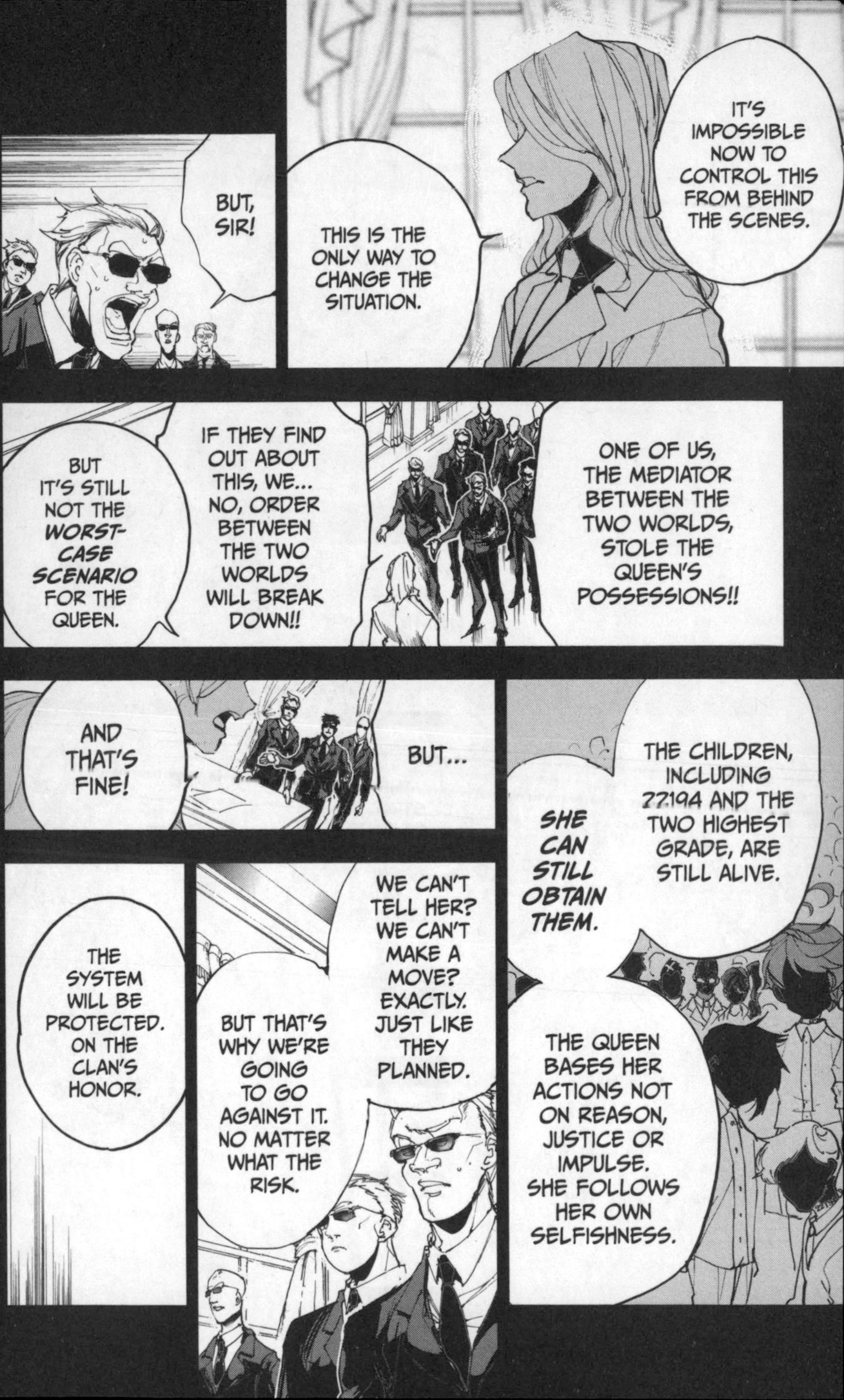
IT'S IMPOSSIBLE NOW TO CONTROL THIS FROM BEHIND THE SCENES.
THIS IS THE ONLY WAY TO CHANGE THE SITUATION.
BUT, SIR!
ONE OF US, THE MEDIATOR BETWEEN THE TWO WORLDS, STOLE THE QUEEN'S POSSESSIONS!!
IF THEY FIND OUT ABOUT THIS, WE... NO, ORDER BETWEEN THE TWO WORLDS WILL BREAK DOWN!!
BUT IT'S STILL NOT THE *WORST-CASE SCENARIO* FOR THE QUEEN.
THE CHILDREN, INCLUDING 22194 AND THE TWO HIGHEST GRADE, ARE STILL ALIVE.
SHE CAN STILL OBTAIN THEM.
THE QUEEN BASES HER ACTIONS NOT ON REASON, JUSTICE OR IMPULSE. SHE FOLLOWS HER OWN SELFISHNESS.
BUT...
AND THAT'S FINE!
WE CAN'T TELL HER? WE CAN'T MAKE A MOVE? EXACTLY. JUST LIKE THEY PLANNED.
BUT THAT'S WHY WE'RE GOING TO GO AGAINST IT. NO MATTER WHAT THE RISK.
THE SYSTEM WILL BE PROTECTED. ON THE CLAN'S HONOR.

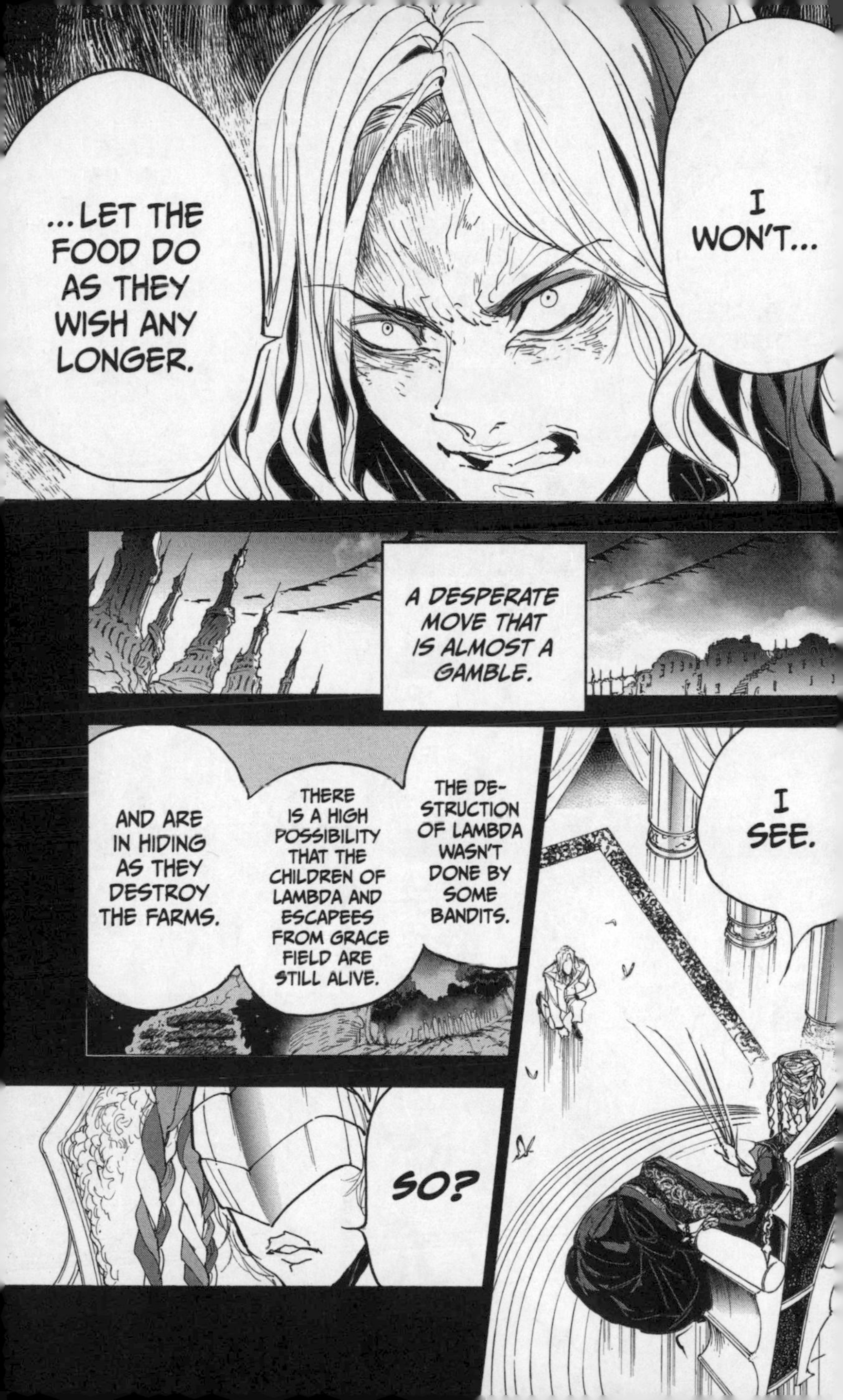
I WON'T...
...LET THE FOOD DO AS THEY WISH ANY LONGER.
A DESPERATE MOVE THAT IS ALMOST A GAMBLE.
I SEE.
THE DESTRUCTION OF LAMBDA WASN'T DONE BY SOME BANDITS.
THERE IS A HIGH POSSIBILITY THAT THE CHILDREN OF LAMBDA AND ESCAPEES FROM GRACE FIELD ARE STILL ALIVE.
AND ARE IN HIDING AS THEY DESTROY THE FARMS.
SO?

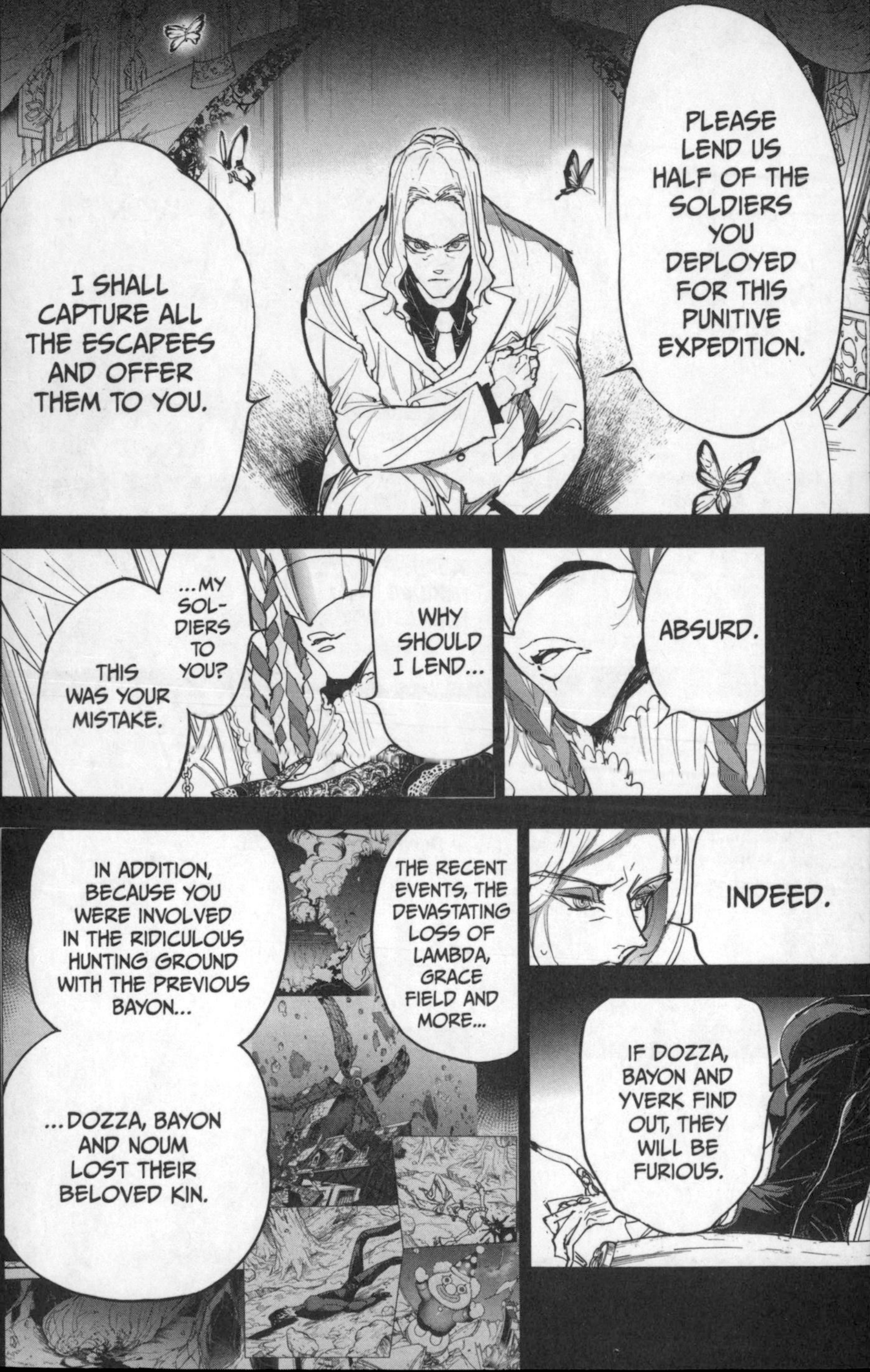
PLEASE LEND US HALF OF THE SOLDIERS YOU DEPLOYED FOR THIS PUNITIVE EXPEDITION.
I SHALL CAPTURE ALL THE ESCAPEES AND OFFER THEM TO YOU.
ABSURD.
WHY SHOULD I LEND...
...MY SOL-DIERS TO YOU?
THIS WAS YOUR MISTAKE.
INDEED.
IF DOZZA, BAYON AND YVERK FIND OUT, THEY WILL BE FURIOUS.
THE RECENT EVENTS, THE DEVASTATING LOSS OF LAMBDA, GRACE FIELD AND MORE...
IN ADDITION, BECAUSE YOU WERE INVOLVED IN THE RIDICULOUS HUNTING GROUND WITH THE PREVIOUS BAYON...
...DOZZA, BAYON AND NOUM LOST THEIR BELOVED KIN.

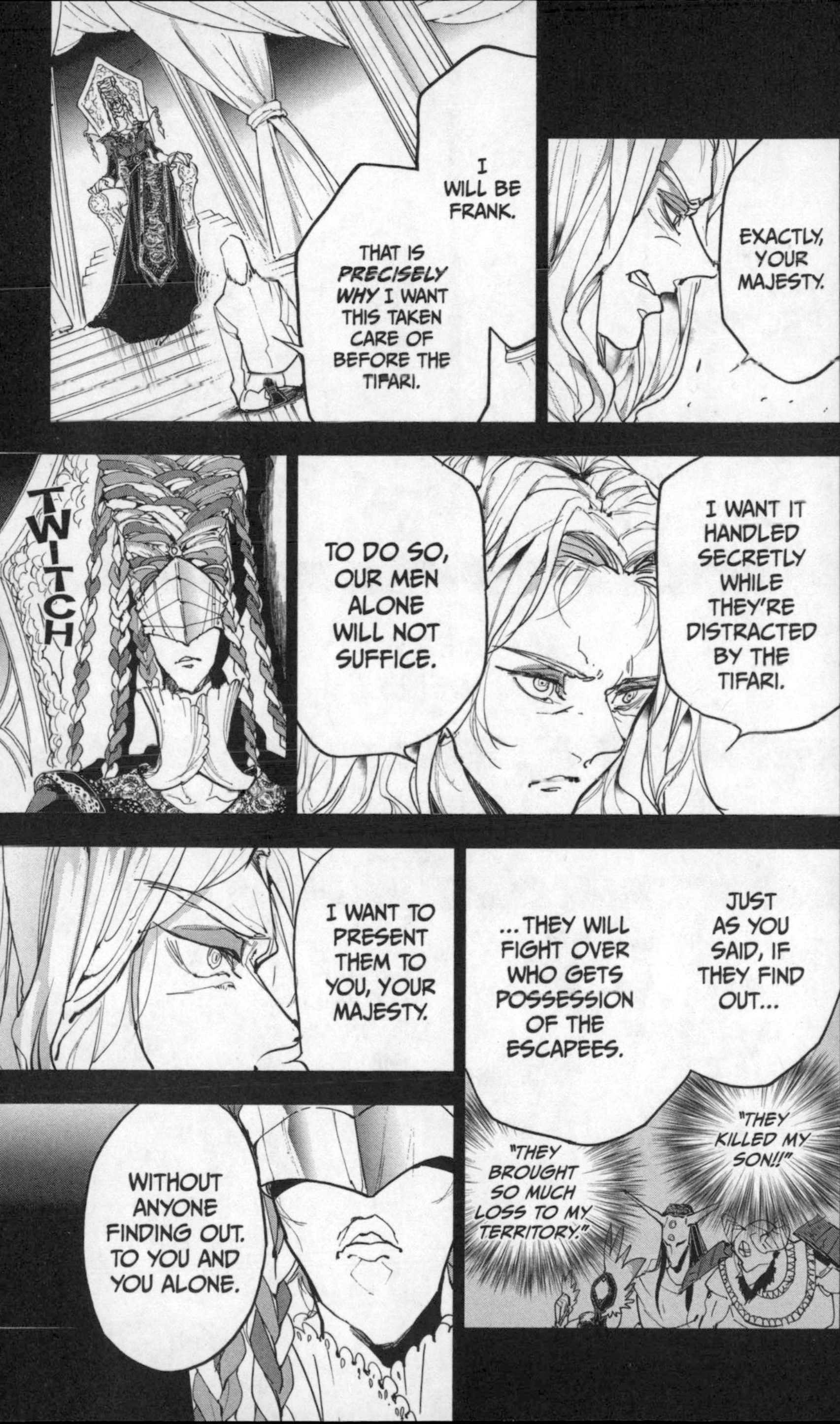
EXACTLY, YOUR MAJESTY.
I WILL BE FRANK.
THAT IS *PRECISELY WHY* I WANT THIS TAKEN CARE OF BEFORE THE TIFARI.
I WANT IT HANDLED SECRETLY WHILE THEY'RE DISTRACTED BY THE TIFARI.
TO DO SO, OUR MEN ALONE WILL NOT SUFFICE.
TWITCH
JUST AS YOU SAID, IF THEY FIND OUT...
...THEY WILL FIGHT OVER WHO GETS POSSESSION OF THE ESCAPEES.
"THEY KILLED MY SON!!"
"THEY BROUGHT SO MUCH LOSS TO MY TERRITORY."
I WANT TO PRESENT THEM TO YOU, YOUR MAJESTY.
WITHOUT ANYONE FINDING OUT. TO YOU AND YOU ALONE.

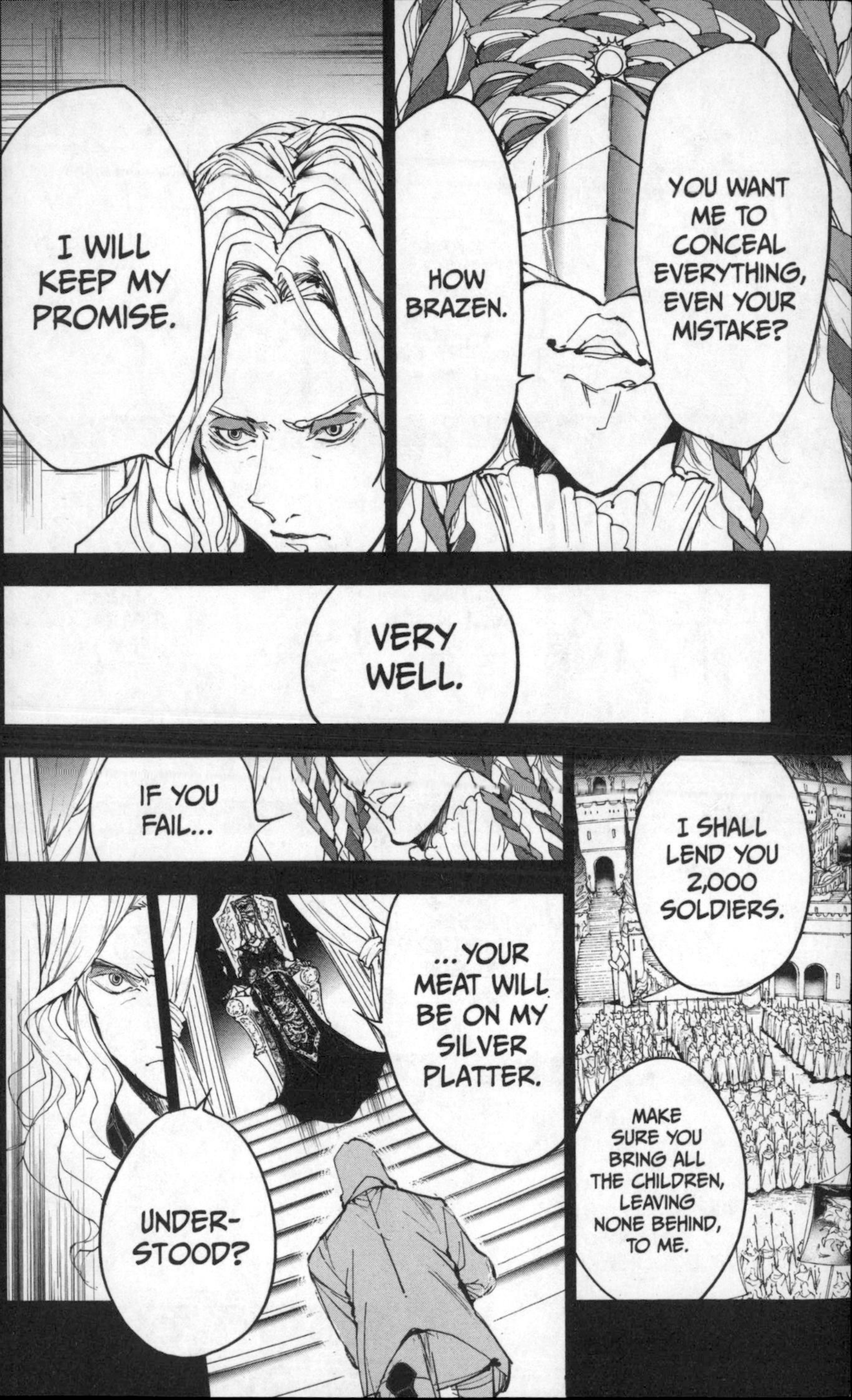
YOU WANT ME TO CONCEAL EVERYTHING, EVEN YOUR MISTAKE?
HOW BRAZEN.
I WILL KEEP MY PROMISE.
VERY WELL.
I SHALL LEND YOU 2,000 SOLDIERS.
MAKE SURE YOU BRING ALL THE CHILDREN, LEAVING NONE BEHIND, TO ME.
IF YOU FAIL...
...YOUR MEAT WILL BE ON MY SILVER PLATTER.
UNDER-STOOD?

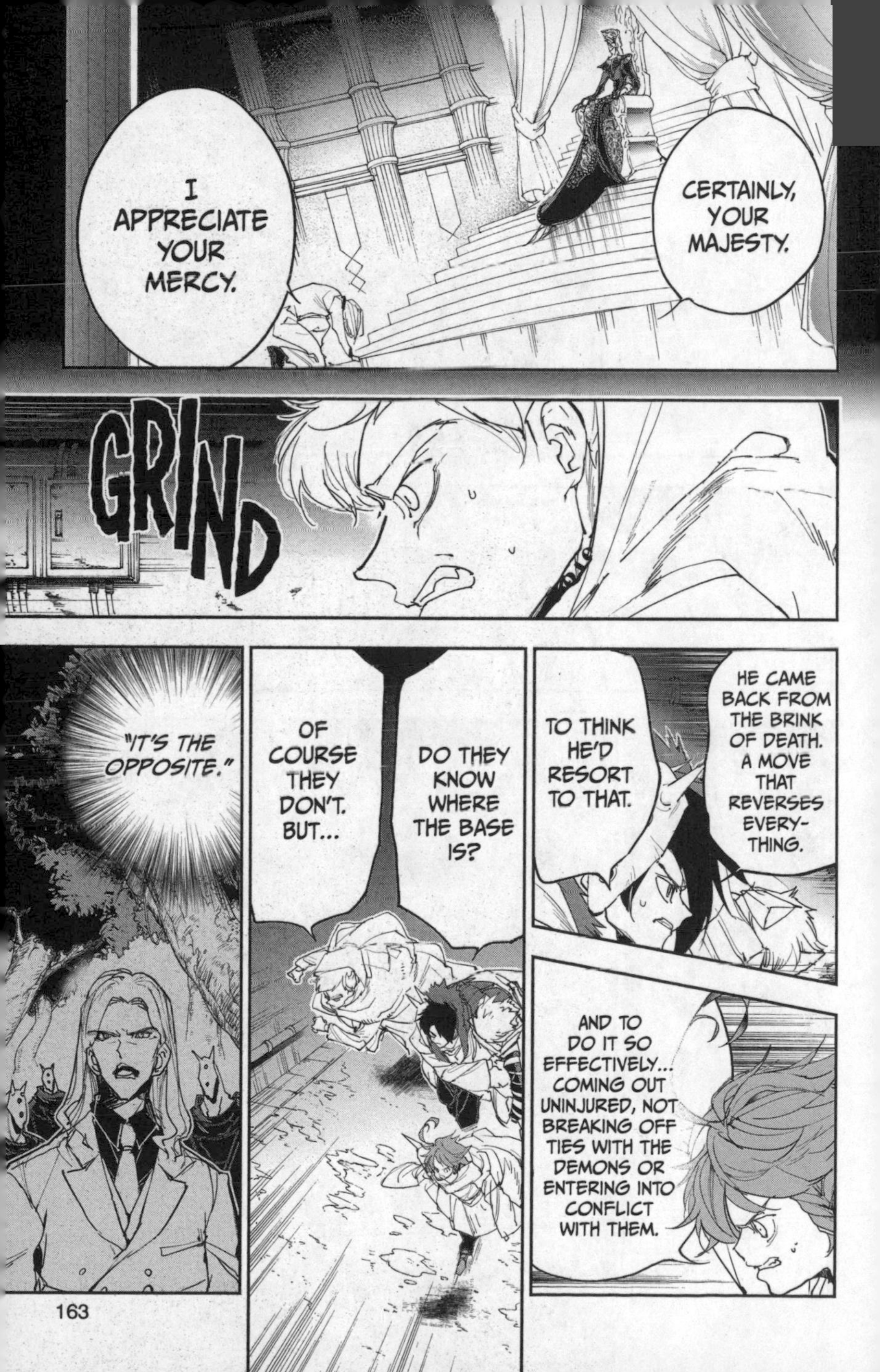
CERTAINLY, YOUR MAJESTY.
I APPRECIATE YOUR MERCY.
GRIND
HE CAME BACK FROM THE BRINK OF DEATH. A MOVE THAT REVERSES EVERYTHING.
TO THINK HE'D RESORT TO THAT.
AND TO DO IT SO EFFECTIVELY... COMING OUT UNINJURED, NOT BREAKING OFF TIES WITH THE DEMONS OR ENTERING INTO CONFLICT WITH THEM.
DO THEY KNOW WHERE THE BASE IS?
OF COURSE THEY DON'T. BUT...
"IT'S THE OPPOSITE."

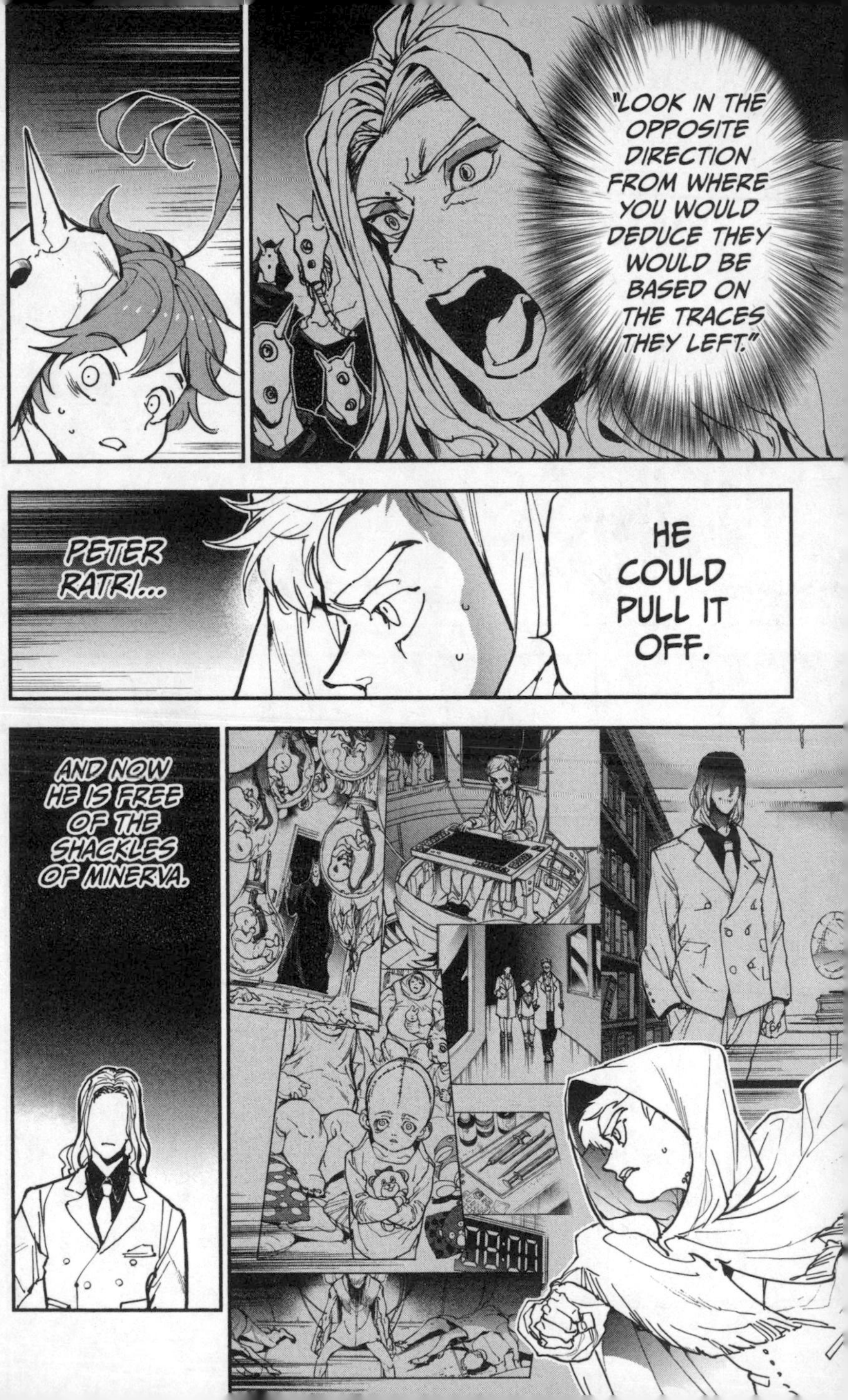
"LOOK IN THE OPPOSITE DIRECTION FROM WHERE YOU WOULD DEDUCE THEY WOULD BE BASED ON THE TRACES THEY LEFT."
HE COULD PULL IT OFF.
PETER RATRI...
AND NOW HE IS FREE OF THE SHACKLES OF MINERVA.

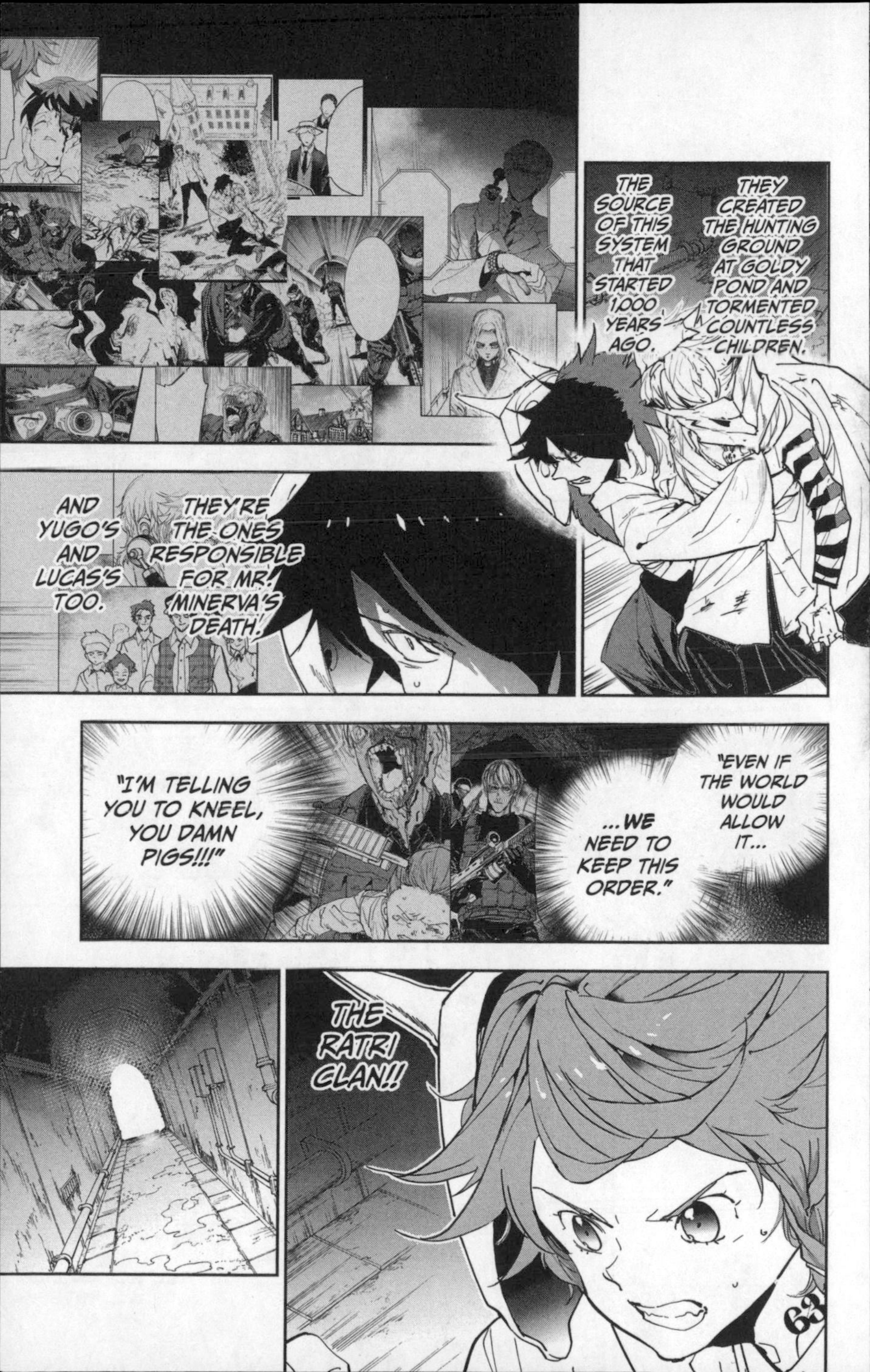
THEY CREATED THE HUNTING GROUND AT GOLDY POND AND TORMENTED COUNTLESS CHILDREN.
THE SOURCE OF THIS SYSTEM THAT STARTED 1,000 YEARS AGO.
THEY'RE THE ONES RESPONSIBLE FOR MR. MINERVA'S DEATH.
AND YUGO'S AND LUCAS'S TOO.
"EVEN IF THE WORLD WOULD ALLOW IT...
...WE NEED TO KEEP THIS ORDER."
"I'M TELLING YOU TO KNEEL, YOU DAMN PIGS!!!"
THE RATRI CLAN!!
63

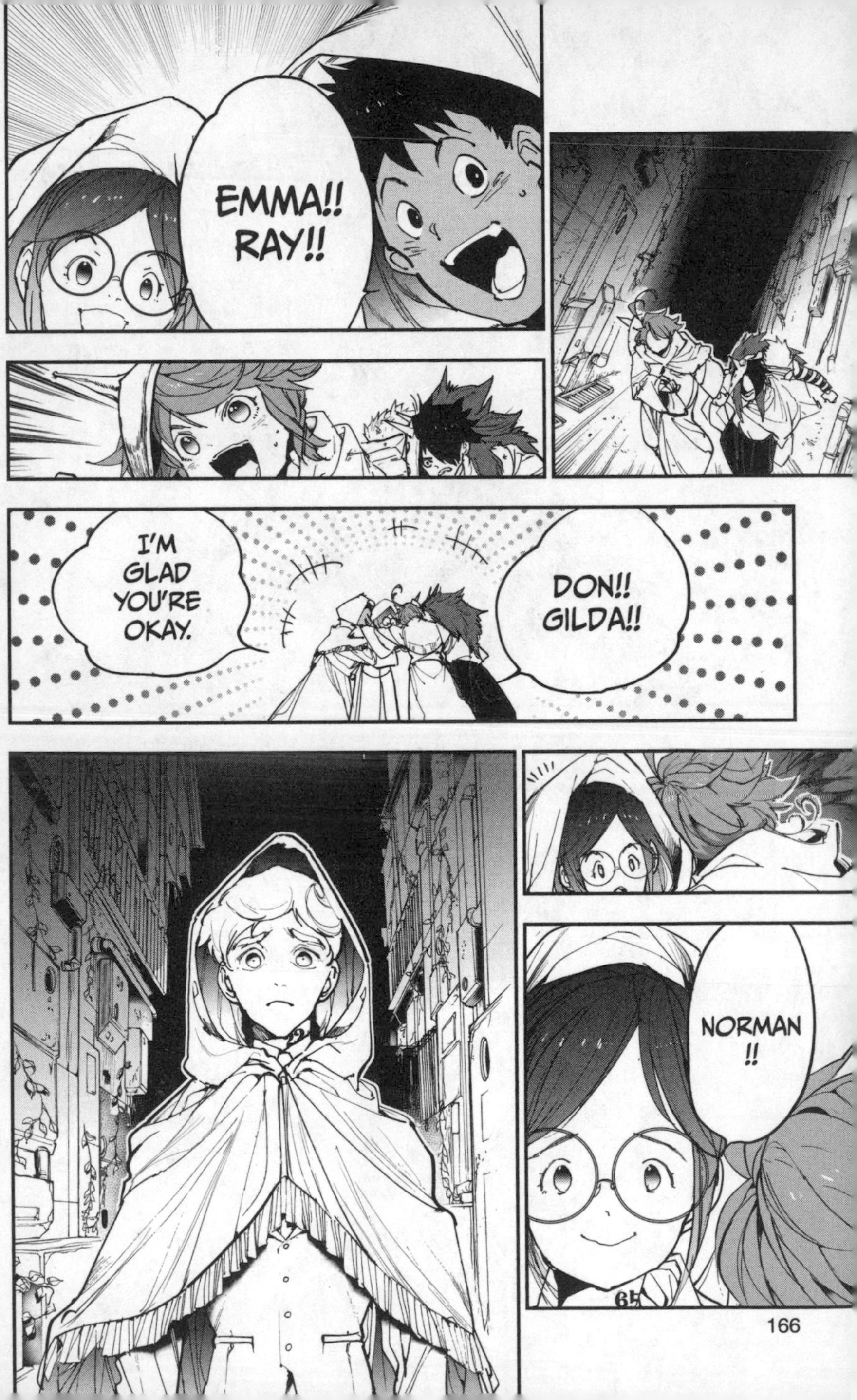
EMMA!! RAY!!
DON!! GILDA!!
I'M GLAD YOU'RE OKAY.
NORMAN!!
65

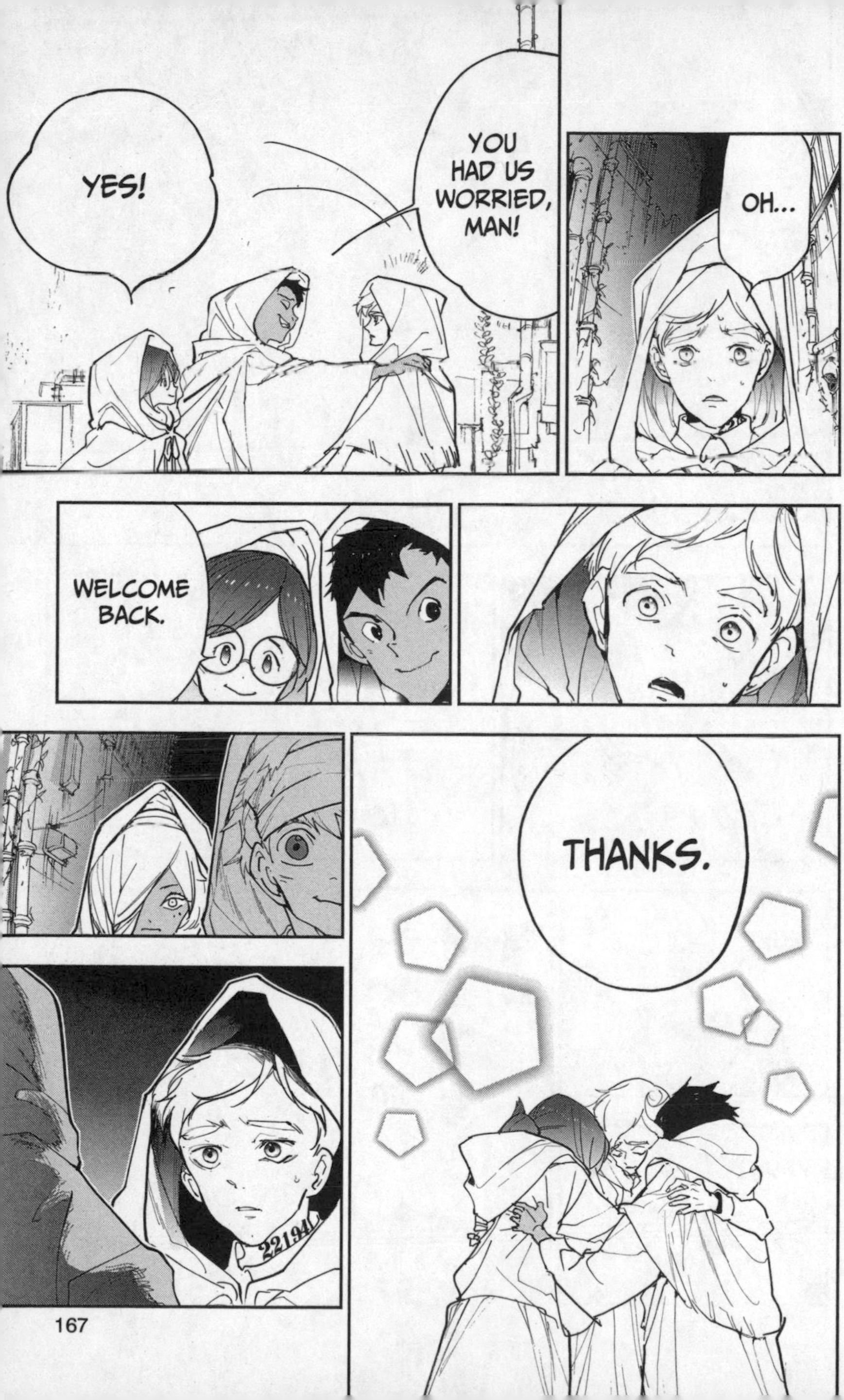
OH...
YOU HAD US WORRIED, MAN!
YES!
WELCOME BACK.
THANKS.

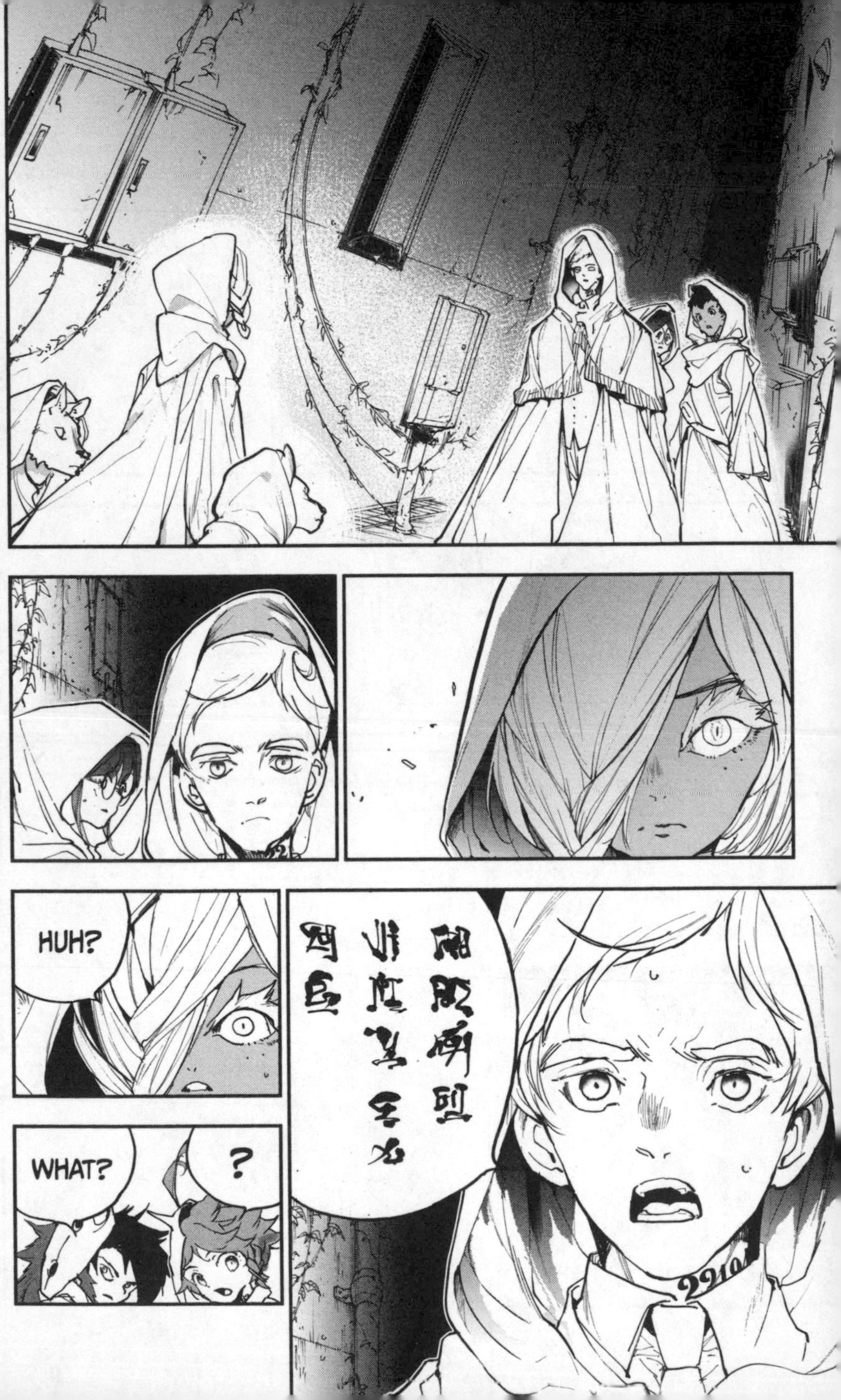
HUH?
WHAT?
?

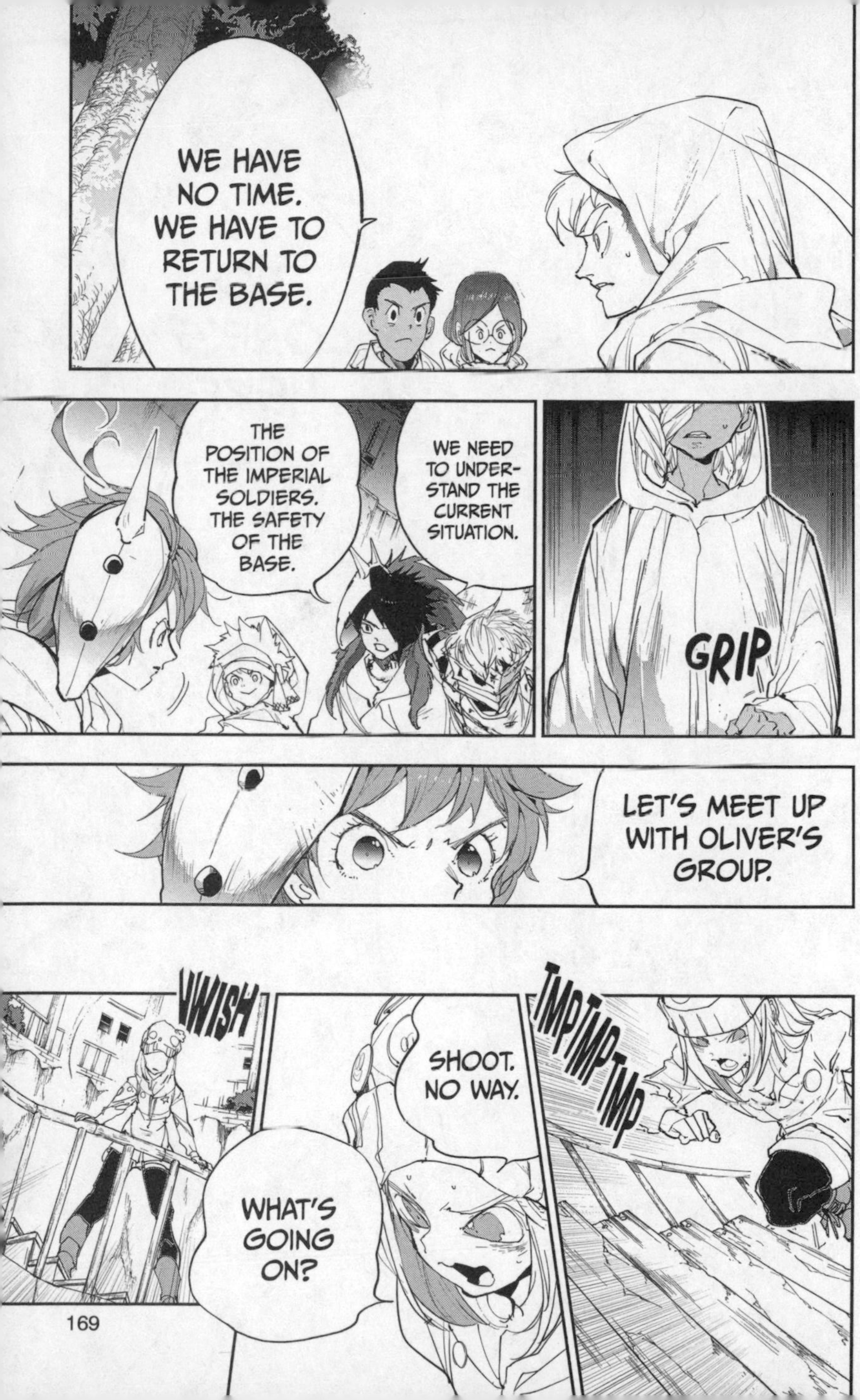
WE HAVE NO TIME. WE HAVE TO RETURN TO THE BASE.
GRIP
WE NEED TO UNDER-STAND THE CURRENT SITUATION.
THE POSITION OF THE IMPERIAL SOLDIERS. THE SAFETY OF THE BASE.
LET'S MEET UP WITH OLIVER'S GROUP.
TMP TMP TMP TMP
SHOOT. NO WAY.
WHAT'S GOING ON?
VWISH

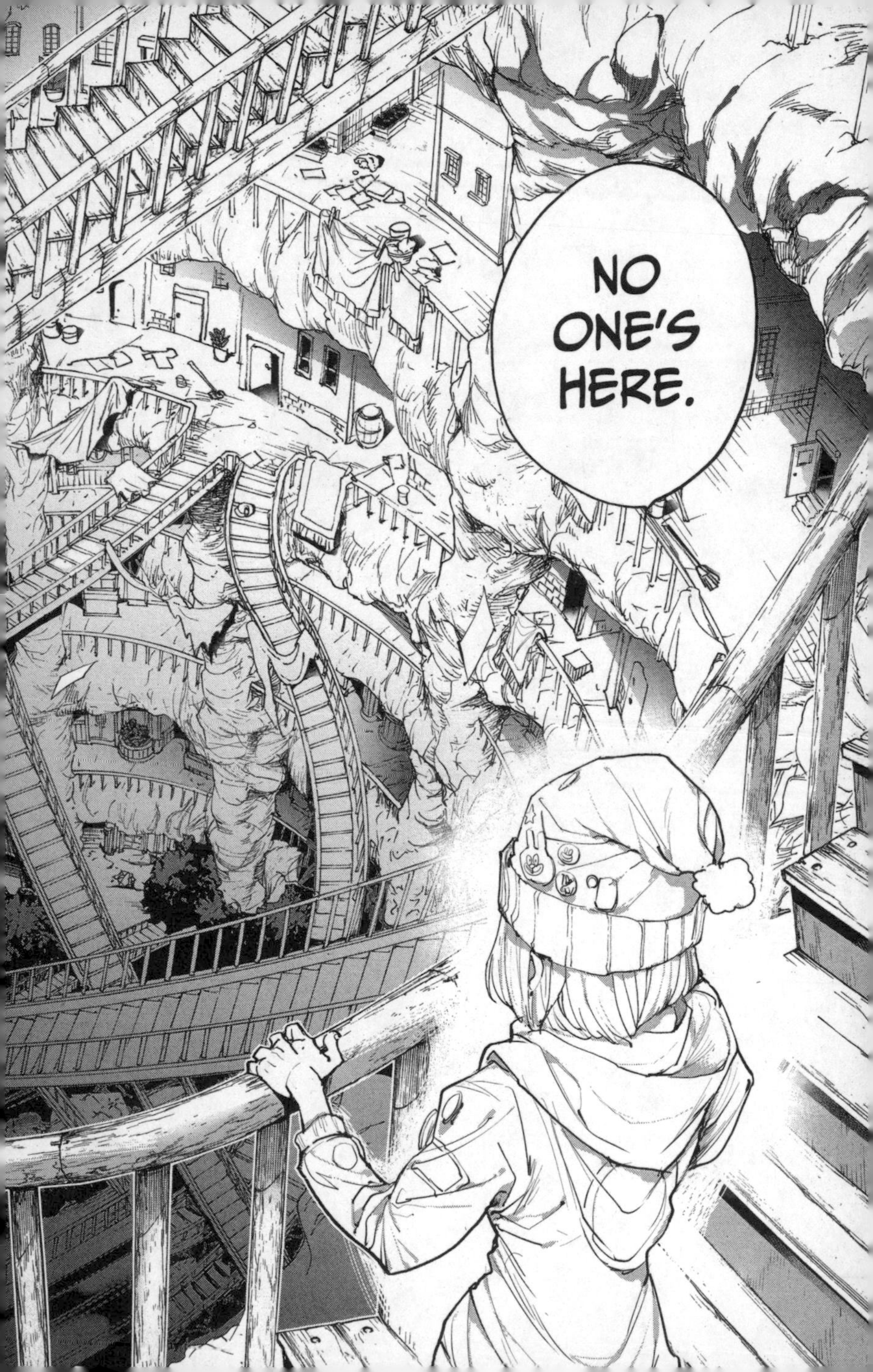
NO ONE'S HERE.

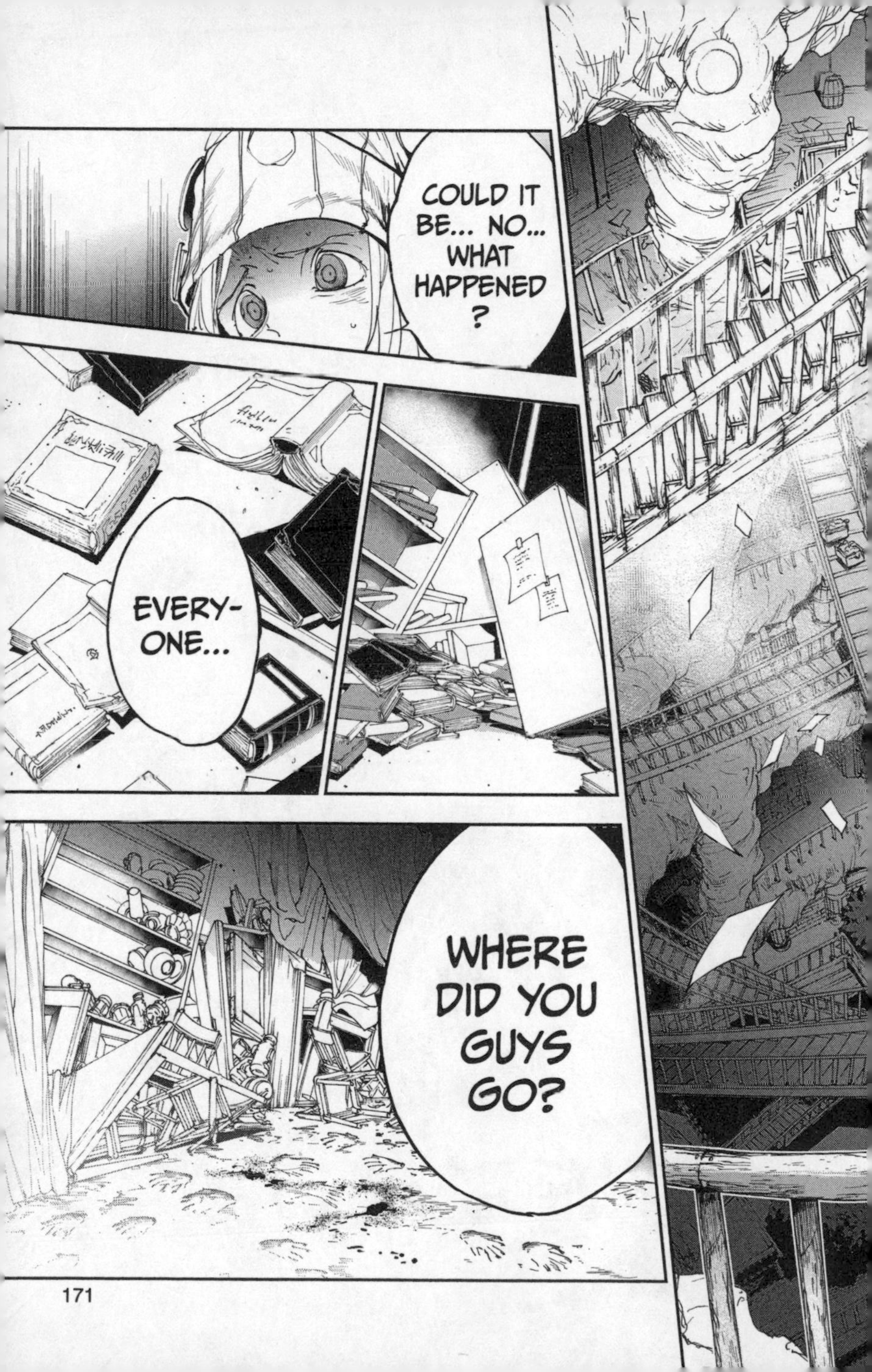
COULD IT BE... NO... WHAT HAPPENED?
EVERY-ONE...
WHERE DID YOU GUYS GO?

THE QUEEN'S HOBBY

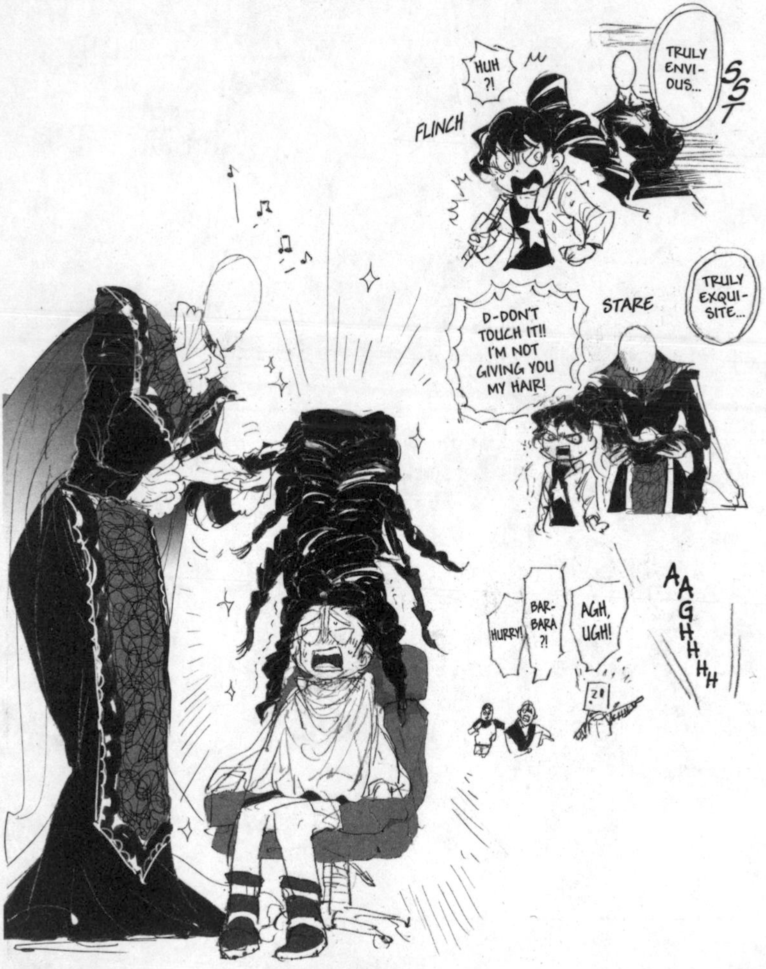
TRULY ENVI-OUS...
SST
HUH ?!
FLINCH
TRULY EXQUI-SITE...
STARE
D-DON'T TOUCH IT!! I'M NOT GIVING YOU MY HAIR!
AAGHHHH
AGH, UGH!
BAR-BARA ?!
HURRY!

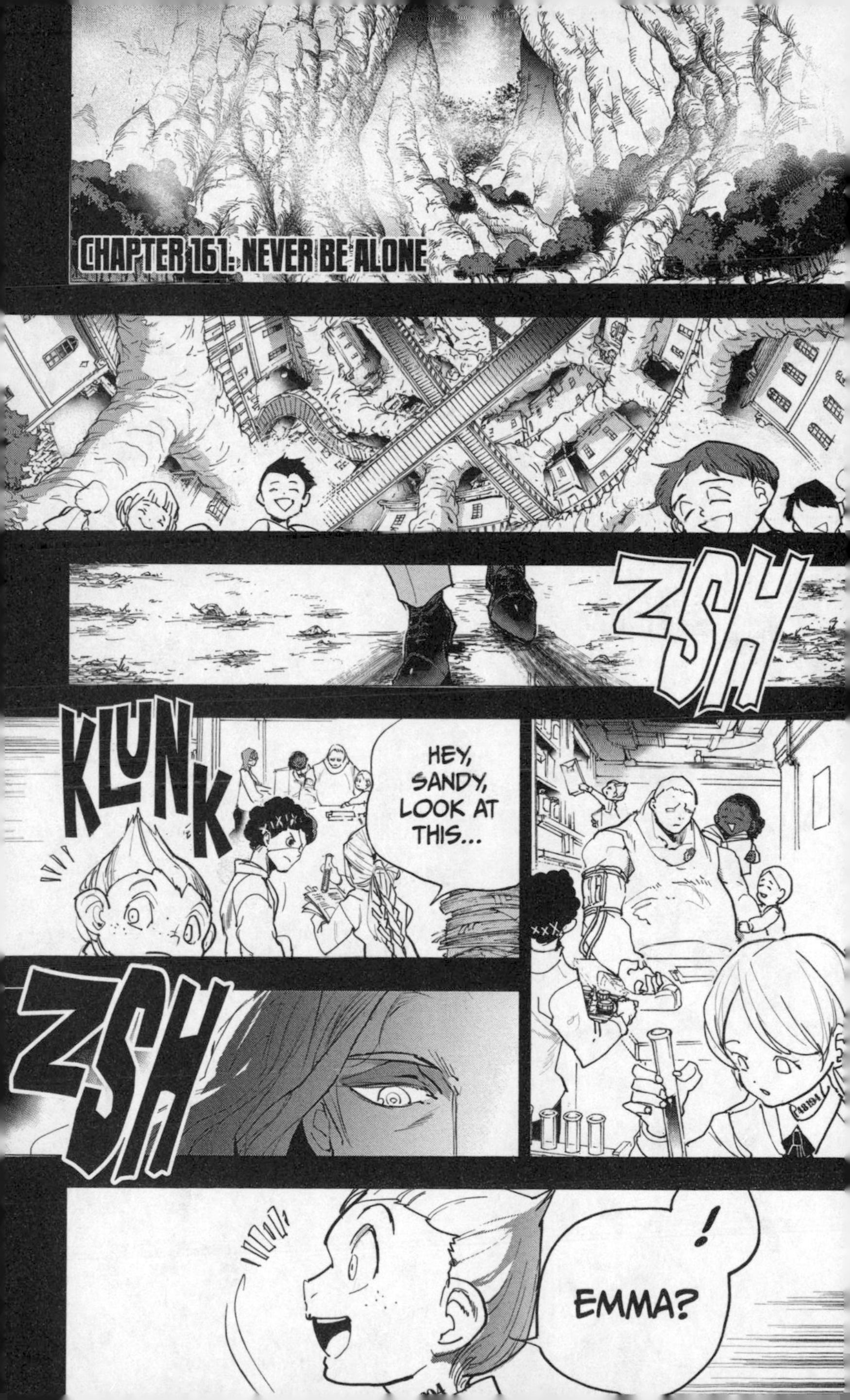
CHAPTER 161: NEVER BE ALONE
ZSH
KLUNK
HEY, SANDY, LOOK AT THIS...
ZSH
!
EMMA?

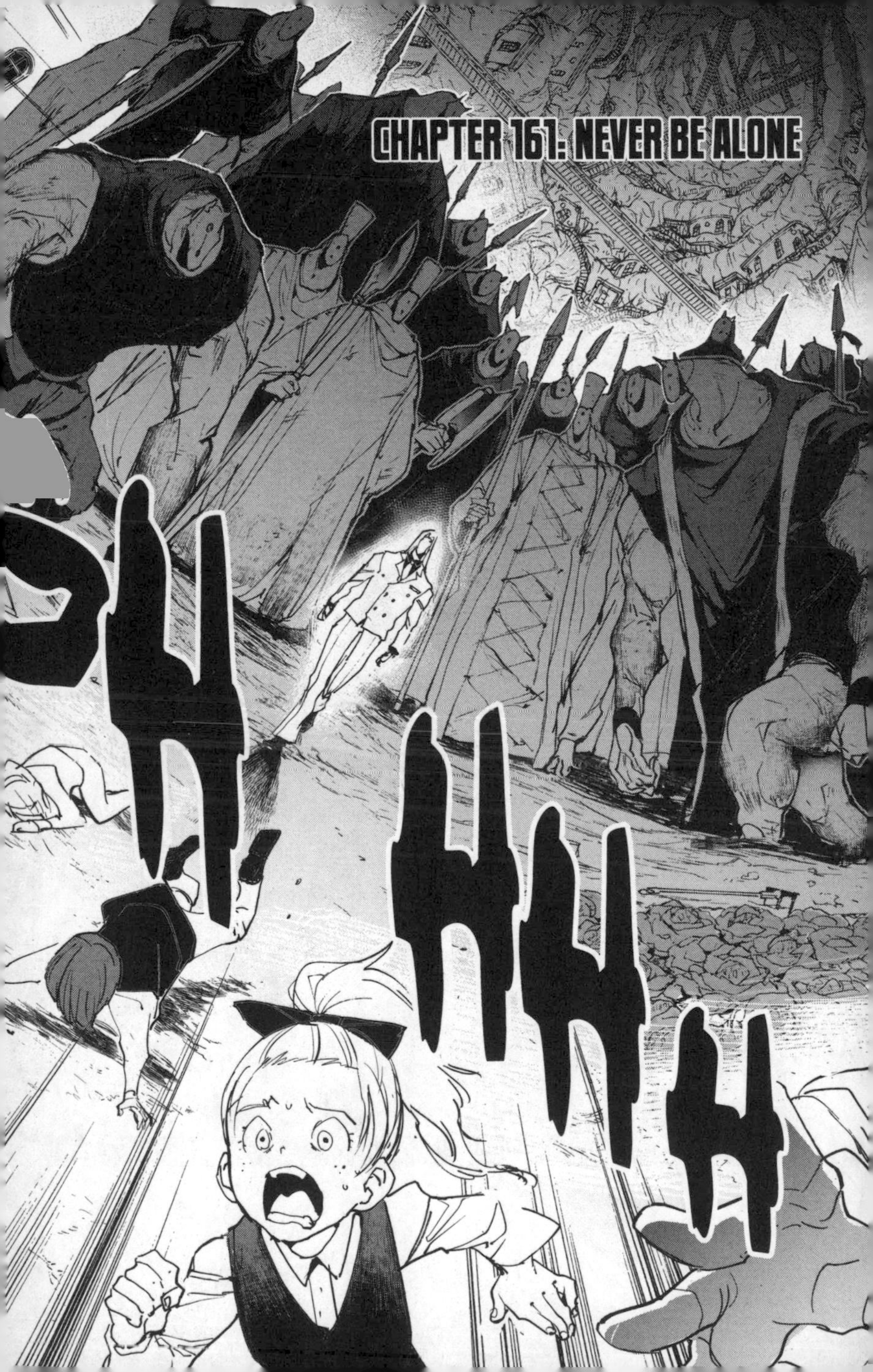
CHAPTER 161: NEVER BE ALONE

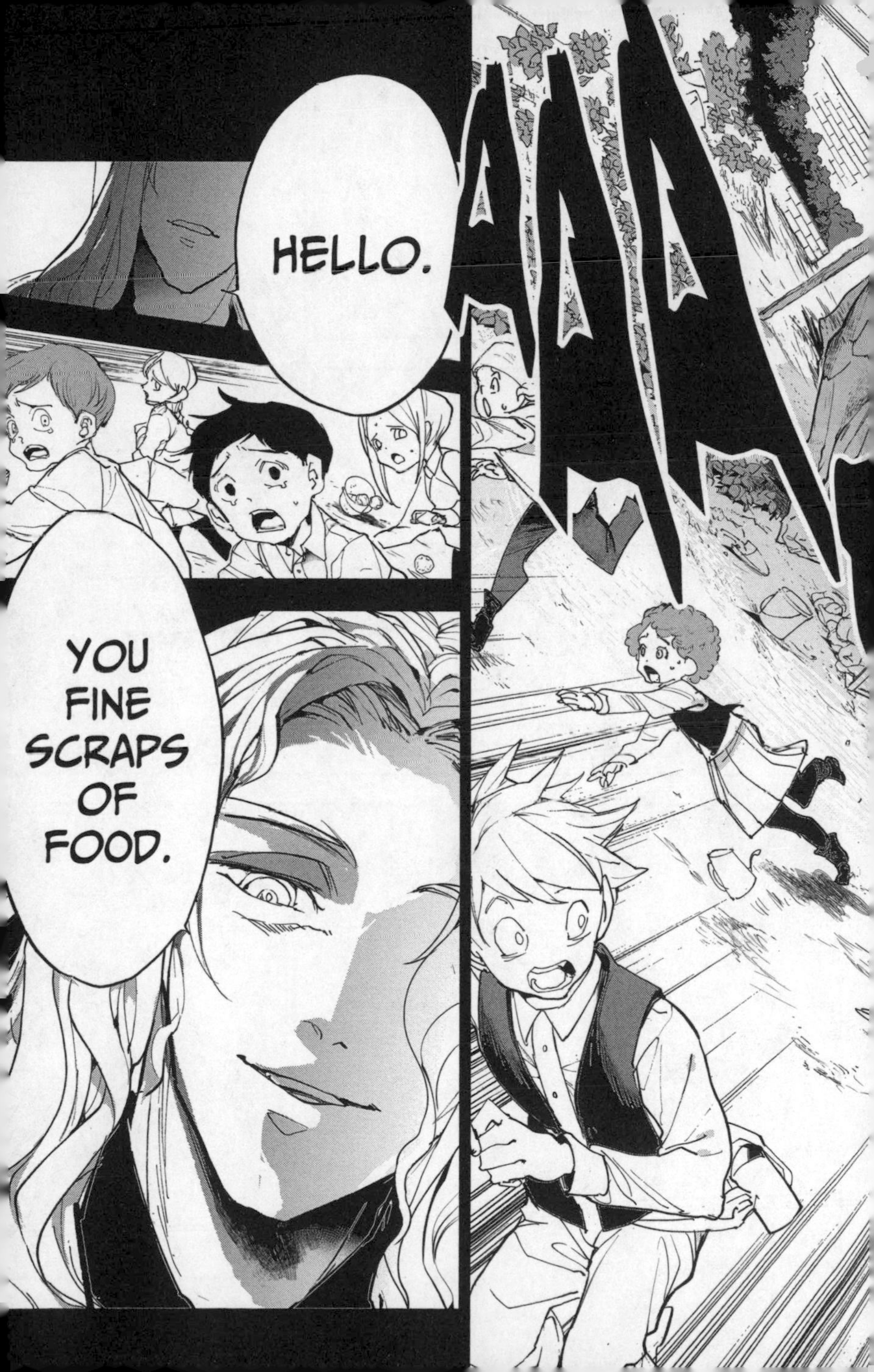
HELLO.
YOU FINE SCRAPS OF FOOD.

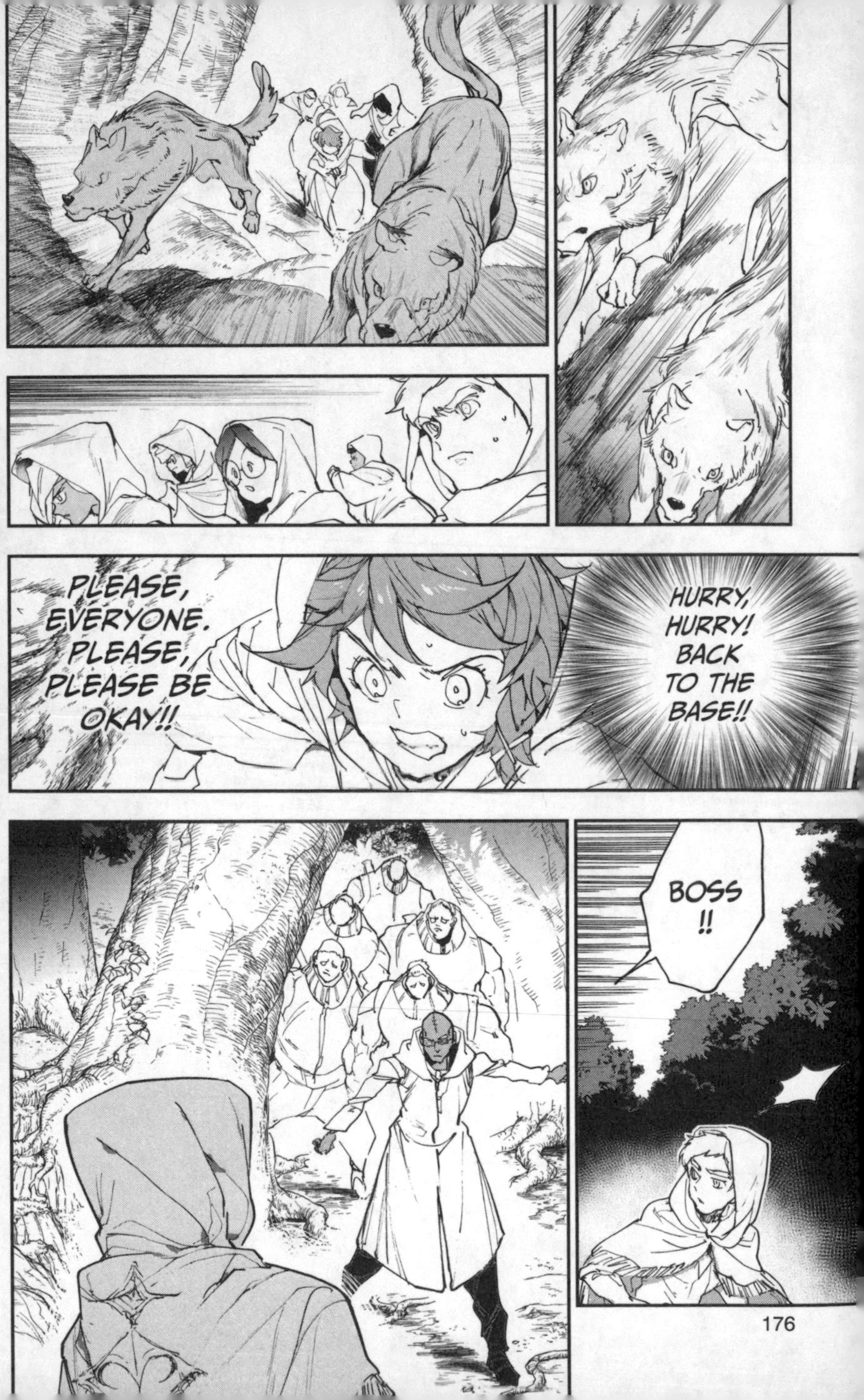
HURRY, HURRY! BACK TO THE BASE!!
PLEASE, EVERYONE. PLEASE, PLEASE BE OKAY!!
BOSS !!

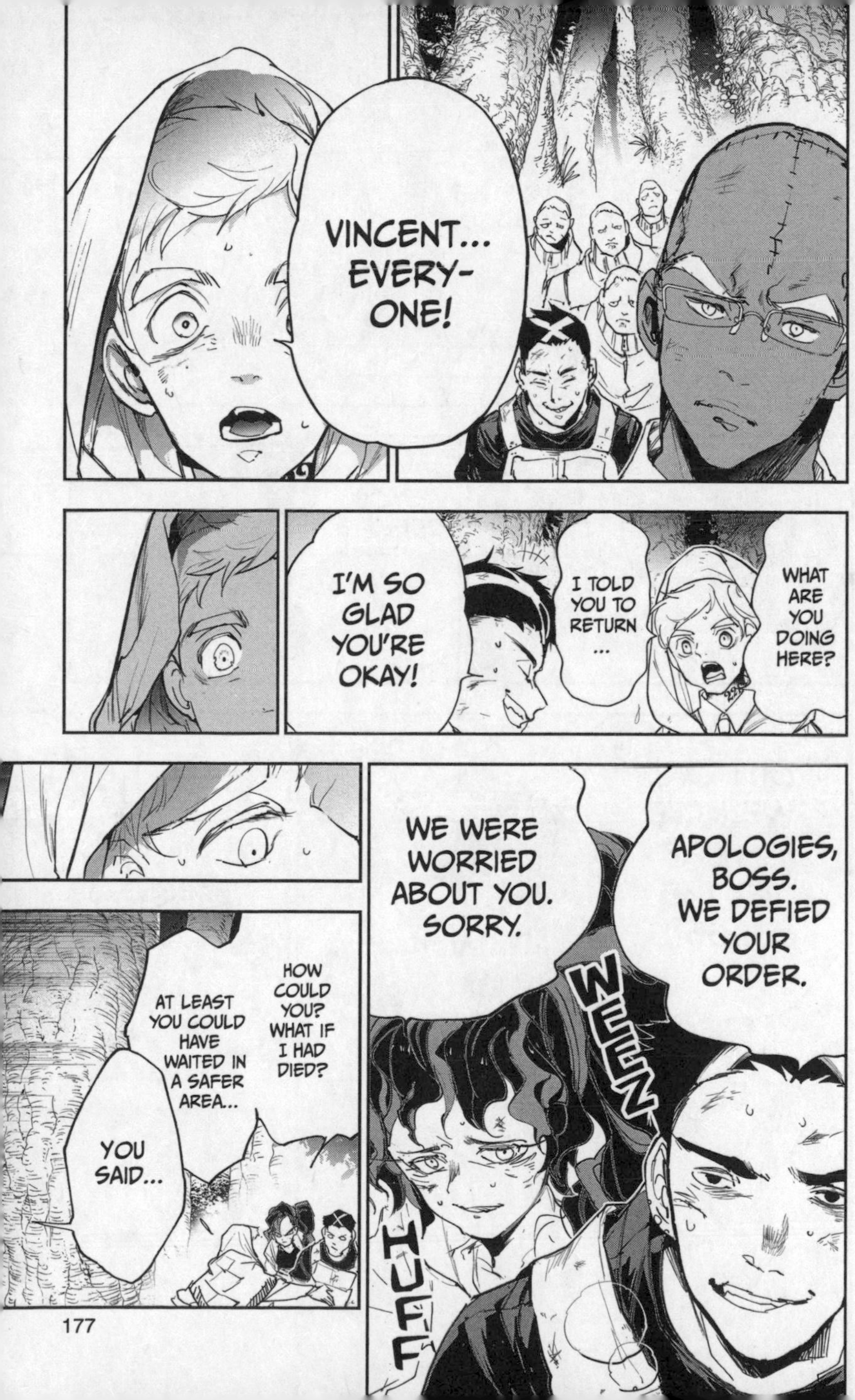
VINCENT... EVERY-ONE!
WHAT ARE YOU DOING HERE?
I TOLD YOU TO RETURN ...
I'M SO GLAD YOU'RE OKAY!
APOLOGIES, BOSS. WE DEFIED YOUR ORDER.
WE WERE WORRIED ABOUT YOU. SORRY.
WEEN
HUFF
HOW COULD YOU? WHAT IF I HAD DIED?
AT LEAST YOU COULD HAVE WAITED IN A SAFER AREA...
YOU SAID...

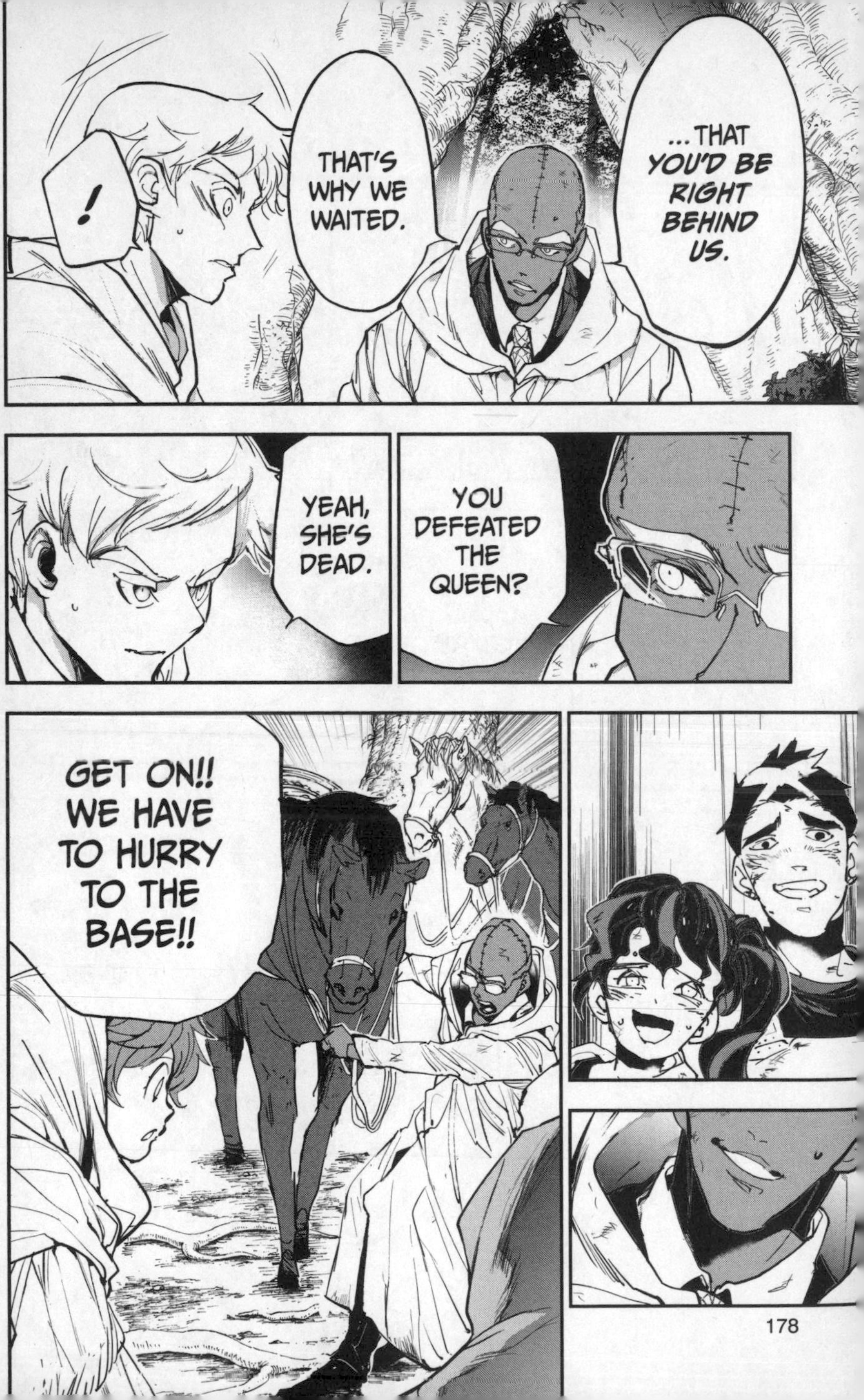
...THAT YOU'D BE RIGHT BEHIND US.
THAT'S WHY WE WAITED.
!
YOU DEFEATED THE QUEEN?
YEAH, SHE'S DEAD.
GET ON!! WE HAVE TO HURRY TO THE BASE!!

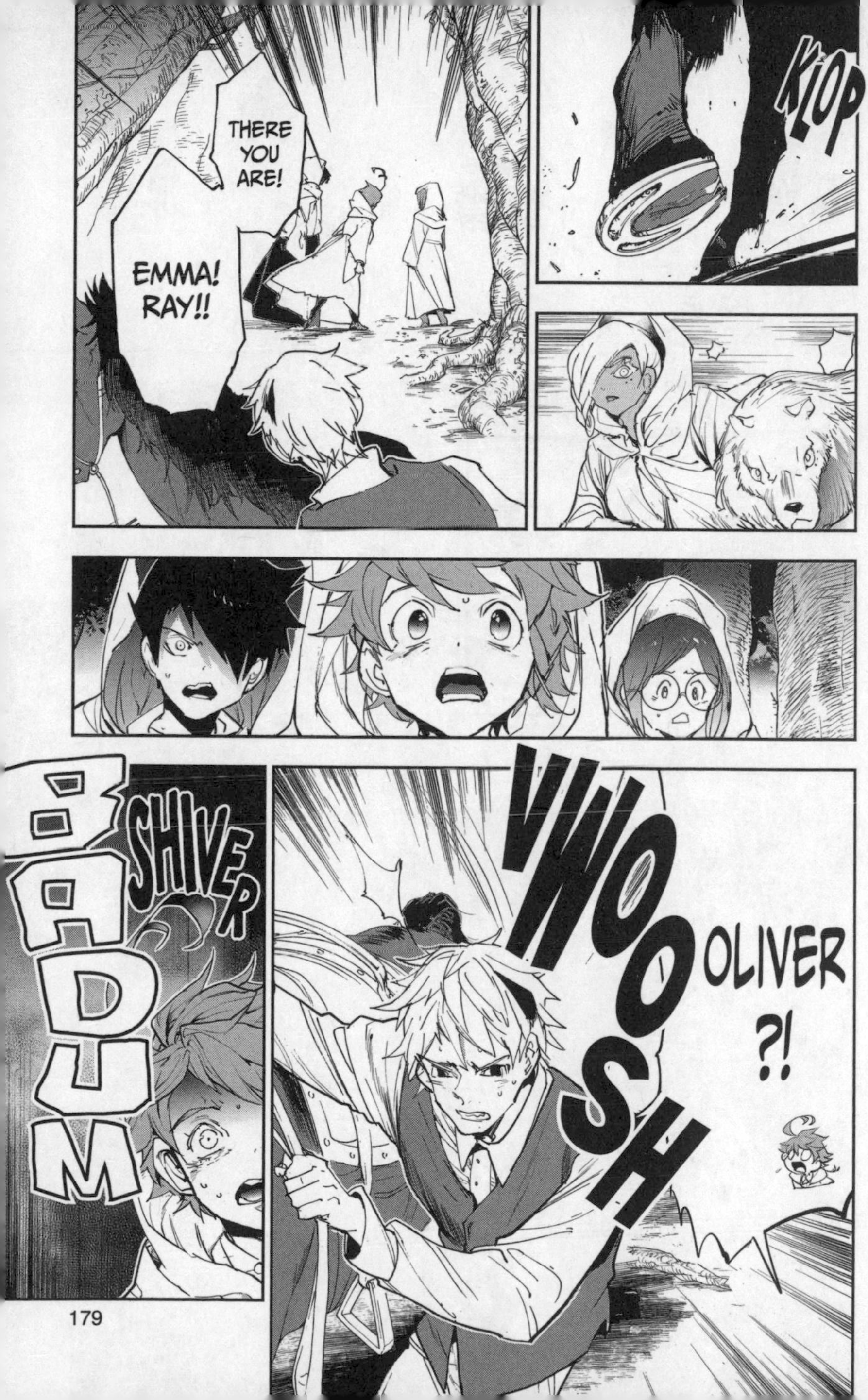
KLOP
THERE YOU ARE!
EMMA! RAY!!
WHOOSH
OLIVER ?!
BADUM
SHIVER

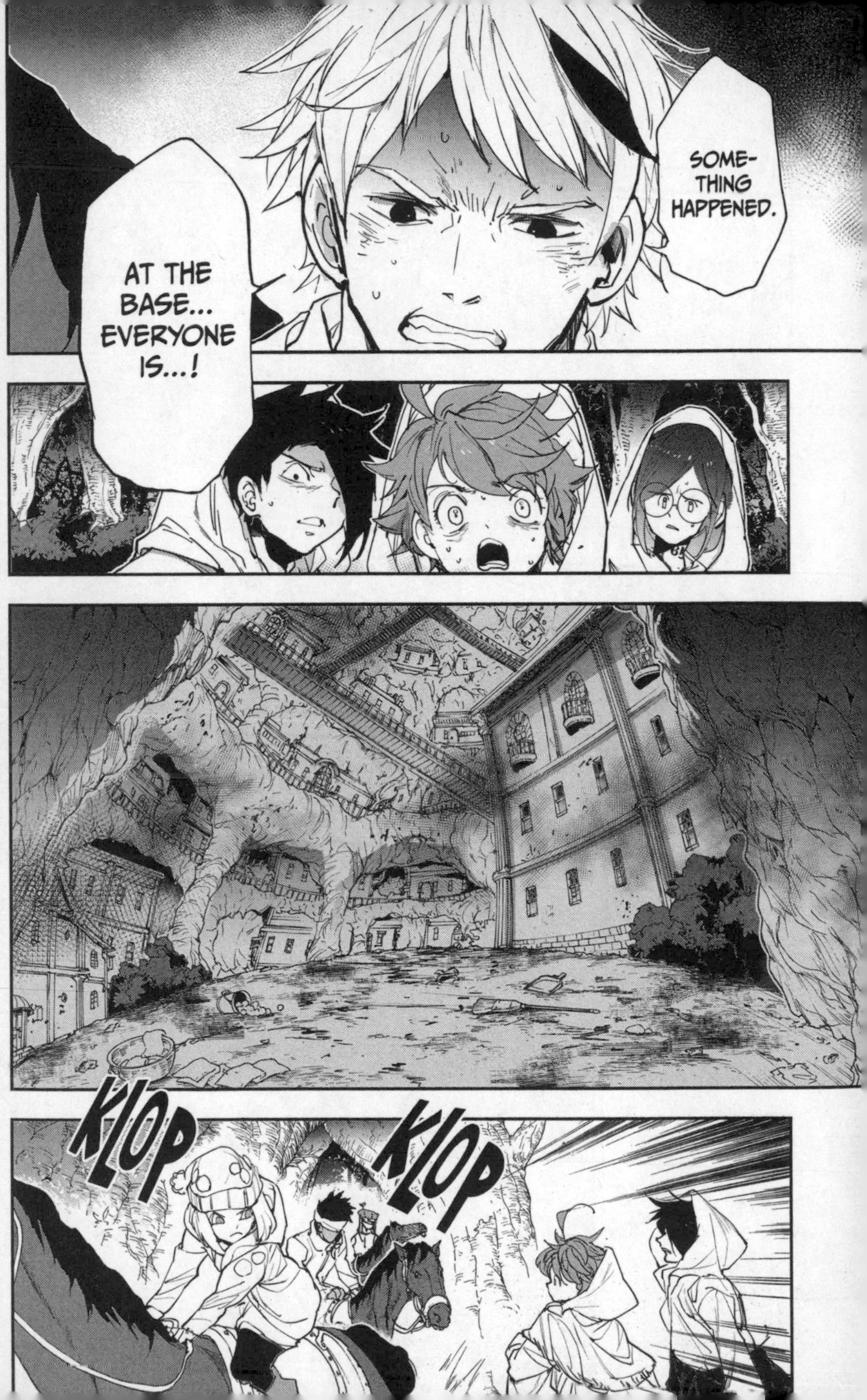
SOME-
THING
HAPPENED.
AT THE
BASE...
EVERYONE
IS...!
KLOP
KLOP

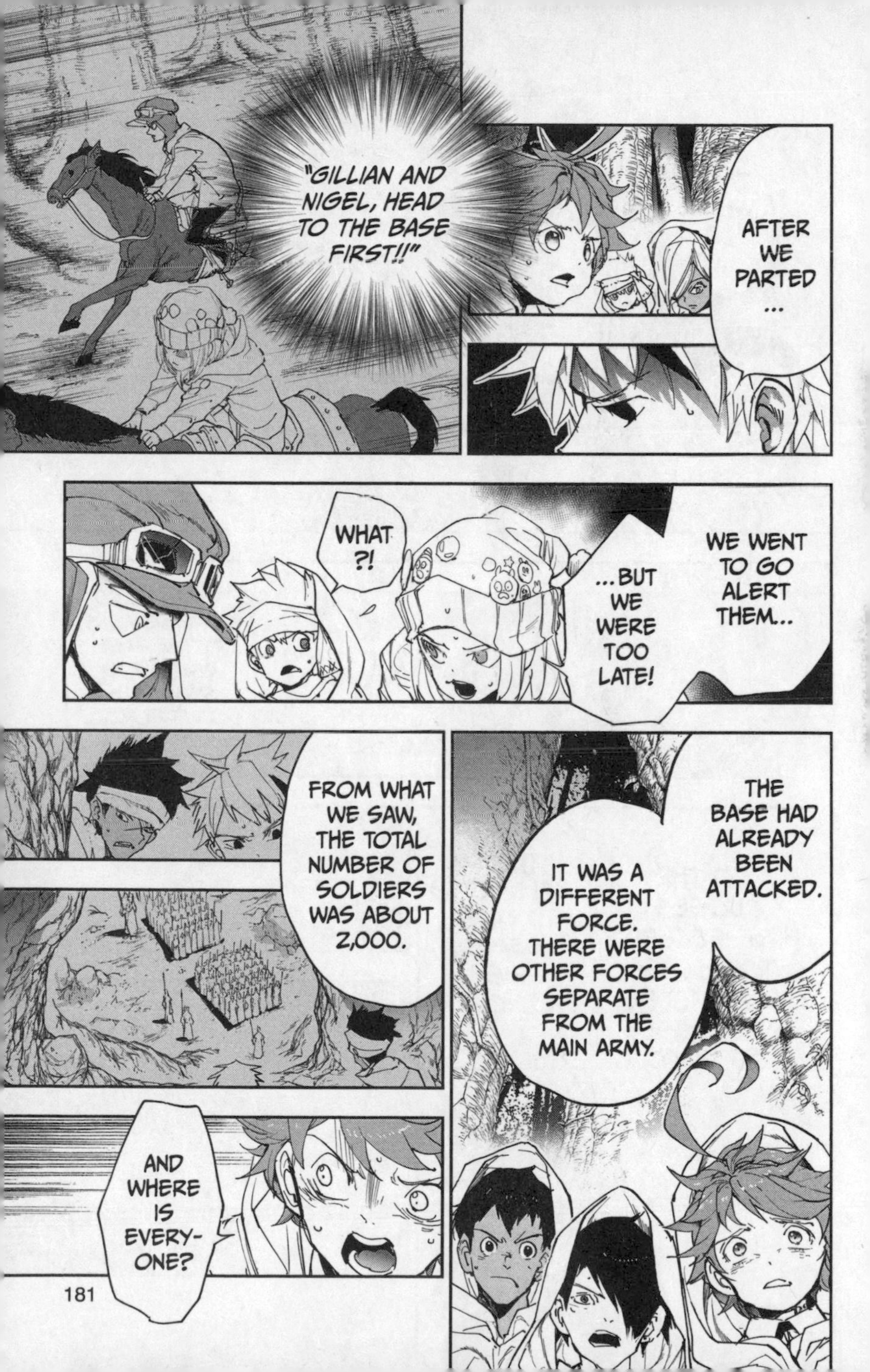
AFTER WE PARTED ...
"GILLIAN AND NIGEL, HEAD TO THE BASE FIRST!!"
WE WENT TO GO ALERT THEM...
...BUT WE WERE TOO LATE!
WHAT ?!
THE BASE HAD ALREADY BEEN ATTACKED.
IT WAS A DIFFERENT FORCE. THERE WERE OTHER FORCES SEPARATE FROM THE MAIN ARMY.
FROM WHAT WE SAW, THE TOTAL NUMBER OF SOLDIERS WAS ABOUT 2,000.
AND WHERE IS EVERY-ONE?

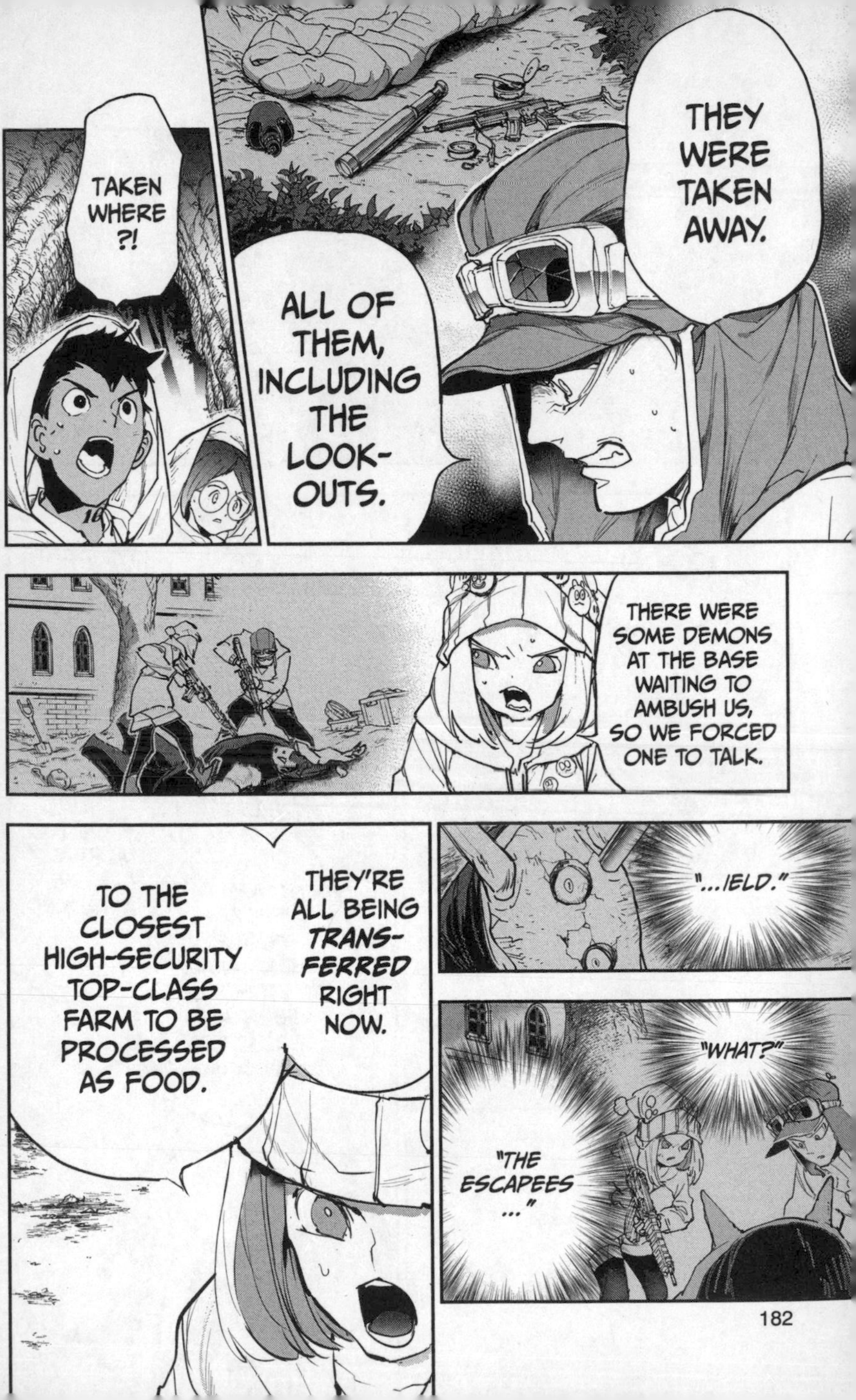
THEY WERE TAKEN AWAY.
ALL OF THEM, INCLUDING THE LOOK-OUTS.
TAKEN WHERE?!
THERE WERE SOME DEMONS AT THE BASE WAITING TO AMBUSH US, SO WE FORCED ONE TO TALK.
"...IELD."
"WHAT?"
"THE ESCAPEES ..."
THEY'RE ALL BEING *TRANSFERRED* RIGHT NOW.
TO THE CLOSEST HIGH-SECURITY TOP-CLASS FARM TO BE PROCESSED AS FOOD.

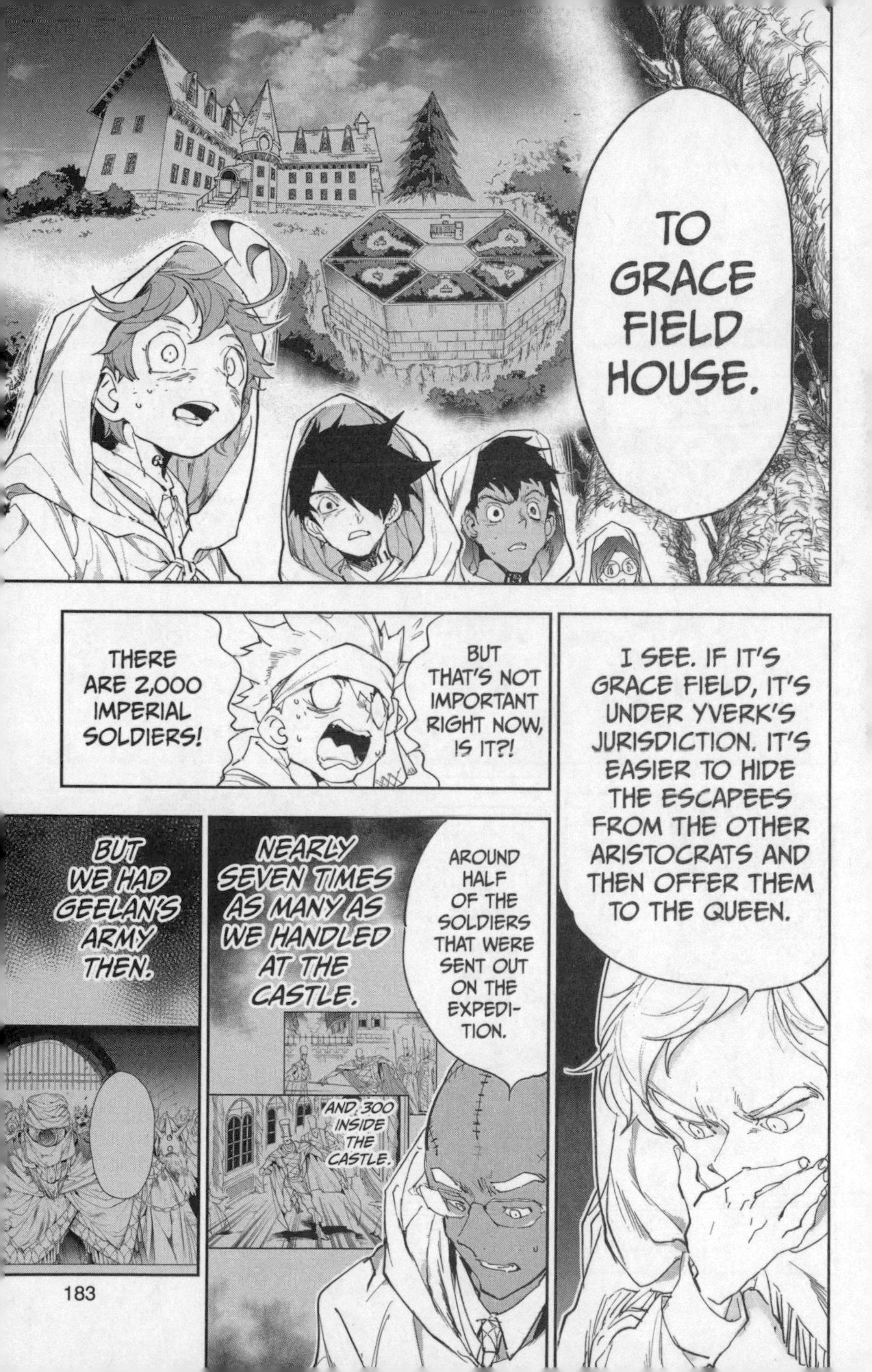
TO GRACE FIELD HOUSE.
I SEE. IF IT'S GRACE FIELD, IT'S UNDER YVERK'S JURISDICTION. IT'S EASIER TO HIDE THE ESCAPEES FROM THE OTHER ARISTOCRATS AND THEN OFFER THEM TO THE QUEEN.
BUT THAT'S NOT IMPORTANT RIGHT NOW, IS IT?!
THERE ARE 2,000 IMPERIAL SOLDIERS!
AROUND HALF OF THE SOLDIERS THAT WERE SENT OUT ON THE EXPEDITION.
NEARLY SEVEN TIMES AS MANY AS WE HANDLED AT THE CASTLE.
AND 300 INSIDE THE CASTLE.
BUT WE HAD GEELAN'S ARMY THEN.

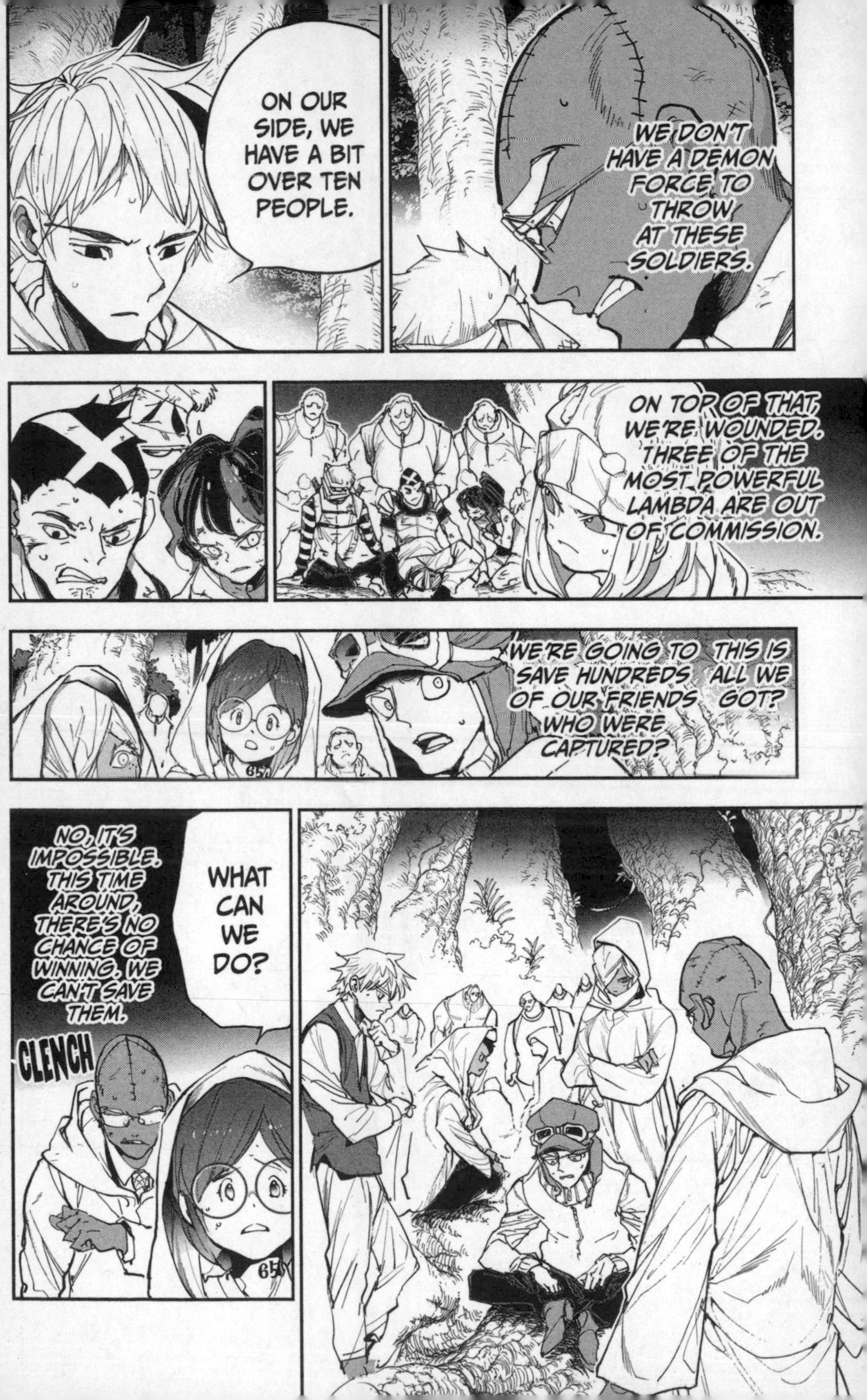
WE DON'T HAVE A DEMON FORCE TO THROW AT THESE SOLDIERS.
ON OUR SIDE, WE HAVE A BIT OVER TEN PEOPLE.
ON TOP OF THAT, WE'RE WOUNDED. THREE OF THE MOST POWERFUL LAMBDA ARE OUT OF COMMISSION.
THIS IS ALL WE GOT?
WE'RE GOING TO SAVE HUNDREDS OF OUR FRIENDS WHO WERE CAPTURED?
WHAT CAN WE DO?
NO, IT'S IMPOSSIBLE. THIS TIME AROUND, THERE'S NO CHANCE OF WINNING. WE CAN'T SAVE THEM.
CLENCH

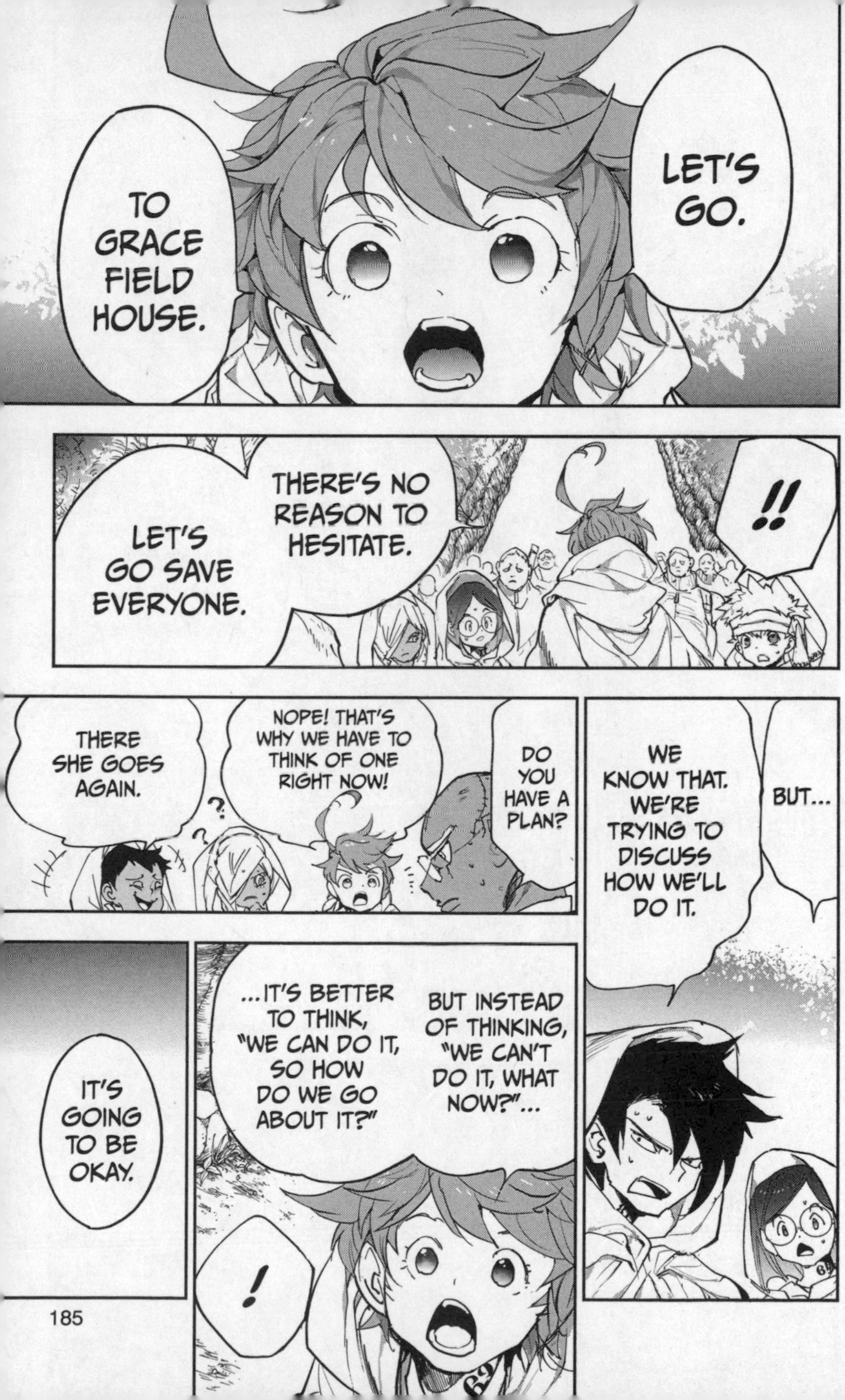
LET'S GO.
TO GRACE FIELD HOUSE.
!!
THERE'S NO REASON TO HESITATE.
LET'S GO SAVE EVERYONE.
BUT...
WE KNOW THAT. WE'RE TRYING TO DISCUSS HOW WE'LL DO IT.
DO YOU HAVE A PLAN?
NOPE! THAT'S WHY WE HAVE TO THINK OF ONE RIGHT NOW!
?
?
THERE SHE GOES AGAIN.
BUT INSTEAD OF THINKING, "WE CAN'T DO IT, WHAT NOW?"...
...IT'S BETTER TO THINK, "WE CAN DO IT, SO HOW DO WE GO ABOUT IT?"
!
IT'S GOING TO BE OKAY.

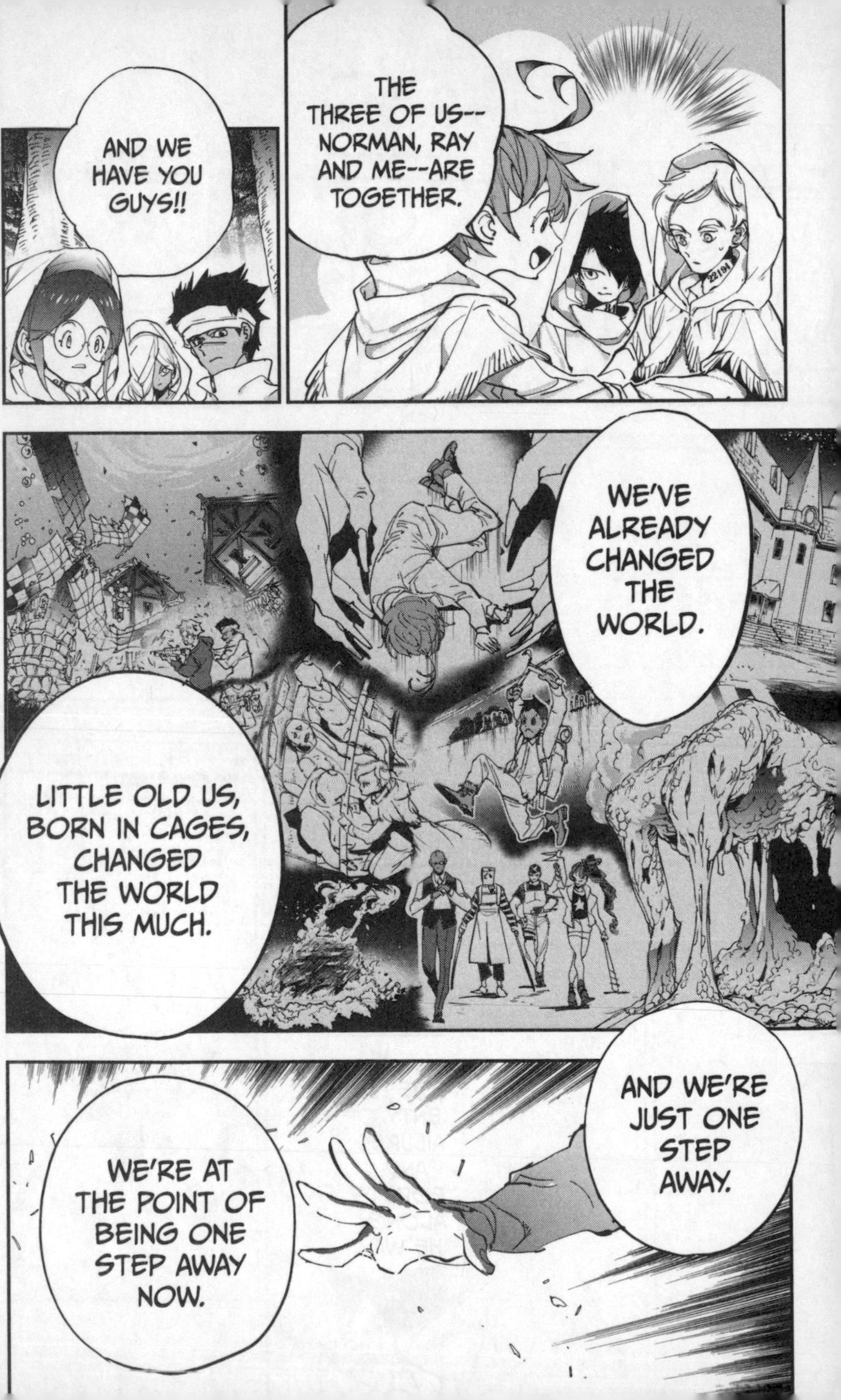
THE THREE OF US--NORMAN, RAY AND ME--ARE TOGETHER.
AND WE HAVE YOU GUYS!!
WE'VE ALREADY CHANGED THE WORLD.
LITTLE OLD US, BORN IN CAGES, CHANGED THE WORLD THIS MUCH.
AND WE'RE JUST ONE STEP AWAY.
WE'RE AT THE POINT OF BEING ONE STEP AWAY NOW.

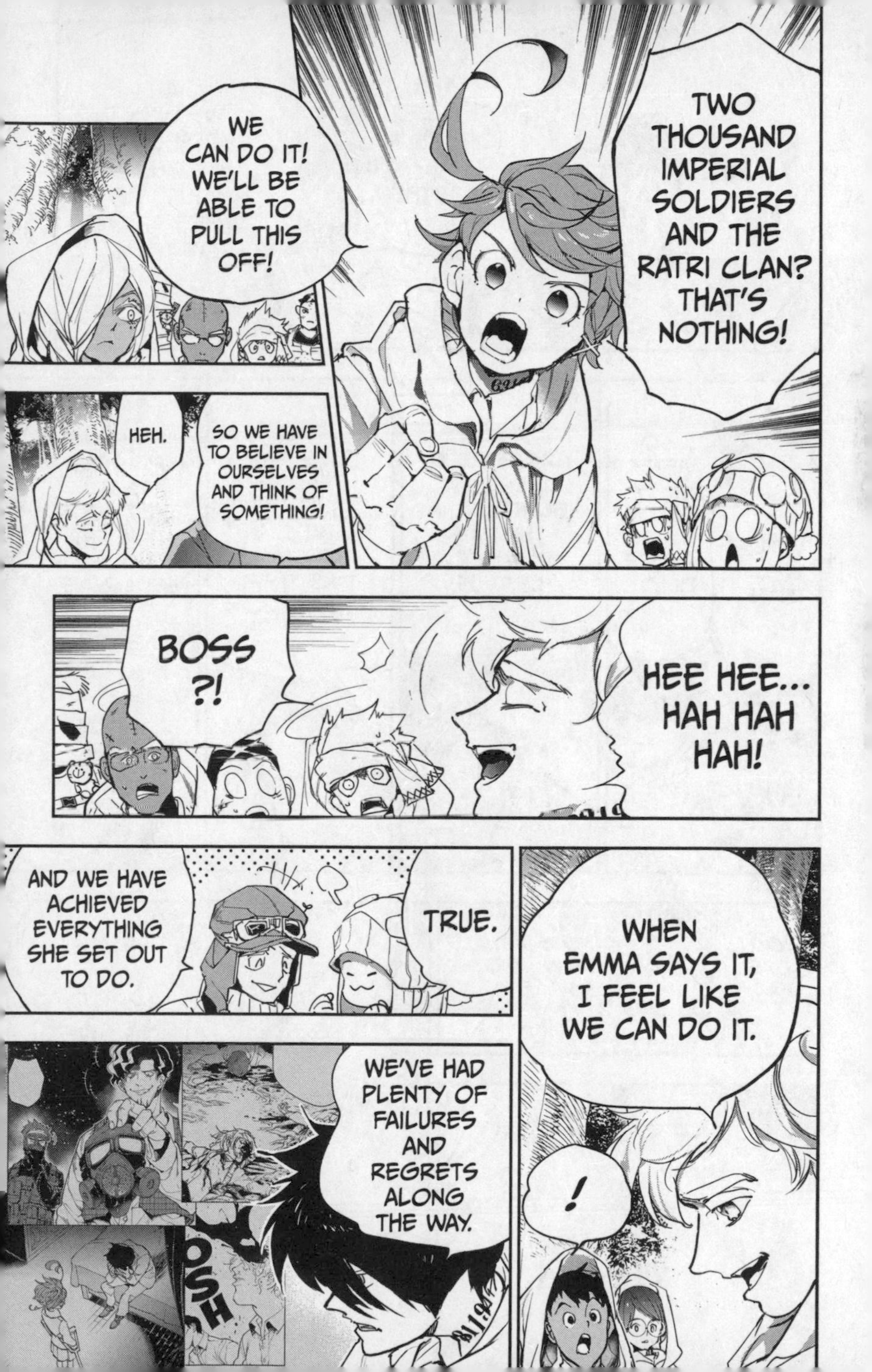
TWO THOUSAND IMPERIAL SOLDIERS AND THE RATRI CLAN? THAT'S NOTHING!
WE CAN DO IT! WE'LL BE ABLE TO PULL THIS OFF!
SO WE HAVE TO BELIEVE IN OURSELVES AND THINK OF SOMETHING!
HEH.
HEE HEE... HAH HAH HAH!
BOSS ?!
WHEN EMMA SAYS IT, I FEEL LIKE WE CAN DO IT.
!
TRUE.
AND WE HAVE ACHIEVED EVERYTHING SHE SET OUT TO DO.
WE'VE HAD PLENTY OF FAILURES AND REGRETS ALONG THE WAY.

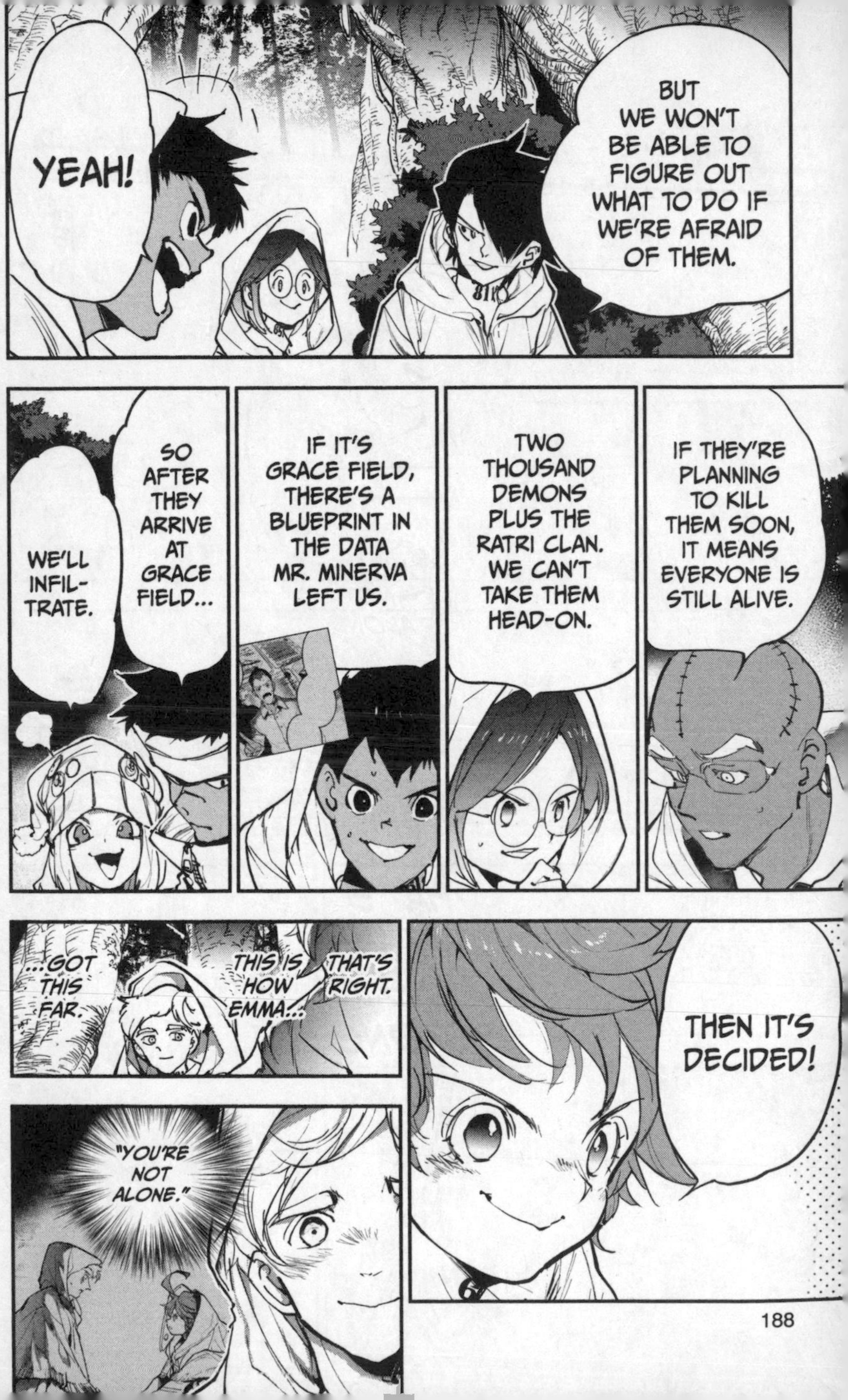
BUT WE WON'T BE ABLE TO FIGURE OUT WHAT TO DO IF WE'RE AFRAID OF THEM.
YEAH!
IF THEY'RE PLANNING TO KILL THEM SOON, IT MEANS EVERYONE IS STILL ALIVE.
TWO THOUSAND DEMONS PLUS THE RATRI CLAN. WE CAN'T TAKE THEM HEAD-ON.
IF IT'S GRACE FIELD, THERE'S A BLUEPRINT IN THE DATA MR. MINERVA LEFT US.
SO AFTER THEY ARRIVE AT GRACE FIELD...
WE'LL INFIL-TRATE.
THEN IT'S DECIDED!
THAT'S RIGHT.
THIS IS HOW EMMA...
...GOT THIS FAR.
"YOU'RE NOT ALONE."

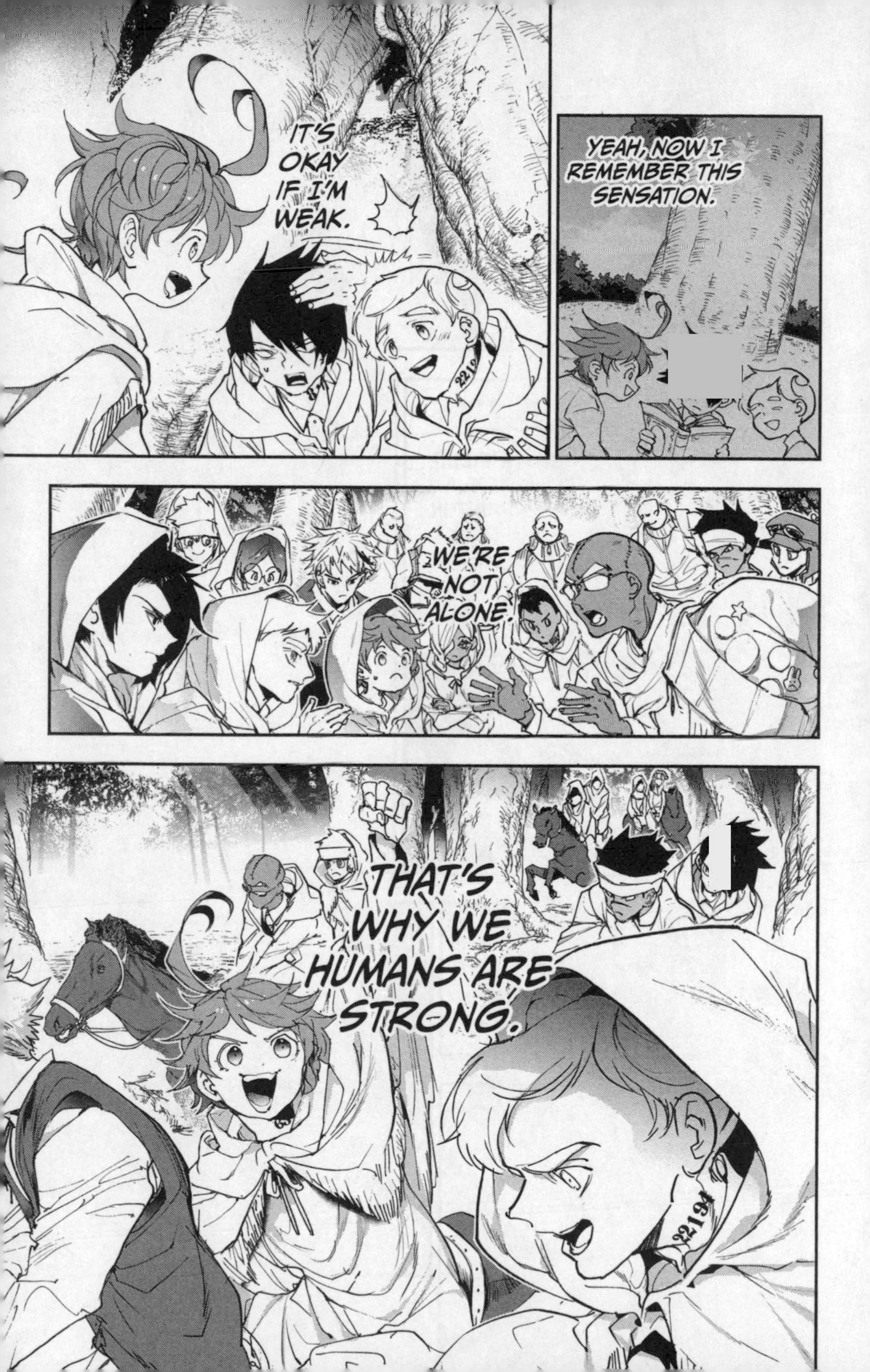
YEAH, NOW I REMEMBER THIS SENSATION.
IT'S OKAY IF I'M WEAK.
WE'RE NOT ALONE.
THAT'S WHY WE HUMANS ARE STRONG.

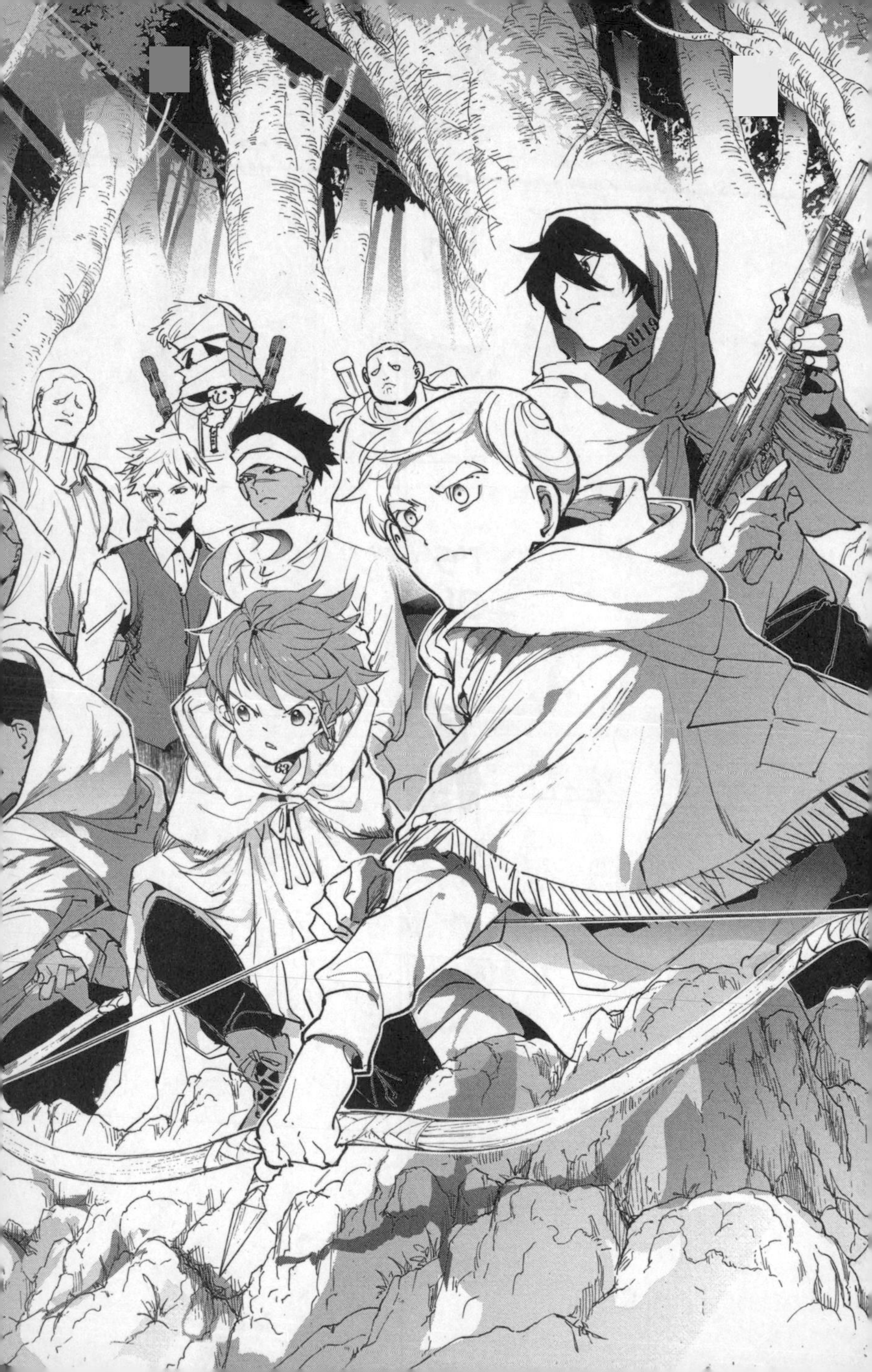

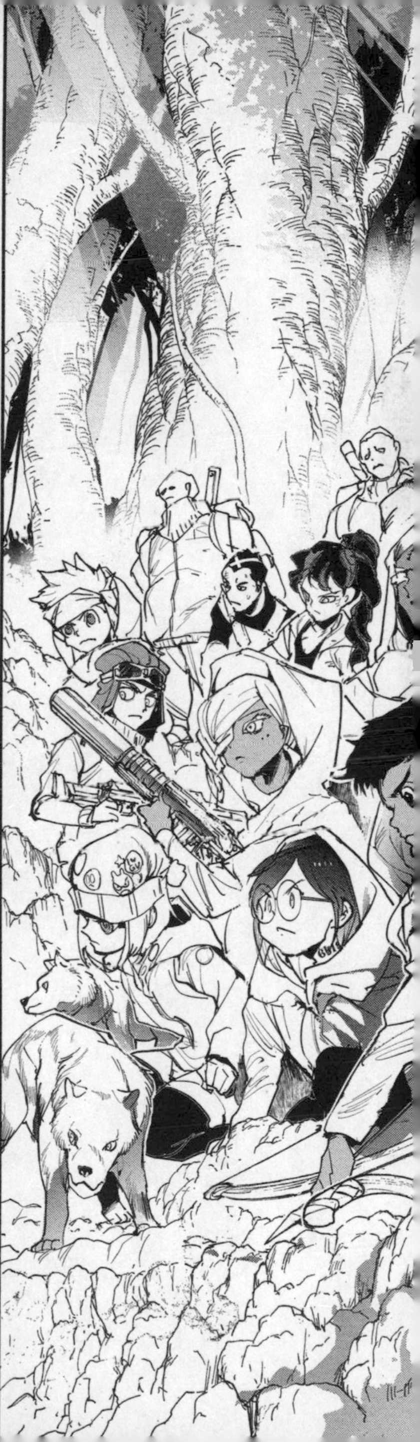

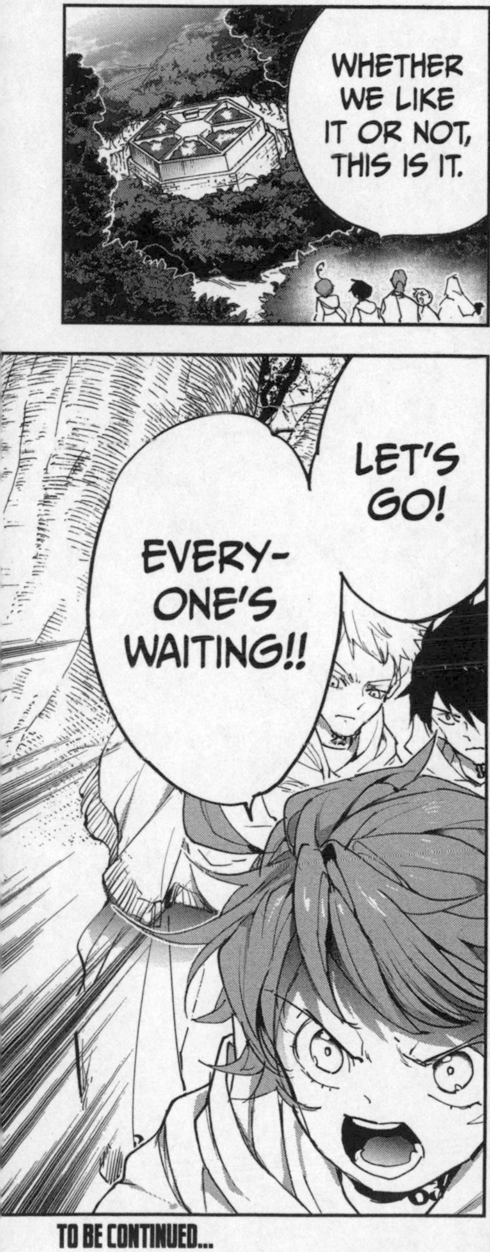
WHETHER WE LIKE IT OR NOT, THIS IS IT.
LET'S GO!
EVERY-ONE'S WAITING!!

TO BE CONTINUED...

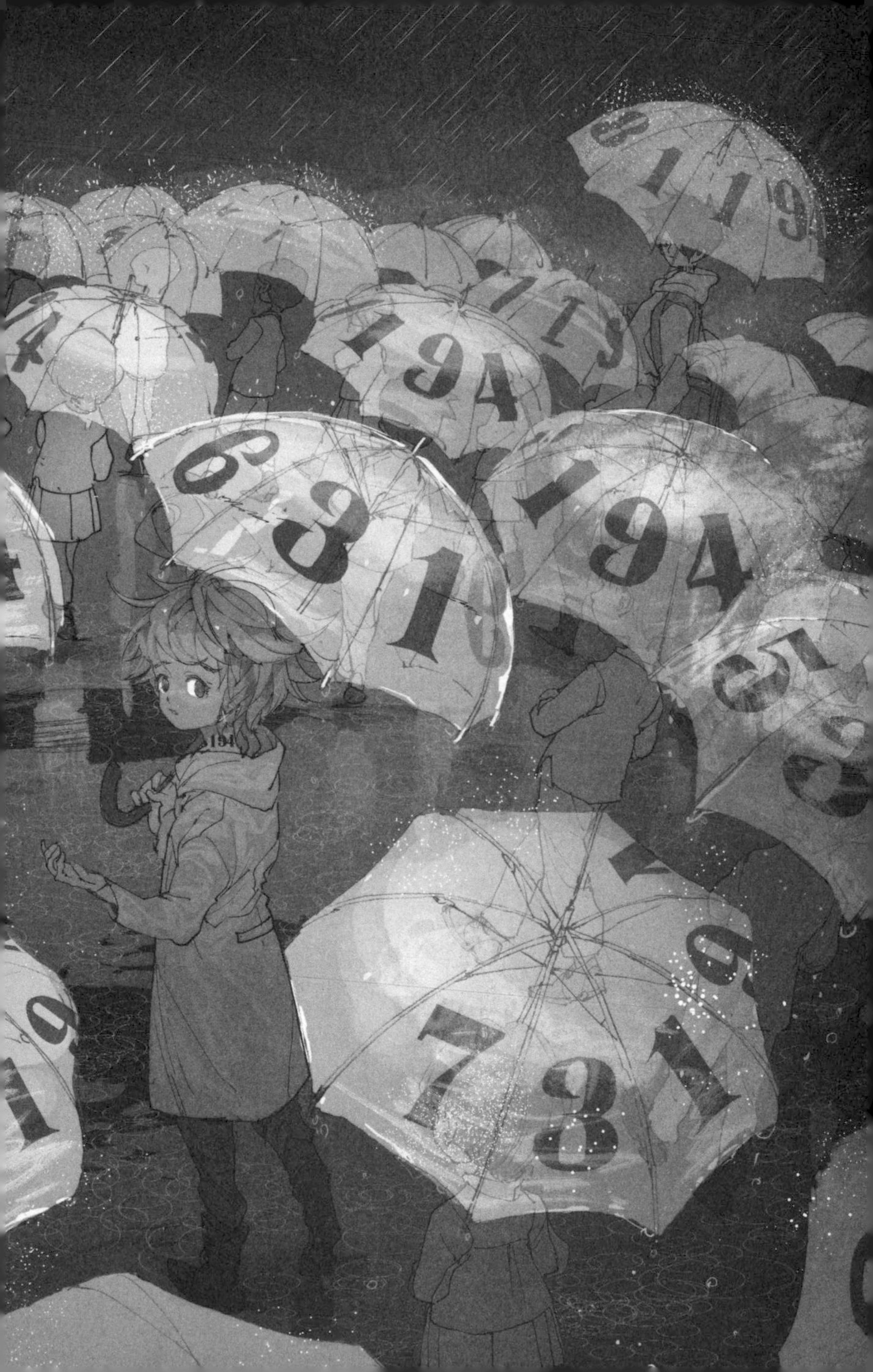

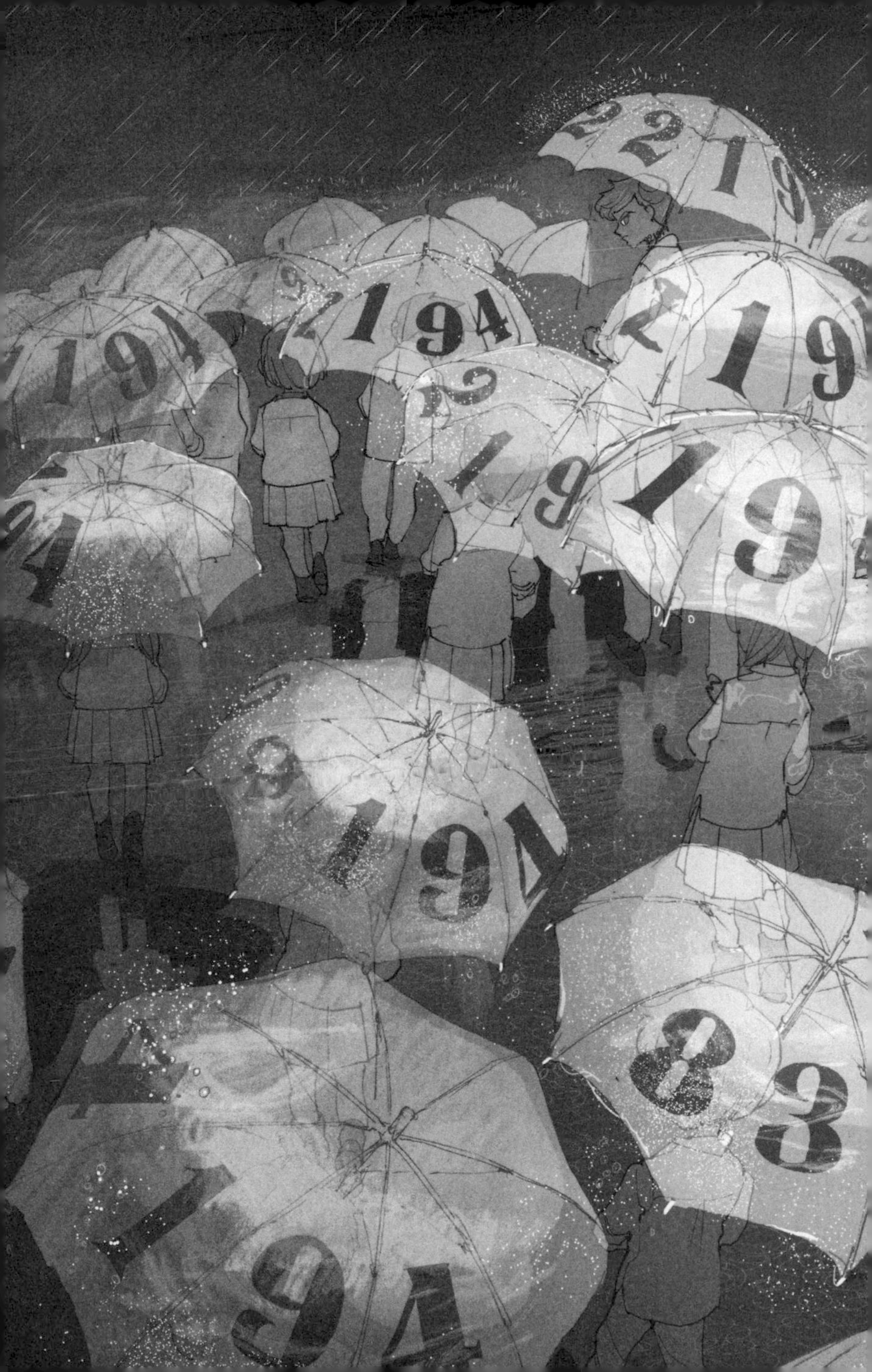

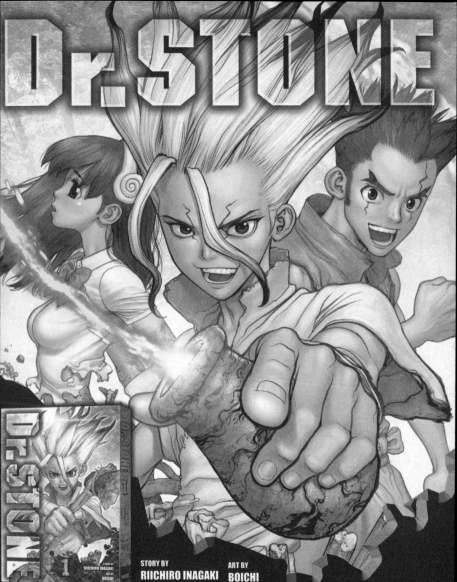

Dr.STONE

STORY BY
RIICHIRO INAGAKI

ART BY
BOICHI

One fateful day, all of humanity turned to stone. Many millennia later, Taiju frees himself from petrification and finds himself surrounded by statues. The situation looks grim—until he runs into his science-loving friend Senku! Together they plan to restart civilization with the power of science!

DR. STONE © 2017 by Riichiro Inagaki, Boichi/SHUEISHA Inc.

Story and Art by
KOYOHARU GOTOUGE

In Taisho-era Japan, kindhearted Tanjiro Kamado makes a living selling charcoal. But his peaceful life is shattered when a demon slaughters his entire family. His little sister Nezuko is the only survivor, but she has been transformed into a demon herself! Tanjiro sets out on a dangerous journey to find a way to return his sister to normal and destroy the demon who ruined his life.

KIMETSU NO YAIBA © 2016 by Koyoharu Gotouge/SHUEISHA Inc.

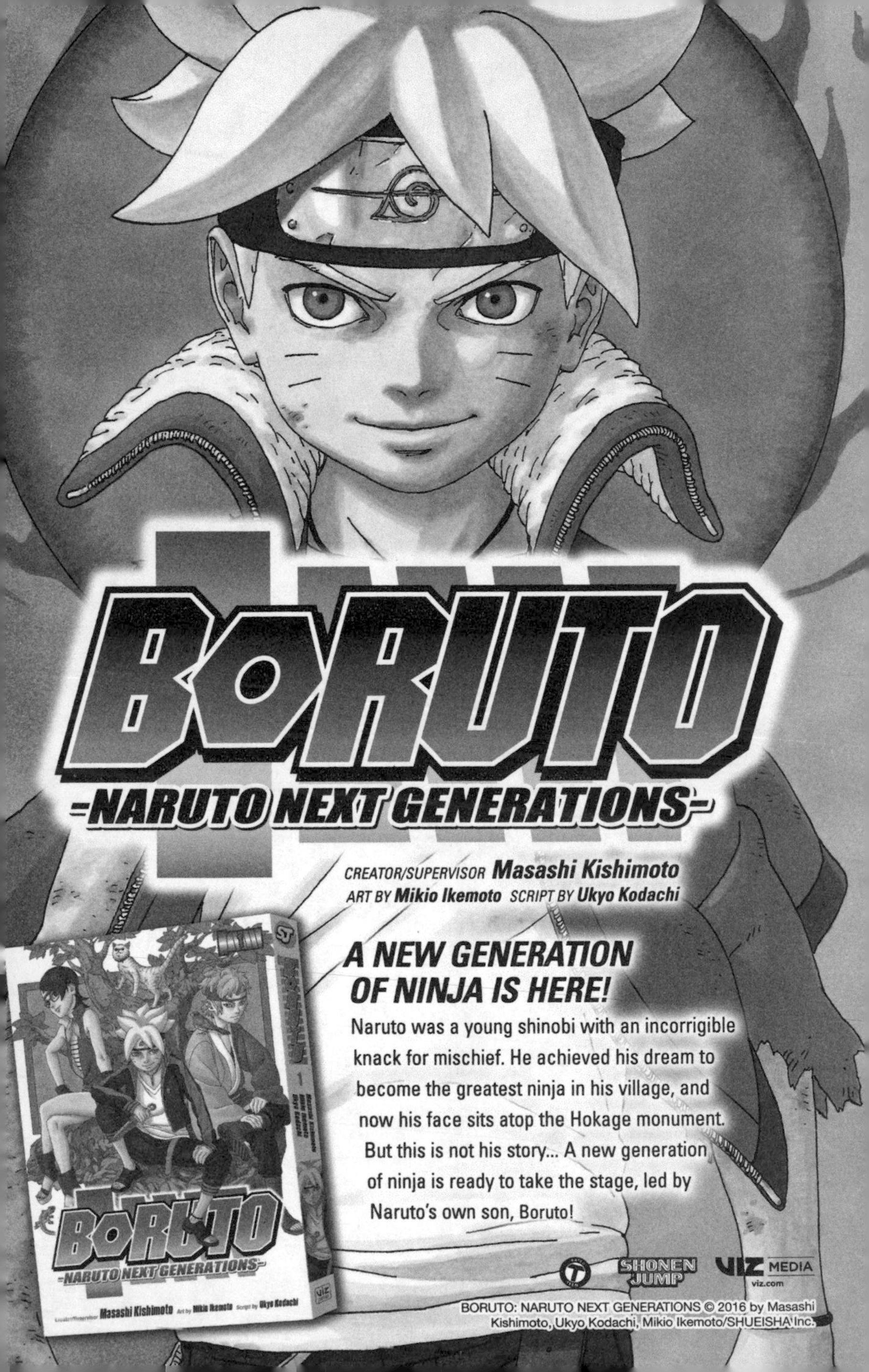
BORUTO
-NARUTO NEXT GENERATIONS-
CREATOR/SUPERVISOR Masashi Kishimoto
ART BY Mikio Ikemoto SCRIPT BY Ukyo Kodachi
A NEW GENERATION OF NINJA IS HERE!
Naruto was a young shinobi with an incorrigible knack for mischief. He achieved his dream to become the greatest ninja in his village, and now his face sits atop the Hokage monument. But this is not his story... A new generation of ninja is ready to take the stage, led by Naruto's own son, Boruto!
SHONEN JUMP
VIZ MEDIA
viz.com
BORUTO: NARUTO NEXT GENERATIONS © 2016 by Masashi Kishimoto, Ukyo Kodachi, Mikio Ikemoto/SHUEISHA Inc.

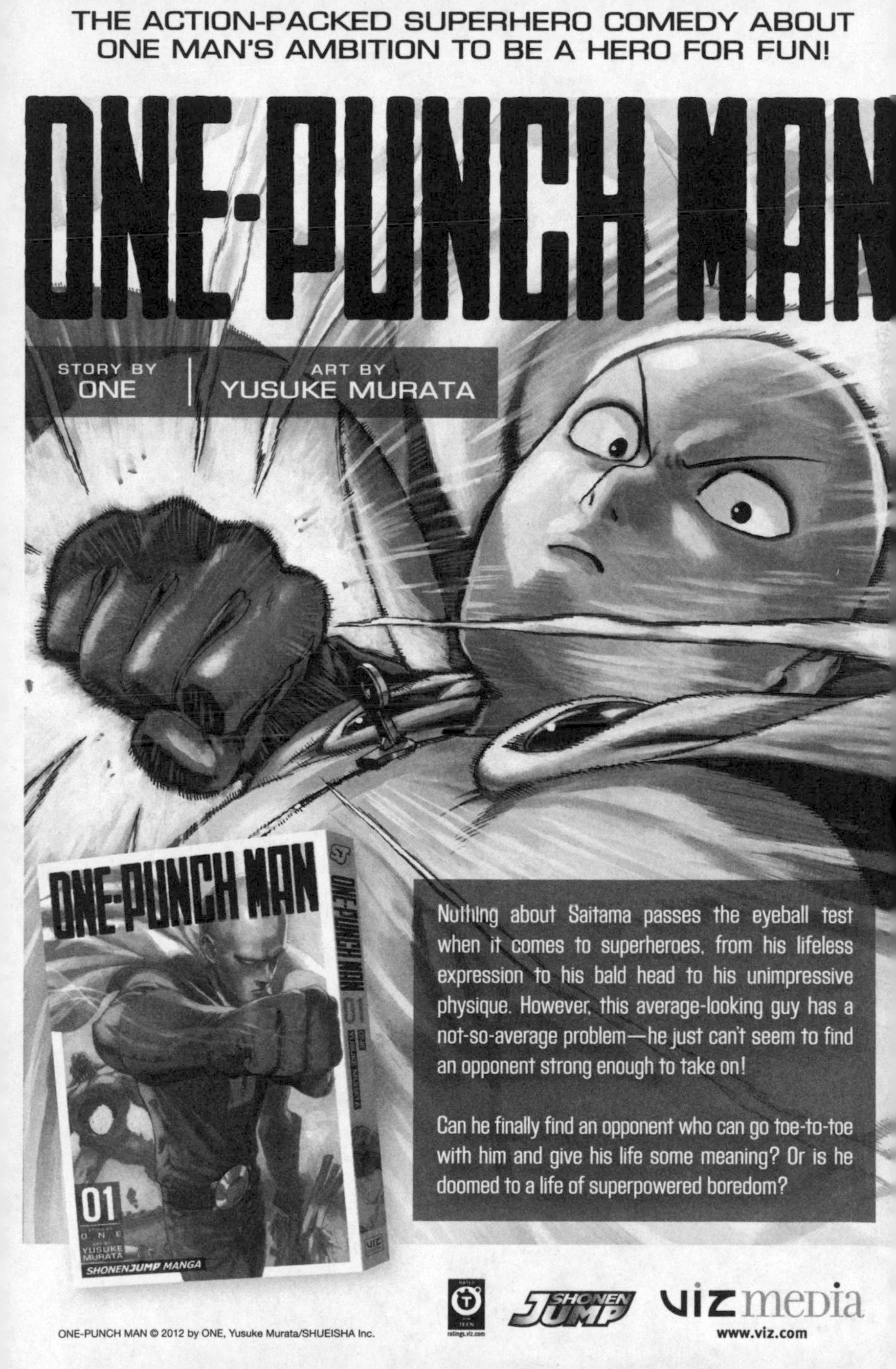
THE ACTION-PACKED SUPERHERO COMEDY ABOUT
ONE MAN'S AMBITION TO BE A HERO FOR FUN!
ONE-PUNCH MAN
STORY BY
ONE
ART BY
YUSUKE MURATA
ONE-PUNCH MAN
01
ONE
YUSUKE MURATA
SHONENJUMP MANGA
Nothing about Saitama passes the eyeball test when it comes to superheroes, from his lifeless expression to his bald head to his unimpressive physique. However, this average-looking guy has a not-so-average problem—he just can't seem to find an opponent strong enough to take on!
Can he finally find an opponent who can go toe-to-toe with him and give his life some meaning? Or is he doomed to a life of superpowered boredom?
ONE-PUNCH MAN © 2012 by ONE, Yusuke Murata/SHUEISHA Inc.
SHONEN JUMP
VIZ media
www.viz.com

ASTRA
LOST IN SPACE

CAN EIGHT TEENAGERS FIND THEIR WAY HOME FROM 5,000 LIGHT-YEARS AWAY?

It's the year 2063, and interstellar space travel has become the norm. Eight students from Caird High School and one child set out on a routine planet camp excursion. While there, the students are mysteriously transported 5,000 light-years away to the middle of nowhere! Will they ever make it back home?!

KANATA NO ASTRA © 2016 by Kenta Shinohara/SHUEISHA Inc.